Time Out

Stockholm

www.tImeout.com/stockholm

Time Out Guides
4th Floor
125 Shaftesbury Avenue
London WC2H 8AD
United Kingdom
Tel: +44 (0)20 7813 3000
Fax: +44 (0)20 7813 6001
Email: guides@timeout.com
www.timeout.com

Published by Time Out Guides, a wholly owned subsidiary
of Time Out Group Ltd. Time Out and the Time Out logo are
trademarks of Time Out Group Ltd.

© **Time Out Group Ltd 2015**
Previous editions 2003, 2005, 2008, 2011.

10 9 8 7 6 5 4 3 2 1

This edition first published in Great Britain in 2015 by Ebury Publishing.
A Random House Group Company
20 Vauxhall Bridge Road, London SW1V 2SA

Random House Australia Pty Ltd 20 Alfred Street, Milsons Point, Sydney,
New South Wales 2061, Australia

Random House New Zealand Ltd 18 Poland Road, Glenfield, Auckland 10,
New Zealand

Random House South Africa (Pty) Ltd Isle of Houghton, Corner Boundary
Road & Carse O'Gowrie, Houghton 2198, South Africa

Random House UK Limited Reg. No. 954009

Distributed in the US and Latin America by Publishers Group West
(1-510-809-3700)

For further distribution details, see www.timeout.com.

ISBN: 978-1-84670-331-7

A CIP catalogue record for this book is available from the British Library.

Printed and bound in China by Leo Paper Products Ltd.

MIX
Paper from
responsible sources
FSC® C020056
www.fsc.org

Contents

56

114

44

67

96

212

Time Out Stockholm

Editorial
Editor Anna Norman
Copy Editor Dominic Earle
Listings Editor Miranda Larbi
Proofreader Tamsin Shelton

Editorial Director Sarah Guy
Group Finance Controller Margaret Wright

Design
Senior Designer Kei Ishimaru
Designers Rob Baalham, Darryl Bell
Group Commercial Senior Designer Jason Tansley

Picture Desk
Picture Editor Jael Marschner
Deputy Picture Editor Ben Rowe
Picture Researcher Lizzy Owen

Advertising
Advertising Jinga Media Ltd (www.jingamedia.com)

Marketing
Senior Publishing Brand Manager Luthfa Begum
Head of Circulation Dan Collins

Production
Production Controller Katie Mulhern-Bhudia

Time Out Group
Chairman & Founder Tony Elliott
Chief Executive Officer Tim Arthur
Chief Financial Officer Matt White
Publisher Alex Batho
Group IT Director Simon Chappell
Group Marketing Director Carolyn Sims

Contributors
This guide was written and updated by Anna Norman, with Nightlife chapter by Angela Marcovic. Thanks to previous *Time Out Stockholm* guide contributors, including Elizabeth Dacey, Chad Henderson, Victoria Hesselius, Victoria Larrson, Jonas Leijonhufvud, Anna Norström, Lisa del Papa, Kristoffer Poppius, James Savage and Stephen Whitlock, whose work forms the basis of the Explore, Arts & Entertainment and In Context sections of the book.

Maps JS Graphics Ltd (john@jsgraphics.co.uk), except page 256: Stockholm Metro Map © 2014 Storstockholms Lokaltrafik

Cover and pull-out map photography Travel Pix Collection/AWL Images Ltd

Back cover photography Clockwise from top left: Oleksiy Mark/Shutterstock.com; Max Plunger; Christian Wilkinson/Shutterstock.com; Steven Schreiber; © Ett Hemm Hotel, Stockholm

Photography pages 2/3 Kalin Eftimov/Shutterstock.com; 4 (top), 56 Henrik Trygg/imagebank.sweden.se; 4 (bottom), 5 (bottom left), 23, 25 (bottom right), 26 (top), 36 (top right and bottom), 58, 79 (bottom), 80, 96, 113, 114, 116, 186/187, 202 Matilda Sveningsson; 5 (top left), 44 Ilona5555/Shutterstock.com; 5 (top right), 24 (middle), 50, 67, 82 Anna Norman; 7 Amy Johansson/Shutterstock.com; 10, 22/23 (top), 54 (bottom), 71 (top and middle), 75, 89 (bottom right), 91 (bottom), 92, 107, 159, 165 Matthew Lea; 10/11 Neirfy/Shutterstock.com; 11, 180, 181 Bengt Nyman/Wikimedia Commons; 12 (top), 25 (bottom left), 38/39, 109 Joppe Wikström/mediabank.visitstockholm.com; 12 (bottom) Katja Halvarsson; 13 (top) Jack Bengtsson; 13 (bottom) Yulia_B/Shutterstock.com; 14 (top), 86 (top) Åke E:son Lindman/ABBA The Museum; 14 (bottom) Dmitry G/Wikimedia Commons; 15 bellena/Shutterstock.com; 16/17 Oleksiy Mark/Shutterstock.com; 18, 22/23 (middle and bottom), 51, 52, 73, 78, 91 (top), 98 (left), 104 (bottom), 105, 115, 118, 131 (right) Olivia Rutherford; 19, 25 (top left), 31, 40, 45, 54 (top), 66, 88, 89 (bottom left), 95 (middle and bottom), 134, 145, 148/149, 167, 169, 182, 204 Tove K Breitstein; 20 Henrik Trygg/VisitSweden; 21, 30 (top right) 42/43, 58/59, 72, 119 Stefan Holm/Shutterstock.com; 24 (top), 27 (top), 142/143, 144 Holger.Ellgaard/Wikimedia Commons; 24 (bottom) Emil Leonardi; 25 (top right) Stefan Evensen; 25 (middle right) Tupungato/Shutterstock.com; 26/27 White Smoke/Shutterstock.com; 27 (middle), 151 Yanan Li/mediabank.visitstockholm.com; 28/29, 82/83 Ola Ericson/imagebank.sweden.se; 30 (top left) Lola Akinmade Åkerström/imagebank.sweden.se; 30 (bottom right) Alex Hinchcliffe; 32, 33, 172/173 Henrik Trygg/mediabank.visitstockholm.com; 34/35 (top) pamuk/Shutterstock.com; 34 (bottom), 95 (top) Åsa Lundén/Moderna Museet; 36 (top left), 128 Niklas Alexandersson; 37 (top), 96/97 Claes Helander; 41 Tsuguliev/Shutterstock.com; 42 (bottom) Anton_Ivanov/Shutterstock.com; 46 (top) Ulf Larsen/Wikimedia Commons; 46 (bottom) Erik Lernestål; 47 (bottom) anshar/Shutterstock.com; 48 (right) Jssfrk/Wikimedia Commons; 49 Prisma/UIG/REX; 57 Vadim Petrakov/Shutterstock.com; 60 b-hide the scene/Shutterstock.com; 64 Lokal Profil/Wikimedia Commons; 65 tuulijumala/Shutterstock.com; 68 (top), 208, 209, 215 Louise Billgert; 69, 98 (right) Gelia/Shutterstock.com; 71 Andrea Belluso; 74 Mikhail Markovskiy/Shutterstock.com; 86 (bottom) Lasse Ansaharju/Shutterstock.com; 89 (top) yoska87/Shutterstock.com; 94, 184, 185 (bottom) Arild Vågen/Wikimedia Commons; 102 Rose-Marie Henriksson/Shutterstock.com; 103 Kei Ishimaru; 117 (right) IBL/REX; 120, 178 Borisb17/Shutterstock.com; 125 Jonas Lindvall; 126 bonchan/Shutterstock.com; 127 (top) Brent Hofacker/Shutterstock.com; 127 (bottom) Björn Tesch/imagebank.sweden.se; 131 (left) Staffan Eliasson/mediabank.visitstockholm.com; 134/135 Ola Ericson/mediabank.visitstockholm.com; 136 Mikael Damkier/Shutterstock.com; 139 Joel Wåreus; 138 Mikael Sjöberg/mediabank.visitstockholm.com; 146 Rovenko Photo/Shutterstock.com; 147 Sheila Larsson; 150 Martin Svalander/imagebank.sweden.se; 152 Hans Ekestang; 154 Shaon Chakraborty; 155 Bonniers Hylen/AFP/Getty Images; 157 Frankie Fouganthin/Wikimedia Commons; 158 Kerstin/Shutterstock.com; 160 Conny Fridh/imagebank.sweden.se; 161 Max Plunger; 166 Steven Schreiber; 168 Alexander Kenney/Kungliga Operan; 171 John Hogg; 176 Christian Wilkinson/Shutterstock.com; 177 Rolf_52/Shutterstock.com; 185 (top) Anssi Koskinen/Wikimedia Commons; 188/189 Wikimedia Commons; 192 akg-images/ullstein bild; 195 © The Art Archive/Alamy; 197 John Hertzberg/Flickr; 199 Ragnar Singsaas/WireImage/Getty Images; 236 Jan Miko/Shutterstock.com

The following images were supplied by the featured establishments: 5 (bottom right), 22, 35 (bottom), 37 (bottom), 48 (left), 53, 55, 68 (bottom), 79 (top), 84, 104 (top), 141, 142, 183, 200/201, 205, 206/207, 212, 213, 216, 218

The Editor would like to thank Tom Janvrin, Andreas Pettersson, Christian Sabe, Hanna Sondell at Visit Stockholm and Matilda Sveningsson.

About the Guide

GETTING AROUND

Each sightseeing chapter contains a street map of the area marked with the locations of sights and museums (❶), restaurants (❶), cafés (❶), bars (❶) and shops (❶). There are also street maps of Stockholm at the back of the book, along with an overview map of the city. In addition, there is a detachable fold-out street map.

THE ESSENTIALS

For practical information, including visas, disabled access, emergency numbers, lost property, websites and local transport, see the Essential Information section. It begins on page 206.

THE LISTINGS

Addresses, phone numbers, websites, transport information, hours and prices are all included in our listings, as are selected other facilities. All were checked and correct at press time. However, business owners can alter their arrangements at any time, and fluctuating economic conditions can cause prices to change rapidly.

The very best venues in the city, the must-sees and must-dos in every category, have been marked with a red star (★). In the sightseeing chapters, we've also marked venues with free admission with a FREE symbol.

PHONE NUMBERS

The area code for Stockholm is 08, but you don't need to use the code when calling from within the city: simply dial the number as listed in this guide.

From outside Sweden, dial your country's access code (00 from the UK, 011 from the US) or a plus symbol, followed by the Swedish country code (46), then 8 (dropping the initial zero) and the number. So, to reach the Nobelmuseet, dial + 46 8 53 48 18 00. For more on phones, including details of local mobile phone access, see p227.

FEEDBACK

We welcome feedback on this guide, both on the venues we've included and on any other locations that you'd like to see featured in future editions. Please email us at guides@timeout.com.

DJURGÅRDEN

LIDINGÖ

HJORTHAGEN

E20

GÄRDET

Försvarshögskolan

Lilla Värten

VALHALLVÄGEN

ÖSTERMALM

LADUGÅRDSGÄRDET

STRANDVÄGEN

Tekniska
Museet

Vasamuseet

Skansen

Moderna
Museet

SKEPPS-
HOLMEN

DJURGÅRDEN

Strömmen

Fotografiska

Saltsjön

STADSGÅRDSLEDEN

222

NACKA

GÖTGATAN

SÖDRA
HAMMARBYHAMNEN

| 0 | | 1 km |
| 0 | | 0.5 mile |

© Copyright Time Out Group 2015

Stockholm's Top 20

*From historic ships
to design boutiques,
we count down
the essentials.*

1 Vasamuseet
(page 90)

If you're only going to visit one museum
when in Stockholm, make it this one. The
Vasamuseet houses the awe-inspiring
17th-century *Vasa* warship that sank
off the coast of Stockholm on its maiden
voyage in 1628 – its 64 cannon and two
gun decks apparently made the huge
wooden boat top-heavy. Left on the
seabed for over 300 years, the incredibly
well-preserved ship was salvaged in the
1960s and has sat in this purpose-built
museum since 1991. Don't miss it.

2 Skeppsholmen
(page 93)

This small island in the heart of the city is one of the most picturesque and laid-back parts of Stockholm. A path running around the island makes for a lovely 30-minute stroll, passing the huge Af Chapman boat hostel, super-stylish Hotel Skeppsholmen, moored houseboats and yachts, and the excellent Hjerta restaurant. Head into the middle of the island for Moderna Museet, Stockholm's best modern art museum, with a colourful sculpture garden that includes works by Picasso and Alexander Calder.

3 Stockholm archipelago
(page 180)

If you're visiting Stockholm during the summer, taking a boat to one of the archipelago islands is an absolute must. Only around 150 of the 30,000 islands and islets are inhabited, but that still gives Stockholmers and visitors a good selection of picture-perfect spots to choose from. Vaxholm is one of the most visited islands and makes for a great day trip; Grinda is often preferred by those looking for more greenery and seclusion.

4 Stadshuset
(page 138)

The Stadshuset (City Hall) is a Stockholm landmark. The huge, red-brick National Romantic edifice was designed by Ragnar Östberg and completed in 1923, and its 106-metre (350-foot) turret affords marvellous views of the Riddarfjärden bay and Gamla Stan. The internal courtyard calls to mind an Italian Renaissance piazza, with watery views through its photogenic pillars and arches. The Nobel Prize banquet is held here every December.

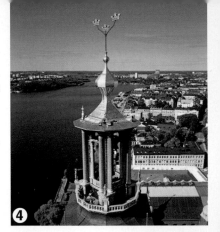

5 Fotografiska
(page 99)

Stockholm's premier photography museum is housed in an art nouveau industrial building on Södermalm's northern shore, which was converted into this excellent contemporary arts space in 2010. The dynamic programme includes four major annual exhibitions, which have so far focused on international photography masters, including Annie Leibovitz, Robert Mapplethorpe and Edward Burtynsky. There's also an excellent shop, a conference space and a café with panoramic views.

6 Rosendals Trädgård
(page 92)

For a taste of the Swedish countryside, head to this idyllic biodynamic garden in the middle of Djurgården, which offers a popular café (which uses produce from the garden), a cute botanical shop and a host of horticultural diversions, including wildflower meadows, a rose garden, vegetable and fruit gardens, and beautiful parkland. It's a lovely area to relax on a sunny Sunday.

7 Traditional cuisine
(page 126)

Despite a recent wave of innovation on the Stockholm eating scene, Swedish cuisine has clung on to many of its traditional dishes, meaning that you'll still find scores of places offering herring, *toast skagen* and Swedish meatballs. For the finest classic Swedish cuisine, book a table at Operabaren (*see p67*) or Den Gyldene Freden (*see p52*). Otherwise, try Strömmingsvagnen (*see p102*), an old-school food truck outside Slussen metro station that's been dishing up fried herring, mashed potatoes and lingonberries to hungry commuters for decades. Pelikan (*see p104*), meanwhile, offers a good middle ground.

9 Monteliusvägen (page 108)

There are myriad lovely views to be had in Stockholm, with panoramic treats often occurring at unexpected moments, such as when strolling or cycling across the Västerbron bridge, or from one of the rides at the Gröna Lund amusement park. The best views, though, are probably from the wooden Monteliusvägen walkway, which runs along the cliffs of northern Södermalm and offers lovely views across the Riddarfjärden bay, taking in the distinctive black rooftops of Gamla Stan.

10 Contemporary cuisine (page 126)

Though you'll probably want to try traditional Swedish cuisine when you're in town (*see p12*), don't miss the new wave of restaurants focused on innovation and stripped-back New Nordic concepts (with small plates, chef-patron interaction, laid-back spaces, seasonal Scandinavian ingredients and foraged produce). Leading the pack for creativity and a sense of occasion is Frantzén (*see p52*), but Lilla Ego (*see p78*), Gro (*see p75*), Smörgåstårteriet (*see p78*), Gastrologik (*see p124*) and Speceriet (*see p125*) are all good bets for contemporary Swedish cooking.

8 Långholmen (page 116)

The small island of Långholmen is something of a green retreat – like a mini Djurgården but without the hordes of tourists. The island sits just above the western end of Södermalm and was home to a prison from the 1720s to the 1970s, which is partly why it's so underdeveloped. Walking paths take you to the Stora Henriksvik café (a definite highlight), the lovely little beach area and past allotment gardens and hidden coves surrounded by trees.

11 Stortorget (page 43)

Gamla Stan is too touristy for many visitors, but its main square – the oldest in Stockholm – shouldn't be missed. The former medieval marketplace is lined with some of the city's most iconic and historic buildings, two excellent cafés (Chokladkoppen and Kaffekoppen) and the Nobelmuseet, housed in the former Stock Exchange. The square is hugely atmospheric around Christmas time, when a handicrafts and food market sets up here.

12 Fika
(page 127)

Fika is often one of the first Swedish words that visitors to the city learn. And with good reason: this ritual of afternoon coffee and cake is much more than just sustenance for locals – it's also an important aspect of social and cultural life. Coffee is good in the majority of Stockholm cafés, but for the best cakes, cinnamon buns and buzzing atmosphere, make a beeline for Blå Porten (*see p92*), Stora Henriksvik (*see p117*), Vete-Katten (*see p68*) or Lisas Café & Hembageri (*see p105*).

13 SoFo
(page 98)

It may now be challenged in the hip stakes by Hornstull, at the western end of Södermalm, but the area known as SoFo, on the island's eastern side, is still a great place to explore if you're looking for stylish clothing and design boutiques, and atmospheric cafés and bars. The focal point of the area is Nytorget, a lovely little park surrounded by cafés, restaurants and traditional wooden buildings.

14 Djurgårdsfärjan
(page 223)

The Djurgården ferry is Stockholm harbour's year-round public transport ferry, used by locals and tourists alike. It runs between Slussen and Allmänna Gränd on Djurgården, next to Gröna Lund amusement park, with an optional stop at the island of Skeppsholmen along the way. Though many visitors enjoy taking one of the visitor-oriented cruise boats

for a complete tour of the city, the Djurgårdsfärgan is a cheap, convenient and authentic way of experiencing Stockholm as a collection of islands.

15 Skansen
(page 89)

If you're in Stockholm with the kids over the summer then Skansen, on Djurgården, should be high on your to-do list. The 'living' historic village and animal park contains more than 150 traditional Swedish buildings – homes, shops, churches, classic cafés and workshops – and is also home to brown bears, moose, wolves and other Scandinavian animals. It's a place that's close to the hearts of many nostalgic Stockholmers.

16 Gröna Lund
(page 87)

This waterside amusement park is Sweden's oldest, built in 1883, and it still retains its old world charm despite many modern new features. You can't fail to hear the happy screams emanating from here on a walk around Djurgården in the summer months. Two intertwined rollercoasters provide plenty of airtime thrills for fanatics, while those looking for tamer pleasures should try the carousels, bumper cars and Ferris wheels. Pop concerts are sometimes held here.

17 Mälarpaviljongen
(page 141)

This bar-café on Kungsholmen's southern shoreline has become more and more popular with visitors over the past few years, mainly due to its floating deck. Watching the sun set with a bottle of wine, while looking out on to the water and enjoying the friendly, mixed crowd, is the sort of experience that Stockholm does so well. No wonder the place has also become a highlight of the city's gay scene.

18 Östermalms Saluhall
(page 130)

Stockholm's poshest food hall is a gastronomic temple to Swedish cuisine that's been pulling in the city's foodies for well over a century. The hall's exquisite carved wooden stalls and high-end culinary pleasures – everything from top-notch coffee and Swedish cakes to sourdough bread and seafood dishes – attract Östermalm ladies who lunch, businessmen and curious tourists. The latter can often be seen wincing at the prices, but it's worth a trip here to see how the other half live in Stockholm.

19 Svenskt Tenn
(page 131)

Stockholm's most famous interiors shop isn't a place for those on a budget, but the newly expanded space is a must for a lesson in Swedish design heritage. Started by pewter artist (*'tenn'* means 'pewter') Estrid Ericson in 1924, the brand is most famous for its bold textile designs by Austrian immigrant Josef Frank, who worked for the company from the 1930s and is celebrated as one of Sweden's greatest designers. Cushions, kitchenware and tableware, wallpaper and furniture are all on sale. Svenskt Tenn celebrated its 90th anniversary in 2014 with a collaborative exhibition with Italian design house Fornasetti.

20 ABBA The Museum
(page 86)

The ABBA museum won't be to everyone's taste, but it's clearly a don't-miss for fans of the Swedish super group – who number in their millions, going by the foursome's phenomenal record sales of the past 40 years. The new museum, located near the water on Djurgården, has been designed as a fun, interactive concept, allowing visitors to experience what it would feel like to be the fifth member of the band.

Stockholm Today

Small country, big ideas.

TEXT: JAMES SAVAGE & ANNA NORMAN

For a country of just over 9.5 million people, Sweden makes a pretty big impression on the world. Few other countries of the same size have produced pop bands to match the success of ABBA, while also boasting international firms of the stature of Ikea, Electrolux and Ericsson. And while the economies of most European countries have declined since 2008, Sweden's has grown – in part due to its separate currency, but also thanks to its strong commodities exports. Although the country's public-private partnership (the 'Swedish Model') has taken a bit of a battering in recent times, the standard of living is still among the highest in the world, and the country remains something of a magnet for foreign politicians in search of an ideology.

Stockholm's trendy SoFo district.

SWEDEN SWINGS

The admiring foreign politicians were, until recently, usually of a left-wing bent. They looked to Sweden to confirm their view that a country could be a socialist paradise and have a thriving economy at the same time. They were sorely disappointed in September 2006 when Sweden, for the first time in 12 years, kicked the Social Democrats out of government and replaced them with a centre-right coalition under Prime Minister Fredrik Reinfeldt. The new government presented a big change, given that the Social Democrats had ruled Sweden for 65 of the previous 74 years, and while the economy has remained stable during his time in power, the gap between rich and poor has widened. Swedes didn't change overnight from being highly taxed lovers of the welfare state to free-wheeling dog-eat-dog capitalists, of course, but it's clear that a new consumer class has been emerging. Time will tell whether the return of the Social Democrats – who narrowly won the 2014 general election under Stefan Löfven – will manage to reverse these social changes and retain the cherished Swedish Model.

CHANGING FACES

The changing nature of Sweden's inhabitants is also confounding the stereotypes. The image of Swedes as blonde, pigtailed Ingas and strapping, bearded Svens is becoming rapidly outdated as the pace of immigration accelerates. Refugees from troubled corners such as Somalia, Iraq and, more recently, Syria have followed earlier immigrants from southern Europe, Turkey and South America. Immigrants now make up more than ten per cent of the country's population, and are the main reason for the population boom of the past few years.

The impact of immigration on politics has also been visible. While most Swedes remain pragmatically liberal on the issue, there are clear pockets of dissent, with anti-immigrant parties – in particular the Sweden Democrats, whose policies include paying for repatriation of immigrants – increasing their share of the vote in the 2006, 2010 and 2014 elections.

CONTINENTAL DRIFT

Sweden shares with its Scandinavian neighbours an ambivalence to the whole

WHO'S HOLDING THE BABY?

Sweden's generous parental leave puts family time first.

What makes women happy, lowers the divorce rate and increases male life expectancy? No, it's not the latest miracle drug. It's dads who spend more time at home raising the kids, according to several recent Swedish studies. And dads in Stockholm have been leading the way for decades. Walk past a coffee shop on a weekday during working hours, and the chances are the establishment will have been colonised by hordes of parents, sipping lattes while their children gurgle contentedly. There's also a better chance in Stockholm than in many other capital cities that those lattes are being sipped by men.

Swedish couples are given 480 days of state-funded leave (where they're paid 90% of their salaries) to look after every child. Most of this can be split between the parents as they see fit, but the mother and father must each take 60 days' leave. If they don't, the other parent cannot take their 60 days. The aim of this is explicit – fathers are expected to do their bit. This 'daddy quota' aims to encourage fathers to take more time off, and a 2014 report in the UK's

Economist suggested that Swedish fathers now take around a quarter of the leave allocation. They're still under pressure to use more, though – not from partners, but from politicians. Certain policy-shapers are proposing that fathers and mothers must split parental time 50-50 or lose the time (and the benefit pay). They believe that only such a drastic measure will help ensure complete gender equality at home and at work.

Summer crayfish party.

EU project. While Swedes are in many ways good Europeans – many speak multiple languages, travel widely and are well informed about international affairs – they have a strong sceptical streak.

Like many Brits, they refer to the rest of Europe as simply 'Europe' or 'the continent', as though it were some distant entity of which they were not really part. This sense of being set apart was one reason why, in a 2003 referendum, Sweden rejected membership of the European single currency, the euro. Since this time, opinion polls have consistently shown that, after another ten years on the outside, opposition to Sweden joining has strengthened.

There is one thing, however, that the Swedes do love about Europe – the Eurovision Song Contest. The Swedish heats for the event, known as *Melodifestivalen* (the Melody Festival), are the most watched entertainment show of all time in Sweden, and remain one of the country's most popular programmes. While some other nations take the pan-European final with a pinch of salt, for the Swedes it's no laughing matter.

NATIONHOOD AND IDENTITY

Sweden comes out well in many international surveys. Generous parental leave helped it to be named the third-best country in the world to be a mother in 2014; other reports in the same year revealed it to have the fourth-highest rate of female representation in parliament and one of the lowest rates of teenage pregnancy in the western world.

Little wonder, then, that Swedes are a nation of unashamed flag-wavers. Drive through a Stockholm suburb on a summer evening and you'll see flags fluttering from many a garden flagpole. Birthday cakes are often decorated with small Swedish flags attached to cocktail sticks, and buses fly the blue-and-yellow ensign to mark occasions ranging from Midsummer Eve to King Carl XVI Gustaf's birthday.

The king and his family might be low-key by European standards, but they remain one of the main focuses of Swedish patriotism. Despite having the last vestiges of formal power removed in 1974, the royals retain a central role in national life. The royal children provide the staple diet for Sweden's army of celebrity magazines, which, after years of endless speculation, were delighted to give extensive coverage to Crown Princess Victoria's 2010 marriage to her former personal trainer Daniel Westling, as well as to the nuptials of the king's youngest daughter, Princess Madeleine, and US investment banker Chris O'Neill three years later. Both daughters have since gone on to give birth to their own mini princesses in 2012 and 2014 respectively. The royals themselves manage to maintain a dignified silence about their private lives, despite the ferocious interest of the press.

CITY AND COUNTRY

Any city that dominates the political, commercial and media life of a country as comprehensively as Stockholm does, tends to have an uneasy relationship with the provinces. This is particularly true in Sweden, which has a population of just 9.5 million spread over the third-largest land area in western Europe.

Stockholm is home to just under a quarter of the Swedish population, and has around twice as many inhabitants as Gothenburg. The Stockholm-centric nature of the media, politics and business grates with many outside the capital, particularly inhabitants of the sparsely populated north. Disdain for the hair-gelled, suited, fake-tanned Stockholmers has even inspired northerners to coin the term *fjollträsk*, roughly translated as 'mire of queens', to describe the capital.

If Stockholmers are viewed in the provinces as effete and snooty, city-dwellers' views of the country are more affectionate. Many families own second homes in the countryside, and the dream of tucking into crayfish next to a simple red wooden cottage by a lake is one that has endured for generations of urban Swedes. This has also contributed to the fact that the environment was a hot issue in Swedish politics long before the current wave of concern about global warming. The country's wealth of lakes and trees, the people's love of outdoor pursuits and the dramatic contrast between Swedish seasons mean that Swedes pay close attention to nature.

'The dream of tucking into crayfish next to a simple cottage by a lake is one that has endured for urban Swedes.'

MONEY MATTERS

Since 2008, Sweden has been prospering, and in 2014 was ranked as the tenth most competitive country in the world by the World Economic Forum. For such a small country, it is home to a large number of international brands. Car-makers Volvo and Saab may have been sold off to US car giants, but furniture retailer Ikea, clothes chains H&M and Gant, and telecoms giant Ericsson all remain in Swedish hands.

However, many Swedish companies owned by the state have been subject to privatisation in recent years, following policies made by the centre-right Alliance government between 2006 and 2014; for instance, Absolut Vodka, the third-largest brand of alcoholic spirits in the world, was bought by Pernod Ricard in 2008.

Music is another area in which Sweden has a global presence. ABBA may have kick-started the success, and Roxette continued it, but since then the music industry has taken on a (some might say more sophisticated) life of its own, and Sweden is now the world's third-largest music exporter, thanks to acts such as The Hives, Robyn and Lykke Li (*see also p163* **Essential Stockholm Music**). It has also been a key player in the digital streaming industry, thanks to the success of Spotify, the commercial music streaming website begun by a Swedish startup in 2008.

Sweden might punch above its weight, but it would be uncharacteristic of Swedes to boast openly of their country's achievements. Yet under the naturally modest outer shell, this is a country that feels comfortable with its place in the world.

Princess Madeleine and Chris O'Neill with their daughter, Leonore.

Itineraries

Plot your perfect trip to Stockholm with our step-by-step planner.

10AM

10AM

NOON

Day 1

10AM Stockholm is compact by city standards, eminently walkable and with an excellent metro system, so it's easy to visit several different areas in one day. It's best to head to the touristy island of Gamla Stan early in the day to avoid the crowds, so start with a coffee and a cinnamon bun at **Fabrique** (see p54), on its western side. There are two shops right nearby that make for a good introduction to Swedish culture: the **English Bookshop** (see p56) has lots of books on Swedish society and culture, while family-owned **E Torndahl** (see p56) sells design-focused Scandinavian gifts. From here, walk along to Stortorget, the historic main square, then head to one of the museums of **Kungliga Slottet** (see p46) – the official residence of the royal family – and the 13th-century **Storkyrkan** (see p51).

NOON Once you've had your fill of Swedish royal history, head south to the much larger residential

4PM

Far left: **Fabrique**. Left (top to bottom): **Kungliga Slottet** and **Storkyrkan**; **Urban Deli**; **Herr Judit**. Below: **Smörgåstårteriet**.

island of Södermalm, for a contrasting taste of contemporary Swedish society. You can walk to the neighbourhood known as **SoFo** (see p98) in around 25 minutes, or otherwise take the green T-bana line south from Gamla Stan to Medborgarplatsen. SoFo is known for its cool fashion boutiques and design shops, but it's also a great option for lunch. **Urban Deli** (see p104), next to laid-back Nytorget square, is an excellent bet for creative dishes and a buzzy vibe.

4PM After lunch, you might like to explore Södermalm further. If you're visiting in the summer and it's a pleasant day, head to the southern tip of Södermalm, near Eriksdalsbadet swimming pool, and take the 45-minute waterside walk from here to **Hornstull** (see p108) on Södermalm's western side.

If you're visiting in the colder months, head to Hornstull via Mariatorget and the vintage shops of Hornsgatan, such as the wonderful **Herr Judit** (see p115). Hornstull is a newly revitalised area with a host of new cafés and restaurants. For *fika* – the Swedish term for a coffee break – try **Mellqvist Café** (see p114) or the bucolic **Lasse i Parken** (see p113).

7PM For an evening meal, head to the mainland part of the city – Norrmalm, Vasastan and Östermalm. You'll find some excellent restaurants in this part of town. **Bakfickan** (see p65) is traditional, while **Gastrologik** (see p124), **Lilla Ego** (see p78) and **Smörgåstårteriet** (see p78) are all decent contemporary bets. If you've still got energy to spend after dinner, the bars of Östermalm beckon – **Riche** (see p125) is a long-running fave.

Top to bottom:
Vasamuseet;
Blå Porten;
Le Rouge.

10AM

Day 2

10AM This relaxed itinerary is suited to a Sunday, when many Stockholmers head over to the large green island of Djurgården, which has walking and cycling paths galore. The island is also home to some of Stockholm's key museums, including **Vasamuseet** (see p90), where this itinerary starts. The building houses an incredible 17th-century wooden warship that sank not far from Stockholm on its maiden voyage in 1628. Arrive here fairly early to reduce the chance of queuing, and to give yourself time to enjoy the ship's intricately carved decorative detail at a leisurely pace.

NOON Nearby museums worth a visit include the **Nordiska Museet** (see p88), celebrating Scandinavian design and culture; **Liljevalchs Konsthall** (see p88), for contemporary art; and **ABBA The Museum** (see p86), the new interactive visitor space dedicated to Sweden's most famous pop group. If you're feeling peckish, there's an excellent option nearby – **Blå Porten** ('Blue Door'; see p92) is an arty café with a lovely courtyard, serving traditional lunch dishes and a tempting range of cakes and desserts. It's not to be missed.

2.30PM You may feel like stretching your legs after lunch, and Djurgården is the ideal island for this. A walk or cycle (there's a 'City Bike' stand on Allmanna Gränd, opposite the Gröna Lund theme park) to **Rosendals**

NOON

Trädgård (see p92) is well worth the effort if you enjoy horticultural havens; the biodynamic gardens feature wildflower meadows and organic vegetable plots, as well as a popular café and botanical shop. Alternatively, if you're up for more cultural pursuits, hop aboard the Djurgårdsfärjan ferry from Allmanna Gränd to Skeppsholmen or Slussen to visit **Moderna Museet** (see p94) or photo museum **Fotografiska** (see p99).

7PM Though Gamla Stan is home to many tourist traps, it also has some excellent restaurants. If you want to splash out on creative Nordic cuisine, then **Frantzén** (see p52) is your place – though you'll need to book in advance to secure a table. Otherwise, try one of two cosy French bistros, **Le Rouge** (see p53) or local fave **Pastis** (see p53). For a post-meal tipple, there's Le Rouge's bar; or if you're looking to party, take the T-bana (red line) from Gamla Stan to Mariatorget and head to cool, industrial-style **Morfar Ginko** (see p114).

7PM

STOCKHOLM FOR FREE
Not everything costs the earth in this city.

SJÖHISTORISKA MUSEET
Although several of Stockholm's museums are free for under-18s (Nobelmuseet, Stockholms Stadsmuseum, Nordiska Museet, Vasamuseet), the Maritime Museum (*see p89*) is one of the only museums in the city with free entry for all. Visit to learn about Sweden's long and dramatic maritime history, and to see the huge number of model ships.

MODERNA MUSEET FRIDAYS
The Museum of Modern Art (*see p94*), on lovely Skeppsholmen, is one of the city's most popular museums. There's normally an admission fee, but it's free for all between 6pm and 8pm on Fridays. Alternatively, you can enjoy the museum's sculpture park, which sits in front of the building, at any time without spending a krona.

RIKSDAGSHUSET
Free 50-minute tours of the Parliament Building (*see p18*) are available in both Swedish and English, from extremely well-informed guides. You'll get an education in the Swedish political system, and see the modern semi-circular main chamber, the grand former entrance with busts of previous prime ministers, and the main parliamentary lobby.

GREEN SPACES
Stockholm's 14 islands each have their own character, and it's this aspect of the city which makes it so special. Djurgården (*see p84*) and Långholmen (*see p116*) are the two most relaxed islands, with a huge amount of greenery. Djurgården, in particular, is a great spot for a walk or bike ride, and encompasses the bucolic (and free) Rosendals Trädgård.

CITY BEACHES
Stockholm in the summer is a truly hedonistic place, when locals can finally strip off the layers and indulge in some wild swimming and sunbathing. There are several good swimming spots around the city, with popular beaches on the northern shore of Långholmen and the southern shores of both Kungsholmen and Södermalm. *See p109* **In the Swim.**

A LOOP OF THE LAKE

Enjoy a watery tour around Riddarfjärden bay.

The water surrounding the 14 islands that make up the city of Stockholm is formed of both sea and lake, which meet at the Slussen locks in the centre, just south of Gamla Stan; the Baltic Sea is on the eastern side while huge Lake Mälaren sits on the western side. The central bay of Mälaren is known as **Riddarfjärden**, and it's this part of the lake that's the focus of this circular walk, which takes in dramatic views and some idyllic refreshment spots. The whole walk takes around 1 hour 40 minutes, not including breaks.

Start at Slussen T-bana station, at the northern tip of Södermalm. The area is currently swamped by cranes as part of the **Future Slussen** construction (see p99). From here, head behind Stockholms Stadsmuseum and west along Hornsgatan, then down the steps of Pustegränd and up steep Bastugatan. Here you'll find a charming neighbourhood of cobbled streets and wooden houses. Continue along to the cliffside boardwalk of **Monteliusvägen** for your first spectacular view of the Riddarfjärden bay, taking in Gamla Stan, Riddarholmen and the City Hall from Stockholm's highest point.

If you haven't yet had a morning coffee, take a small detour to arty **Magnolia Café** (see p114), situated on the nearby steps of Blecktornsgränd. Otherwise, walk all the way along Monteliusvägen, enjoying the views, and then down on to the lakeside Söder Malastrand. Walk all the way along until you get to the little Pålsundsbron bridge, which takes you to **Långholmen** (see p116). The walk from Slussen to here takes about 30 minutes.

Långholmen is a lovely island for a stroll on a sunny day. If you're here in the summer months and fancy a dip, then head to the little beach on its northern side. Next to the beach is the delightful **Stora Henriksvik** café (see p117), housed in a 17th-century house with an idyllic garden. Once you've had your fill of woodland paths and secluded coves, head east along one of the paths that leads to the huge **Västerbron** bridge (see p116), which runs over the centre of Långholmen, connecting Södermalm to Kungsholmen. Walking across exposed Västerbron can be a blustery experience, but you'll be rewarded with panoramic views across the lake.

View from Monteliusvägen.

Rålambshovsparken

Stadshuset.

rectangular shape that forms the lake loop. The red-brick National Romantic building has a 106m (348ft) tower that can be climbed, for a small fee, for breathtaking views. But its inner open courtyard is just as rewarding, with an Italian piazza feel and lovely views of the water through its colonnade, which separates the courtyard from the sculpture-filled garden by the lake.

To complete the loop, you'll need to cross over the Stadshusbron bridge, and then Vasabron, to Gamla Stan. From here, walk

At the northern end of Västerbron, head east into **Rålambshovsparken** (see p136), a waterside park in Kungsholmen that's popular with joggers and skateboarders. A boules bar opens here in summer, when there's also open-air theatre, beach volleyball and a sociable vibe.

Leave the park at its south-east corner and you'll come on to a lovely lakeside footpath that runs parallel to Kungsholmen's Norr Mälarstrand. The path leads all the way to Stadshuset, Stockholm's landmark City Hall. On the way you'll encounter waterside café-bars – if you need a break, stop at the ever-popular **Mälarpaviljongen** (see p141), with its floating deck – as well as a host of joggers, power-walkers and, in the warmer months, kayakers. The views over the Riddarfjärden bay are fantastic, and you can look back at Västerbron, Långholmen and northern Södermalm to assess your progress so far.

Upon reaching **Stadshuset** (see p138), you'll have done three sides of the rough

over Riddarholmsbron, to get to the small adjacent island of **Riddarholmen** (see p56), a sanctuary of cobbled streets, medieval churches and 17th-century palaces. Down by the water on Evert Taubes Terrass is one of the city's best views – across Riddarfjärden towards the main section of Lake Mälaren. From here, head back to the southern end of Gamla Stan, near to where you started. Good refreshment spots nearby include **Fabrique** (see p54) and the **Flying Elk** (see p52).

Diary

*From summer fun
to winter cheer.*

Swedes hold hard to traditions and the calendar is dotted with beloved, quintessentially Swedish events such as Valborgsmässoafton (Walpurgis Night) and Luciadagen (Lucia Day); both great opportunities for visitors to dabble in Swedishness. The calendar isn't all age-old tradition, though. There are plenty of events with a more contemporary flavour – such as Stockholm Pride Week and the Supermarket art fair – and the calendar continues to diversify. There are also plenty of sporting events, and not just for spectators: if you're feeling fit, you might want to enter the Midnattsloppet (Midnight Race) or even the Stockholm Marathon.

Midsummer Eve.
See p31.

Spring

Stockholm Design Week
Stockholmsmässan AB, Mässvägen 1, Älvsjö; and venues throughout the city (www.stockholm designweek.com). **Date** early Feb.

All of Sweden's top creatives are in town for this world-class design event, which centres around the Stockholm Furniture Fair and Nordic Light Fair (www.stockholmfurniturelightfair.se), which take place at the Stockholmsmässan trade centre, south-west of Södermalm. Shops, showrooms, museums and galleries put on special events and parties throughout the week, with both industry figures and the general public attending.

Påsk (Easter)
Date Mar/Apr.

For many Swedes, Easter's greatest significance is getting a four-day weekend, well timed to polish up the boat or tidy up the garden. Still, the painting and eating of eggs is a hallowed tradition at the Easter *smörgåsbord*, along with salmon and pickled herring prepared in endlessly creative ways. On Maundy Thursday or Easter Saturday, young girls dress up and paint themselves as Easter witches, and then go around begging sweets from generous neighbours, handing over home-made Easter cards in exchange.

Market
Liljevalchs, Djurgårdsvägen 60, Djurgården (www.market-art.se). Bus 44, or tram 7, or ferry from Slussen. **Date** late Apr. **Map** p242 H11.

The Nordic region's leading fair for contemporary art moved to a new venue on Djurgården in 2014.

Supermarket
Supermarket will move to a new venue from 2015; check the website for more details (www.supermarket artfair.com). **Date** late Apr.

This artist-run initiative was established in 2006 as Minimarket (in response to the more commercial Market art fair, *see above*). Now called Supermarket, it has grown into an increasingly international art fair in its own right. Installations aim for the unexpected, with something for everyone during the three days.

Valborgsmässoafton (Walpurgis Night)
Throughout the city. **Date** 30 Apr.

Though they once protected Swedes from witches, the bonfires of Valborgsmässoafton now mark the end of winter and the coming of spring. Walpurgis Night is celebrated all over Sweden, but for visitors to Stockholm the place to be is either the open-air Skansen museum (*see p89*), where fireworks add extra sparkle to the evening's festivities, or Evert Taubes Terras on Riddarholmen (*see p57*).

Left:
Walpurgis Night (see p29).
Above:
Stockholm Marathon.
Right:
Parkteatern.

Första Maj (May Day)

Date 1 May.

If you happen to be in Stockholm on May Day, you'll probably run into marchers waving banners in Sergels Torg and other large squares throughout the city. The first of May has been celebrated in various ways since 1890. In the early 19th century, May Day was a hugely popular festival in Djurgården park and featured a royal procession. By the late 19th century, though, it had turned into a rally of industrial workers. It's a lot more low-key these days, but it's still an important event for left-wing Stockholmers. Due to the cold weather, there's no maypole dancing – that's saved for Midsummer Eve (see p31).

Stockholm Marathon

Start point: Lidingövägen, Hjorthagen. Finish point: Stockholms Stadion, Hjorthagen (54 56 64 40, www.marathon.se). **Map** p246 C9.
Date end May.

Few cities can match the breathtaking beauty of this marathon route, which takes runners along waterside Strandvägen, Norr Mälarstrand and Skeppsbron. Head for Lidingövägen to watch the race start, or if you want to glimpse the winner at the finish line, position yourself at Stockholms Stadion on Vallhallavägen.

Summer

Parkteatern (Park Theatre)

Parks throughout the city (www.stadsteatern. stockholm.se). **Date** June-Aug.

There's been free outdoor theatre in Stockholm's parks since 1942, and many performances can be enjoyed by non-Swedish speakers, such as circus shows, music concerts and dance. There are workshops on everything from playing steel drums to klezmer or Swedish folk dance.

Stockholm Early Music Festival

Tyska Brinken 13, Gamla Stan (www.semf.se).
T-bana Gamla Stan or bus 3, 53, 59. **Map** p241 J7.
Date early June.

This four-day event attracts an impressive roster of established and new artistic talent from Sweden and Europe performing a programme of music from the Middle Ages, Renaissance and Baroque periods. The festival takes place in Gamla Stan.

Skärgårdsbåtens Dag (Archipelago Boat Day)

Strömkajen, Norrmalm (662 89 02). T-bana Kungsträdgården or bus 2, 55, 62, 65, 76, 96.
Map p241 G8/H8. **Date** 2nd Wed in June.

If the idea of travelling aboard one of Stockholm's old-fashioned steamboats appeals, there's no better day to do it than Archipelago Boat Day. A parade of vessels make their way from Strömkajen to Vaxholm in the early evening. For those who don't catch a ride, good places to view the boats are Strömkajen, Skeppsholmen, Kastellholmen and Fåfängen. The boats arriving in Vaxholm are greeted by live music and an outdoor market; visitors have a couple of hours to explore Vaxholm before returning to Stockholm.

Above
and left:
**Archipelago
Boat Day.**

Nationaldag (National Day)
Date 6 June.
Sweden's National Day celebrates Gustav Vasa's election as King of Sweden on 6 June 1523 and the adoption of a new constitution on the same date in 1809. For a glimpse of the royal family in their traditional blue-and-yellow folk costumes, visit the open-air Skansen museum (*see p89*), where, since 1916, the King of Sweden has presented flags on this day to representatives of various organisations and charities.

Midsommarafton (Midsummer Eve)
Date Friday closest to 24 June.
The longest day of the year has been revered in Scandinavia since the days of pagan ritual. Modern Swedes flock to their summer cottages and Stockholmers set sail for quiet coves in the archipelago to commemorate this fertility feast.

INSIDE TRACK
A SEASONAL FEAST

If you're in Stockholm in August, an absolute don't-miss is one of the city's legendary crayfish parties. A late summer phenomenon that marks the closing of the season, the crayfish are eaten outdoors in a setting traditionally decorated with colourful paper lanterns. Paper hats are also worn. The crayfish are eaten cold, with dill, and with your fingers. Beer and schnapps are also consumed in large quantities, adding to the sense of camaraderie. Although crayfish have been eaten in Sweden since the 16th century, the parties were the preserve of the upper classes until the 20th century, when the festivities were taken on by the hoi polloi.

PUBLIC HOLIDAYS

New Year's Day (Nyårsdagen)
1 Jan

Epiphany (Trettondedag Jul)
6 Jan

Good Friday (Långfredagen)
3 Apr 2015, 25 Mar 2016

Easter Sunday (Påskdagen)
5 Apr 2015, 27 Mar 2016

Easter Monday (Annandag Påsk)
6 Apr 2015, 28 Mar 2016

May Day (Första Maj)
1 May

Ascension Day (Krist Himmelfärds Dag)
14 May 2015, 5 May 2016

National Day (Nationaldagen)
6 June

Midsummer Eve (Midsommarafton)
19 June 2015, 24 June 2016

Midsummer Day (Midsommardagen)
20 June 2015, 25 June 2016

All Saints' Day (Alla Helgons Dag)
31 Oct 2015, 5 Nov 2016

Christmas Eve (Julafton)
24 Dec

Christmas Day (Juldagen)
25 Dec

Boxing Day (Annandag Jul)
26 Dec

New Year's Eve (Nyårsafton)
31 Dec

People in traditional dress dance around the flower-decorated maypole. It's said that if an unmarried girl picks seven different flower types and puts them under her pillow on Midsummer Eve, she will dream of her future husband.

Stockholm Pride Week

Östermalms Athletics Ground, Fiskartorpsvägen 2, Östermalm (www.stockholmpride.org). Bus 55. **Date** early Aug.

Since its birth in 1998, Stockholm Pride Week has grown into the biggest gay Pride celebration in Scandinavia. The festival includes art exhibitions, films, parties and, on the Saturday, the big parade. *See also p158* **In the Know**.

Midnattsloppet (Midnight Race)

Start: Ringvägen. Finish: Hornsgatan (771 84 08 40, www.midnattsloppet.com). **Map** Start & finish p249 L5. **Date** mid Aug.

This popular night-time race could only be possible in the land of the midnight sun. More than 40,000 runners of all ages navigate a 10km (six-mile) course around the island of Södermalm. But it's much more than a race – and thousands of spectators get in on the act with cheering, music and partying. To catch the starting gun, position yourself at Ringvägen, just south of the Zinkensdamm athletics field, at 10pm and then wait for the first runners to cross the finish line at Hornsgatan, not far from the starting point.

Autumn

Lidingöloppet

Around Lidingö (765 26 15, www.lidingoloppet.se). **Date** weekend in late Sept.

The world's biggest cross-country race has become a tradition for Swedes. The first Lidingöloppet was held in 1965, and every year thousands of runners from some 30 different countries pass the finish line on Grönsta Gärde.

Stockholm Jazz Festival

Various venues (www.stockholmjazz.com). **Date** mid Oct.

The Stockholm Jazz Festival is one of Sweden's premier live music festivals with more than 100 concerts. It's prestigious enough to pull in some big international artists (Jamie Cullum appeared in 2014).

Stockholm Open

Kungliga Tennishallen, Lidingövägen 75, Norra Djurgården (31 94 02 50, www.stockholm open.se). Bus 73, 291, 293. **Map** p247 B11. **Date** mid Oct.

In 1969, veteran tennis star Sven Davidson received a letter from American colleagues asking him to arrange a competition in Sweden with tennis pros and amateurs from all over the world. The event now pulls in around 40,000 spectators each year.

Luciadagen.

Stockholm International Film Festival

Various venues around Stockholm (677 50 00, www.stockholmfilmfestival.se). **Date** early Nov.

The ten-day Stockholm Film Festival aims to launch young filmmakers and broaden the forum for innovative high-quality films in Scandinavia. It may not be Cannes, but it can still attract some big names: past guests have included Quentin Tarantino, the Coen brothers and Danish director Lars von Trier.

Winter

Advent

Date Dec.

You can tell Christmas is approaching when you start to spot Advent candles or Advent stars hanging in the windows of homes, shops and offices. Nearly every home has one, usually a little box with four candle-holders nestled in moss and lingonberry sprigs. The first candle is lit on the First Sunday of Advent and allowed to burn down only one quarter, so that it won't burn out before the fourth candle is lit.

Skansen Christmas Market

For listings, see p89. **Date** early-end Dec.

Skansen's Christmas market is held at weekends throughout December until Christmas Eve (the only day Skansen is closed). Look out for Swedish craft products, traditional Christmas ornaments made of straw, hand-dipped candles and Christmas fare such as smoked sausage, eel, salmon, *pepparkakor* (gingersnaps), *glögg* (mulled wine) and saffron buns.

Christmas.

Nobeldagen (Nobel Day)

Konserthuset, Hötorget, Norrmalm & Stadshuset, Hantverkargatan 1, Kungsholmen (Nobel Foundation 663 09 20, www.nobel.se). **Date** 10 Dec. The year's Nobel Prize laureates are honoured in a ceremony at Konserthuset (*see p167*). In the evening, the royal family attends a banquet at Stadshuset (City Hall; *see p138*). Tickets for this glittering affair are usually only granted to the privileged few, though 250 of the 1,300 seats are reserved for lucky students. The rest have to be content with watching the proceedings on television and sighing over the fabulous menu. *See also p49* **The Noblest of Them All**.

Luciadagen (Lucia Day)

Date 13 Dec.

Among the best-known of Sweden's festivals, Lucia is celebrated in the heart of the winter darkness. The Lutheran Swedes adopted the Sicilian St Lucia because Lucia is connected with *lux*, the Latin for light. All over Sweden, a procession of singers, dressed in white, full-length chemises with red ribbons around their waists, are led by a woman dressed as Lucia, with a crown of lit candles on her head.

Jul (Christmas Day)

Date 24-26 Dec.

The main celebration is at home, held on Christmas Eve (though restaurants all over the city offer the traditional, overflowing *Julbord* or *smörgåsbord* for most of December). A traditional *Julbord* (Christmas table) is typically eaten in three stages. You start with herring and salmon, then move on to the meats (meatballs, sausages and ham), accompanied by 'Jansson's Temptation' – an anchovy, potato and cream casserole. You polish it all off with a sweet berry-filled pastry. Christmas Day itself is usually a quiet day.

▶ *For information on Skansen's excellent Christmas market, see p32.*

Nyårsafton (New Year's Eve)

Date 31 Dec.

The New Year's Eve celebration in Sweden is a public and raucous contrast to the quiet and private Christmas festivities that have gone before. Visitors can join the crowds at Skansen (*see p89*), where New Year's Eve has been celebrated every year since 1895. At the stroke of midnight, a well-known Swede reads Tennyson's 'Ring Out, Wild Bells'. Throughout the city, crowds fill the streets, feasting on seafood at various restaurants and moving from one club or bar to another.

SINGING FOR SWEDEN

Skansen plays host to Stockholm's ever-popular annual sing-along.

Sweden is a nation filled with people who love to sing, and not just in the shower. It's estimated that between 600,000 and 700,000 Swedes sing weekly in choirs, and that fondness for choral singing goes some way towards explaining the enduring popularity of **Allsång på Skansen** (www. skansen.se), a sing-along tradition at Skansen (*see p89*) reminiscent of the BBC's *The Good Old Days*.

Attending Allsång på Skansen is an annual pilgrimage for some Swedes. For many others it's the 'must-do' of a summer visit. The long-running sing-along show was an instant success in May 1935, when the audience was invited to sing along with its musical director, Sven Lilja. Televised since 1979, the show now has two million viewers for its summer broadcasts, as dedicated families all over Sweden devote Tuesday evenings to belting out oldies-but-goodies in front of the TV.

In the early years, the musical selection always remained the same mixture of popular numbers. But by the time of Sven Lilja's death in 1951 tastes had changed, and the songs changed with them. Traditions die hard, though, and the repertoire remains classically Swedish, although the artists performing are as likely to be today's teenage heart-throbs as stars of yesteryear. This strategy of appealing to young and old has been a win-win for both pop music artists and die-hard fanatics, and the Allsång tradition, which could so easily have become fodder for fuddy-duddies, is currently enjoying über pop-cult status.

Allsång på Skansen takes place eight times between late June and mid August. For exact dates, visit the Skansen website.

Stockholm's Best

There's something for everyone with our hand-picked highlights.

Sightseeing

VIEWS
Monteliusvägen p108
The boardwalk of northern Södermalm gives spectacular views of Gamla Stan.
Västerbron p136
A view from the bridge, between Kungsholmen and Södermalm.
Kastellholmen p94
Enjoy Djurgården views from the cliffs of this tiny island.
Fotografiska café p99
Big picture windows offer panoramic views.

ART & DESIGN
Moderna Museet p94
Fotografiska p99
Liljevalchs Konsthall p88

Artipelag p183
Millesgården p145

HISTORY
Nordiska Museet p88
Sweden's national museum of cultural history.
Historiska Museet p121
The country's largest archaeological museum.
Kungliga Slottet p46
The imposing 18th-century royal palace.
Sjöhistoriska Museet p132
An extensive display of model boats tells the story of Sweden's maritime heritage.

ICONS
Vasamuseet p90
This preserved 17th-century warship is simply unmissable.

Moderna Museet.

Nordiska Museet.

Lux Dag för Dag.

Stadshuset p138
The red-brick City Hall hosts the annual Nobel Prize banquet.
ABBA The Museum p86
Become the fifth member of ABBA at this new interactive museum.
Storkyrkan p51
The site of coronations and royal weddings.
Globen p147
The world's largest hemispherical building.

HORTICULTURAL HAVENS
Rosendals Trädgärd p92
These organic gardens house an idyllic café and a botanical shop.
Stora Henriksvik p117
This old-school Långholmen café has a lovely garden.
Tanto allotment gardens p112
Much-coveted allotment gardens in southern Södermalm.
Bergianska Trädgården p145
Botanists and picnickers love this botanical garden.

CHILDREN
Skansen p151
Traditional buildings and Scandinavian animals.
Junibacken p150
Mini indoor theme park devoted to Pippi Longstocking.
Tekniska Museet p152
Inquisitive kids can roam for hours at this science and technology museum.
Gröna Lund p150
A waterside theme park that's been going for decades.

SWIMMING SPOTS
Långholmsbadet p109
Eriksdalsbadet p109
Smedsuddsbadet p109
The Archipelago p180

Eating & drinking

BLOWOUTS
Mathias Dahlgren p66
Michelin-starred dining in the Grand Hôtel.
Frantzén p52
The best place to sample contemporary Scandinavian cooking.
Operakällaren p67
The Opera House's most illustrious restaurant.
Esperanto p124
Swedish and Japanese cuisine of the highest order.
AG Restaurang p139
Nose-to-tail dining in an industrial space.

LOCAL VIBES
Smörgåstårteriet p78
Creative Swedish cooking in a small space in Vasastan.
Hjerta p95
Hjerta has an unmistakably 'Skeppsholmen' vibe, with watery views to match.
Gastrologik/ Speceriet p124
New Nordic cuisine in Östermalm, with a firm focus on local veg.
Lux Dag för Dag p147
Top-notch Lilla Essingen restaurant with its very own veg patch.
Lilla Ego p78
Bare-brick walls and seasonally inspired dishes in Vasastan.
Bistro Süd p112
A friendly and reliable Södermalm classic.

TRADITIONAL SWEDISH
Pelikan p104
Den Gyldene Freden p52
Bakfickan p65
Lisa Elmqvist p125
Operabaren p67

Riche.

Svenskt Tenn.

Lasse i Parken.

BUDGET
Strömmingsvagnen p102
A humble herring cart that's long been a local fave.
Bon Bon p124
Tapas-style Swedish and French plates.
Nalle & Kroppkakan p147
Pork- or mushroom-filled *kroppkakor* (potato dumplings).
Flying Elk p52
A London-style gastropub, run by the owners of Frantzén.
La Neta p104
Tacos and quesadillas.

VEGETARIAN
Lao Wai p75
Chinese vegetarian restaurant with a deservedly strong following.
Hermans Trädgårdcafé p105
Wholesome vegetarian food and panoramic city views.
Gro p75
Honest cooking focused on vegetables.

FIKA
Blå Porten p92
Lasse i Parken p113
Chokladkoppen p54
Sturekatten p128
Lisas Café & Hembageri p105

BARS
Mälarpaviljongen p141
Alfresco imbibing on the Kungsholmen waterfront.
Riche p129
This media bar is a long-time Stockholm favourite.
Kvarnen p106
A Södermalm beer hall that draws the crowds.
Hotellet p129
A hotspot for young professionals and partygoers.
Morfar Ginko & Papa Ray Ray p114
These neighbouring Södermalm bars have widespread appeal.

Shopping

SHOPPING STREETS & AREAS
Biblioteksgatan, Norrmalm p69
For Sweden's most stylish fashion brands.
SoFo, Södermalm p98
Edgier fashion and design boutiques.
Nybrogatan, Östermalm p129
For high-end designer interiors shops.
Western Södermalm p108
Vintage shops and emerging labels.

Södra Teatern.

Frantzén.

Urban Deli p104
This gourmet shop-deli-café has an NYC feel.
Hötorgshallen p70
A culinary trip around the world.

Nightlife

JAZZ
Glenn Miller Café p164
Fasching p164
Nalen p164
Stampen p164

CLUBS & LIVE MUSIC
Södra Teatern p165
The city's best space for international acts.
Pet Sounds Bar p165
Intimate indie-rock gigs.
Debaser Medis p164
Rock, pop, hip hop and reggae.
Marie Laveau p161
One of Söder's best clubs.
Landet p165
Mix with a trendy Midsommarkransen crowd.
Café Opera p160
A posh Stockholm classic.

Arts

PERFORMING ARTS
Berwaldhallen p166
Stockholm's acclaimed modernist concert hall.
Kungliga Operan p167
The lavish Royal Opera House.
Konserthuset p167
Home to the Royal Philharmonic.
Strindbergsmuseet p65
Strindberg's former home.

FESTIVALS
Parkteatern p30
Stockholm Jazz Festival p32
Stockholm International Film Festival p32
Stockholm Design Week p29

DESIGN & INTERIORS
E Torndahl p56
Gamla Stan's design-led, family-owned gift shop.
Svenskt Tenn p131
A Stockholm classic that should not be missed.
Granit p107
This Swedish chain sells minimalist stationery, homewares and accessories.
Nordiska Galleriet p130
Furniture, lights and gifts from Nordic and international designers.
Modernity p130
One for mid-century modern furniture fans.

LOCAL BRANDS
Hope p70
This Swedish fashion label goes from strength to strength.

Our legacy p115
Stylish menswear label with a boutique in Södermalm.
Acne p69
The clothes aren't cheap, but it's the definitive Swedish fashion label.
Fjällräven Kånken p72
These 1970s backpacks, sold at Naturkompaniet, are timelessly cool.
Byredo p70
A fragrance house with divine perfumes and candles.
Happy Socks p70
The Swedish brand that's taken the sock world by storm.
Weekday p73
Edgy, fashion-led and affordable garments in high-energy spaces.

BOOKS & MUSIC
Papercut p115
Pet Sounds p107
Hedengrens Bokhandel p130
English Bookshop p56

FOOD & DRINK
Riddarbageriet p130
Superior sourdough loaves and fabulous cakes.
Östermalms Saluhall p130
Stockholm's oldest, poshest and priciest food hall.

Explore

Gamla Stan & Riddarholmen

Gamla Stan – meaning 'Old Town' – is the living embryo of Stockholm's birth more than 750 years ago. The island straddles the strategic gateway between the global reaches of the Baltic Sea and the expansive inland trade routes of Lake Mälaren. Many of its structures stand on foundations from the 17th and 18th centuries, packed into narrow, meandering cobbled streets that today echo with the footfalls of tourists and the lucky few who are residents. The Swedish monarchy have had their 'official' home here for hundreds of years, and the immense Kungliga Slottet (Royal Palace) is still the main sight.

Cut off from Gamla Stan by several lanes of traffic and a narrow canal, the tiny island of Riddarholmen is a sanctuary of cobbled streets, 17th-century palaces and lovely water views. Most of its buildings house government offices.

Nobelmuseet.

Don't Miss

1 **Frantzén** For a Michelin-starred contemporary Swedish feast (p52).

2 **Livrustkammaren** The Royal Armoury is stuffed with weapons (p47).

3 **Nobelmuseet** For an education in the history of the famous prizes (p47).

4 **E Torndahl** Design-focused gifts crafted in Scandinavia (p56).

5 **Riddarholmskyrkan** One of the city's most distinctive churches (p57).

Gamla Stan.

Storkyrkan. See p51.

GAMLA STAN & HELGEANDSHOLMEN

Before Stockholm sprawled out to neighbouring farmland, the whole city was once limited to this small island, referred to historically as 'the city between the bridges'. A fortress was built on the island's north-eastern shore around the 11th century, but there's no record of an actual city on Gamla Stan until Birger Jarl's famous letter of 1252, which mentioned the name 'Stockholm' for the first time. The island city grew into a mess of winding streets and ramshackle houses until most of the western half burned down in 1625. City planners finally crafted a few right angles and tore down the crumbling defensive wall around the island to make room for waterfront properties for the city council.

Kungliga Slottet sits on a hill at the highest point in Gamla Stan, where the old fortress of

Tre Kronor, which was almost completely destroyed – except for the north wing – by a fire in 1697, once stood. Royal architect Nicodemus Tessin the Younger designed the new palace, giving it a Roman Baroque exterior. The architect Carl Hårleman completed Tessin's work in 1754.

The low, yellowy-brown building is imposing rather than pretty; its northern façade looms menacingly as you approach Gamla Stan over the bridges from Norrmalm. The square central building around an open courtyard is flanked by two wings extending to the west and two more to the east. Between its eastern wings lie the gardens of Logården, and between the curved western wings is an outer courtyard; the ticket/information office and gift shop are located in the south-western curve. The southern façade with its triumphal central arch is the most attractive; it runs along Slottsbacken, the hill that leads up from Skeppsbron and the water to the back of Storkyrkan. This large space was kept open to make it easier to defend the palace. The obelisk in front of the church, designed by Louis Jean Desprez, was erected in 1799 as a memorial to those who fought in Gustav III's war against Russia in 1788-90.

Although the palace is the official residence of the royal family, the King, Queen and Heir Apparent, Princess Victoria, live on the island of Drottningholm (itself well worth a visit; see p176); Prince Carl-Philip has moved to the chic address of Slottsbacken 2, just across from the main entrance to the palace, and his sister Princess Madeleine has also flown the family coop to be nearer to the city's pulse. Visitors are welcome to roam around the sumptuous **Representationsvåningarna** (Royal Apartments) and museums. The **Museet Tre Kronor** explores the history of the palace, while the **Skattkammaren** (Treasury), **Livrustkammaren** (Royal Armoury) and

Gustav III's Antikmuseum (Museum of Antiquities) show off its prized possessions. If you plan on seeing most of the palace, buy the combined ticket (rather than individual tickets for each attraction), which provides admission to everything except the Livrustkammaren. The limited opening hours and sheer size of the place mean that you'll probably have to visit a couple of

times if you want to see it all. Another royal museum, the **Kungliga Myntkabinettet**, is located on Slottsbacken, opposite the entrance to the Royal Armoury.

There are plenty of other sights on Gamla Stan apart from the Royal Palace. At the top of Slottsbacken stands the imposing yellow bulk of Stockholm's de facto cathedral, **Storkyrkan**, the scene of royal weddings and coronations. Trångsund, the street at the front of the church, leads down to Gamla Stan's main square, **Stortorget** (*photo p44*). A former marketplace, it's surrounded by colourful 18th-century buildings, many containing cafés: the two located at the western end of the square, **Chokladkoppen** and **Kaffekoppen**, are the best. The notorious Stockholm Bloodbath – in which more than 80 noblemen, priests and burghers were hanged or decapitated at the command of the Danish King, Christian II – occurred in Stortorget in 1520. You can see a cannonball in the façade of the building at Stortorget 7, on the corner with Skomakargatan. It is said to have been fired at Christian II at the time of the Bloodbath, but in fact was placed much later as a joke, probably in 1795 by a furniture dealer named Grevesmühl.

The large white building in the square is the former Stock Exchange, designed by Erik

EXPLORE

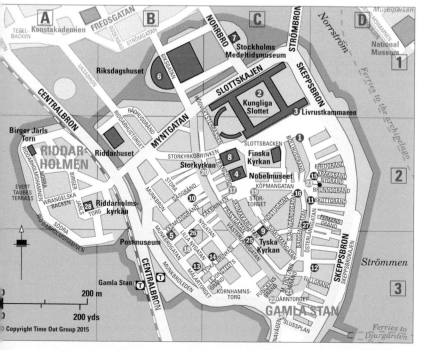

Stortorget. See p43.

See p43.

EXPLORE

Lallerstedt (not to be confused with one of Sweden's most famous chefs by the same name); it now houses the high-tech **Nobelmuseet**, telling the history of the esteemed Nobel Prizes. The museum is due to move to an exciting new purpose-built space in 2018 (*see p49* **The Noblest of Them All**). The Swedish Academy of Sciences permanently occupies the upper floor. Lallerstedt also designed the 1778 well in the centre of the square. Due to the land rising, the well dried up in the 19th century and was moved to Brunkebergstorg in Norrmalm, but it was moved back again in the 20th century.

Gamla Stan's main thoroughfares of Västerlånggatan, Österlånggatan, Stora Nygatan and Lilla Nygatan run north–south along the island. Crowded Västerlånggatan draws tourists to its many small shops, while the parallel street – narrow, curving Prästgatan – is a quiet alternative to the hubbub and far more atmospheric, giving you a much better idea of life in the crowded medieval city. At the southern end of Västerlånggatan is Mårten Trotzigs Gränd, the city's narrowest street at only 90 centimetres (three feet) wide. You'll notice it from the number of tourists gathered around its entrance, taking snaps of the photogenic steep steps. Just down from here is Järntorget, one of the island's main squares, where you can sit outdoors and enjoy the excellent cakes and pastries of **Sundbergs Konditori**.

There are only a handful of hotels on Gamla Stan; two of them – the **Victory Hotel** (www.thecollectorshotels.se) and the **Scandic Gamla Stan** (*see p209*) – are located on Lilla Nygatan, as is the surprisingly interesting **Postmuseum**. On nearby Stora Nygatan (Nos.10-12) you can visit the **Forum för Levande Historia** (Living History Forum; 723 87 50, www.levandehistoria.se, open noon-5pm Mon-Fri). Opened in 2004, it's a government exhibition centre and library focusing on human rights, prejudice and genocide.

The island's churches include the **Tyska Kyrkan** (German Church) and the **Finska Kyrkan** (Finnish Church) – proof of Sweden's long connections with its European neighbours. The latter is housed in a 1640s building opposite the Kungliga Slottet; originally a ball-games court for the palace, it has been the religious centre of the Finnish community since 1725.

IN THE KNOW
CHANGING THE GUARD

The **Högvakten** (Royal Guard; 402 63 17) has been stationed at the palace since 1523 and is a popular tourist attraction. The guard changes posts every day in summer but less frequently in winter (June-Aug 12.15pm Mon-Sat, 1.15pm Sun; Sept-May 12.15pm Wed, Sat, 1.15pm Sun), to the sound of a marching band. Around 20 soldiers in full livery go through their paces in the palace's outer western courtyard. The whole thing lasts about 35 minutes.

Gamla Stan also contains a number of beautiful palaces, all former homes of the aristocracy. On the island's north-western tip on Riddarhustorget is **Bondeska Palatset**, designed by Tessin the Elder and the seat of the Supreme Court since 1949, and the lovely **Riddarhuset** (723 39 90, www.riddarhuset.se). The nobility governed from here until parliamentary reforms in 1866 knocked them down a notch or two. They still own the place, though, and will let you visit during lunch hour (11.30am-12.30pm Mon-Fri, admission 60kr, 40kr reductions) to admire their coats of arms (more than 2,000 in all), signet collection and early 17th-century chair with ivory engravings. Another way to see inside is to attend a concert by the **Stockholm Sinfonietta** (*see p167*).

Finally, there's **Helgeandsholmen**, the tiny oval-shaped island that's connected to the southern end of Norrmalm and the northern end of Gamla Stan by two bridges: a pedestrian one at the western end and a car/pedestrian one at the eastern end. The **Riksdagshuset** (Parliament Building) dominates the whole western half of the island. As you walk north, the new parliament building is to your left and the old one to your right, joined by two stone arches. The older section, completed in 1905, was designed by Aron Johansson, with two chambers for a bicameral parliament, Baroque motifs and a grand staircase. At the same time he also designed a curved stone building across the street for the Bank of Sweden. After the country changed over to a unicameral

system in 1971, the bank moved out, the roof was flattened and the parliament's new glass-fronted debating chamber built on top.

This being Sweden, it's a pretty open system of government. There's a very detailed website (with text in Swedish and English), as well as an information centre (Storkyrkobrinken 7, www.riksdagen.se), and the parliament building is open for guided tours year round (for more information call 786 48 62). You can also visit the public gallery when parliament is in session and listen to debates.

Beneath the lawns at the other end of the island, the **Stockholms Medeltidsmuseum** provides a fascinating insight into life in medieval Stockholm.

Sights & Museums

Kungliga Myntkabinettet

Slottsbacken 6 (51 95 53 04, www.myntkabinettet. se). T-bana Gamla Stan or bus 2, 43, 55, 76, 96. **Open** 11am-5pm daily. **Admission** 70kr; 50kr reductions; free under-19s, all Mon & daily June-mid Aug. Free with SC. **Map** p43 C2 ❶
The Royal Coin Cabinet, a museum of rare coins and monetary history, is surprisingly large, filling three floors in a building directly south of the palace. The darkened ground floor displays numerous coins from around the world in different contexts, from the first coin made in Greece in 625 BC to what is claimed to be the world's biggest coin, which weighs in at a hefty 19.7kg (43lb).

Kungliga Slottet.
See p46.

EXPLORE

Kungliga Slottet

Bordered by Slottsbacken, Skeppsbron, Lejonbacken & Högvaktsterrassen (402 61 30, www.royalcourt. se). T-bana Gamla Stan or bus 2, 43, 55, 76, 96. **Open** *Representationsvåningarna, Museet Tre Kronor & Skattkammaren* mid Sept-mid May Tue-Sun 10am-4pm; mid May-mid Sept 10am-5pm daily (Royal Apartments can close for official engagements, check online for details). *Gustav III's Antikmuseum* mid May-mid Sept 10am-5pm daily. **Admission** 150kr; 75kr reductions; free under-7s (tickets valid for 7 days). Free with SC. **Map** p43 C1 ❷ *Photos p45.*

Representationsvåningarna

Entrance in western courtyard.
The Royal Apartments occupy two floors of the palace and are entered by a grand staircase in the western wing. Since it's the stories behind the rooms and decorations that make the palace especially interesting – such as Gustav III's invitation to aristocrats to watch him wake up in the morning – taking a guided tour is highly recommended. Banquets are held several times a year in Karl XI's Gallery in the State Apartments on the second floor. Heads of state stay in the Guest Apartments during their visits to the capital, and for this reason part or all of the palace may be occasionally closed. Downstairs in the Bernadotte Apartments, portraits of the current dynasty's ancestors hang in the Bernadotte Gallery. Medals and orders of various kinds are awarded in the Apartments of the Orders of Chivalry, and paintings of coats of arms decorate its walls. Until 1975, the monarch opened parliament each year in the Hall of State, and directly across from this lies the Royal Chapel with pew ends made in the 1690s for the Tre Kronor castle. Services are held every Sunday and all are welcome to attend.

Museet Tre Kronor

Entrance on Lejonbacken.
A boardwalk built through the palace cellars, along with several models, enables visitors to see how war, fire and wealth have shaped the palace as it is today. An old well from the former courtyard, a 13th-century defensive wall and the arched brick ceilings are evidence of how the palace was built up around the fortress that was once there. Panels describe life within the castle, archaeological discoveries and building techniques.

Gustav III's Antikmuseum

Entrance on Lejonbacken.
This museum of Roman statues and busts, in two halls in the north-east wing of the palace, has been laid out to look exactly as it did in the 1790s when King Gustav III returned from Italy with the collection, which includes *Apollo and His Nine Muses* and the sleeping *Endymion*. The repairs and additions made to the statues at the time have been left

Livrustkammaren.

intact, as well as the odd combinations of pieces, such as table legs on fountains. Nothing is labelled, in accordance with the period, so you should try and take the 20-minute tour (conducted in English) or borrow a pamphlet if you want to make the most of your visit.

Skattkammaren

Entrance on Slottsbacken.
The regalia of past Swedish royal families sparkles behind glass, with orbs, sceptres and crowns in adults' and children's sizes. The crowns are still in use for the monarch's inauguration and were present at the wedding of Carl Gustav and Silvia. The museum also contains Gustav Vasa's etched sword of state from 1541, the coronation cloak of Oscar II and the ornate silver baptismal font of Karl XI.

EXPLORE

Livrustkammaren

Entrance on Slottsbacken 3 (402 30 30, www. livrustkammaren.se). T-bana Gamla Stan or bus 2, 43, 55, 76, 96. **Open** *Jan-Apr* 11am-5pm Tue, Wed, Fri, Sat; 11am-8pm Thur. *May, June* 11am-5pm daily. *July, Aug* 10am-6pm daily. *Sept-Dec* 11am-5pm Mon-Wed; 11am-8pm Thur. **Admission** 90kr; free under-19s & all 5-8pm Thur Aug-Apr. Free with SC. **Map** p43 C1 ❸

The Royal Armoury is one of the palace's best museums – don't miss it. Sweden's oldest museum, which was founded in 1633, is stuffed full with armour, weapons and clothes from the 16th century onwards, and is housed in the palace's former cellars, which were used for storing potatoes and firewood. With wonderfully descriptive texts, the museum's first room shows what a bloody and dangerous business being a king once was. It contains the masked costume King Gustav III wore when he was assassinated in 1792, and the stuffed body of Streiff, the horse that Gustav II Adolf was riding when he was killed in battle in 1632. Don't overlook the glass jar preserving the stomach contents of one of the conspirators to Gustav III's murder. Other rooms display splendid mounted knights, suits of armour, swords and muskets. Two rooms of clothes and toys – including a miniature carriage – describe the lost childhoods and early responsibilities of the royal children. The ceremonial coaches lie beneath the main floor, in another hall. Guided tours in English are at 3pm (mid June-late Aug), and audio guides are available for 20kr.

Nobelmuseet

Stortorget (53 48 18 00, www.nobelmuseum.se). T-bana Gamla Stan or bus 2, 3, 43, 53, 55, 76, 96.

**IN THE KNOW
ROYAL SCULPTURE**

Since June 2010, Gamla Stan has had a new public sculpture. Called **Kyrka** (Church), the bronze sculpture depicting church bells is the work of Ernst Billgren, one of Sweden's best-known artists, to commemorate the royal wedding of Princess Victoria and Daniel Westling, her former personal trainer. The sculpture can be found on the quay below the Royal Palace.

Open *June-Aug* 10am-8pm daily. *Sept-May* Tue 11am-8pm; Wed-Sun 11am-5pm. **Guided tours** (in English) *June-Aug* 10.15am, 11.15am, 1pm, 3pm, 4pm, 6pm daily. *Sept-May* 11.15am, 1pm, 3pm Tue-Sun. **Admission** 100kr; 70kr reductions; free under-18s. Free with SC. **Map** p43 C2 ❹

The Nobel Museum opened in 2001 to commemorate the centenary of the Nobel Prizes. Although the museum is not that large, its two theatres showing short films about the laureates, television clips about the prizes and a computer room with an 'e-museum' bombard you with enough information to keep you entertained for a while. You can also listen to acceptance speeches over the years in audio booths, including that of Martin Luther King, Jr in 1964. Alfred Nobel's books, lab equipment and two packs of dynamite are displayed in a side room, along with his death mask and a copy of the first page of his four-page will, which called for the creation of the prizes. An exhibit on the Nobel banquet

EXPLORE

Riksdagshuset. *See p48.*

Stockholms Medeltidsmuseum.

EXPLORE

includes a glassed-in table setting and videos of the event. For more on the Nobel Prize, *see p49* **The Noblest of Them All**.

▶ *The Nobel Museum will be moving to a new, purpose-built building at Nybroviken (near the Grand Hôtel), with building work planned for completion in December 2018; see p49 for more information.*

Postmuseum

Ralambshovsleden 6, Lilla Nygatan 6 (436 44 39, www.postmuseum.posten.se). T-bana Gamla Stan or bus 3, 53. **Sept-Apr** 11am-4pm Tue-Sun; 11am-7pm Wed. **Admission** 60kr; 50kr reductions; free under-18s. Free with SC. **Map** p43 B3 ❺

Life-size scenes depicting more than 360 years of the Swedish postal service make the main exhibit of this museum unexpectedly enjoyable. A mounted postal carrier, a farm boy running with the mail and a postal train wagon, among other tableaux, illustrate the effect that the postal service has had on people's lives over the centuries. From 1720 until 1869, the city's only post office was housed on this spot. Lilla Posten downstairs includes a miniature post office for kids and the gift shop sells stationery and, of course, stamps.

FREE Riksdagshuset

Riksgatan 3 (786 40 00, www.riksdagen.se). T-bana Kungsträdgården or bus 43, 62, 65. **Open** (guided tours only) *End June-Aug* noon, 1pm, 2pm, 3pm Mon-Fri. *Oct-June* 1.30pm Sat, Sun. **Admission** free. **Map** p43 B1 ❻

Free 50-minute guided tours of the Riksdagshuset (Parliament Building) are given in Swedish and English. The guides are exceptionally well informed and the tour is interesting enough – if you don't mind a little education. You'll see the modern semicircular main chamber; at the front is a large tapestry, *Memory of a Landscape* by Elisabet Hasselberg Olsson, woven in 200 shades of grey. Beneath the chamber lies the former bank hall, now a lobby for the parliamentarians. In the old building, where the tour begins and ends, visitors are shown the grand former main entrance with its marble columns and busts of prime ministers, as well as the old dual chambers (now used as meeting rooms). *Photo p47.*

Stockholms Medeltidsmuseum

Strömparterren, Norrbro (508 31 620, www. medeltidsmuseet.stockholm.se). **Open** noon-5pm Tue, Thur-Sun; noon-7pm Wed. **Admission** 100kr. Free with SC. **Map** p43 C1 ❼

During an excavation of Helgeandsholmen during the late 1970s for the construction of a new parking garage for MPs, archaeologists discovered thousands of artefacts from medieval Stockholm. So, instead of the garage, parliament decided to build this underground museum, which underwent a recent refurbishment, reopening in 2010. The Medeltidsmuseum (Medieval Museum) contains more than 850 objects, a hidden passage to the castle and a 14th-century cemetery wall. Displays inform visitors about the emergence and medieval development of Stockholm.

▶ *The museum also runs 90-minute guided tours of Gamla Stan (2,000kr-3,000kr per group); call 508 31 620 to book (9am-noon Mon-Fri).*

THE NOBLEST OF THEM ALL

The man behind the prestigious awards – and the future of the prizes.

Born in Stockholm in 1833, Alfred Nobel spent his teenage years in Russia and early adulthood in the USA. On returning to Sweden, the chemist, engineer and inventor devoted himself to the study of explosives, inventing dynamite, which he patented in 1867. In 1888, he read his own obituary in a French newspaper, which had been erroneously published after his brother, Ludvig, died while visiting France. The scathing article condemned Alfred as a 'merchant of death', leading him to rethink how he was living his life and how he'd like to be remembered. Upon his actual death in 1896, Alfred Nobel, whose grave sits in Norra begravningsplatsen, bequeathed his huge fortune (around 1.8 billion kronor in today's money) as an endowment to humanity. His last will specified that the generated interest 'shall be annually distributed in the form of prizes to those who, during the preceding year, shall have conferred the greatest benefit on mankind'. He specified five categories; physics, chemistry, medicine, literature and peace. The first prizes, set at 150,782 kronor, were awarded in 1901.

The Nobel Prizes today are still each field's most prestigious annual award. The Peace Prize is awarded in Oslo, Norway, while the other prizes are awarded in Stockholm on 10 December (the anniversary of Nobel's death) in the Stockholm Concert Hall (with a Nobel banquet, attended by the Swedish royal family, taking place in Stockholm City Hall). Each recipient receives around 10 million kronor from the Nobel Foundation.

A purpose-built 'Nobel Center', which will be the new focus of the Nobel Prize in Stockholm, is in the wings, planned for completion in 2018. The exciting and ambitious new space, designed by David Chipperfield Architects Berlin, will sit at Nybroviken (near the Grand Hôtel), and the aim is for it to host thought-provoking events, talks and conferences, and, of course, the Nobel Prize itself. The Nobelmuseet (*see p47*) will also move here. Visit www.nobelcenter.se for more information, including a timeline for the building.

FAMOUS WINNERS

Famous Nobel laureates include Marie Curie (Physics 1903, Chemistry 1911); Rudyard Kipling (Literature 1907); Albert Einstein (Physics 1921); Alexander Fleming (Medicine 1945); Martin Luther King, Jr (Peace 1964); Nelson Mandela (Peace 1993); Doris Lessing (Literature 2007); Al Gore (Peace 2007); and Barack Obama (Peace 2009). Jean-Paul Sartre declined the Literature Prize in 1964.

CONTROVERSIAL WINNERS

The most notorious Nobel Prize recipient is **Fritz Haber**, dubbed the 'father of chemical warfare'. Haber received the 1918 chemistry prize at the end of World War I, during which he developed chlorine gas, which killed thousands in the trenches in Belgium. More than 60 years later, people continue to lobby for the posthumous revocation of **Egas Moniz**'s 1949 prize in medicine, awarded for his discovery of the lobotomy. Opponents cite the misuse of his procedure, which condemned patients to a near zombie-like existence. Other controversial laureates have included **Henry Kissinger** and **Lê Duc Tho** (the latter declined the prize). They were awarded the Peace Prize for negotiating a ceasefire between North Vietnam and the US in 1973, despite hostilities still occurring. Two Norwegian Nobel Committee members resigned over the award.

NOBEL BY NUMBERS

Nobel Laureates 851 individuals, 25 organisations
Female Laureates 45
Youngest Laureate Lawrence Bragg (25yrs; Physics 1915)
Oldest Laureate Leonid Hurwicz (90yrs; Economic Sciences 2007)

EXPLORE

A VIEW FROM ABOVE

Three ways to get a bird's eye view of the city.

EXPLORE

There are a large variety of ways to tour Stockholm, and a boat tour of the city and its surrounding archipelago is an essential activity on any visitor's itinerary. Innovative walking tours, too, such as the **Millennium Tours** (see p103), inspired by Stieg Larsson's extraordinarily popular books, are a good way of finding out about aspects of the city that you might miss if touring alone. However, two tours have been under the spotlight recently, both offering a bird's eye view of the city – although from two very different angles.

The rooftop tours offered by **Takvandring** (www.takvandring.com; *pictured*) are a good starting point for learning about the history of Stockholm. Tours take place in Riddarholmen, on the roof of the seven-storey Old Parliamentary Building, next to Riddarholmskyrkan (see p57), and take in interesting views of the rooftops of Gamla Stan, as well as of the surrounding areas. The amiable guides provide interesting and humorous facts and anecdotes about the evolution of Stockholm (for instance, explaining why the rooftops are painted black). With secure 'catwalks' firmly anchored to the roof, there is virtually no risk involved – though those who suffer from vertigo might want to think twice before

booking. Tours, which are available in mixed groups of English and German (Apr-June Fri; July, Aug Mon, Thur, Fri, Sun) or English and Swedish (July, Aug Tue, Wed, Sat), cost 595kr per person and last for about 75 minutes.

Another way to see Stockholm from above is by booking on the **SkyView** (0771 811 000, www.globearenas.se/en/skyview) attraction, which takes you on a ride over the spherical Ericsson Globen (see p147), a Stockholm landmark. Reaching a height of 130 metres (425 feet), the two glass 'gondolas', which each have space for 16 people, offer commanding views of the Stockholm horizon and the surrounding area (which, it should be noted, isn't the most classically scenic part of the city). Rides depart every ten minutes, and the entire experience takes around 30 minutes. What's more, holders of the Stockholm Card can ride for free.

Stockholm is also one of the few European cities to allow hot-air balloons to fly over its centre. The season is May and September, and flights are generally in the early evening. You need to book at least two weeks in advance (bad weather can result in cancellations). Try **Far & Flyg** (645 77 00, www.farochflyg.se), which charges 2,345kr for a one-hour flight plus a champagne picnic.

Storkyrkan
Storkyrkobrinken, Trångsund 1 (723 30 00, www. stockholmsdomkyrkoforsamling.se). T-bana Gamla Stan or bus 2, 3, 43, 53, 55, 76, 96. **Open** *Sept-May* 9am-6pm daily. *June* 9am-7pm Mon-Fri; 9am-4pm Sat, Sun. *July, Aug* 9am-6pm Mon-Fri; 9am-4pm Sat, Sun. **Guided tours** (no extra fee) check website for times. **Admission** 40kr; free under-18s & all Sun or for prayer. *Tour of the Tower* 60kr. Free with SC. **Map** p43 C2 ❽

Dating from the mid 13th century, 'the Great Church' is the oldest congregational church in Stockholm and the site of past coronations and royal weddings. A huge brick church with a rectangular plan, it's been extended and rebuilt numerous times. Between 1736 and 1742, its exterior was renovated from medieval to Baroque to match the neighbouring palace, and in 1743 the tower was raised to its current height of 66m (216ft). Inside, the style is primarily Gothic with Baroque additions – such as the extravagant golden booths designed for the royal family by the palace architect Tessin the Younger. The main attraction is Bernt Notke's intricately carved wooden statue, *St George and the Dragon*, which is decorated with authentic elk antlers. The statue symbolises Sten Sture's victory over the Danes in a battle in 1471, and was given to the church by Sture himself in 1489. (A bronze copy of the statue can also be found in Köpmantorget, not far from the church.) Don't miss the famous *Parhelion* painting, which shows an unusual light phenomenon – six sparkling halos – that appeared over Stockholm on 20 April 1535. It's one of the oldest depictions of the capital, though the painting is a 1630s copy of the earlier original. From July to mid August, theology students give guided tours (in Swedish and English) of the church's tower (9am & 1pm Mon-Fri, 40kr including entry fee to the church, call 723 30 00 to

book), which involves climbing 200 steps on narrow wooden staircases for an amazing view of the black roofs of Gamla Stan. *Photo p42.*

FREE Tyska Kyrkan
Svartmangatan 16 (411 11 88, www.svenska kyrkan.se/deutschegemeinde). T-bana Gamla Stan or bus 2, 3, 43, 53, 55, 76, 96. **Open** 9am-3pm Tue, Thur; 9am-noon Wed; 9am-2pm Fri (outside of religious services). **Admission** free. *Concerts* 50kr. **Map** p43 C2 ❾

At the height of the Hanseatic League, when Stockholm had strong trade links with Germany, many German merchants settled in this area of Gamla Stan. They originally worshipped at the monastery on what is now Riddarholmen, but moved to St Gertrude's guildhouse after its expansion in the 1580s. Baroque renovations in 1638-42 gave the German Church its present appearance; its tower was rebuilt after a fire in 1878. Tessin the Elder designed the royal pews, and Jost Henner created the richly decorated ornaments and figures on the portal. The church is best viewed from Tyska Brinken, where the tower rises up 96m (315ft) from the narrow street. At the church's summer concerts, you can listen to a replica of a 17th-century organ, constructed for the church in 2004 at a cost of ten million kronor. There's also a café in summer.

Restaurants

19 Glas Bar & Matsal
Stora Nygatan 19 (723 19 19, www.19glas.com). T-bana Gamla Stan or bus 3, 53. **Open** noon-midnight Mon-Sat. **Set menu** 499kr. **Map** p43 B2 ❿ **Contemporary**

The size of a living room, 19 Glas used to be able to host only 19 guests (hence the name). Coming here

19 Glas Bar & Matsal.

Den Gyldene Freden.

EXPLORE

The menu goes from classic French to more modern Mediterranean influences, and it's all well cooked, tasty and not overworked. Next door, Grill Ruby is noisier and more fun, and it's all about the meat, so vegetarians should steer clear. With each cut you get a wide choice of tapas, salsas and other accompaniments. The weekend brunch is recommended.

★ Den Gyldene Freden

Österlånggatan 51 (24 97 60, www.gyldenefreden. se). T-bana Gamla Stan or bus 2, 43, 55, 76, 96. **Open** 11.30am-2.30pm, 5-10pm Mon-Wed; 11am-2.30pm, 5-11pm Thur, Fri; 1-11pm Sat. **Main courses** 180kr-380kr. **Map** p43 D3 ⓬
Traditional Swedish
This first-class restaurant is housed in an 18th-century building owned by the Swedish Academy, and the dimly lit interior lends a suitably grandiose atmosphere to a meal here. Since it first opened in 1722, large sections of Stockholm's cultural elite have dined here – singer-poet Carl Michael Bellman, painter Anders Zorn and singer-composer Evert Taube were regular customers. As you'd expect, the menu is stocked with traditional Swedish dishes, including smoked reindeer, meatballs and plenty of herring and salmon.

Flying Elk

Mälartorget 15 (20 85 83, www.theflyingelk.se). T-bana Gamla Stan. **Open** 5pm-midnight Mon, Tue; 5pm-1am Wed-Fri; noon-1am Sat, Sun. **Main courses** 159kr-345kr. **Map** p43 B3
⓭ **Gastropub**
With the same owners as Frantzén, this Old Town gastropub with chunky wooden tables had an auspicious start when it opened in 2013, and it remains a solid bet in an area crowded with tourist traps. British influences are evident in both the atmosphere and the menu, but the place still allows space for some local interpretation: 'God Save the Elk' is the unofficial slogan, and dishes include the likes of posh fish and chips with curry remoulade, pan-fried local char with new potatoes, and an Eton mess that definitely isn't for purists. Camden Town Brewery beer is on offer, and an 'Iron Lady Burger' is the speciality on Sundays.

★ Frantzén

Lilla Nygatan 21 (20 85 80, www.restaurant frantzen.com). T-bana Gamla Stan. **Open** 6.30pm-midnight Tue-Fri; 3pm-midnight Sat. **Tasting menu** 2,300kr. **Map** p43 C3
⓮ **Contemporary**
Awarded the best restaurant accolade by Sweden's *White* guide, the national food bible, and two Michelin stars, this restaurant, previously called Frantzén & Lindeberg, is a must for foodies. The owners grow their own vegetables and herbs in the restaurant garden, while other raw materials come from local farmers, fishermen and wine-makers. The amuse-bouches are extremely imaginative

is a bit like visiting someone at home. The menu changes each night – a four- or seven-course journey into whatever locally produced ingredients the owner has found that day. The wine list is well put together and the two-course set lunch is good value.

Bistro Ruby & Grill Ruby

Österlånggatan 14 (20 57 76/60 15, www.grill ruby.com). T-bana Gamla Stan or bus 2, 43, 55, 76, 96. **Open** *Bistro Ruby* 5-11pm Mon-Sat. *Grill Ruby* 11am-1am daily; brunch 11.30am-4pm Sat, Sun. **Main courses** *Bistro Ruby* 195kr-295kr. *Grill Ruby* 174kr-478kr. **Map** p43 D2 ⓫ **French/North American**
These two sister restaurants set out to combine Paris and Texas. Bistro Ruby offers European formality in a pleasant environment ideal for a quiet chat.

(macaroon with foie gras and pear, for instance), with the set menu amounting to a cutting-edge taste extravaganza. A dinner experience here certainly generates conversation.

Le Rouge

Brunnsgränd 2-4 (505 244 30, www.lerouge.se). T-bana Gamla Stan or bus 2, 43, 55, 76, 96. **Open** 6pm-1am Tue; 5pm-1am Wed-Sat. *Food served* until 11pm. **Set menu** 650kr. **Map** p43 D2 **⑮ French**
Melker Andersson's Le Rouge allows you to step into the world of French decadence from the Moulin Rouge era. The chef's fine dining restaurant is all red velvet, low lighting and waitresses in can-can clothes. The food is pretty good, too – traditional French, with lots of meat and fish dishes. Le Bar

Rouge (*see p55*), in the same building, is one of Stockholm's most popular drinking spots, with good cocktails and a cheaper food menu.

Pastis

Baggensgatan 12 (20 20 18, www.pastis.se). T-bana Gamla Stan or bus 2, 43, 55, 76, 96. **Open** *Takeaway* 11.30am-3.30pm Mon-Fri. *Restaurant* 5-11pm Mon-Sat. **Main courses** 195kr-290kr. **Map** p43 C2 **⑯ French**
Favoured by locals, this cute corner bistro in the heart of the Old Town serves up a good selection of French classics (bouillabaisse, steak tartare, foie gras, beef bourguignon) from a charming old building. The authentic atmosphere makes it feel like it's been here for decades, but the restaurant actually

Frantzén.

EXPLORE

Chokladkoppen.

opened in 2009, and has been steadily building up a local clientele. There are outdoor tables in summer.

Cafés

For ice-cream and fresh waffles, stop at **Café Kåkbrinken** (Västerlånggatan 41, 411 61 74), near **Sundbergs Konditori** (*see p55*).

★ Chokladkoppen

Stortorget 18 (20 31 70, www.chokladkoppen.se). T-bana Gamla Stan or bus 2, 3, 43, 53, 55, 96. **Open** *Winter* 10am-10pm Mon-Thur; 10am-11pm Fri; 9am-11pm Sat; 9am-10pm Sun. *Summer* 9am-11pm daily. **Map** p43 C2 ⓱
Just how good can a hot chocolate really be? To find out, skip Gamla Stan's tourist traps and head for this place on Stortorget, the charming square at the centre of Gamla Stan. Colourful Chokladkoppen has a trendy feel and a traditional interior, and is popular with Stockholm's gay crowd. The laid-back service suffers at weekends when it gets ridiculously busy. In summer, the tables outside are a prime spot. It also serves fantastic cakes and snacks – don't miss the utterly divine white chocolate cheesecake.
▶ *Sister café Kaffekoppen, next door at no.18, has a similarly cosy feel and serves decent savoury dishes.*

★ Fabrique

Lilla Nygatan 12 (20 81 44, www.fabrique.se). T-bana Gamla Stan or bus 3, 53. **Open** 7.30am-7pm Mon-Fri; 8am-6pm Sat, Sun. **Map** p43 B3 ⓲
This successful bakery mini-chain sells superior sandwiches, buns and pastries, as well as a range of quality fruit juices and yoghurts. The interior of the corner building is entered from Schönfeldts Gränd, and has a clean industrial look, with white wall tiles, chequered floors and vintage tables and chairs. There are other handy locations on Götgatan in Södermalm, Odenplan and Nybrogatan; check the website for the full list.
Other locations throughout the city.

Grillska Husets Konditori

Stortorget 3 (684 233 64). T-bana Gamla Stan or bus 2, 3, 43, 53, 55, 71, 76, 96. **Open** *Café* 9am-6pm Mon-Fri; 10am-6pm Sat, Sun. *Lunch* served 11am-2pm weekdays. *Bakery* 8am-6pm Mon-Fri; 9am-4pm Sat. **Map** p43 C2 ⓳
This café and bakery in a corner of Stortorget is run by a charitable group that works with the homeless. For a real treat, walk through the downstairs café and follow signs through to the tranquil first-floor terrace, which is one of Gamla Stan's best-kept secrets. With good-value pastries and friendly service on offer, spend your change here and make a difference.

Muren

Västerlånggatan 19 (10 80 70). T-bana Gamla Stan or bus 3, 53, 55, 76, 96. **Open** 10am-7pm Mon-Thur, Sun; 10am-8pm Fri, Sat. **Map** p43 B2 ⓴

EXPLORE

Navigate the cobblestones to this café, which transforms itself from a trendy café in winter into a popular ice-cream parlour in summer. Remnants of the building's 13th-century wall remain intact (though not visible), hence the name. This gay-friendly establishment serves the usual selection of sandwiches and pastries when in café mode; otherwise it dishes up one of the largest selections of ice-cream in the capital.

Sundbergs Konditori

Järntorget 83 (10 67 35). T-bana Gamla Stan or bus 2, 3, 43, 53, 55, 59, 71, 76, 96. **Open** 9am-8.30pm Mon-Fri; 9.30am-8.30pm Sat, Sun. **Map** p43 C3 ㉑

This place has served hot coffee from a copper samovar for more than 200 years. Believed to be Stockholm's oldest *konditori*, it was founded in 1785 by Johan Ludvig Sundberg. According to local lore, King Gustav III had a secret passageway from the Kungliga Slottet straight to the bakery. Don't expect newfangled frappuccinos and smoothies here: come to Sundbergs for traditional cakes and atmosphere. This is a good starting point for navigating the curiosities and cobbles of nearby Västerlånggatan, Gamla Stan's busiest street.

Bars

In the Old Town, most of the bars are situated around Kornhamnstorg or Järntorget. If you're a jazz fan, try the bar at **Stampen** jazz pub (www.stampen.se), which is pretty lively.

Engelen

Kornhamnstorg 59B (0771 826 826, www.engelen.se). T-bana Gamla Stan or bus 2, 3, 53, 55, 59, 73, 76, 96. **Open** *Bar* 4pm-12.30am Mon-Thur, Sun; 4pm-2.30am Fri, Sat. *Food served* until 11pm Sun-Thur; midnight Fri, Sat. **Minimum age** 23. **Admission** (after 8pm) 80kr Mon-Thur, Sun; 120kr Fri, Sat. **Map** p43 C3 ㉒

Posing as a rustic tavern (both bar and steak restaurant), Engelen caters firmly to groups of passing tourists and middle-aged locals looking to get down and party. The main room has a stage where Sweden's top covers bands play familiar tunes from 8.30pm to midnight most days. When that's finished, guests move down to the vaulted nightclub in the 15th-century cellar, where chart tracks are mixed with a selection of popular classics.

Le Bar Rouge

Österlånggatan 17 (505 244 60, www.lerouge.se). T-bana Gamla Stan or bus 2, 43, 55, 76, 96. **Open** 6pm-1am Tue; 5pm-1am Wed-Sat. *Food served* until 11pm. **Minimum age** 18. **Map** p43 D2 ㉓

At this sultry brasserie, you won't find any traces of Scandinavian minimalism. The place is draped in plush red velvet, the floors are covered with gaudy flower-patterned carpeting and there are plenty of gold details. So for a healthy dose of Moulin Rouge, and a break from the reigning taut Swedish interior design sensibilities, enjoy your favourite libation here. An excellent French restaurant, Le Rouge, is part of the same complex; *see p53.*

Fabrique.

EXPLORE

EXPLORE

Riddarholmen.

Medusa

Kornhamnstorg 61 (no phone, www.medusabar. com). T-bana Gamla Stan or bus 2, 3, 53, 55, 76, 96. **Open** *Bar* 1pm-3am daily. *Food served* until midnight daily. **Minimum age** 18. **Admission** free. **Map** p43 C3 ㉓

A small bar with a cavernous basement, Medusa is Gamla Stan's heavy-metal hangout. The upstairs bar plays basic rock music to a mixed crowd of tourists and local headbangers. Downstairs in the catacombs, the music is louder and harder.

Shops & Services

★ E Torndahl

Västerlånggatan 63 (10 34 09, www.etorndahl.se). T-bana Gamla Stan or bus 2, 43, 55, 76, 96. **Open** 10am-6pm Mon-Sat; 11am-6pm Sun. **Map** p43 C3 ㉕ **Gifts & souvenirs**

This family-owned Scandinavian design shop beats most of the other Gamla Stan gift shops hands down, with a lovely selection of homewares, jewellery and accessories. The graphics-led posters will appeal to both adults and children, while the handcrafted wooden moose ornaments make for a nice change from the ubiquitous Dala horse souvenirs.

★ English Bookshop

Lilla Nygatan 11 (790 55 10, www.bookshop.se). T-bana Gamla Stan or bus 2, 43, 55, 76, 96. **Open** 10am-6.30pm Mon-Fri; 11am-4pm Sat; noon-3pm Sun. **Map** p43 B3 ㉖ **Books**

This well-stocked and exclusively English-language bookshop is the sister venue of an established Uppsala bookshop of the same name. You'll find a well-edited selection of fiction, including plenty of new titles, as well as books on history, art and design, current affairs, cookery and travel, with a good number of books on Swedish culture. Staff are friendly and helpful, and the shop also sells copies of the *Guardian Weekly*.

Kalikå

Österlånggatan 18 (20 52 19, www.kalika.se). T-bana Gamla Stan or bus 2, 43, 55, 76, 96. **Open** 11am-5pm Mon-Fri; 11am-4pm Sat. **Map** p43 C2 ㉗ **Children**

With clothes, hats, finger puppets and stuffed toys all in brightly coloured 1970s-style velour, you can reincarnate your youngster as a hippie kid. The lovely shop also sells science kits, tea sets, children's musical instruments and giant bubble-blowing kits.

RIDDARHOLMEN

Riddarholmen's main attraction is the medieval brick church, **Riddarholmskyrkan**. Next to the church is **Birger Jarls Torg**, the site of an 1854 statue of Stockholm's founder, Birger Jarl. The huge white **Wrangelska Palatset** stands to the west of the statue. Constructed as a nobleman's residence in the mid 17th century, it was extensively rebuilt a few decades later by Tessin the Elder, under its new owner,

Riddarholmskyrkan.

EXPLORE

Field Marshal Carl Gustaf Wrangel. The palace became the home of the royal family for several years after the Tre Kronor fire of 1697.

On the other side of the square is the well-preserved, pink-coloured **Stenbockska Palatset**, built in the 1640s by state councillor Fredrik Stenbock, and extended and renovated in succeeding centuries. Several of the palaces of Riddarholmen are today used by the Swedish courts and government authorities. They are seldom open to the public, but taking a walk around them is highly recommended.

Down by the water on **Evert Taubes Terrass**, you'll find one of the best views in Stockholm, looking out across the choppy water of Riddarfjärden and towards the shores of Lake Mälaren. The terrace is named after the much-loved Swedish poet and troubadour Evert Taube (who died in 1976) and there's a bronze sculpture of him, lute in hand, near the water. It's also a prime spot to celebrate the arrival of spring on Walpurgis Night, with a bonfire by the water and communal singing. Author and dramatist August Strindberg was born here in 1849. A plaque in Swedish on a nearby wall commemorates the site of his birth.

North along the waterfront, on Norra Riddarholmshamnen, is the distinctive circular **Birger Jarls Torn**. The only remnant of the defensive fortifications built by Gustav Vasa around 1530 (along with part of the Wrangelska Palatset), it was given its name in the 19th century

when it was mistakenly thought to have been built under Birger Jarl 600 years earlier. It's not open to the public.

Sights & Museums

Riddarholmskyrkan

Birger Jarls Torg (402 61 30, www.royalcourt.se). T-bana Gamla Stan or bus 3, 53. **Open** *Mid May–mid Sept* 10am-5pm daily. Closed mid Sept-mid May. **Tours** in English 12pm daily. **Admission** 50kr; 25kr reductions; free under-18s. Free with SC. No cash. **Map** p43 A2 ㉓

The black, lattice-work spire of Riddarholmskyrkan is one of Stockholm's most distinctive sights, visible from all over the city. Construction on the church started in the late 13th century as a monastery for Franciscan monks. The church's benefactor, King Magnus Ladulås, is buried in the church along with 16 other monarchs, including Gustav III, Gustav II Adolf and, the last to be buried here in 1950, Gustav V. Since the 17th century, only two Swedish monarchs have not been buried here. Additions have been made to the church over time, in part to make room for more graves, since an estimated 500-1,000 people are buried in its floors and vaults. The southern wall was moved back in the 15th century, the tower was added in the late 16th century, and work began in 1838 on the current cast-iron spire after lightning struck the original. Colourful plaques of the Serafim order, which are awarded to Swedish nobility and visiting heads of state, decorate the walls of the church.

Norrmalm & Vasastan

Most of downtown Norrmalm resulted from a massive 'renewal' campaign in the 1960s, in which nearly all of the district's older buildings were torn down in favour of boxy office space. The area continues to develop today, with a growing number of shops and modern hotels. It's also known for its restaurants, nightclubs, and some key museums and sights. Most visitors to Stockholm arrive in Norrmalm, zoomed in on the Arlanda Express to its terminal next to Central Station. Stepping out from here, you immediately see the kind of functionalist concrete buildings that dominate the area.

Much of Vasastan (formerly Vasastaden), to the north of Norrmalm, was built in the late 1800s to accommodate Stockholm's growing population. Aside from its main thoroughfares of Sveavägen, Odengatan and St Eriksgatan, the area has stayed primarily residential, with several beautiful parks.

EXPLORE

Lilla Ego.

Don't Miss

1 **Mathias Dahlgren** Treat your tastebuds to a Scandi splurge (p66).

2 **Lilla Ego** Stripped-back restaurant with a cosy vibe and creative food (p78).

3 **Gustaf Vasa Kyrka** Beautiful Baroque church with a dominating 60-metre dome (p74).

4 **NK** Shop in style at Stockholm's equivalent of Selfridges (p72).

5 **Sosta** Standing room only at Sweden's finest espresso bar (p80).

Sergels Torg.

EXPLORE

NORRMALM

Those wanting to head straight into the very heart of the shopping district should take **Klarabergsgatan** from Central Station, which ends at Sergelses Torg. To see the water and the more picturesque areas of Norrmalm, head south on the eastern side of Vasagatan. Swing round the corner when you reach the **Sheraton Stockholm Hotel** and wajapalk one block up Jakobsgatan to avoid the horrible tangle of highways and viaducts. The nearby **Konstakademien** (Royal Academy of Art), on parallel Fredsgatan, occupies a renovated palace designed by Tessin the Elder in the 1670s.

Many of Sweden's government departments are nearby, such as the two buildings – one light orange and the other red – called **Rosenbad**, which house the offices of the prime minister. A stone walkway and bicycle path follow the northern shore of **Norrström** – from Rosenbad to the tip of the Blasieholmen peninsula. East on Fredsgatan is **Gustav Adolfs Torg**, named after King Gustav II Adolf, who greatly expanded the city in the early 17th century; a statue of the King stands in the centre of the square. Not far away there are Mediterranean antiquities in the **Medelhavsmuseet** and dance costumes in the **Dansmuseet**.

On the square's eastern flank is the grand **Kungliga Operan** (*see p167*), which was styled after the Royal Palace in the late 19th century, with a splendid chandelier-strewn gold foyer 28 metres (92 feet) long. The original opera building, where King Gustav III was assassinated in 1792, looked exactly like **Arvfurstens Palats**, the building across from it, which was constructed in the 1780s and is now used by the Ministry for Foreign Affairs. The Opera House contains several restaurants, varying in splendour and price; the fanciest, and one of Sweden's best, is **Operakällaren**. From the front of the opera house you get a beautiful view across the water towards Kungliga Slottet; behind it stands the earthy red Gothic structure of **St Jacobs Kyrka**.

The rectangular park of **Kungsträdgården** (King's Garden) stretches north from here. This is a popular venue for open-air events and fairs. Originally a vegetable garden for the royal castle in the 15th century, the park later developed into a pleasure garden and opened to the public in the 18th century. A century later, French-born King Karl XIV Johan tore out the trees, erected a statue of his adoptive father, Karl XIII, and converted the garden into a field for military exercises. After his death it was turned back into a park. The statue of Karl XII – his finger pointing to his old battlegrounds in Russia – was added in 1868 near the water.

Two tree-lined avenues shade the restaurants and glassed-in cafés along the park's western and eastern edges. At the top end of the park, in front of a shallow pool with three fountains, is the touristy Friday's American Bar, while Volvo's newest and oldest cars are displayed in a showroom nearby. In winter, there's skating on the park's ice rink.

The crowded thoroughfare of **Hamngatan** crosses over the top of Kungsträdgården. The street's highlight is **NK**, Sweden's first and most exclusive department store. For cheaper shops, try the **Gallerian** mall just up the street. A couple of blocks west along from NK is **Sergels Torg**. This two-level area of glass, concrete and underground shops was built after the bulldozer extravaganza of the 1960s. The sunken modernist square of black-and-white triangles is a popular spot for political demonstrations; the rather grubby, tall glass tower surrounded by fountains in the middle of the traffic island was designed by sculptor Edvin Öhrström in 1972.

Architect Peter Celsing was responsible for **Kulturhuset**, the seven-storey structure that stands behind Sergels Torg like a great glass wall, which he built in the early 1970s. Today it's home to Stockholm's main tourist office, as well as Sweden's only comic book library, **Serieteket**. Also here is one of Stockholm's biggest theatres, **Stadsteatern** (*see p168*). Take the escalators up to the galleries on the upper floors to check out one of the many temporary art exhibitions, as well as the National Museum's temporary design space, housed here during its extensive refurbishment. The top-floor **Café Panorama** has a great view. There's also a library, an internet café and a branch of **DesignTorget**.

Several main streets converge on Sergels Torg, including Klarabergsgatan and Sveavägen. The block-long, windowless **Åhléns** department store occupies the north-west corner of the former, just one of scores of shopping options. The more downmarket pedestrian street of **Drottninggatan** is lined with shops from its start at the water's edge all the way north to Tegnérgatan, and is permanently heaving with hungry shoppers.

North from Sergels Torg five glass office buildings stand in a row towards the open space of Hötorget; built in the 1950s, they're city landmarks – whether people want them to be or not. **Hötorget** is home to the **PUB** department store and an outdoor market selling fruit, flowers and a bit of everything. The indoor, international food hall, **Hötorgshallen**, bustles beneath the **Filmstaden Sergel** multiplex (*see p156*). On another side stands the **Konserthuset** (*see p167*). Stockholm's main concert hall is apparently a prime example of Swedish neo-classical style, but to the untrained eye the 1926 building looks suspiciously like a bright blue box with ten grey pillars attached to it.

Further north on Drottninggatan, **Centralbadet** is a lovely, art nouveau bathhouse built in 1905, with café tables in its pretty front courtyard. Nearby, **Dansens Hus** (*see p171*) is the capital's main venue for modern dance. To the east of Dansens Hus, on Sveavägen, stands

the classical **Adolf Fredriks Kyrka**. It has a Greek cross plan and a beautifully painted ceiling; assassinated prime minister Olof Palme is buried in the cemetery here. On the corner of Drottninggatan and Tegnérgatan is the building in which August Strindberg spent the last four years of his life. His apartment is now home to the **Strindbergsmuseet** – a must for fans of Sweden's greatest author. On Drottninggatan, near the museum, a few of Strindberg's famous quotes have been printed on the street in Swedish.

Down at the southern tip of Norrmalm, the **Blasieholmen** peninsula pokes out into the water towards Skeppsholmen. At the end of this spur of land stands the imposing limestone façade of Sweden's largest art museum, the **Nationalmuseum**, closed until 2017 for a huge refurbishment. North along the waterfront, on Strömkajen, in front of the five-star **Grand Hôtel** (*see p209*), is the boarding point for sightseeing boats and ferries to the archipelago. Another wharf for ferries (to the archipelago and, in summer, to Djurgården and Slussen) is across the peninsula at the small harbour of Nybroviken.

Overlooking the lawns of Berzelii Park is **Berns Salonger**, a legendary venue since the 1860s. It's still a nightlife favourite, and its magnificent salons, gilded and topped with crystal chandeliers, now play host to one of Stockholm's largest restaurants (**Berns Asia**, as well as **Bistro Berns**), plus several bars.

Sights & Museums

Dansmuseet

Drottninggatan 17 (441 76 50, www.dansmuseet.se). T-bana Centralen or Kungsträdgården or bus 43, 62, 65. **Open** 11am-5pm Tue-Fri; noon-4pm Sat, Sun. **Admission** 80kr; 60kr reductions; free under-18s. **Map** p63 E6 **❶**

EXPLORE

EXPLORE

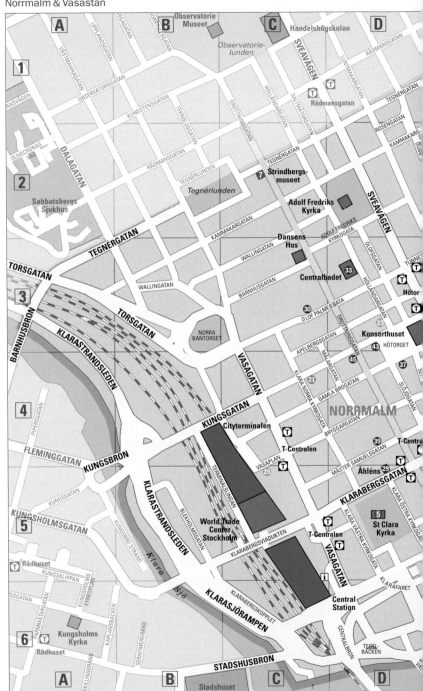

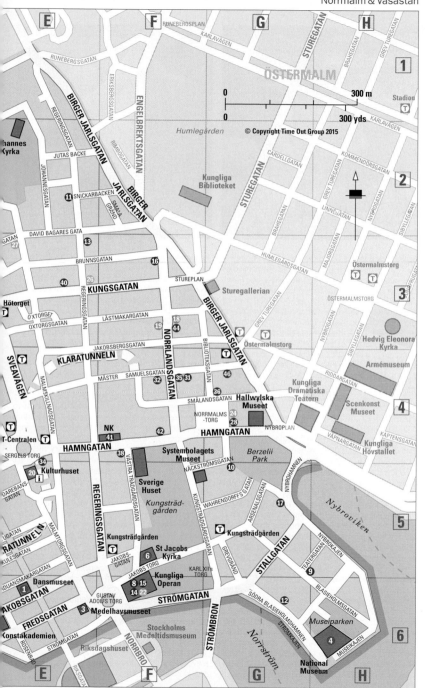

EXPLORE

Medelhavsmuseet.

EXPLORE

Now housed in a new building on Drottninggatan, the Dance Museum displays costumes from Swedish and Russian ballets, paintings and sketches related to dance, and traditional masks and costumes from Africa, Thailand, China, Japan and Tibet. Rolf de Maré, who managed the Swedish Ballet in Paris in the 1920s, opened the museum in the French capital in 1933. When the museum closed in the 1940s, the contents relating to Swedish and non-European dance were relocated to Stockholm. The collection is small but well presented. A variety of free dance films are also screened regularly. Be sure to visit the well-stocked café too.

Konstakademien

Fredsgatan 12 (23 29 25, www.konstakademien.se). T-bana Kungsträdgården or T-Centralen or bus 43, 62, 65. **Open** 11am-5pm Tue-Fri; noon-4pm Sat, Sun. **Admission** 100kr; 80kr reductions; free under-21s. Free with SC. **Map** p63 E6 ❷
The Royal Academy of Fine Arts was founded by King Gustav III in 1773 and moved into its current premises in 1780. In 1978, it was separated from the Royal University College of Fine Arts, which is today on Skeppsholmen. The building is currently housing the Nationalmuseum's temporary themed exhibitions while the latter's building at Blasieholmen undergoes a four-year renovation (*see right*). The academy's terrace bar is very popular in summer.

Medelhavsmuseet

Fredsgatan 2 (456 12 98, www.medelhavsmuseet.se). T-bana Kungsträdgården or bus 43, 62, 65. **Open** noon-8pm Tue-Fri; noon-5pm Sat, Sun. **Admission** 80kr; free under-18s. Free with SC. **Map** p63 E6 ❸
Artefacts from Greece, Rome, Egypt and Cyprus are housed in the Museum of Mediterranean Antiquities. Displayed in the main hall are a variety of busts and statues, while other rooms contain Islamic art, early medical instruments, ancient

sarcophagi and a reconstruction of an Egyptian tomb. The Gold Room, a vault holding ancient wreaths of gold, is open between 12.30pm and 1pm or 2.30pm and 3pm. The second-floor Bagdad café serves Mediterranean specialities for lunch.

Nationalmuseum

Södra Blasieholmshamnen (51 95 43 00, www. nationalmuseum.se). T-bana Kungsträdgården or bus 2, 62, 65, 76, 96. **Open** Closed until 2017. **Map** p63 H6 ❹
Sweden's largest museum is currently closed for a huge and much-needed refurbishment. It is expected to reopen in 2017 with a new state-of-the-art climate control system – which will allow the museum to exhibit more climate-sensitive works – and a more integrated display system. More visitor amenities and open public spaces are also planned for the renovated space. Until this time, temporary thematic exhibitions based on the museum's collections are being held at Konstakademien (Swedish Royal Academy of Fine Arts; *see left*) and Kulturhuset (*see p168*). The latter is displaying collaborative design exhibitions with the museum. The vast majority of the Nationalmuseum's paintings, sculptures, drawings and decorative arts, dating from the Middle Ages to the present, will be unavailable to the public during the renovations, though.

The creation of the Nationalmuseum was the largest governmental investment in culture in 19th-century Sweden, and although its collection may not be as impressive as some of Europe's big art museums, there are works by Rembrandt, Rubens, Gauguin, Goya and Degas, as well as substantial collections of 17th-century Dutch, 18th-century French and 18th/19th-century Swedish art, plus a huge collection of 20th-century Scandinavian design pieces. The building itself, designed in 1866 to look like a northern Italian Renaissance palace, remains a Stockholm landmark.

FREE St Clara Kyrka

Klarabergsgatan 37 (411 73 24, www.klarakyrka.se).
T-bana T-Centralen or bus 53, 56, 59, 65, 69.
Open 10am-5pm Mon-Fri, Sun; 5-7.30pm Sat.
Admission free. **Map** p62 D5 ❺

The copper spire of this brick church across from
Central Station rises from a cluster of dull, box-like
1960s buildings. St Clara Kyrka was one of many
churches built in the late 16th century during the
reign of Johan III, who had a Catholic wife and a
love of architecture. He decided to build here in the
1570s as it was the site of a former convent torn
down in the Reformation. Dutch architect Willem
Boy designed the church, and Carl Hårleman, who
also completed the interior of the Kungliga Slottet
(*see p46*), redesigned its roof and spire after a fire in
the mid 18th century. Inside the sunlit church, the
ceiling is painted with biblical scenes. The congre-
gation gives out bread and coffee to the needy, so the
graveyard and nearby steps are often occupied by
homeless people.

FREE St Jacobs Kyrka

Västra Trädgårdsgatan 2 (723 30 38, www.
stockholmsdomkyrkoforsamling.se). T-bana
Kungsträdgården or bus 43, 62, 65. **Open**
11am-5pm Mon-Wed, Sat; 11am-6pm Thur, Fri,
Sun. *Worship in English* 6pm Sun. **Admission**
free. **Map** p63 F5 ❻

This red church overlooking Kungsträdgården was
commissioned in 1588 by King Johan III. The project
was abandoned four years later when Johan died,
but was resumed in 1630 and completed in 1643. The

St Clara Kyrka.

IN THE KNOW IT'S ALL GREEK

Ivar Tengbom modelled the **Konserthuset**
(*see p167*) on the temples of ancient Greece,
and the artworks inside depict figures and
scenes from Greek mythology. Tengbom's
son, Anders, renovated the building in 1972
to improve the acoustics. Einar Forseth
(who also decorated the Golden Hall at the
Stadshuset) created the floor mosaics in the
entrance hall and main foyer, and Carl Milles
sculpted the bronze statue of Orpheus near
the front steps. There are guided tours
(50kr) on Saturdays when there's a concert,
but it's more fun to attend a performance.

church is named after the patron saint of pilgrims,
who is depicted in the sandstone sculpture above
the southern entrance carrying a walking staff. The
church underwent several interior renovations in the
19th century, including the addition of five stained-
glass panels behind the altar, depicting scenes from
the New Testament. Sunday services are held in
English at 6pm.

Strindbergsmuseet

Drottninggatan 85 (411 53 54, www.
strindbergsmuseet.se). T-bana Rådmansgatan
or bus 59, 65. **Open** *Sept-June* noon-4pm
Tue-Sun. *July, Aug* 10am-4pm Tue-Sun. Closed
Christmas. **Admission** 60kr; 40kr reductions;
free under-19s. Free with SC. *Guided tours* 20kr
(phone ahead to book). **Map** p62 C2 ❼

August Strindberg moved into an apartment in
the Blå Tornet (Blue Tower) in 1908; it was his last
home and is now a museum. Much of it is taken up
with temporary exhibits on Strindberg as a writer,
dramatist, photographer and painter, but his tiny
apartment is the main reason for visiting. An air of
reverence dominates: you have to put white slippers
on over your shoes to protect the floor, and his bedroom, study and sitting room are preserved as they
were at the time of his death, his pens still neatly
lined up on his writing desk. It's an atmospheric and
moving place: you can just imagine the ailing play-
wright standing on the balcony to greet a procession
of well-wishers on his last birthday, 22 January 1912.
He died just a few months later, on 14 May, aged 63.

Restaurants

Bakfickan

Kungliga Operan, Karl XIIs Torg (676 58 00,
www.operakallaren.se). T-bana Kungsträdgården
or bus 2, 43, 62, 76, 96. **Open** 11.30am-11pm Mon-
Fri; noon-10pm Sat. **Main courses** 170kr-325kr.
Map p63 F6 ❽ **Traditional Swedish**

In the Opera House, alongside Operakällaren and
Operabaren (for both, *see p67*), you'll find Bakfickan

EXPLORE

Bakfickan. See p65.

(Hip pocket), the little brother of the trio that shares the same giant kitchen. Head here for quality traditional Swedish fare if you've been turned away from the more upscale Opera establishments for wearing trainers. *See also p79* **Staying in Pocket**.

B.A.R.

Blasieholmsgatan 4A (611 53 35, www.restaurang bar.se). T-bana Kungsträdgården or bus 2, 62, 65, 76, 96. **Open** *11.30am-2pm, 5pm-1am Mon-Fri; 4pm-1am Sat; 5-9pm Sun.* **Main courses** *125kr-195kr.* **Map** p63 H5 ❾ **Seafood**
This seafood restaurant has its own aquarium, from which customers can select something for their dinner plate. The day's fish options are listed on a blackboard, with other options available from the à la carte. The quality of the cooking is generally reliable, while the long bar is ideal for pre-drinks, especially if you fancy hobnobbing with the city's fashionable set.

Berns Asia/Bistro Berns

Berzelii Park (56 63 22 22/00, www.berns.se). T-bana Kungsträdgården or bus 2, 52, 55, 62, 69, 76, 96. **Open** *Berns Asia 6.30-10am, 11.30am-1am Mon-Thur; 6.30-10am, 11.30am-3am Fri; 7.30-11am, 11.30am-3am Sat; 7.30-11am, 11.30am-1am Sun. Bistro Berns 11.30am-10pm Mon; 11.30am-midnight Tue-Fri; noon-midnight Sat; noon-midnight Sun.* **Main courses** *Berns Asia 175kr-420kr. Bistro Berns 125kr-329kr.* **Map** p63 G5 ❿ **Asian/French**
Sir Terence Conran did an admirable job in transforming this jaw-droppingly grand ballroom into a restaurant several years ago. The food is crossover pan-Asian cuisine, tasty but slightly uneven. Avoid the main courses and go for a share of dim sum (prices start at 38kr).The various bars are always packed, and there's also a landmark hotel attached

(*see p211*). Inside the front glass veranda is Bistro Berns, a classic French bistro with dishes such as steak tartare and entrecôte de Berns served in a chatty environment with easygoing attitude.

Martins Gröna

Regeringsgatan 91 (411 58 50, www.martins grona.com). T-bana Hötorget or bus 2, 43, 96. **Open** *11am-2pm Mon-Fri. Closed July.* **Lunch** *95kr.* **Map** p63 E2 ⓫ **Vegetarian**
This small, unpretentious vegetarian restaurant is one of the most pleasant places to eat lunch in the city centre. Each day there's a choice of just two dishes (or you can have a mix of both), served with home-baked bread and tea and coffee. It's not sophisticated fare, but it's tasty and filling.

Mathias Dahlgren

Grand Hôtel, Södra Blasieholmshamnen 6 (679 35 84, www.mathiasdahlgren.com). T-bana Kungsträdgården or bus 2, 43, 55, 62, 65, 76, 96. **Open** *Food Bar noon-2pm, 6pm-midnight Mon-Fri; 6pm-midnight Sat. Dining Room 7-11pm (last seating 9pm) Tue-Sat.* **Main courses** *Food Bar 145kr-295kr.* **Set menus** *Dining Room 1,500kr-3,250kr.* **Map** p63 G6 ⓬ **Contemporary**
Mathias Dahlgren is one of Sweden's most respected chef, and the critics' darling. His Grand Hôtel restaurant is a two-room affair: Matbaren (Food Bar), with one Michelin star, is a stripped-down room with bare wooden tables and a steel bar; while Matsalen (Dining Room), with two stars, is classy and elegant. The modern Scandinavian food is faultless: smoked

Mathias Dahlgren.

salmon from Tromsö, Norway; mussels from New Bedford, USA; even oven-baked wild chocolate from Bolivia. Head to the Dining Room for a splurge or, for a more affordable experience, perch in the Food Bar.

Nalen
Regeringsgatan 74 (50 52 92 01, www.nalen. com). T-bana Hötorget or bus 1, 2, 43, 56, 96. **Open** 11am-3pm, 4-11pm Mon-Fri; 5-11pm Sat. Closed July. **Main courses** 155kr-275kr. **Set menu** 400kr-495kr. **Map** p63 E3 ⑬ **Traditional Swedish**
This restaurant shares space with the old jazz haunt Nalen (*see p164*), and it's worth scouting out even if you're not coming for the entertainment. Nalen offers classic Swedish cuisine with the best of native ingredients, such as reindeer, pike-perch and herring, at reasonable prices. Staff are attentive, and the Irish coffee is the best in town.

Operabaren
Kungliga Operan, Karl XIIs Torg (676 58 08, www.operakallaren.se). T-bana Kungsträdgården or bus 2, 43, 55, 62, 76, 96. **Open** 11.30am-11pm Mon-Wed; 11.30am-1am Thur, Fri; 12.30pm-1am Sat. Closed July. **Main courses** 195kr-345kr. **Map** p63 F6 ⑭ **Traditional Swedish**
Operabaren is one of the city's true gems – and perhaps the finest place to come for traditional Swedish meatballs. Sitting on the old leather sofas and admiring the magnificent Jugendstil interior is like travelling back in time. Service from the white-jacketed waiters is impeccable, prices are fair and the food never disappoints.

Operakällaren
Kungliga Operan, Karl XIIs Torg (676 58 01, www.operakallaren.se). T-bana Kungsträdgården or bus 2, 43, 55, 62, 76, 96. **Open** 6-10pm Tue-Sat. Closed July. **Set menu** 995kr-1,300kr. **Map** p63 F6 ⑮ **Mediterranean**
Operakällaren is one of Sweden's best restaurants, with one Michelin star and a history and setting to match. As the name (Opera Cellar) implies, it's located in the Opera House, which has been open for business since 1787 – although the present building was erected in 1895. The restaurant was created in the 1960s by legendary chef Tore Wretman, who, more than any other person, is responsible for turning the Swedes into foodies. Today you'll find mouthwatering dishes such as chanterelle-filled quail, and dry-aged Gotland beef with marrow sauce. The desserts are sublime. This is a luxury establishment on all counts – food, service and wine. The prices are equally spectacular.

Pontus!
Norrlandsgatan 33 (54 52 73 00, www.pontus frithiof.com). T-bana Östermalmstorg or bus 2, 55, 96. **Open** 11.30am-2pm, 6-10pm Mon, Tue; 11.30am-2pm, 6-11pm Wed-Fri; 6-11pm Sat.

Bianchi Café & Cycles.

Main courses 185kr-595kr. **Map** p63 F3 ⑯ **Swedish/French**
This huge, three-storey restaurant close to Stureplan combines three concepts in one place. There's the oyster bar, with the freshest Swedish molluscs; a cocktail bar, which also serves dim sum, sashimi and sushi; and a dining room serving modern cuisine. The dramatic decor – rooms are plastered with custom-made wallpaper depicting many of founder Pontus Frithiof's favourite books – is as much a draw as the excellent food, which is divided up by menus for Harvest, Catch and Season.

Wedholms Fisk
Nybrokajen 17 (611 78 74, www.wedholmsfisk.se). T-bana Kungsträdgården or bus 2, 52, 62, 76, 96. **Open** 11.30am-2pm, 6-11pm Mon; 11.30am-11pm Tue-Fri; 5-11pm Sat. **Main courses** 265kr-595kr. **Map** p63 G5 ⑰ **Seafood**
The standard of seafood in Stockholm is high, and it's at its highest at Wedholms Fisk. Located close to the waterfront in the heart of the city, this is a classic restaurant, both in terms of the decor and cuisine. Dishes are simple and unfussy: when fish is this good, it needs little doing to it. Needless to say, quality like this doesn't come cheap; be prepared for the bill.

Cafés

Bianchi Café & Cycles
Norrlandsgatan 20 (08 611 21 00, www.bianchi cafecycles.com). T-bana Östermalmstorg. **Open** 7.30am-7pm Mon-Fri; 11am-7pm Sat. **Map** p63 F3 ⑱
Cycling enthusiasts can get a bike and caffeine hit at this new airy café, staffed mainly by Italians. Stylish Bianchi bikes, apparel and accessories (all for sale) dot the split-level space, which serves a popular Italian lunchtime buffet on weekdays (11am-2pm), as well as salads, bruschetta, ciabatta and piadina.

The repairmen tinkering away behind a glass wall create a nice vibe for those who choose to eat in. If you prefer to take away, head to the deli section in the front bar area, which offers everything from buffalo mozzarella to truffle honey.

Joe & the Juice

Norrlandsgatan 21 (08 611 21 00, www.joejuice. com). T-bana Östermalmstorg. **Open** 8am-7pm Mon-Fri; 10am-6pm Sat; 11am-5pm Sun. **Map** p63 F3 ⑲

This branch of the Danish juice chain recently opened in an area surprisingly lacking in good cafés. The concept has been a success due to its quality raw materials and fun, high-energy vibe. As well as the normal range of juices and smoothies – with novelty names such as 'Hangover Heaven' and 'Immunity' – there's also a wholesome range of sandwiches.

Theatre Bar

2nd Floor, Kulturhuset, Sergels Torg 3 (14 56 06, www.gladaankan.se). T-bana T-Centralen or bus 43, 52, 56, 59, 69, 91. **Open** 11am-7pm Mon-Fri. *Lunch served* 11am-2pm. **Map** p63 E5 ⑳

This café, set in Stockholm's famous Kulturhuset, allows you to sip your latte while flicking through newspapers from all over the world. There's a fantastic view of the fountain and glass structure at Sergels Torg too. If you're looking for something more substantial than a sandwich, head to Café Panorama on the top floor.

Vete-Katten

Kungsgatan 55 (20 84 05, www.vetekatten.se). T-bana Hötorget or bus 1, 56, 59, 91. **Open** 7.30am-7.30pm Mon-Fri; 9.30am-5pm Sat, Sun. **Map** p62 C4 ㉑

This old-fashioned tearoom serves classic Swedish pâtisseries such as *prinsesstårta* ('princess tart' – a cream-filled cake encased in green marzipan). You can also buy biscuits, bread, cinnamon, vanilla and cardamom rolls, plus home-made ice-cream. The café's pretty courtyard has outside tables in the summer.

Bars

Café Opera

Kungliga Operan, Karl XIIs Torg (676 58 07, www. cafeopera.se). T-bana Kungsträdgården or bus 2, 43, 55, 62, 76, 96. **Open** *Bar* 10pm-3am Wed-Sun. **Minimum age** 20. **Admission** (after 10pm) 220kr. **Map** p63 F6 ㉒

In the back of the Royal Opera House, Café Opera is one of the most elegant and exclusive venues in town. A restaurant by day, in the evening it's an extravagant party bar with a big dancefloor. The interior is a luxurious mix of Scandinavian chic and remodelled Baroque. The crowd ranges from twenty-something trend-followers to scantily clad women and older men in suits.

Gold Bar.

Dubliner

Holländargatan 1 (679 77 07, www.dubliner.se). T-bana Hötorget or bus 1, 56, 59. **Open** 3pm-midnight Mon, Tue; 3pm-1am Wed, Thur; 2pm-3am Fri; noon-3am Sat; 1-10pm Sun. *Food served* until 10pm Mon, Tue; 11pm Wed-Sat; 9pm Sun. **Minimum age** 20. **Admission** (after 9pm) 100kr Fri, Sat. **Map** p62 D3 ㉓

Previously situated in Östermalm, the Dubliner is as close as you'll come to an Irish pub in Stockholm. It's fairly rowdy and, while the waitresses are Swedes, most of the bar staff speak English only – a mix of Aussies, Brits and Irishmen. The stage features covers bands and traditional Irish acts. It has a big screen so it's also a good place to catch major sporting events. There are seven beers on tap, including Guinness, Kilkenny and John Smith's.

Gold Bar

Nobis Hotel, Norrmalmstorg 2-4 (614 10 00, www.nobishotel.se). T-bana Östermalmstorg or bus 2, 43, 52, 55, 62, 69, 76, 96. **Open** 5pm-1am Mon-Thur; 4pm-1am Fri, Sat; 5pm-midnight Sun. **Map** p63 G4 ㉔

Nobis Hotel's (*see p209*) exquisitely designed Gold Bar has been the place for international fashionistas since it opened in late 2010. The bar is buzzing on Friday and Saturday nights with a glamorous crowd that includes both hotel guests and locals. Bar manager Robby Radovic qualified for the Swedish national bartender team on the back of his Que Tal cocktail for the bar, consisting of rum, lime juice, sugar syrup and saffron – but all the cocktails served here are top notch. Decent Italian snacks help to bolster the punch of the drinks.

Icebar

Nordic C Hotel, Vasaplan 4 (50 56 35 20, www. icebarstockholm.se). T-bana T-Centralen or bus 1, 53, 65, 69. **Open** 11.15am-midnight Mon-Thur, Sun; 11.15am-1am Fri, Sat. **Admission** 195kr incl 1 vodka drink. **Map** p62 C5

You can be as cool as you like about this slightly gimmicky attraction, designed by the people behind the Icehotel in Jukkasjärvi in the far north of Sweden, but the minute you don your silver high-tech poncho and sip from your ice glass, you'll be giggling and snapping photos with the rest of them. This tiny sub-zero bar, maintained at a chilly -4°C (23°F), is in a corner of the Nordic C Hotel. With 20 minutes of chilling usually enough for most, the turnover is high. Loud music and fine Absolut shooters (one included in the steep entrance fee) keep spirits high. If you're part of a large group it's wise to book (online or by phone) in advance.

Kåken

Regeringsgatan 66 (20 60 10, www.kaken. niklas.se) T-bana Hötorget or bus 1, 2, 55, 56. **Open** *Bar* 6pm-2am Wed-Sat. *Food served* until 11pm. **Minimum age** 23. **Map** p63 E3

The so-called 'Back Pocket' of celebrity chef Niklas Ekstedt's restaurant 1900 was an instant hit among hip, young-ish and well-to-do media types when it opened in 2009. Dark wood, muted colours and dim lighting add a timeless noir vibe. The drinks list is composed of tried-and-true classics such as whisky sour. The generous porch is where it's at during the warmer months.

KGB

Malmskillnadsgatan 45 (20 91 55, www.kgb.nu). T-bana Hötorget or bus 1, 56. **Open** *Bar* 5-10pm Mon, Tue; 5-11pm Wed, Thur; 4pm-2am Fri; 5pm-2am Sat. *Food served* until 10pm daily. **Minimum age** 18. **Map** p63 E3

Wanna party like the Cold War isn't over? This Russian-inspired party-hard institution is filled with Soviet-era kitsch, Lenin propaganda posters and uniforms. This is where party animals go to drink multiple beers and shots of vodka, and maybe down a bowl of magenta borscht. A crash course in Russian is offered in the toilets.

Shops & Services

Norrmalm's most upmarket shopping streets are located close to the border with Östermalm – head, in particular, to **Mäster Samuelsgatan** and **Biblioteksgatan** for mid-range and designer brands. For the cheaper chain shops, meanwhile, try busy, pedestrianised **Drottninggatan**, one of Stockholm's longest streets.

Acne

Hamngatan 10-14 (20 34 55, www.acnestudios. com). T-bana Östermalmstorg or bus 2, 43, 55, 59, 62, 76, 96. **Open** 10am-8pm Mon-Fri; 10am-6pm Sat; noon-5pm Sun. **Map** p63 G4 **Fashion**

Cutting-edge Swedish fashion label Acne started out as an advertising agency, became a jeans manufacturer and is now an all-round designer, although it's still best known for its innovative denim. This branch is located in the building where, in 1973, a robbery and hostage situation introduced the world to the concept of 'Stockholm Syndrome'.

Other locations Norrmalmstorg 2, Norrmalm (611 64 11); Nytorgsgatan 36, Södermalm (640 04 70).

EXPLORE

Åhléns. See p70.

▶ *The Acne Archives store on Torsgatan in Vasastan (No.53, 30 27 23) is a must for fans of the label, selling samples and items from past collections. There's also an Acne Outlet store at Barkarby Outlet (Majorsvägen 2-4, 760 53 09).*

Åhléns

Klarabergsgatan 50 (676 60 00, www.ahlens.se). T-bana T-Centralen or bus 52, 56, 59, 65. **Open** 10am-9pm Mon-Fri; 10am-7pm Sat; 11am-7pm Sun. **Map** p62 D5 ㉙ **Department store**
You can't get much more central than Åhléns, which is located in a massive brick building next to Sergels Torg. It's an excellent mid-range department store with a good cosmetics and perfume section, a well-stocked homewares department and a large CD shop. The clothing department stocks threads by Swedish designers and international labels. You can get a luxurious facial in the Stockholm Day Spa and there's a big supermarket, Hemköp. *Photo p69.*

Alfa Antikvariat

Olof Palmes gata 20B (21 42 75). T-bana Hötorget or bus 59. **Open** 10am-6pm Mon-Fri; 10am-4pm Sat. **Map** p62 C3 ㉚ **Books**
This used bookshop has a good English department, with lots of English-language paperbacks available. Since a large part of the stock comes from book reviewers, the books are often in better condition and more up-to-date than you might expect.

Antikt, Gammalt & Nytt

Mäster Samuelsgatan 11 (678 35 30). T-bana Östermalmstorg or bus 2, 55, 96. **Open** 11am-6pm Mon-Fri; 11am-4pm Sat. **Map** p63 F4 ㉛ **Jewellery**
This is the place to go when you need an antique rhinestone tiara or a glass brooch in any colour, size or price range. The shop was dreamed up by Tore and Mats Grundström when they discovered a warehouse full of long-forgotten 1940s gear. You'll have to fight over all the best pieces with stylists and other dedicated followers of fashion.

Byredo

Mäster Samuelsgatan 6 (54 03 99 40, www.byredo. com). T-bana Östermalmstorg or bus 2, 55, 59, 62, 96. **Open** 11am-6.30pm Mon-Fri; 11am-5pm Sat. **Map** p63 F4 ㉜ **Perfume**
The Byredo fragrance house was founded in 2006 by Ben Gorham, and has achieved enormous success in its short life span (it's one of the bestselling perfume brands at London's Liberty department store). The company creates perfumes, bodycare products, home fragrances and accessories – the 'Bibliothèque' candle is utterly divine.

★ Centralbadet

Drottninggatan 88 (54 52 13 00, www. centralbadet.se). T-bana Hötorget or bus 1, 47, 52, 53. **Open** 7am-9pm Mon-Fri; 9am-9pm Sat; 9am-6pm Sun. *Last entry* 90mins before closing; pools close 1hr before. **Admission** 120kr-320kr. **Minimum age** 18. **Map** p62 D3 ㉝ **Spa/pool**
In 1904, Jugendstil architect Wilhelm Klemming realised a dream about an 'open window to nature' when he designed Centralbadet. Set back from the street in a pretty garden, it has beautiful art nouveau interiors and a fairly inexpensive café. Dip in the pool or jacuzzi, experience different types of sauna, have a massage (a 50-minute Swedish massage costs 650kr) or a treatment (aromatherapy bath costs 755kr). Friendly staff and an air of faded grandeur make it more appealing than fashionable Sturebadet (*see p131*).

DesignTorget

Sergelgången 29, Sergels Torg (21 91 50, www. designtorget.se). T-bana T-Centralen or Hötorget or bus 52, 56, 59, 65. **Open** 10am-8pm Mon-Fri; 10am-6pm Sat; 11am-6pm Sun. **Map** p63 E5 ㉞ **Design/homewares**
The concept of DesignTorget is that promising new designers can sell their work on a commission basis alongside established companies. At this branch opposite Kulturhuset you'll find an assortment of jewellery, household goods, ceramics, textiles and furniture, as well as some original gifts.
Other locations throughout the city.

Happy Socks

Mäster Samuelsgatan 9 (611 87 02, www.happy socks.com). T-bana Östermalmstorg or bus 2, 55, 96. **Open** 11am-7pm Mon-Fri; 11am-5pm Sat. **Map** p63 F4 ㉟ **Fashion**
This Swedish sock brand, known for its colourful designs, has grown exponentially since its launch a few years ago. Its socks and tights are stocked in shops all around the city, but this is the brand's only standalone store in Stockholm. A new, colourful underwear line was launched in 2014.

Hope

Smålandsgatan 14 (410 64 123, www.hope-sthlm. com). T-bana Östermalmstorg or bus 2, 52, 55, 62, 96. **Open** 10am-7pm Mon-Fri; 10am-5pm Sat; noon-5pm Sun. Closed Sun in July. **Map** p63 G4 ㊱ **Fashion**
Hope is a stylish Swedish label created and run by the designers Ann Ringstrand and Stefan Söderberg, catering to women and men. It's characterised by well-made, modern utility wear, with influences including vintage uniforms and traditional jackets. This flagship store stocks the full collection.
Other locations Odengatan 70, Vasastan (410 64 123); Götgatan 34 (410 64 123), Södermalm.

Hötorgshallen

Hötorget (no phone, www.hotorgshallen.se). T-bana Hötorget or bus 1, 56, 59. **Open** *Winter* 10am-6pm Mon-Thur; 10am-6.30pm Fri; 10am-4pm Sat. *Summer* 10am-6pm Mon-Fri; 10am-3pm Sat. **Map** p62 D4 ㊲ **Food hall**

EXPLORE

CHAIN GANG

Sweden does budget and mid-range chain stores especially well.

FACE Stockholm.

Swedish budget brand **H&M** needs no introduction; there are branches all over Stockholm, but the latest designs normally arrive at the Hamngatan store (No.22) first, which also has a children's department. Norrmalm's Biblioteksgatan is the best street to head to for both Swedish and international mid-range chains. H&M's more grown-up label **COS** appeared in London before it reached Stockholm, but the city now has a store on Biblioteksgatan (No.3, www.hm.com). The shop is sandwiched

between a branch of Swedish cosmetics brand **FACE Stockholm** (No.1, www.face stockholm.com) and edgy US chain **Urban Outfitters** (No.5, www.urbanoutfitters.com), with the latter housed in the lovely old Roda Kvarn (Red Mill) cinema. At No.2, on the other side of Biblioteksgatan, is **Filippa K** (611 88 03, www.filippa-k.com), the shop to head to for good-quality wardrobe staples – practically every Swede owns a Filippa K piece. Nearby, at No.6, is **J Lindeberg** (www.jlindeberg.com), a mainstream Swedish fashion brand for men and women that's known for its smart office-style clothes and simple cuts, while at No.11 is another H&M group store, the on-trend womenswear label **& Other Stories** (www.stories.com). Head around the corner for menswear specialist **Tiger of Sweden**, on Jakobsbergsgatan (No.8, www.tigerof sweden.com); suits are the trademark here, though the brand has also now branched into womenswear. Another Swedish chain with an international presence is **Lindex** (www.lindex.se), a reasonably priced fashion brand for women and children that's especially popular for underwear and swimwear. There are 11 branches in Stockholm, including Kungsgatan (No.48) and Odengatan (No.69). Last but not least is global king of flat-packing, **Ikea**. In Sweden, Ikea is more than just a furniture store, it's a way of life. It's well worth visiting a branch on home turf even if you're not after any homewares, just to see how the Swedes spend their weekends. The store in Skärholmen (Modulvägen 1, Kungens Kurva, www.ikea.com), south-west of Södermalm, is one of the biggest.

EXPLORE

Filippa K.

NK.

A visit to Hötorgshallen is a culinary trip around the world. Built in the 1950s, the hall was renovated in the 1990s and its international character has grown along with immigration to Stockholm. You can buy everything from Middle Eastern falafel to Indian spices, as well as fantastic fish and meat, and there are several good places to grab lunch. Outside there's a bustling fruit, vegetable and flower market on Hötorget (*see p61*), which first opened as a market in the 1640s.

Illums Bolighus Stockholm

Hamngatan 27 (718 55 00, www.illumsbolighus. se). T-bana Kungsträdgården or Östermalmstorg or bus 2, 43, 52, 55, 62, 69, 76, 91. **Open** 10am-7pm Mon-Fri; 10am-5pm Sat; 11am-5pm Sun. **Map** p63 F4 ❸ **Furniture/homewares**
Open since autumn 2010 in Sweden House, this is Stockholm's first branch of the excellent Danish furniture and interior design store. Stock includes upmarket furniture, ceramics, glass and lighting fixtures by renowned Scandinavian designers.

Kartbutiken

Mäster Samuelsgatan 54 (20 23 03, www. kartbutiken.se). T-bana T-Centralen or bus 53, 56, 59, 65, 69. **Open** 10am-6pm Mon-Fri; 10am-4pm Sat; noon-4pm Sun. **Map** p62 D4 ❸ **Books/Travel**
This travel specialist has a good range of maps, guidebooks, travel accessories, atlases and globes, as well as marine charts for the more intrepid traveller.

Naturkompaniet

Kungsgatan 26 (24 19 96, www.naturkompaniet.se). T-bana Hötorget or bus 1, 56, 291. **Open** 10am-7pm Mon-Fri; 10am-5pm Sat; noon-4pm Sun. **Map** p63 E3 ❹ **Outdoors**

Everything you need for that outdoors or camping weekend, from outdoor clothing and Blundstone boots to mushroom foraging equipment and travel guides. Naturkompaniet, whose symbol is a bear, specialises in the Swedish brand Fjällräven, famous both for its outstanding quality and timeless 1970s cut; a huge range of the brand's now-trendy colourful Kånken backpacks are on display here.
Other locations Kungsgatan 4A, Norrmalm (723 15 81); Sveavägen 62, Norrmalm (24 30 02); Hantverkargatan 38-40, Kungsholmen (651 35 00); Odengatan 50, Vasastan (673 11 60).

★ NK

Hamngatan 18-20 (762 80 00, www.nk.se). T-bana Kungsträdgården or Östermalmstorg or bus 2, 43, 52, 55, 62, 69, 76, 91. **Open** 10am-8pm Mon-Fri; 10am-6pm Sat; 11am-5pm Sun. **Map** p63 F4 ❹
Department store
Eternally elegant, Nordiska Kompaniet is one of the city's most treasured institutions. The famous revolving sign on the roof – with the letters NK on one side and a clock on the other – is visible from all over town. A sort of Swedish Selfridges, it's a first-class store, particularly good for clothes (lots of Scandinavian labels), Swedish souvenirs (crafts, homewares and glassware in the basement) and gourmet food. There's a decent in-house supermarket, a books section with a good selection of fiction titles in English, and a concession of Swedish stationery brand Bookbinders – established in 1927, and selling some of the best-quality paper, books, boxes and folders in Stockholm.

Polarn o Pyret

Hamngatan 10 (411 41 40, www.polarno pyret.se). T-bana Östermalmstorg or bus 2,

52, 55, 62, 69, 59, 76, 96. **Open** 10am-8pm Mon-Fri; 10am-6pm Sat; noon-5pm Sun. **Map** p63 F4 ❷ **Children**

Polarn o Pyret (the Pal & the Tot) became famous in the 1970s when its striped, long-sleeved T-shirts dressed a generation of kids. With a retro revival in the new millennium, today's grown-ups and children can be seen sporting Polarn o Pyret's soft fabrics and simple styles. And, of course, stripes.

Other locations Gallerian, Hamngatan 35, Norrmalm (411 22 47); Västermalmsgallerian, Kungsholmen (653 57 30); Fältöversten, Karlaplan 13, Östermalm (660 62 75); Ringen, Götgatan 98, Södermalm (642 03 62).

PUB
Hötorget 13-15 (789 19 30, www.pub.se). T-bana Hötorget or bus 1, 56, 59. **Open** 10am-7pm Mon-Fri; 10am-6pm Sat; 11am-5pm Sun. **Map** p62 D3 ❸ **Department store**

Facing the bustling outdoor fruit and veg market at Hötorget, PUB has evolved into a trendy 'lifestyle store' over the past few years. Greta Garbo once worked in the millinery department and modelled hats for the store's catalogue.

Svensk Hemslöjd
Norrlandsgatan 20 (23 21 15, www.svensk hemslojd.com). T-bana Östermalmstorg. **Open** 10am-6pm Mon-Fri; 11am-4pm Sat. **Map** p63 F3 ❷ **Crafts/homewares**

Founded in 1899, Svensk Hemslöjd (Swedish Handicrafts) is the place to head for hand-made Swedish homewares, textiles, yarns and traditional gifts, with a wide range of cushions, wool blankets, candleholders and superior Dala horses.

Weekday
Drottninggatan 63 (08 411 29 70, www.weekday. com). T-bana Hötorget or T-Centralen or bus 1, 56, 59. **Open** 10am-7pm Mon-Fri; 10am-6pm Sat; 11am-5pm Sun. **Map** p62 D4 ❹ **Fashion**

This is Stockholm's biggest stockist of Swedish brand Cheap Monday, known for its cool, well-cut and cheap jeans. Other items sold here are equally stylish and affordable, featuring sharp silhouettes and edgy graphics. All Weekday stores are spacious and full of energy.

Other location Götgatan 21, Södermalm (642 17 72).

Whyred
Mäster Samuelsgatan 3 (660 01 70, www. whyred.se). T-bana Östermalmstorg or bus 2, 55, 96. **Open** 10am-7pm Mon-Fri; 10am-5pm Sat; noon-4pm Sun. **Map** p63 G4 ❹ **Fashion**

This flagship of the stylish Swedish clothes brand opened in a former tailor's in 2010. The collection features well-cut clothes for men and women, with extremely desirable takes on urban classics such as the parka jacket, chelsea boots and chinos. Tasteful tones, stripes and quality materials feature heavily.

Other location Bruno, Götgatsbacken 36, Södermalm (see p106).

VASASTAN

In southern Vasastan lies the small park of **Tegnérlunden**. At one end a man-made stream flows out of a gazebo; at the other there's a statue of a naked August Strindberg sitting on a rock (*photo p74*). The **Strindbergsmuseet** is on the corner of Drottninggatan and Tegnérgatan, and further east on Tegnérgatan you'll find a good

Whyred.

EXPLORE

EXPLORE

selection of pubs, restaurants and antiques shops. From here, turn left on tree-lined Sveavägen – designed to look like a Parisian boulevard – and walk two blocks to the north.

The south-east corner of the hillside park, **Observatorielunden**, is dominated by the grand **Handelshögskolan** (Stockholm School of Economics). It was designed by Ivar Tengbom, who was also architect of the Konserthuset. Up the steep steps on top of the hill is the **Observatorie Museet** (Drottninggatan 120, www.observatoriet.kva.se) overlooking a reflecting pool. The observatory itself closed down in 2014, with no information about when, or if, it might reopen. However, its **Himlavalvet Café** (11am-5pm Mon-Fri; 11am-6pm Sat, Sun; closed Jan, Feb) remains open.

Standing proudly at the park's north-east corner, Gunnar Asplund's bright orange **Stadsbiblioteket** (Stockholm Public Library) is one of Sweden's best-known architectural works, instantly identifiable by its round central building. Several blocks north on Sveavägen is the quiet, hilly park of **Vanadislunden**.

If you head west from the library along busy Odengatan, you'll reach the triangle-shaped Odenplan square, bordered by the beautiful Baroque **Gustaf Vasa Kyrka** and surrounded by the rumble of passing buses. Several budget hotels are located in this area.

Two blocks further west is the green retreat of **Vasaparken**, with outdoor summer cafés and a football field/ice-skating rink, depending on the season. The easternmost section of the park was recently renamed **Astrid Lindgren's Terrace** after the author of the *Pippi Longstocking* children's book series, who died in 2002; she lived just across the street. The small **Judiska Museet** is nearby, and at the western end of the park there's the bustling intersection of St Eriksplan. To the south is the shiny contemporary building that houses **Sven-Harrys Konstmuseum**, Stockholm's newest privately owned art museum, as well as high-end apartments.

The neighbourhood of **Birkastan**, west of St Eriksplan, was originally built during the early 20th century for the working classes, but the charming cafés and restaurants around Rörstrandsgatan are becoming increasingly fashionable. If you take St Eriksgatan south, you'll end up on Kungsholmen.

Sights & Museums

Bonniers Konsthall
Torsgatan 19 (736 42 48, www.bonnierskonsthall. se). T-bana St Eriksplan or bus 3, 70, 77, 94. **Open** noon-7pm Wed-Fri; 11am-5pm Sat, Sun. **Admission** 70kr; 50kr reductions; free under-18s. Map p76 D6 ❼

This contemporary art gallery is at the heart of the growing Vasastan art district. Founded by Jeanette Bonnier, the non-profit institution is run by the Bonnier Group, one of Scandinavia's biggest media concerns. There's a programme of talks, artists in conversation and innovative exhibitions of international and Swedish art.

FREE Gustaf Vasa Kyrka
Karlbergsvägen 1-5 (50 88 86 00, www.gustaf vasa.nu). T-bana Odenplan or bus 2, 40, 65. **Open** usually 11am-6pm Mon-Thur; 10am-6pm Fri; 11am-6pm Sat, Sun. **Admission** free (concerts & activities free-100kr). Map p77 E4 ❽

The striking 60m (200ft) dome of Gustaf Vasa Kyrka rises far above Odenplan. This white church in the Italian Baroque style is, without doubt, Vasastan's most beautiful building. Completed in 1906, Gustaf Vasa Kyrka stands on a triangular island near the intersection of two busy streets. The spectacular 1731 altarpiece is Sweden's largest Baroque sculpture, originally created for Uppsala Cathedral. It depicts Jesus on the cross in front of a relief of Jerusalem. The ceiling frescoes in the dome show scenes from the New Testament.

Judiska Museet
Hälsingegatan 2 (31 01 43, www.judiska-museet. se). T-bana Odenplan or bus 4, 53, 69, 70, 94. **Open** noon-4pm Mon-Fri, Sun. **Admission** 70kr; 40kr-50kr reductions; free under-12s. *Guided tours* 1.30pm Wed, Sun. Free with SC. Map p76 D4 ❾

August Strindberg statue, Tegnérlunden. See p73.

Gustaf Vasa Kyrka.

This small museum contains venerable religious objects and a permanent exhibition on the Holocaust. A Torah, an 18th-century menorah and a variety of yarmulkes (skullcaps) are displayed, plus a wooden Mizrach plaque from the first synagogue in Stockholm, dating from 1795.

Sven-Harrys Konstmuseum

Eastmansvägen 10-12 (www.sven-harrys.se). T-bana Odenplan or St Eriksplan or bus 3, 4, 40, 53, 69. **Open** *11am-7pm Wed-Fri; 11am-5pm Sat, Sun.* **Admission** *60kr; free under-19s.* **Map** p76 D5 ⑩

This six-storey art museum and exhibition space opened in spring 2011 in an impressive purpose-built building near Vasaparken – a five-minute walk away from Bonniers Konsthall (*see p74*). Swedish building contractor Sven-Harry Karlson has amassed a personal collection of 20th-century Scandinavian art over some 40 years, and it's these works that form the basis of the museum. As well as fuctioning as a museum and gallery space, the building also houses a restaurant and upmarket apartments.

Restaurants

Döden i Grytan

Norrtullsgatan 61 (32 50 95, www.dodenigrytan.se). T-bana Odenplan or bus 2, 40, 65. **Open** *5.30pm-midnight Mon-Sat; 5-10pm Sun. Kitchen closes 11pm Mon-Sat; 9.30pm Sun.* **Main courses** *155kr-475kr.* **Map** p76 D2 ㊴ **Italian**

Don't let the strange name (Death in the Pot) or dead-end street location put you off – this is a welcoming neighbourhood Italian with friendly service and great food. The focus is on first-class meat – bistecca Fiorentina, salsiccia in all shapes and sizes, and pasta all'amatriciana – and the portions are enormous, so don't even think of attempting the full four-course Italian dinner. The same family runs another excellent Italian, nearby Den Gamle och Havet (Tulegatan 27, 661 53 00, www.visomkanmat. se), which means 'the Old Man and the Sea'.

★ Gro

St Eriksgatan 67 (643 42 22, www.gro restaurang.se). T-bana St Eriksplan or bus 3, 4, 21, 48, 72, 77, 94. **Open** *11.30am-3pm Tue, Wed, Fri; 11.30am-3pm, 6-11pm Thur.* **Main courses** *100kr.* **Map** p76 B5 ㊵ **Contemporary Scandinavian**

Vegetables are the focus of this lunchtime restaurant, opened by chefs Magnus Villnow (formerly at Rolfs Kök) and Henrik Norén (previously at F12) in 2013. The duo both cook and serve the dishes – possible due to the fact that there are only around 20 seats, which gives the place a sociable and homely atmosphere. The excellent lunches consist of three small plates (one of which often contains meat) and a dessert, and are all about honest cooking using local produce. If you can't make it for lunch, the place is also open on Thursday evenings. Don't come here expecting a boozy affair – the drinks list is very short and doesn't include wine – but do come expecting to have your passion for good food reaffirmed.

Ki-mama

Observatoriegatan 13 (33 34 82, www.kimamma.se). T-bana Odenplan or bus 2, 40, 65. **Open** *11.30am-9pm Mon-Fri; 3-9pm Sat, Sun.* **Main courses** *80kr-195kr.* **Map** p77 E5 ㊳ **Asian**

This top sushi spot offers a good selection of fish, cut in the regular Swedish size (Swedish sushi tends to be too big to eat in one bite), and reasonable prices. Ki-mama is deservedly popular among locals, although more at lunch than dinner due to its early closing time, and the fact that it's unlicensed. Ramen dishes are also on the menu.

▶ *Ki-mama's sister restaurant, Ramen Ki-mama (Birger Jarlsgatan 93, 15 55 39), serves up noodle soups and ramen, and has an alcohol licence.*

★ Lao Wai

Luntmakargatan 74 (673 78 00, www.laowai.se). T-bana Rådmansgatan or bus 43, 59. **Open** *11am-2pm, 5.30-10pm Mon-Sat. Kitchen closes 9pm.*

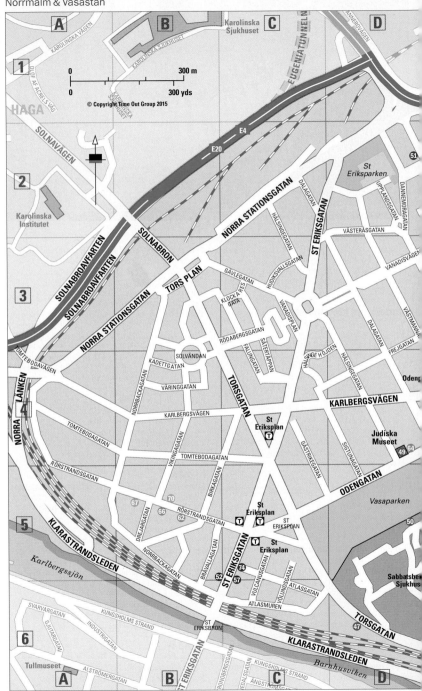

EXPLORE

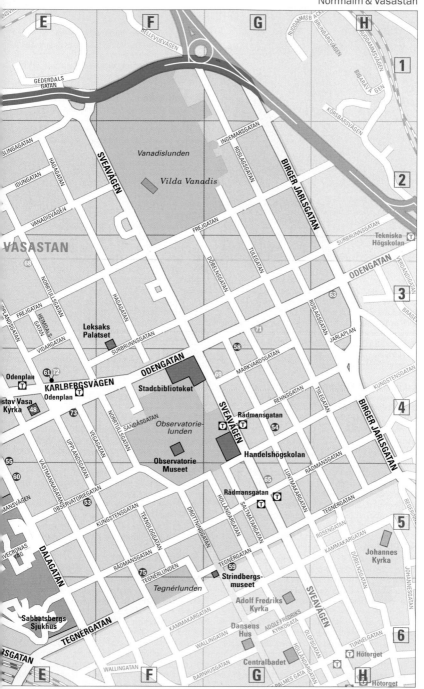

EXPLORE

Lao Wai. See p75.

Closed July, 1st wk Aug. **Main courses** 175kr-215kr. **Map** p77 G4 ❸ **Asian/Vegetarian**
Stockholm's best vegetarian restaurant is slightly hidden away, in a simply decorated space, but it's well worth seeking out. The base is Chinese, but with influences from several other Asian cuisines. Try the Jian Chang tofu (smoked tofu with shiitake mushrooms, sugar snap peas and fresh spices). The tea menu is also spectacular.

Le Bistro de Wasahof
Dalagatan 46 (32 34 40, www.wasahof.se).
T-bana Odenplan or bus 4, 53, 69, 70, 72, 94.
Open 5pm-midnight Mon, Tue; 5pm-1am Wed-Sat.
Kitchen closes 11pm Mon, Tue; 11.30pm Wed-Sat.
Main courses 174kr-314kr. **Set menus** 295kr-515kr. **Map** p77 E4 ❺ **Seafood**
This restaurant acts as a second home to writers, actors, singers and well-dressed wannabes. A bar and bistro, its main contribution to the culinary scene is its seafood – it imports oysters from France and the Swedish west coast. Next door, hipper sibling Musslan (No.46, 34 64 10, www.musslan.se) serves a younger crowd with the same menu.

★ Lilla Ego
Västmannagatan 69 (27 44 55, www.lillaego. com). T-bana Odenplan or bus 2, 42, 69, 70.
Open 5-11pm Tue-Sat. **Small plates** 115kr-325kr. **Map** p77 E4 ❺ **New Nordic**
The contemporary Scandinavian interior (bare-brick walls, white wooden chairs, sheepskin throws) gives this small neighbourhood restaurant a cosy, honest and hopeful vibe. And the food is indeed fantastic, combining top-notch seasonal ingredients with skilful technique and passionate creativity. The frequently changing menu is written on the wall, and might include plates such as pickled herring with

egg yolk and swede, lamb with celeriac or turbot with a seafood broth; the chefs try to engage with the diners by sometimes serving them themselves. Lilla Ego has been a huge hit since opening in late 2013, so book in advance – or try for a seat at the bar.

Lilla Pakistan
St Eriksgatan 66 (30 56 46, www.lillapakistan. com). T-bana St Eriksplan or bus 3, 4, 72, 77, 94.
Open 5-10pm Mon-Thur; 5-11pm Fri, Sat. **Main courses** 145kr-225kr. **Tasting menu** 495kr.
Map p76 C5 ❺ **Asian**
Little Pakistan offers authentic Pakistani and northern Indian dishes. Everything is tasty and well prepared, right down to the amuse-bouches. There are a couple of vegetarian options too. Don't miss the lassi.

Malaysia
Luntmakargatan 98 (684 396 46, www.restaurang-malaysia.se). T-bana Odenplan or bus 2, 4, 42.
Open 10am-2.30pm, 5-10pm daily. **Main courses** 135kr-250kr. **Map** p77 G3 ❺ **Asian**
This restaurant is an eye-opener, with deep-fried frog's legs and tofu listed on the menu next to chicken satay and own-made dumplings. All the exotic ingredients – kelp, tapioca, curry leaves – are prepared with care and served with a friendly smile. It's not cheap, but it's worth the expense. There's an ambitious vegetarian selection too.

Rolfs Kök
Tegnérgatan 41 (10 16 96, www.rolfskok.se).
T-bana Rådmansgatan or bus 59, 65. **Open** 11.30am-1am Mon-Fri; 5pm-1am Sat, Sun. Closed July. **Main courses** 225kr-595kr. **Map** p77 G5 ❺ **Contemporary**
A favourite haunt for lunching business executives, this Stockholm design classic is well worth a visit for both the interesting food (a mix of traditional and contemporary Swedish) and decor. Chairs hang on the grey concrete walls, to be quickly taken down if more diners arrive. Solo eaters are lined up at the long bar overlooking the open kitchen. Enjoy fresh fish with tender meat, as East Asian ideas combine with southern European tricks. The creative somersaults usually succeed, and a visit to Rolfs Kök is always a treat. Owner-chef Johan Jureskog also runs AG Restaurang in Kungsholmen (*see p139*).

★ Smörgåstårteriet
Dalagatan 42 (94 91 13, www.smorgastarteriet.se).
T-bana Odenplan or bus 40, 53, 69. **Open** 11.30am-2pm Mon; 11.30am-2pm, 5-10.30pm Tue-Fri; 5-10.30pm Sat. **Tasting menu** 595kr.
Main courses 315kr. **Map** p77 E5 ❺ **Contemporary Scandinavian**
The five-course tasting menu at Smörgåstårteriet (named after a traditional Swedish sandwich-style cake) is the definite highlight of this superb restaurant; the dishes, conceived around landscapes and places in Sweden, are designed for sharing, and their

STAYING IN POCKET

Want to eat out for less? Head for the city's bakfickor.

Eating out in Stockholm can be a huge strain on the wallet, but a recent shift in approach from many restaurateurs favours those on a budget. The term *'bakfickan'* – meaning 'back pocket', and referring to a more informal sister venue of a fine-dining restaurant – has been a feature of the city's eating out scene for years. But a new trend has seen a rise in the number of *bakfickor* as celebrated chefs push aside ostentation and formality to experiment with a more laid-back and personal approach. 'Back pockets' that should be on your radar include **Speceriet** (see *p125*), the *bakfickan* of Michelin-starred Gastrologik); **Råkultur** (see *p124*), sister venue of Esperanto; and **Pocket**, owned by Pontus Frithiof of Pontus! (see *p67*). What's more, this trend has also led to the opening of a wave of unpretentious, stripped-back

Lux Dag för Dag.

neighbourhood restaurants such as **Lilla Ego** (see *p78*) and **Lux Dag för Dag** (see *p147*). The latter is a rethink of former fine dining restaurant Lux; owner-chef Henrik Norström has gone for a more accessible, affordable concept in the new restaurant, making it very much in alignment with the times.

culinary creativity and sublime flavour combinations always generate discussion. Wine pairing is an important and highly enjoyable part of any meal here, and the excellent list includes lots of organic bottles. Service is polite and friendly. *Photos p80.*

Tranan
Karlbergsvägen 14 (52 72 81 00, www.tranan.se). T-bana Odenplan or bus 2, 4, 40, 65, 96. **Open** 11.30am-1am Mon-Fri; noon-1am Sat; noon-11pm Sun (July, Aug 5-11pm daily). **Main courses** 155kr-345kr. **Map** p77 E4 ③ **Contemporary**
Once a working-class pub, Tranan has changed dramatically to reach out to the professionals who now inhabit Vasastan. The transformation has been managed well, and Tranan has become one of the

(Lilla Ego.)

city's classics – though success has taken a toll on the service. The *isterband* (lard sausage – tastier than it sounds) is great, as is the *silltallrik* (herring plate). There's a trendy bar in the basement (see *p81*).

Cafés

Café Levinsky's
Rörstrandsgatan 9 (30 33 33, www.cafelevinskys.se). T-bana St Eriksplan or bus 3, 4, 42, 72, 77. **Open** 7.30am-9.30pm Mon-Thur; 7.30am-9pm Fri; 9am-9pm Sat; 9.30am-8.30pm Sun. **Map** p76 B5 ⑥
If you've got a smoothie craving, head to Levinsky's (try the blueberry and banana). Alongside the usual salad, sandwich and cake offerings, Levinsky's offers tasty own-made burgers, as well as weekend brunch.
▶ *For dessert, pop round the corner to Stockholms Glasshus (Birkagatan 8, 30 32 37, www.glasshus.se) for home-made ice-cream in flavours you'd previously only dreamed about.*

Lindquists
Odengatan 27 (08 411 59 55, www.lindquists.nu). T-bana Rådmansgatan or bus 42, 53. **Open** 6.30am-8pm Mon-Fri; 7.30am-6pm Sat, Sun. **Map** p77 H3 ⑥
One of a dying breed of old-school bakery-cafés, Lindquists is as traditional as they come. Divided into two sections – a takeaway bakery/pâtisserie counter, and a sit-down café area kitschly decorated with pictures of the Swedish royal family – it's a great spot for traditional Swedish delicacies such as *semlor* (cream-filled buns). The passionfruit cheesecake is also heavenly.

EXPLORE

Ritorno

Odengatan 80-82 (32 01 06, www.ritorno.se). T-bana Odenplan or bus 4, 53, 69, 70, 72, 94. **Open** *Sept-June* 7am-10pm Mon-Thur; 7am-8pm Fri; 8am-6pm Sat; 10am-6pm Sun. *July-Aug* 7am-6pm Mon-Fri; 10am-4pm Sat, Sun. **Map** p76 D4 ❹

Time stands still at this 1950s café, where beautiful old jukeboxes are still in working order. The regulars voiced a collective outcry when a revamp was suggested, so the battered leather sofas and kitsch decor remain. Ritorno offers everything from traditional shrimp sandwiches to calorie-dripping Danish pastries with funny names, such as 'one of those' and 'sumthing sweet'. If you don't drink coffee, try the apple soda Pommac. The café doubles as a gallery and the paintings on show are for sale.

★ Sosta

Sveavägen 84 (www.sosta.se). T-bana Rådmansgatan or bus 59. **Open** 8am-6.30pm Mon-Fri; 10am-5.30pm Sat. **No credit cards**. **Map** p77 G5 ❺

This is a standing room-only espresso bar known all over Sweden for its extraordinary coffee and low prices – although some say it's as famous for the well-dressed baristas making the doppios and serving cornettos. Try the focaccias or the home-made strawberry sorbet and you'll realise that Sosta is the closest you'll get to Italy in Scandinavia.

Xoko

Rörstrandsgatan 15 (31 84 87, www.xoko.se). T-bana St Eriksplan or bus 3, 4, 42, 77. **Open** 7am-7pm Mon-Fri; 8am-6pm Sat, Sun. **Map** p76 B5 ❻

This café and bakery is quite simply a visual and gastronomic feast. Situated in Birkastan, Stockholm's most bohemian quarter, Xoko's quirky interior – all illuminated sci-fi circles – is worth a visit in itself. But as Xoko is owned by one of Sweden's leading chocolatiers, there are plenty of other reasons to drop by – not least for the delicious *semlor*, considered some of the best in town.

Bars

Nightlife in Vasastan is quite spread out, with most of the bars on Rörstrandsgatan or within a few blocks of the busy intersection of Odengatan and Sveavägan.

Bagpipers Inn

Rörstrandsgatan 21 (31 18 55, www.bagpipers.se). T-bana St Eriksplan or bus 42, 72. **Open** *Bar* 4pm-1am Mon-Thur; 3pm-1am Fri; 2pm-1am Sun. *Food served* until midnight daily. **Minimum age** 18. **Map** p76 B5 ❼

The bartenders wear kilts at this Scottish-themed pub decorated with dark wood, green walls and knick-knacks from the Highlands. There's a decent

Smörgåstårteriet. *See p78.*

selection of beer, with around a dozen brews on tap, many from the UK and Ireland. The crowd consists mainly of thirtysomethings and out-of-towners drawn by the cosy atmosphere. The Bagpipers Inn is usually packed at the weekends.

Cliff Barnes

Norrtullsgatan 45 (31 80 70, www.diff.se). T-bana Odenplan or bus 2, 40, 65. **Open** *Bar* 11am-2am Mon; 11am-11pm Tue; 11am-midnight Wed, Thur; 11am-1am Fri; 11am-1am Sat. *Food served* until 11pm Mon, Tue; until closing Wed-Sat. **Minimum age** 23. **Map** p77 E3 ⑯

On the outskirts of Vasastan, in what was once a home for widows, Cliff Barnes is a down-to-earth party bar-restaurant. The worn wooden floors, high ceilings and large vaulted windows make it ideal for enthusiastic beer drinking and loud conversation. At 11pm on Fridays and Saturdays, the lights are turned down and the music (popular classics from the 1960s and '70s) is turned up. Although several large signs clearly forbid it, dancing on the tables is not uncommon. Cliff Barnes takes its name from JR's unlucky arch rival in *Dallas*, and a framed portrait of Ken Kercheval (the actor who portrayed Barnes) decorates the bar's main wall.

La Habana

Sveavägen 108 (16 64 65, www.lahabana.se). T-bana Rådmansgatan or bus 2, 4, 42, 53, 72, 94, 96. **Open** *Bar* 5-11pm Mon, Tue; 5pm-1am Wed-Sat. *Food served* until 11pm Tue-Sat. **Minimum age** 18. **Map** p77 G4 ⑱

As one of a handful of Cuban bars in Stockholm, La Habana makes a refreshing alternative to the otherwise largely mainstream places in the area. The interior is all dark wood and white walls, but the crowd, the drinks and the music are much more colourful as Latin Americans and Swedes meet and mix. The small basement bar serves up great mojitos, and the floor comes alive with salsa dancing later on.

Paus

Rörstrandsgatan 18 (34 44 05, www.restaurang paus.com). T-bana St Eriksplan or bus 42, 72. **Open** *Bar* 5pm-midnight Mon-Wed; 5pm-1am Thur-Sat. *Food served* until 11.30pm Mon-Sat. **Map** p76 B5 ⑰

Well placed on a quiet residential street of cafés and bars, Paus has a cream-coloured interior with large monochrome paintings and a giant mirror wall. It specialises in mixing up quality cocktails but doesn't take itself too seriously, evident in its laid-back, neighbourhood feel.

Storstad

Odengatan 41 (673 38 00, www.storstad.se). T-bana Rådmansgatan or bus 2, 4, 42, 53, 72, 94, 96. **Open** *Bar* 4pm-midnight Mon; 4pm-1am Tue-Thur; 4pm-3am Fri, Sat. *Food served* until 11pm Mon-Sat. **Map** p77 G3 ⑪

The hip mix with the suit-and-tie brigade at the hottest bar in Vasastan. Storstad (literally 'Big Town') has a chic white interior, huge windows and a large L-shaped bar that allows for a great deal of person-to-person interaction. This is a trendy spot and features the usual guest DJs playing all the right tunes, but it's not as reserved as similar venues – some might even call it a classy pick-up bar. For a darker version of the same thing, check out its sister bar, Olssons Video, next door.

Tranan

Karlbergsvägen 14 (52 72 81 00, www.tranan.se). T-bana Odenplan or bus 2, 4, 40, 65, 96. **Open** *Bar* 5pm-1am Mon-Sat; 5-10pm Sun. *Food served* until closing. **Minimum age** 23. **Map** p77 E4 ⑫

Described as a 'modern classic' in the local entertainment guides, Tranan is the quintessential Stockholm bar. In the basement of the well-respected Tranan restaurant, it combines minimalist chic with the cosy feel of a cellar. A DJ spins as twentysomethings congregate around the sturdy wooden tables. Never too surprising, Tranan still manages to hold its own as one of the most enduring bars in Stockholm.

Shops & Services

For the **Acne Archives** shop, *see p70*.

Plagg

Odengatan 75 (31 90 04, www.plagg.se). T-bana Odenplan or bus 2, 4, 40, 65. **Open** 10am-6.30pm Mon-Fri; 10am-4pm Sat, Sun. **Map** p77 E4 ⑰ **Fashion**

At Plagg, the smart-looking 21st-century woman gets classy clothing from designers such as Denmark's DAY/Birger et Mikkelsen or Sweden's hugely successful Filippa K. The selection is larger than you think when you see the size of the shop.

Other locations St Eriksgatan 37, Kungsholmen (650 31 58); Rörstrandsgatan 8, Vasastan (30 58 01).

Record Hunter

St Eriksgatan 70 (08 32 20 23, www.record hunter.se). T-bana St Eriksplan or bus 3, 4, 49, 77, 94. **Open** noon-6pm Mon-Fri; 11am-4pm Sat; noon-4pm Sun. **Map** p76 C5 ⑭ **Music**

Stockholm's best second-hand record store, in terms of scope, friendliness and prices. Every genre is stocked, and there are bargains aplenty. Be sure to inspect records carefully for scratches.

Schönherrs Foto

Upplandsgatan 16 (33 64 80, www.schonherrsfoto.se). T-bana Rådmansgatan or bus 40, 53, 59, 65. **Open** 9am-6pm Mon-Fri. **Map** p77 F5 ⑮ **Photography**

With a large range of second-hand Hasselblads and Leicas, this well-established shop is a godsend for serious photographers and old-school romantics. The new digital cameras and accessories are equally covetable, and the staff here know their stuff.

EXPLORE

Djurgården & Skeppsholmen

If you begin to feel cramped by the narrow streets and tourist crowds of Gamla Stan, head for the green oasis of Djurgården. The island, a short walk from downtown, has many of Stockholm's best museums (including the world-class Vasamuseet), as well as lovely cafés, picnic spots, walking and cycling paths and Gröna Lund amusement park. The rest of the island is part of Ekoparken, the National City Park. Its acres of undeveloped land are a much-loved retreat from the rest of the city.

Once an important naval base and shipyard, the small island of Skeppsholmen is now known for its cultural institutions, many housed in ex-naval buildings, with the highlight being the Moderna Museet. It's also a lovely place for an amble, either along the western shore with views of Gamla Stan or along the wooden boardwalk of the eastern shore, where private and historic boats are docked.

EXPLORE

Rosendals Trädgård.

Don't Miss

1 **Vasamuseet** The jaw-dropping 17th-century warship (p90).

2 **Rosendals Trädgård** Organic dishes and a garden idyll (p92).

3 **Moderna Museet** Contemporary art in an old naval building (p94).

4 **Hjerta** Top-notch food and delightful Skeppsholmen views (p95).

5 **Blå Porten** Classic Swedish fare and a much-loved courtyard (p92).

DJURGÅRDEN

Crossing to the island from Strandvägen, over Djurgårdsbron – where you can rent bicycles, paddleboats and canoes, and get tourist information from the new **Visit Djurgården** office (*see right* **In the Know**) – you'll see the magnificent **Nordiska Museet** directly in front of you. This city landmark was designed in the style of a Nordic Renaissance palace and holds historical and cultural objects from all over Scandinavia. The path to the right of the bridge leads you to **Junibacken**, a children's fantasy land with a train ride through the stories of Astrid Lindgren's books.

Further on lies the don't-miss **Vasamuseet** (*see p91* **Salvaged from the Sea**), home of the vast *Vasa* warship, which sank just off the island of Beckholmen on her maiden voyage in 1628. Fittingly, the purpose-built museum occupies the site of the former naval dockyard. If you're going to visit just one museum in Stockholm – and there are plenty to choose from – make it this one.

Djurgårdsvägen, the main route into and around the island, passes by the vast Nordiska Museet, the western entrance to Skansen and the quaint, old-fashioned **Biologiska Museet**, devoted to Scandinavian wildlife. Further south, the beautiful **Liljevalchs Konsthall** stands on the corner of Djurgården's most developed area. It's one of the best exhibition spaces in Sweden, with contemporary shows that change every three months. Next to the building is the lovely café **Blå Porten** (Blue Gate), named after the 19th-century gate near Djurgårdsbron.

Behind Blå Porten is the **Aquaria Vattenmuseum**, which sits on the water next to the depot for the island's old-fashioned trams, in a stretch known as Galärskjulen. Its waterfront café has spectacular views to Skeppsholmen. This stretch of waterfront has become more developed in the past few years. It's now home to **Båthall 2**, the Maritime Museum's boathouse displaying historical vessels, and, a little further along towards Vasamuseet, the new

Spritmuseum, containing the Absolut Art Collection, a traditional Swedish restaurant, tasting rooms and engaging exhibitions.

Squeals, laughter and live music can be heard coming from the summer-only **Gröna Lund** amusement park, a couple of blocks to the south. Opposite the park is **ABBA The Museum**, the high-profile attraction that finally opened in 2013 after a decade in the planning. There are several hamburger and pizza places here, as well as the 1920s Hasselbacken restaurant on the hill across the street, next to the **Cirkus** concert/ theatre venue (*see p163*).

East of Gröna Lund, Djurgårdsstaden is the island's only real residential area. Most of the houses and cottages along this district's narrow streets were built between the mid 1700s and the early 1800s as housing for shipyard workers. About 200 people live here today and the apartments are much sought after. This residential area is often overlooked by tourists, which makes a walk through its well-preserved, historic streets all the more charming. Whipping posts like the one in the district's tiny square, Skampålens Torg, once stood in public places around the city.

Continuing along Djurgårdsvägen, you soon arrive at the main entrance to **Skansen**. Stockholm's number one attraction pulls in 1.4 million visitors a year, and is a mix of open-air history museum, amusement park and zoo,

EXPLORE

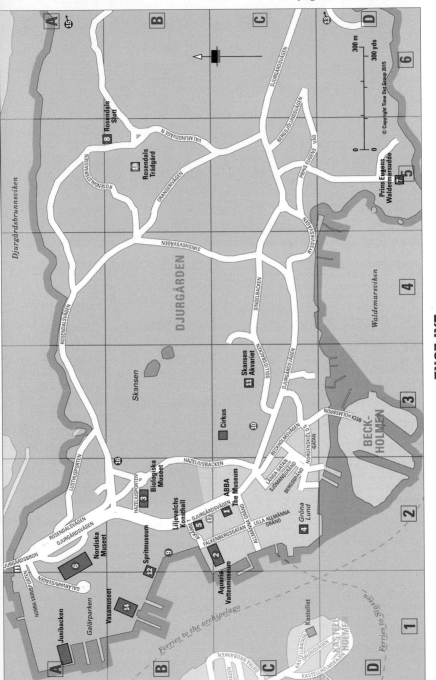

EXPLORE

Djurgårdsbrunnsviken

A

19

8 Rosendals Slott

18 Rosendals Trädgård

ROSENDALSTERRASSEN

ORANGERIVÄGEN

VALMUNDSVÄGEN N

DJURGÅRDSVÄGEN

BERGS MJÖLUNDSVÄGEN

SIRISHOVSVÄGEN

DJURGÅRDEN

PRINS EUGENS VÄG

Prins Eugens Waldemarsudde 7

5

ROSENDALSVÄGEN

Skansen

Waldemarsviken

PYSSINGSVÄGEN

4

SINGELBACKEN

11 Skansen Akvariet

SOLLIDSBACKEN

DJURGÅRDSVÄGEN

BECKHOLMSBRON

13

D

6

© Copyright Time Out Group 2015

300 m

300 yds

0

0

BECK-HOLMEN

3

LUSTHUSPORTEN

16

HAZELIUSPORTEN

HAZELIUSBACKEN

10 Cirkus

BECKHOLMSVÄGEN

NORDENSKIÖLDSGATAN

LÅNGA GATAN

SJÖMANSGRÄND

BERGSBRAND

2

ROSENDALSVÄGEN

DJURGÅRDSVÄGEN

3 Biologiska Museet

Liljevalchs Konsthall

5 DJURGÅRDSVÄGEN

1 ABBA The Museum

FALKENBERGSGATAN

ALMÄNNA GRÄND

LILLA ALLMÄNNA GRÄND

4 Gröna Lund

JURGÅRDSBRON

NORRA VANNPORTEN

GALÄRVARVSVÄGEN

Galärparken

6

Nordiska Museet

Spritmuseum

12

9

2

Aquaria Vattenmuseum

Ferries to the archipelago

A

Junibacken

Galärparken

Vasamuseet

14

Ferries to Slussen

KASTELLHOLMSKAJEN

ÖSTRA BROBÄNKEN

KASTELLBACKEN

Kastellet

KASTEL-HOLMEN

SLOTTSVÄGEN

C

D

ABBA The Museum.

covering almost the entire width of Djurgården. It includes the **Skansen Akvariet**, which houses monkeys, crocodiles and bats, but you'll have to pay a separate fee to see this.

The number 7 tram route goes to Ryssviken, from where you can walk south to the palatial mansion of **Prins Eugens Waldemarsudde**, which has amazing views of the water, or walk north for about ten minutes to the café at **Rosendals Trädgård**, a lovely spot for a bite to eat. Nearby is **Rosendals Slott**, the summer retreat of Karl XIV Johan, the French marshal who was elected as Sweden's crown prince in 1810 and later went on to be crowned king.

To explore further east, you'll need to be prepared to walk, cycle or drive. To reach the eastern half of Djurgården by bus, you'll have to plan ahead and take line 69 from the northern side of Djurgårdsbron. The bus takes you to the south-eastern tip of the island, where Nordic art is displayed at swanky **Thielska Galleriet** and waterfront cafés at Blockhusudden look out towards the Fjäderholmarna islands. The southern shore of this area of Djurgården is lined with the homes and estates of Stockholm's extremely wealthy.

Most of eastern Djurgården is a designated nature reserve with a marsh, old oak trees and paths for horses, bikes and hikers. The narrow canal, Djurgårdsbrunnskanalen, which first opened in 1834, is a pleasant place for a stroll, lined with trees and ending with a small footbridge near the sea.

Sights & Museums

ABBA The Museum
Djurdgårdsvägen 68 (121 328 60, www.abba themuseum.com). Bus 44, or tram 7, or ferry

from Slussen. **Open** *1 May-31 Aug* 10am-8pm daily. *Sept-mid Jan* 10am-6pm Mon, Tue, Sat, Sun; 10am-8pm Wed-Fri. *Halloween & Christmas* 10am-6pm daily. See website for 2015 opening information. **Admission** 195kr; 145kr reductions; free under-7s. **No cash. Map** p85 C2 ❶

This genuinely interactive museum in the Swedish Hall of Fame (also included in the ticket) has been designed around the idea of giving visitors a sense of what it would be like to be the fifth member of Sweden's most famous pop group: visitors can try on the quartet's colourful satin outfits, enter replica versions of the band's studio and dressing room, and even perform classic tunes on stage. Some of the museum's more novel touches include the

EXPLORE

installation of a special telephone for which only Björn, Benny, Agnetha and Anni-Frid have the number – if it rings, a visitor will find themselves talking directly to a member of the band – and a piano supposedly linked to Benny's own ivories, which sounds when he rehearses in his studio. There's also a cinema screening Lasse Hallström's much-loved music videos, and a dancefloor. The museum opened in 2013, after a decade or so in the planning (it was originally due to be housed in the building that's now home to Fotografiska; *see p99*), and has succeeded in finally providing an ABBA attraction that appeals to both diehard fans, and families with children who probably haven't even heard of the 1970s pop sensation that went on to sell some 379 million records. Refreshments come in the form of a steak restaurant, and there's a museum shop – no true ABBA fan leaves the place empty-handed. The Swedish Music Hall of Fame, meanwhile, gives a chronological tour of Swedish pop music, from Roxette to First Aid Kit via The Cardigans.

▶ *Dedicated ABBA fans might want to stay at the Melody Hotel (see p215), which has direct access to the museum.*

Aquaria Vattenmuseum

Falkenbergsgatan 2 (708 70 00, www.aquaria.se). Bus 44, or tram 7, or ferry from Slussen. **Open** *Mid June-mid Aug* 10am-6pm daily. *Mid Aug-mid June* 10am-4.30pm Tue-Sun (daily during school hols). **Admission** 100kr; 30kr-80kr reductions; free under-3s. Free with SC. **Map** p85 C2 ❷

A waterfall cascades over the entrance to this unusual aquarium, which is next to the Vasamuseet. In the rainforest exhibit, you can go eyeball to eyeball with 1.5m (5ft) catfish, then step into a realistic jungle, with dripping plants, chirping insects and rain showers every ten minutes. Elsewhere, tropical fish swim in a long aquarium, and a mountain waterfall splashes down into a pool of trout. Environmental concerns are highlighted; a sign next to an open manhole encourages you to climb down for a 'sewer adventure', where you see the effects of pollution and acid rain. The water views from the café make it a good pit stop.

Biologiska Museet

Hazeliusporten 2 (442 82 15, tours 442 82 70, www.biologiskamuseet.com). Bus 44, 47, or tram 7, or ferry from Slussen or Nybroviken. **Open** *Apr-Sept* 11am-4pm daily. *Oct-Mar* noon-3pm Tue-Fri; 11am-3pm Sat, Sun. **Admission** 65kr; 25kr reductions; free under-6s. Free with SC. **Map** p85 B2 ❸

Designed in the style of a medieval Norwegian church, the dark brown, shingled Biological Museum is a sanctuary of peace in this otherwise bustling section of Djurgården. Beneath its A-framed roof, three dioramas depict Scandinavian wildlife. The ground floor features a valley in east Greenland and an Arctic cave, as well as a box containing a

'*skvader*' – a fantasy hybrid of a hare and a grouse. Up the double-helix staircase lies the main attraction, a 360° diorama viewable from two platforms of the Swedish outdoors, including coastline, cliff and forest, where you can spot bears, birds, deer and other immobile critters. Artist Bruno Liljefors (whose depictions of nature hang in the National Museet) painted the detailed backdrop. Except for replacing a few of its stuffed animals, the museum has remained unchanged since it opened in 1893. It's worth poking your head in for a few minutes, but no more.

Gröna Lund

Allmänna Gränd (708 70 00, www.gronalund.se). Bus 44, or tram 7, or ferry from Slussen or Nybroplan. **Open** *May-late Sept* days & times vary; call or check website for details. *Late June-mid Aug* typically 10am-11pm Mon-Thur, Sat; 10am-10pm Sun. Closed end Sept-end Apr. **Admission** 110kr; free under-6s & over-65s; one-day bracelet (all rides) 310kr. Free with SC. **Map** p85 C2 ❹

Perched on the edge of Djurgården, with great views across the water, Gröna Lund (Green Grove) is Sweden's oldest amusement park. Built in 1883 and owned by the same family ever since, its historic buildings and well-preserved rides retain an old-world charm. You can even travel here by boat the way people did more than 100 years ago. Among the older favourites are carousels, bumper cars and Ferris wheels, while the newer fairground thrills come from two rollercoasters intertwined, and the free-fall 'power tower', Europe's highest at (gulp) 80m (264ft), with four of its seats modified to tilt forward. The Kvasten (Broom) rollercoaster takes thrill-seekers over the park with their feet dangling in the air at 55km/h (35mph), while a much tamer Tuff-Tuff-Train is a rollercoaster designed for tots.

IN THE KNOW GETTING THERE

In summer, tram 7 is forever packed with tourists on their way to Djurgården, yet the green island can be easily and pleasantly reached on foot, via the Djurgårdsbron bridge, or on the Djurgårdsfärjan ferry from Slussen (run by Waxholmsbolaget, 679 58 30, www.waxholmsbolaget.com; free with an SL card). The ferry arrives/departs at a jetty near Gröna Lund, and stops off at Skeppsholmen on the way. If you're heading to the eastern side of Djurgården, take tram 7 from Norrmalm to Ryssviken (there's no Tunnelbana station on or near Djurgården). Bus 44 runs along Djurgårdsvägen as far as Skansen. The only transport that goes to Skeppsholmen, meanwhile, is the number 65 bus, which runs along the south side of Norrmalm.

EXPLORE

EXPLORE

You can buy multi-ride booklets or pay for each ride separately. Stick around for an evening pop concert, held about once a week. For more information on children's activities at the park, *see p150*.

Liljevalchs Konsthall

Djurgårdsvägen 60 (50 83 13 30, www.liljevalchs. se). Bus 44, 69, 76, or tram 7, or ferry from Slussen or Nybroplan (summer only). **Open** 11am-7pm Tue, Thur; 11am-5pm Wed, Fri-Sun. **Admission** 80kr; 60kr reductions; free under-18s. Free with SC. **Map** p85 B2 ❺

This 1916 building, owned by the City of Stockholm, is a fine example of Swedish neo-classicism. Originally built from a donation by the businessman Carl Fredrik Liljevach, it attracts a wide audience to its 12 exhibition rooms, where you can view themed and solo shows (which change every three months) by Swedish and international artists.

Nordiska Museet

Djurgårdsvägen 6-16 (51 95 46 00, www. nordiskamuseet.se). Bus 44, 69, 76, or tram 7, or ferry from Slussen or Nybroplan (summer only). **Open** 10am-5pm daily. **Admission** 100kr; free under-18s. Free with SC. **Map** p85 A2 ❻

The Nordiska Museet, Sweden's national museum of cultural history, was the brainchild of Artur Hazelius, who also created Skansen. Everything about the place is big: the building itself, designed by Isak Clason and completed in 1907, is massive, though only a quarter of the originally intended size. On entering the aptly named Great Hall, visitors are greeted by Carl Milles' colossal pink statue of a seated Gustav Vasa. (In his forehead is a chunk of oak from a tree planted by the King himself, so legend has it.) The museum's collection of artefacts is immense. Permanent exhibitions include Swedish traditions, manners and customs, fashion and folk costumes, recreated table settings from the 16th to the 20th centuries, and the Sami people. There are also marvellously detailed doll's houses and a collection of doom-laden paintings and photos by Strindberg that do nothing to dispel his madman image. The Textile Gallery features 500 textiles dating from the 1600s onwards. Lekstugan, the play area aimed at kids aged five to 12, is always popular.

Prins Eugens Waldemarsudde

Prins Eugens väg 6 (54 58 37 00, www. waldemarsudde.se). Bus 44, or tram 7, or ferry from Slussen or Nybroplan (summer only). **Open** 11am-5pm Tue, Wed, Fri-Sun; 11am-8pm Thur. **Admission** 100kr; 80kr reductions; free under-19s. **Map** p85 D5 ❼

This beautiful waterfront property, comprising a grand three-storey mansion and an art gallery, was owned by Prince Eugen from 1899 until his death in 1947. The prince, a well-known Swedish landscape painter and the brother of King Gustav V, moved into the mansion upon its completion in 1904. The house's architect, Ferdinand Boberg, later designed the NK department store. The light, simply decorated rooms on the ground floor are furnished as the prince left them. Temporary art exhibitions, featuring the likes of Anders Zorn, Ernst Josephson, Isaac Grünewald and Carl Larsson, as well as the prince's wonderful landscape paintings, are displayed upstairs and in the gallery next door. The gallery was built in 1913 when Prince Eugen ran out of display space for his art collection. The prince designed the classical white flowerpots for sale in the gift shop himself. The mansion and artworks are impressive, but the grounds and views are even more so. Sculptures by Auguste Rodin and Carl Milles adorn the park, which is a great spot to relax, and a path leads to an 18th-century windmill.

Nordiska Museet.

Skansen

Rosendals Slott

*Rosendalsvägen 49 (402 61 30, www.royal
court.se). Tram 7 to Bellmansro (then 700m walk,
follow signs to Rosendal).* **Open** (by guided tour
only) *June-Aug* noon, 1pm, 2pm, 5pm Tue-Sun.
Admission 100kr; 50kr reductions; free under-7s.
Free with SC. **Map** p85 B5 **8**

King Karl XIV Johan's summer retreat, this light
yellow building with grey pillars is designed in
the Empire style, its wall paintings and decorative
scheme reflecting the King's military background.
The cotton fabric around the dining room is pleated
to resemble an officer's tent, and the frieze in the
Red Salon shows the Norse god Odin's victory over
the frost giants. The fable of Eros and Psyche is
told on the beautifully painted domed ceiling in the
Lantern Room. The palace was designed by Fredrik
Blom, who also created the Historiska Museet
and Skeppsholm church; it was prefabricated in
Norrmalm then shipped out to Djurgården in pieces.
Karl Johan always remained a Frenchman at heart:
he never ate Swedish food and sometimes forced his
less fragrant guests to wash their hands in cologne.
The 45-minute tour offered in summer is the only
way to see the inside of the palace.

FREE Sjohistoriska at Galärvarvet

*Galärvarvet (www.sjohistoriska.se). Bus 44 or
tram 7.* **Open** *May-Sept* 10am-5pm Tue-Sun.
Admission free. **Map** p85 B2 **9**

There are two ships docked near the Vasamuseet
that are both free to visit. The lightship *Finngrundet*

(1903) was anchored in the ice-free part of Sweden's
Gulf of Bothnia before lightships were replaced
by lighthouses, and has recently reopened after
a three-year restoration. The *St Erik* (1915) was
Sweden's first ice-breaker, and was used to keep
the archipelago channels clear. They're also known
as Museifartygen and Museipiren respectively.
Also here is Båthall 2, the Maritime Museum's
(Sjohistoriska) charming boathouse museum. There
are some 50 vessels on display, with steam launches,
workboats, leisure craft and more from the 18th,
19th and 20th centuries.

★ Skansen

*Djurgårdsslätten 49-51 (442 80 00, www.
skansen.se). Bus 44, or tram 7, or ferry from
Slussen or Nybroplan.* **Open** *Jan, Feb, Nov, Dec*
10am-3pm Mon-Fri; 10am-4pm Sat, Sun. *Mar,
Apr, Oct* 10am-4pm daily. *May-mid June* 10am-
7pm daily. *Mid June-Aug* 10am-10pm daily.
Sept 10am-6pm daily. **Admission** 60kr-170kr;
25kr-60kr reductions; free under-6s. Free with SC.
Map p85 C3 **10**

Founded in 1891 by Artur Hazelius, also responsible for the Nordiska Museet, Skansen is a one-stop
cultural tour of Sweden. The 150-plus traditional
buildings – homes, shops, churches, barns and
workshops – are organised as a miniature Sweden,
with buildings from the north of the country at
the north, those from the middle in the middle,
and so on. Most of the structures, situated along
paths lined with elm, oak and maple trees, date

EXPLORE

from the 18th and 19th centuries. The striking 14th-century Norwegian storage hut that overlooks Djurgårdsbrunnsviken is the oldest; newest is the ironmonger's shop and the co-op grocery store from the 1930s. Most complete is the 1850s quarter, with cobblestoned streets and artisans' workshops, including a baker, glass-blower and potter. Watch them work, then buy the proceeds. Nearly all of the buildings are original and were moved here whole or piece by piece from all over Sweden. Skansen's staff – dressed in folk costumes – spin wool, tend fires and perform traditional tasks (Oct-Apr 11am-3pm; May-Sept 11am-5pm).

Animals from all over Scandinavia, including brown bears, moose and wolves, are kept along the northern cliff in natural habitats. There's also a petting zoo with goats, hedgehogs and kittens, and an aquarium/zoo, Skansen Akvariet, near the southern entrance. An old-fashioned marketplace sits at the centre of the park, and folk-dancing demonstrations – with foot-stamping and fiddle-playing – take place in summer on the Tingsvallen stage.

Hunger pangs can be satisfied at a variety of places; Restaurang Solliden serves classic Swedish dishes and has a wonderful view of Djurgården and southern Stockholm. The 19th-century Gubbhyllan building to the left of the main entrance houses a Tobacco and Match Museum – it was a Swede who invented the safety match – and an old-fashioned café that serves simple dishes. Skansen is a popular destination on Sweden's national holidays since most of them, including Midsummer and Lucia, are celebrated here in traditional style.

▶ *The Christmas market is a massive draw at Skansen (see p32). Also, on summer Tuesdays, be sure to stick around for 'Allsång på Skansen', a sing-along concert on the Solliden stage that's broadcast nationally at 8pm (see also p33 Singing for Sweden).*

Skansen Akvariet
Djurgårdsslätten 49-51 (660 10 00, www. skansen-akvariet.se). Bus 44, 47, or tram 7, or ferry from Slussen or Nybroplan. **Open** *May* 10am-5pm Mon-Fri; 10am-6pm Sat, Sun. *1st 3wks June* 10am-6pm Mon-Fri; 10am-7pm Sat, Sun. *Midsummer-end July* 10am-8pm daily. *Aug* 10am-6pm Mon-Fri; 10am-7pm Sat, Sun. *Sept-Dec* 10am-4pm Mon-Fri; 10am-5pm Sat, Sun. *Christmas* 10am-4pm Sat, Sun. **Admission** 120kr; 60kr reductions; free under-6s. Free with SC. **Map** p85 C3 ⓫

Some of the smallest monkeys you've ever seen are on show in this zoo and aquarium inside Skansen. Bright orange tamarins and pygmy marmosets hang from trees behind glass, and you can walk up the steps of a giant treehouse where more than three dozen striped lemurs hop around while chewing on fresh vegetables. The less friendly-looking baboons crawl around a steep hill in another exhibit, complete with a crashed jungle jeep hanging from a branch.

You can even pet a boa constrictor and a tarantula. There's lots to see – snakes, a nocturnal room full of bats, and two crocodiles (given by Fidel Castro to a Russian cosmonaut before ending up here). If you don't want to pay the separate entrance fee, you can watch the baboons and lemurs from outside.

Spritmuseum
Djurgårdsvägen 38 (12 13 13 00, www.sprit museum.se). Bus 44 or tram 7. **Open** *1 June-31 Aug* 10am-6pm Mon, Wed-Sun; 10am-8pm Tue. *1 Sept-31 May* 10am-5pm Mon, Wed-Sun; 10am-8pm Tue. **Admission** 100kr; free under-12s. Free with SC. **Map** p85 B2 ⓬

Spritmuseum is the new version of the former Vin & Sprithistoriska Museet, which was previously housed on Dalagatan in Vasastan. Whereas the old museum was a (surprisingly engaging) examination of the history of the production of alcohol in Sweden, the new museum is more contemporary in its focus, looking at the culture of alcohol consumption through a series of temporary exhibitions. When they work, the exhibitions are both playful and informative, though the promotion of the Absolut brand is slightly jarring in some instances. Afterwards, you can head to the tasting room or the restaurant to put the culture of alcohol consumption into practice.

Thielska Galleriet
Sjötullsbacken 8 (662 58 84, www.thielska-galleriet.se). Bus 69. **Open** noon-5pm Tue, Wed, Fri-Sun; noon-8pm Thur. Check website for guided tour times & dates (price included in entrance fee). **Admission** 80kr; 50kr reductions; free under-18s. Free with SC. **Map** p85 D6 ⓭

Wealthy banker and art collector Ernest Thiel built this palatial home on the eastern tip of Djurgården in the early 1900s. The eclectically styled building, with influences from the Italian Renaissance and the Orient, was designed by Ferdinand Boberg, who built Prins Eugens Waldemarsudde at roughly the same time. Thiel lost most of his fortune after World War I, and the state acquired the property in 1924. This museum opened two years later, displaying his collection of turn-of-the-19th-century Nordic art, including works by Carl Larsson, Bruno Liljefors and Edvard Munch (a close friend of Thiel). Although six works by some of these artists, valued at 24 million kronor, were stolen in the middle of the night on 20 June 2000 – a crime that remains unsolved – there are still plenty of paintings to see. Thiel's bathroom has been turned into a small café serving cinnamon rolls and meat pies, and the urn containing his ashes lies beneath a statue by Rodin in the park. If you haven't seen enough Scandinavian art at the National Museet, this gallery should satisfy you.

★ Vasamuseet
Galärvarvsvägen 14 (51 95 48 00, www. vasamuseet.se). Bus 44, 69, 76, or tram 7, or ferry from Slussen or Nybroplan (summer only).

SALVAGED FROM THE SEA

This huge 17th-century warship was saved by a lack of salt.

Entering Scandinavia's most popular museum (*see p90*) for the first time is a jaw-dropping experience, as you take in the monstrous size of the 17th-century *Vasa* – the largest (69 metres/226 feet long) and best-preserved ship of its kind in the world.

Built in the 1620s, when Sweden was at war with Poland, the *Vasa* had two gun decks and 64 cannon, making it the mightiest ship in the fleet. Unfortunately, though, the gun decks and heavy cannon made the ship top-heavy. During a stability test, in which 30 men ran back and forth across the deck,

she nearly toppled over. Still, the King needed his ship and the maiden voyage went ahead. But only a few minutes after the *Vasa* set sail from near present-day Slussen on 10 August 1628, she began to list to one side. The gun ports filled with water and the ship sank after a voyage of only 1,300 metres (just under a mile). Of the 150 people on board, as many as 50 died – the number would have been much higher if the ship had reached Älvsnabben in the archipelago, where 300 soldiers were waiting to board.

The *Vasa* was returned to the surface to royal fanfare in 1961, and was installed in her custom-designed museum in 1991. In 2011, the museum celebrated the 50th anniversary of her salvage from the seabed with a series of special exhibitions. A project to expand the museum was finished in 2013, allowing for 2,000 visitors at a time (400 more than before); however, be warned that queues in summer can still be very long – so try to visit early or shortly before closing time.

The reason the *Vasa* was so well preserved at her recovery in 1961 – 95 per cent of the ship is original – is because the Baltic Sea is insufficiently saline to contain the tiny shipworm, which destroys wood in saltier seas. Yet her health is still a matter of concern. She was diagnosed with a near fatal disease in 2000 when she became her own worst enemy, producing sulphuric acid that began dissolving her mighty timbers from the inside out. But true to all great drama queens, the *Vasa* beat her affliction.

Upon arrival, head first for the theatre to see a short film about the *Vasa* and her discovery by amateur naval historian Anders Franzén. On your own or with a tour (there are several daily in English), you can walk around the exterior of the warship and view the upper deck and keel from six different levels. The ornate stern is covered with sculptures intended to express the glory of the Swedish King and to frighten enemies. No one's allowed on board, but you can walk through a recreation of one of the gun decks.

In an eerie exhibit down by the keel, the skeletons of ten people who died aboard the *Vasa* are on display, as are reconstructed models of how they would have looked alive. The museum's restaurant has a dockside view, and its new gift shop is stocked with everything the *Vasa* enthusiast might need.

EXPLORE

Blå Porten.

Open *Sept-May* 10am-5pm Mon, Tue, Thur-Sun; 10am-8pm Wed. *June-Aug* 8.30am-6pm daily. **Guided tours** (in English, included with admission) *Sept-May* 11.30am, 1.30pm, 3.30pm Mon-Fri; 10.30am, 11.30am, 12.30pm, 1.30pm, 2.30pm, 3.30pm Sat, Sun. *June-Aug* Every half hour. **Admission** 130kr; 100kr reductions & all 5-8pm Wed; free under-18s. Free with SC. **Map** p85 B1 ⑭

See p91 **Salvaged from the Sea**.

Restaurants

Djurgårdsbrunn Wärdshus
Djurgårdsbrunnsvägen 68 (624 22 00, www. djurgardsbrunn.com). Bus 69. **Open** 5-11pm Wed-Sat. *Brunch* noon-4pm Sat, Sun. Hours may vary; call or check online for details. Closed mid Nov-mid May. **Main courses** 195kr-265kr. **Weekend brunch** 285kr. **Map** p85 A6 ⑮ **Traditional Swedish**
At Djurgårdsbrunn you can easily spend hours sitting outside eating, drinking and enjoying the view across the canal. The food and decor make it feel like a lodge in the archipelago or a traditional countryside inn. Either way, it's an easy, pleasant walk from the city centre.

Ulla Winbladh
Rosendalsvägen 8 (53 48 97 01, www.ullawinbladh. se). Tram 7 or bus 44. **Open** 11.30am-10pm Mon; 11.30am-11pm Tue-Fri; 12.30-11pm Sat; 12.30-10pm Sun. **Main courses** 185kr-315kr. **Map** p85 B2 ⑯ **Traditional Swedish**
Despite its picturesque setting, old-fashioned Ulla Winbladh (named after a much-loved friend of Swedish national poet and composer Carl Michael Bellman) doesn't quite live up to its reputation. The kitchen seems to cut corners a little too often, and the service can sometimes be unfriendly. The safest bets are the classic meatballs or fried *strömming* (Baltic herring), eaten outdoors in summer or in the cosy dining room in winter.

Cafés

In addition to the places listed below, many of Djurgården's museums have good cafés. Worth a visit are the café at the **Aquaria Vattenmuseum**, with its waterfront views; Café Ektorpet, set outside an 18th-century cottage on a hill overlooking the water, at **Prins Eugens Waldemarsudde**; or one of **Skansen's** numerous cafés and eateries, the best of which is Café Petissan, situated in in a cosy building from the late 17th century.

★ Blå Porten
Djurgårdsvägen 64 (663 87 59, www.blaporten. com). Bus 44, 47, or tram 7, or ferry from Slussen. **Open** *May-Aug* 11am-8pm Mon, Wed, Fri-Sun; 11am-9pm Tue, Thur. *Sept-Apr* 11am-7pm Mon, Wed, Fri-Sun; 11am-9pm Tue, Thur. **Map** p85 B2 ⑰
The 'Blue Door' is Stockholm's most romantic café. Next door to prominent art gallery Liljevalchs Konsthall (*see p88*), this beautiful piazza-like garden is a secret hideaway in the heart of the island. The interior isn't that exciting, so you should probably choose somewhere else on a rainy day. There's a medieval-style table inside with a mouthwatering display of desserts, and traditional Swedish lunch dishes available throughout the day. If you're visiting Vasamuseet, Skansen or Gröna Lund, then Blå Porten is the perfect stop.

★ Rosendals Trädgård
Rosendalsterrassen 12 (54 58 12 70, www. rosendalstradgard.se). Tram 7. **Open** *Feb-Mar* 11am-4pm Tue-Sun. *Apr* 11am-5pm Tue-Sun. *May-Sept* 11am-5pm Mon-Fri; 11am-6pm Sat, Sun. *Oct* 11am-4pm Tue-Fri; 11am-5pm Sat, Sun. *Nov* 11am-4pm Tue-Sun. Closed Dec, Jan. **Map** p85 B5 ⑱
The green-fingered café located in this upmarket garden centre offers some of the finest cakes and sandwiches in town – all of them organic and grown

or baked on the premises. Rosendals Trädgård is well known for its seasonal desserts, and its recipes fill the pages of bestselling cookbook *Rosendals trädgårdscafé*. In summer, people devour fruit pie at picnic tables or on the grass under the apple trees; in winter they keep warm with a mug of *glögg* (mulled wine) in the greenhouses. There's a small shop selling jam, bread and flowers (which you can pick yourself). The place is a little tricky to find, so be prepared to ask for directions.

Shops & Services

Djurgården is not a shopping destination. However, **Skansen** does have a very good shop selling traditional and contemporary Swedish handicrafts, jewellery, condiments and tools. It's open to the general public and situated outside the main entrance. And the Garden Shop at upmarket garden centre **Rosendals Trädgård** is also worth a look if you're into rustic tools, French soaps and home-made herbal teas, salts and oils.

SKEPPSHOLMEN

Crossing the narrow bridge from Blasieholmen, you'll see the **Östasiatiska Museet** on the hill to your left, housed in a long yellow building designed by Kungliga Slottet architect Nicodemus Tessin the Younger in 1700. The white, Empire-style **Skeppsholmskyrkan** – officially known as Karl Johans Kyrka – stands nearby; designed for the navy by Fredrik Blom, it was completed in 1842 but has now been deconsecrated. The three-masted schooner **Af Chapman**, which is now a youth hostel (*see p215*), is docked to your right. Behind the church stands the **Moderna Museet** (Museum of Modern Art), occupying an earth-toned building designed by Spanish architect Rafael Moneo and completed in 1998; the adjoining **Arkitektur – och Designcentrum** (ArkDes; previously Arkitekturmuseet) is housed in a former naval drill hall. On the north-east corner of Skeppsholmen, **Panoptikon Fotografins Hus** (Slupskjulsvägen 26, 611 69 69, www.panoptikon. nu) exhibits contemporary photography in a long hall where the navy previously manufactured mines and torpedoes. The annual **Stockholm Jazz Festival** is held further south on the eastern shore. On the south-western corner of Skeppsholmen are **Kungliga Konsthögskolan** (Royal University College of Fine Arts), housed in beautifully restored 18th-century naval barracks, and the headquarters of the Swedish Society of Crafts and Design, **Svensk Form**. A newer addition to the island is the contemporary-styled

EXPLORE

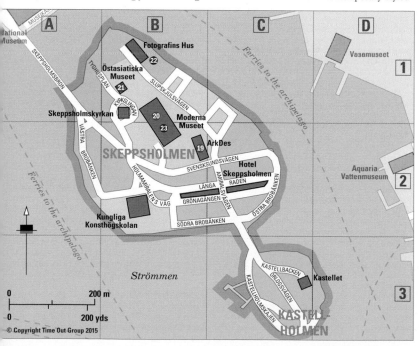

Skeppsholmen.

Hotel Skeppsholmen (*see p213*), on the southern side – one of the nicest places to rest your head in Stockholm.

Situated to the south of Skeppsholmen, and connected to it by a bridge, the tiny granite island of **Kastellholmen** is named after a castle built here in the 1660s. The castle was blown up in 1845 after an accident in a cartridge-manufacturing laboratory. A year later, Fredrik Blom designed a new, medieval-style castle with two red towers, one tall and one squat (not open to the public); the castle's cannons are fired on Sweden's national day on 6 June, as well as on the birthdays of the King, Queen and Crown Princess. Kastellholmen makes for a lovely short stroll, and provides excellent views of Gröna Lund and the sea from its rocky eastern side.

Arkitektur – och Designcentrum (ArkDes)

Exercisplan 4 (58 72 70 40, www.arkdes.se). Bus 65. **Open** 10am-8pm Tue; 10am-6pm Wed-Sun. **Admission** 80kr; free under-19s & all 4-6pm Fri. Free with SC. **Map** p93 B2 ⑲

The Centre of Architecture and Design, in a long hall linked to Moderna Museet (*see right*), has recently widened its scope (and changed its name) as part of a new government initiative to strengthen the interest in and status of Swedish design. As well as its permanent displays of famous Swedish buildings and architectural projects – including Stockholm's Stadshuset (City Hall), the Royal Palace and the five office buildings at Hötorget – the museum now also holds temporary exhibitions that run the full design gamut, from bicycle design to the work of Konstantin Grcic. However, this move has been controversial overall, with the new centre encountering some criticism from the design world (*see p205*). With the dismissal of the museum's director in 2014,

its future trajectory is uncertain, and part of a general debate over the future of the nation's design collections and industry.

★ Moderna Museet

Slupskjulsvägen 7 (51 95 52 00, www.moderna museet.se). Bus 65 or ferry from Slussen. **Open** 10am-8pm Tue; 10am-6pm Wed, Thur, Sat; 10am-8pm Fri. *Guided tours in English* July-Sept 2pm Tue, Thur; 1pm Sun. **Admission** 120kr; 100kr reductions; free under-18s & all 6-8pm Fri. Free with SC. **Map** p93 B1 ⑳

When it opened in 1958, Moderna Museet soon gained a reputation as one of the world's most groundbreaking contemporary art venues. Housed originally in an old, disused naval exercise building, the museum's heyday came in the 1960s and '70s when it introduced Andy Warhol, Jean Tinguely, Robert Rauschenberg, Niki de Saint Phalle and many more to an astonished Swedish audience. The construction of Moneo's new museum building was completed in 1998, but it closed four years later owing to structural problems, including a mould infestation. The museum reopened in 2004 with a brighter interior, a more open floor plan, an espresso bar and – most importantly – no mould. Its collection of 20th-century art, featuring works by greats such as Picasso, Dali, Pollock and de Chirico, is arranged in reverse chronological order on the main floor. The terrace of the museum's restaurant offers beautiful views. Though admission to the museum is no longer free, the '1st at Moderna' series on the first of every month offers a free look at a new exhibition.

Östasiatiska Museet

Tyghusplan (456 12 00, www.mfea.se). Bus 65. **Open** 11am-8pm Tue; 11am-5pm Wed-Sun. **Admission** 80kr; free under-19s. Free with SC. **Map** p93 B1 ㉑

The main focus of the Östasiatiska Museet (Museum of Far Eastern Antiquities) is a permanent exhibition on prehistoric China, presenting artefacts unearthed in the 1920s in a Chinese village by the museum's founder, Johan Gunnar Andersson. The exhibit, displayed in a dimly lit room echoing with sounds and voices, includes 3,000- to 4,000-year-old tools and pottery, descriptions of burial traditions, and the symbols, as well as patterns, of prehistoric earthenware. The museum also has a large collection of Far Eastern Buddhist sculptures. The shop sells Japanese tea sets, books on Asian art, religions and design, and kimonos.

Restaurants

The restaurant at **Hotel Skeppsholmen** (*see p213*) is open to non-guests, and serves well-executed classic Swedish fare; its terrace is normally packed in the summer months.

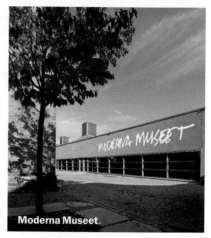

Moderna Museet.

★ Hjerta
Slupskjulsvägen 28 (611 41 00, www.restaurang hjerta.se). Bus 65. **Open** noon-11pm daily.
Main courses 185kr-275kr. **Map** p93 B1
㉒ Modern European/Swedish
One of Stockholm's best summer eating spots, Hjerta (Heart) is a friendly proposition offering laid-back Swedish and Modern European fare (*toast skagen*, sourdough pizza, fish and chips with smoked mayonnaise) made with top-quality ingredients. The food is excellent, but the place is as much about the setting as the cooking – the restaurant's outdoor wooden bench-style tables overlook the moored boats along Skeppsholmen's shore, and provide the perfect spot from which to see the sun setting over the water. In the colder months, the action moves into the stylish interior.

Moderna Museet
Slupskjulsvägen 7-9 (52 02 36 60, www.momumat. se). Bus 65 or ferry from Slussen. **Open** 11am-8pm Tue; 11am-5pm Wed-Sun. *Brunch* 11am-5pm Sat, Sun. **Main courses** 120kr. **Map** p93 B2
㉓ Contemporary
The Moderna Museet has an ordinary museum café, of course, but also a dining room with white-cloth service and excellent food. It's only open for lunch, but at the weekend serves one of the city's best buffet brunches (135kr). There are two sittings, one at 11.30am and the other at 2pm, and reservations are necessary. The food is (naturally) a modern take on Scandinavian classics and the desserts are particularly glorious.

Shops & Services

There are no standalone shops on Skeppsholmen, but the museum shop at **Moderna Museet** is worth checking out for art- and design-related posters, books, homewares and knick-knacks.

EXPLORE

Södermalm & Långholmen

Södermalm's working-class heritage no longer deters the posh folk from crossing the water locks at Slussen to eat, drink, live and be merry in the city's most colourful district. Cool restaurants, cafés, bars and shops continue to mushroom on the island that's known more simply as 'Söder', while a world-class photography museum, Fotografiska, has cemented the island's status as a cutting-edge cultural hub. A development of the past decade has been the rise of Hornstull, in the west, now one of the hippest parts of the island.

Across from Hornstull, to the north, lies the narrow island of Långholmen (Long Island), almost a mile in length. Thanks largely to the presence of a jail here, Långholmen remained undeveloped for many years, and, as a result, is something of a green retreat. Its sandy beaches are a favoured summer bathing spot.

Stora Henriksvik.

Don't Miss

1 Fotografiska One of the world's best photography museums (p99).

2 Stora Henriksvik Fresh air and fine coffee combined (p117).

3 Monteliusvägen Stunning city views from this cliffside boardwalk (p108).

4 Urban Deli New York-style deli treats (p104).

5 Hornstull Hipster heaven in this Söder neighbourhood (p108).

Fotografiska.

EASTERN SÖDERMALM

The first place you'll arrive at from Gamla Stan is the transport interchange of **Slussen** – a busy Tunnelbana and bus station. Major construction works – for both the new Citybanan railway tunnel and the controversial Future Slussen redevelopment plan – are under way here, meaning that building works will be a feature of the area until at least 2020 (*see p99* **In the Know**). But while Slussen isn't currently the most attractive introduction to Söder's charms, it does contain one of the island's essential museums, the **Stockholms Stadsmuseum**, where you can learn about the city's history since it was founded back in 1252. The famous 38-metre (125-foot) black steel Katarinahissen lift that towers over it, and which visitors used to use to get panoramic views of the city, is no longer in use (and probably, according to local reports, retired). But you can still enjoy the view with a meal (or drink) at the attached **Eriks Gondolen** restaurant. A short walk east along the waterfront from Slussen takes you to the high-profile **Fotografiska** photography museum; open since summer 2010, it's put Slussen on the international art scene map.

Head directly south of Slussen (east of Mariatorget), meanwhile, and you're faced with a steep climb up the pedestrian section of Götgatan, Södermalm's busiest shopping street, which runs down the length of the island. Heading east from this end of Götgatan, walk up Urvädersgränd past the rarely open **Bellmanhuset**, former home of 18th-century balladeer Carl Michael Bellman, to **Mosebacketorg**. This busy cobbled square has been Söder's entertainment centre since the mid 19th century, and is bordered by one of Stockholm's most popular nightlife haunts, **Södra Teatern**. The venue covers everything from clubbing to drinking, cutting-edge performance to live music; in summer, the

terrace provides a great view of Stockholm's harbour. Further south is the landmark **Katarina Kyrka**, masterfully restored in the 1990s to its original Baroque splendour, as well as a preserved early 18th-century neighbourhood on **Mäster Mikaels Gata**, which was named after the city's first paid executioner. Mäster Mikaels Gata and Fjällgatan were connected before the hill was blasted away at the turn of the 19th century in order to create the Renstiernas Gata main road.

Once back on Götgatan, continue downhill and you'll reach lively **Medborgarplatsen**, which houses a small galleria, an indoor farmers' market and two cinema complexes. This large square has undergone a renaissance in recent times, and expansive outdoor seating has been added to the stylish restaurants facing the Medborgarhuset civic hall. Constructed in 1939, the yellow-brick building houses a library, swimming pool and concert venue **Debaser Medis** (*see p164*). A memorial to assassinated Swedish Foreign Minister Anna Lindh, who gave her last speech on the steps of Medborgarhuset, was inaugurated hastily near the steps on 10 September 2004, the first anniversary of her death.

Across the street, the minaret of the city's mosque, **Stockholmsmoskén**, rises over **Björns Trädgard** park, a welcoming space for all ages that now also features a skate park. South-east from here lies the trendy shopping area dubbed **SoFo**, standing for the grid of streets south of Folkungatan, which have a high concentration of independent artists and designers. The area around Nytorget – a lovely garden square lined with traditional wooden houses on its western side – is something of a focal point for the area, particularly since the opening of the **Urban Deli** restaurant-grocery.

Devotees of public transport, from old-fashioned to modern, should visit the entertaining (and child-friendly) **Spårvägsmuseet**, located over in the eastern reaches of the island, near nothing but residential apartments. If you'd rather explore the southern end of Götgatan, you'll be rewarded with a superb swimming complex, **Eriksdalsbadet**, which has Olympic-sized indoor and outdoor pools. The latter is a huge hit in summer. Another of the city's sports arenas, **Globen** (*see p147*), is clearly visible from this part of Södermalm. The huge dome hosts major competitions and concerts, and is one of Stockholm's landmark buildings.

Sights & Museums

Bellmanhuset

Urvädersgränd 3 (767 85 58 00, www.bellmanhuset. se). T-bana Slussen or bus 2, 3, 53, 71, 76, 96. **Open** (guided tours only, in Swedish) 1pm 1st Sun of mth; check website for details. **Admission** 100kr. **No credit cards. Map** p100 A1 ❶
This small house just off Götgatan is the only remaining home of legendary Swedish songwriter and poet Carl Michael Bellman (1740-95). During his tenancy, between 1770 and 1774, he wrote much of his *Fredmans Epistlar*, a book of songs about Stockholm's drunks and prostitutes that parodies the letters of the apostle Paul in the New Testament.
▶ *Stora Henriksvik (see p117) also has a small permanent exhibition relating to Carl Bellman and Stockholm during his lifetime.*

★ Eriksdalsbadet

Hammarby Slussväg 20 (50 84 02 58, www. eriksdalsbadet.se). T-bana Skanstull or bus 3, 4, 55, 74, 94. **Open** 6.30am-9pm Mon-Thur; 6.30am-8pm Fri; 9am-6pm Sat, Sun. Call or visit website to check outdoor pool opening hours. **Admission** *Indoor pool* 90kr; 60kr reductions. *Outdoor pool* 75kr; 55kr reductions. **Map** p100 B6 ❷
This is the main arena for Swedish swimming competitions. It also has adventure pools for children and a seasonal outdoor pool (get there early on warm days to avoid the crowds, and bring a padlock for the lockers), plus a spa and gym. The park surrounding the outdoor pool is popular for summer picnics and sunbathing, and also serves as the site for the annual Popaganda music festival (www.popaganda.se).

★ Fotografiska

Stadsgårdshamnen 22 (50 900 500, www. fotografiska.eu). T-bana Slussen or bus 2, 3, 43, 53, 55, 71, 76. **Open** 9am-9pm Mon-Wed, Sun; 9am-11pm Thur-Sat. **Admission** 120kr; 90kr reductions; free under-12s. **Map** p100 D2 ❸
Housed in a huge art nouveau industrial building built in 1906, the Fotografiska national museum of photography opened to great fanfare in May 2010, quickly becoming one of Scandinavia's – and the world's – foremost centres for contemporary photography. With restoration costs to the former customs house's interior amounting to around 250

million kroner, the stakes were high, but the museum has been a great success, attracting hundreds of thousands of visitors a year.

The inaugural show featured works by some of the world's most respected photographers, including Annie Leibovitz, Lennart Nilsson, Joel-Peter Witkin and Vee Speers. And the high-profile programming has continued, with exhibitions by English photographer Sarah Moon, Scottish fashion and portrait photographer Albert Watson, Canadian landscape photographer Edward Burtynsky, and late New York photographer Robert Mapplethorpe. As well as showcasing renowned international names, Fotografiska aims to promote a good range of Swedish photographers, and to encourage debate and innovation within the field through an active programme of exhibitions, seminars and courses.

Four major exhibitions are held annually, plus 15 to 20 smaller shows (with an emphasis on provocative documentary works). As well as the 2,500sq m (27,000sq ft) of exhibition space, Fotografiska also houses an academy, bistro, café (with superb waterside views), bar, events spaces, a commercial gallery, and an excellent book and souvenir shop. Note that the Stockholm Card is not valid for entry to the museum.

KA Almgren Sidenväveri Museum

Repslagargatan 15A (642 56 16, www.kasiden.se). T-bana Slussen or bus 2, 3, 53, 71, 76, 96. **Open** 10am-4pm Mon-Fri; 11am-3pm Sat. *Guided tours* 1pm Mon, Wed, Sat. Closed July. **Admission** 75kr. Free with SC. **Map** p100 A2 ❹

**IN THE KNOW
FUTURE SLUSSEN**

Slussen has waited decades for a much-needed facelift – and finally it seems about to happen. In 2009, city authorities announced an architectural collaboration between Foster+Partners and Swedish firm Berg Arkitektkontor would be responsible for creating a modern civic quarter in the area adjacent to the navigation lock between the Baltic and Lake Mälaren. The plan, called Future Slussen, was delayed for several years due to various controversies and feuds about the future of the area, but construction finally began in 2014. The new Slussen will feature an accessible quayside, new public spaces, pedestrian and cycle routes, and some prominent contemporary architecture. Slussen's infrastructure will also be improved to minimise the threat of flooding and create a 21st-century transport interchange. The project has a series of planned deadlines, with the final stages not expected to be completed until 2020 at the earliest.

EXPLORE (vertical, right margin)

Södermalm & Långholmen

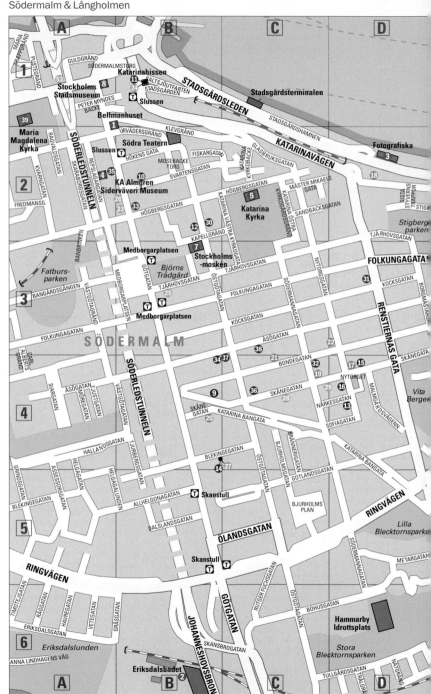

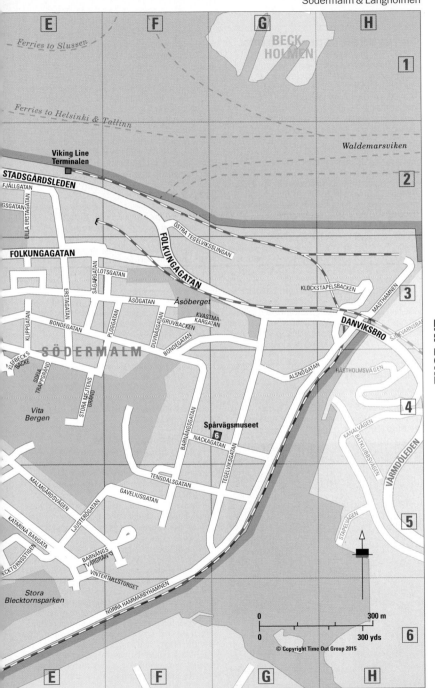

EXPLORE

IN THE KNOW HERRING WAGON

The Strömmingsvagnen herring wagon, which sits just outside Slussen T-bana station, has been dishing up fried herring, mashed potato, lingonberries and crispbread to hungry commuters for decades. Head here for an affordable taste of classic Swedish cuisine.

Knut August Almgren stole the technology for this former silk-weaving factory back in the late 1820s. While recovering from tuberculosis in France, he posed as a German-speaking Frenchman and gained access to factories where the innovative Jacquard looms were being used. He took notes, smuggled machinery out of the country and opened a factory in Sweden in 1833. The factory here closed down in 1974, but was then reopened as a working museum in 1991 by a fifth-generation Almgren. It reproduces silk fabrics for stately homes around Scandinavia, including the Royal Palace. The renovated additional floor houses an exhibition on the history of silk weaving in Sweden, along with a collection of silk portraits, landscapes and fabrics. You can watch its 160-year-old looms in action; they produce 2m (6.5ft) of fabric per day. Silk scarves and other handwoven fabrics are on sale in the gift shop if you fancy a souvenir.

FREE Katarina Kyrka
Högbergsgatan 13 (743 68 00, www.svenska kyrkan.se/katarina). T-bana Medborgarplatsen or Slussen or bus 2, 3, 53, 71, 76, 96. **Open** 11am-5pm Mon-Sat; 10am-5pm Sun. **Admission** free. **Map** p100 C2 ⑤

Katarina Kyrka.

As Södermalm's population grew, it was agreed in the mid 17th century to split Maria Magdalena parish and build a new church. Katarina Kyrka, completed in 1695, was designed by Jean de la Vallé in Baroque style with a central plan. A huge fire in 1723 destroyed the church's cupola and half the buildings in the parish. A more recent fire in 1990 burned down all but the walls and side vaults. Architect Ove Hildemark reconstructed the church (based on photos and drawings) using 17th-century building techniques. The yellow church with flat white pillars now looks much as it did before, but with a distinctly modern interior. Many victims of the Stockholm Bloodbath of 1520 were buried in the large cemetery.

Spårvägsmuséet
Tegelviksgatan 22 (686 17 60, www.sparvagsmuseet. sl.se). Bus 2, 53, 66, 71, 96. **Open** 10am-5pm Mon-Fri; 11am-4pm Sat, Sun. **Admission** 50kr; 25kr reductions; free under-7s. Tickets also valid for Toy Museum next door. **Map** p101 G4 ⑥

What the Transport Museum lacks in descriptive texts and focused exhibits, it makes up for in quantity – more than 60 vehicles are stored in this former bus station in eastern Söder. Rows of carriages, trams and buses from the late 1800s to the present cover the development of Stockholm's transport system. For 1kr you can stand in a tramcar from the 1960s and pretend to drive as a grainy film of city streets flashes before you. Children can also try on a ticket collector's uniform and ride a miniature Tunnelbana train (10kr). There's a café and a shop selling transport-related paraphernalia, including an excellent selection of Brio trains. The museum is perfect for a rainy-day visit – borrow a guidebook in English from the cashier, since most of the exhibits are labelled in Swedish.

FREE Stockholms Moskén
Kapellgränd 10 (50 91 09 00, www.ifstockholm.se). T-bana Medborgarplatsen or bus 59, 66. **Visiting hours** 10am-6pm daily. *Prayers* 5 times daily; call or visit website for details. **Admission** free. **Map** p100 B3 ⑦

The conversion of Katarinastation, a former power station, into Stockholm's first mosque led to heated architectural debates. Prior to its inauguration in 2000, Stockholm's Muslim community worshipped in cellars and other cramped spaces, jokingly claiming to be Sweden's biggest underground movement. Ferdinand Boberg, the architect behind Rosenbad and NK (*see p72*), designed Katarinastation. Inspired by Andalusian Moorish architecture, he decorated the lofty main hall in mosaic brick, with floor-to-ceiling vaulted windows. Fittingly, the original structure faces Mecca. As long as shoes are removed and women covered up (robes provided), visitors may view the prayer hall and lecture hall. Before you leave, take a look at the massive copper doors facing Östgötagatan, embedded with numerous mundane objects by the process of blast-moulding.

Stockholms Stadsmuseum.

Stockholms Stadsmuseum
Ryssgården (50 83 16 20, www.stadsmuseum. stockholm.se). T-bana Slussen or bus 2, 3, 53, 71, 76, 96. **Open** 11am-5pm Tue, Wed, Fri, Sat, Sun; 11am-8pm Thur. *Tours* (in English) July, Aug 2pm Tue, Thur, Sun. **Admission** 130kr; free under-20s. Free with SC. **Map** p100 A1 ❽
Nicodemus Tessin the Elder designed this building in the 1670s. After a fire in 1680, the renovations were supervised by his son, Tessin the Younger, architect of the Royal Palace. Renovations in 2003 spruced up the entrance and the peaceful courtyard, where you can sit and enjoy goodies from the café, which is decorated with fixtures from an early 20th-century bakery. Temporary exhibitions are on the ground floor. A series of rooms named Stockholm Through All Times is a journey through the growth of the city from medieval times to the 17th century. The third floor takes you through the realistic models of a Stockholm factory from 1897, plus a city registrar's office and schoolroom from the same period. Don't miss peeking into the two reconstructed flats from the 1940s; one of these tiny rooms housed a family, plus additional lodgers. On the ground floor, Torget, a children's play area, recreates a city market square and is open at weekends. This is Söder's best museum and a great place to learn about the city. It also has free WiFi.
▶ *The museum also offers two-hour guided Stieg Larsson Millennium Trilogy tours in English at 11.30am on Saturdays (plus 6pm Wed July-Sept), or you can purchase a map (also available from Arlanda Airport and the Stockholm Tourist Centre in Vasagaten) and follow the tour route on your own. Visit the museum's website for further details. See also p117.*

Restaurants

Chutney
Katarina Bangata 19 (640 30 10, www.chutney.se). T-bana Medborgarplatsen or bus 59, 66. **Open**

11am-10pm Mon-Fri; noon-10pm Sat; noon-9pm Sun. **Main courses** 90kr-140kr. **Map** p100 B4 ❾ **Vegetarian**
A favourite with the eco crowd, with environmentally conscious art on the walls and vegan food on the plates. Service is friendly, portions are huge and prices are decent. Good for lunch or an early dinner after doing the SoFo shopping rounds.

Crêperie Fyra Knop
Svartensgatan 4 (640 77 27, www.creperie fyraknop.se). T-bana Slussen or bus 2, 59, 66. **Open** 5-11pm Mon-Fri; noon-11pm Sat, Sun. **Main courses** 72kr-112kr. **Map** p100 B2 ❿ **Mediterranean**
If you're French and homesick, or looking for an inexpensive but romantic meal, this could be the place. The decor in the two dark, cosy little rooms is kitsch, complete with old fishing nets and lifebelts. The savoury and sweet crêpes are delicious, and cheap enough that you can go drinking in one of the nearby bars afterwards.

Eriks Gondolen
Stadsgården 6 (641 70 90, www.eriks.se). T-bana Slussen or bus 2, 3, 43, 53, 55, 71, 76. **Open** 11.30am-2.30pm, 5-11pm Mon; 11.30am-2.30pm, 5pm-1am Tue-Fri; 4pm-1am Sat. **Main courses** 215kr-335kr. **Set menu** 495kr. **Map** p100 B1 ⓫ **Swedish**
It's difficult to imagine a restaurant with a more spectacular view. The Gondolen bar and restaurant are both suspended over Slussen, underneath the Katarinahissen walkway, with views over Gamla Stan and the water. Enter via the bridge from Mosebacke Torg (the Katarinahissen lift is now closed). The menu offers both French and Swedish dishes. This is where locals bring their foreign friends or business associates to wow them on their arrival in town. The place is run by Anna Lallerstedt, daughter of former owner and famous chef Erik Lallerstedt.

EXPLORE

Pelikan.

La Neta

Östgötagatan 12B (640 40 20, www.laneta.se).
T-bana Medborgarplatsen or bus 59, 66, 96.
Open 11am-9pm Mon-Fri; noon-9pm Sat;
noon-4pm Sun. **Map** p100 B2 ⑫ **Mexican**
The Mexican street food trend has hit Stockholm,
and this taqueria pulls in the corn-hungry crowds,
who devour the fairly authentic selection of soft
tacos on offer. The interior suits the no-frills cuisine,
made up of rows of wooden bench tables.

Nytorget 6

Nytorgsgatan 6 (640 96 55, www.nytorget6.com).
T-bana Medborgarplatsen or bus 59, 66, 96. **Open**
7.30-10.30am, 11am-4pm, 5-11pm Mon-Fri; 10am-
4pm, 5-11pm Sat, Sun. **Main courses** 125kr-199kr.
Map p100 D4 ⑬ **Swedish/Mediterranean**
This relative newcomer, next to Nytorget Urban Deli,
offers a smart yet rustic vibe and reasonable prices,
with an all-day menu and a wide range of dishes
that run the gamut from eggs benedict and burgers
to Swedish meatballs, pasta dishes and grilled tuna.
There are outdoor tables at the front during the summer, and the restaurant is also a popular nightlife spot,
with two cocktail bars and contemporary variety acts.

★ Pelikan

Blekingegatan 40 (55 60 90 90, www.pelikan.se).
T-bana Skanstull or bus 55, 59, 66, 76. **Open** 5pm-
midnight Mon, Tue; 5pm-1am Wed-Sun. *Kitchen
closes* 11pm daily. **Main courses** 179kr-315kr.
Map p100 B4 ⑭ **Traditional Swedish**
Not many restaurants feel as genuinely Swedish as
this beer hall in Södermalm. Its elegant painted ceilings and wood-panelled walls haven't changed since
the days before Söder became trendy, back when
restaurants served only *husmanskost*. Classics on
offer here include meatballs with lingonberries and
pickled cucumber. Ice-cold schnapps is compulsory.
For the bar, *see p106.*

Sardin

*Skånegatan 79 (644 97 00, www.restaurang
sardin.se). T-bana Medborgarplatsen or bus 3,*

59, 66, 76, 96. **Open** 5pm-12.30am Mon-Sat.
Tapas 22kr-165kr. **Map** p100 D4 ⑮ **Spanish**
With just 18 seats, guests are tightly packed into
this tiny restaurant where the walls are decorated
with sardine tins. It's a cute and cosy place, serving
good-value food and with warmer staff than most
Stockholm restaurants.

★ Urban Deli

Nytorget 4 (08 599 091 80, www.urbandeli.org).
T-bana Skanstull or Medborgarplatsen or bus 3,
59, 66. **Open** 8am-11pm Mon, Tue, Sun; 8am-
midnight Wed, Thur; 8am-1am Fri, Sat. **Main
courses** 185kr-215kr. **Map** p100 D4 ⑯ **Global**
This new deli-restaurant-café-shop has been a huge
hit since opening a few years ago, offering a New
York-style take on the traditional Swedish locale,
with concrete floors and industrial fittings. Both
the lunch and dinner menus feature a good range

Urban Deli.

EXPLORE

of seafood (lobster, crab, scallops and mussels, as well as the more ubiquitous smoked salmon and shrimp salad), and make use of the extensive range of Spanish charcuterie and Mediterranean cheeses from the attached grocery. Asian influences also appear. A good spot for dinner, lunch or weekend brunch – if you can manage to get a table.

▶ *For more information on the Urban Deli shop, see p114* **In the Know**.

Cafés

Restaurant-bar-shop **Urban Deli** (*see p104*) is a great spot for brunch, lunch or *fika*, and also houses a branch of top-notch bakery Bröd & Salt (www.brodsalt.se).

★ Gildas Rum
Skånegatan 79 (714 77 98, www.gildasrum.se). T-bana Skanstull or bus 59, 66, 96. **Open** 7.30am-10pm Mon-Fri; 8.30am-10pm Sat, Sun. **Map** p100 D4 ⑰

One of Södermalm's most popular cafés, Gildas Rum is a hive of activity, full of freelancer types, many of whom have offices/studios in the surrounding area. A seat outside provides prime people-watching opportunities, with Nytorget opposite. The decor is very much Stockholm new wave, with Scandinavian clean lines eschewed for a more kitschy, colourful design – think patterned floor tiles, striped wallpaper, red cushions and candlesticks. Coffee is top notch and the sandwiches are delicious.

Hermans Trädgårdcafé
Fjällgatan 23B (643 94 80, www.hermans.se). T-bana Slussen or bus 2, 3, 53, 76, 96. **Open** 11am-9pm daily. *Lunch served* 11am-3pm. **Map** p100 D2 ⑱

This vegetarian café boasts amazing views over the Stockholm skyline – you can pick out nearly all the major landmarks, together with the cruise ships and tourist boats shuttling in and out of the harbour. The café offers a buffet menu at lunch and in the evening, and you can opt for just a main course or include one of the delicious fruit pies.

Il Caffè
Södermannagatan 23 (462 95 00, www.ilcaffe.se). T-bana Medborgarplatsen or bus 59, 66. **Open** 8am-8pm Mon-Fri; 9am-7pm Sat, Sun. **Map** p100 C4 ⑲

This trendy space, serving excellent toasted sandwiches (with ingredients such as parma ham, bresaola, mozzarella and pesto), is very much of its neighbourhood, full of cool locals with their laptops. The coffee is excellent and the service refreshingly down-to-earth.

Other location Bergsgatan 17, Kungsholmen (652 30 04).

▶ *Il Caffè shares a space with a takeaway branch of high-end bakery Fabrique.*

Louie Louie.

Lisas Café & Hembageri
Skånegatan 68 (640 36 36). T-bana Medborgarplatsen or bus 59, 66. **Open** 6.30am-3pm Mon-Fri; 7.30am-3pm Sat. **No credit cards**. **Map** p100 B4 ⑳

Motherly Lisa has been getting up at 4am every morning for the last 15 years to serve the residents of Södermalm. She has around 250 photos of regulars gracing the walls of her café and claims she can tell you a story about every one of them. Cinnamon buns (*kanelbulle*) are the house speciality, but ask for a latte at your peril, since any coffee with warmed-up milk is barred from her menu – she champions the survival of the plain coffee. Lisas Café & Hembageri is as local as they come and continues to weather the storm of competition from the area's trendy cafés.

Louie Louie
Bondegatan 13 (640 02 71, www.louielouie.se). T-bana Medborgarplatsen or bus 59, 66. **Open** 8am-6pm Mon-Fri; 10am-6pm Sat, Sun. **Map** p100 C4 ㉑

Named after the rock 'n' roll song, Louie Louie is a homage to indie-rock Americana. The cute, kitsch space has a friendly feel, and is frequented by groups of trendy twentysomethings. The café offers decent coffee, plus sandwiches, pastries, salads and tarts, while a small in-house record store and occasional live music events create a lively vibe.

String
Nytorgsgatan 38 (714 85 14, www.cafestring.com). T-bana Medborgarplatsen or bus 3, 59, 66, 96. **Open** 9am-8pm Mon-Fri; 10am-7pm Sat, Sun. **Map** p100 D3 ㉒

Once a furniture shop that served coffee to its customers, String is now a café that also sells furniture. Everything from the deckchair you sit on to the plate you eat off is for sale, and this is also the closest you'll get to having your coffee in a shop window. String is as fun and hip as its fan base, whose favourite hangover cure is the weekend breakfast buffet. Live music sessions and stand-up comedy are occasionally held here.

EXPLORE

Bars

Nightlife hotspots on Söder are Götgatan and the area around Medborgarplatsen. Several small bars are scattered south of Folkungagatan. The **Clarion Hotel** (*see p217*), further south still, also has two lively bars. Note that many of the venues listed below also function as restaurants.

Fenix

Götgatan 40 (640 45 06, www.fenixbar.se). T-bana Slussen or Medborgarplatsen or bus 2, 3, 43, 53, 55. **Open** *Bar* 3pm-1am Mon-Fri; noon-1am Sat, Sun. *Food served* until 10pm daily. **Minimum age** 18. **Map** p100 B2 ㉝

This gaudy party bar offers a thoroughly refreshing alternative to the tasteful minimalism of many Stockholm drinking dens. With red walls, crazy artwork and mosaic decorations, it attracts a crowd of twenty- and thirtysomethings dressed for a night out. The cavernous basement features a dancefloor and lounge area.

Gondolen

Stadsgården 6 (641 70 90, www.eriks.se). T-bana Slussen or bus 2, 3, 43, 53, 55, 71, 76. **Open** *Bar* 11.30am-11pm Mon; 11.30am-1am Tue-Fri; 4pm-1am Sat. *Food served* until closing. **Map** p100 B1 ㉞

At the top of the historic Katarinahissen lift (sadly no longer in use), Gondolen is an ideal place for a tall drink. The bar sits under the walkway – it's reached via the restaurant's free lift at Stadsgården 6 – and provides a panoramic view of Djurgården to the east and Riddarfjärden to the west. Drinks are reasonably priced, despite the feeling of international luxury.

Kvarnen

Tjärhovsgatan 4 (643 03 80, www.kvarnen.com). T-bana Medborgarplatsen or bus 59, 66. **Open** *Kvarnen* 11am-3am Mon-Fri; noon-3am Sat; noon-1am Sun. *Food served* until 11pm daily. **Minimum age** 21 (Mon-Thur), 23 (Fri, Sat). **Map** p100 B3 ㉟

Originally a beer hall, Kvarnen (Windmill) has evolved into one of the most popular late-night pubs on Söder, and even features in Stieg Larsson's bestseller *The Girl with the Dragon Tattoo*. The lofty main room, filled with rows of tables and loud chatter, plays no music and retains the look and feel of a beer hall. It is flanked by two more recent additions: the small Mediterranean-themed H20 bar in what used to be a kitchen, and the flame-inspired Eld (Hell) bar in the basement. Show up early at the weekend to avoid the queue.

Ljunggren

Götgatan 36 (640 75 65, www.restaurang ljunggren.se). T-bana Slussen or bus 2, 3, 43, 53, 55, 59, 66. **Open** *Bar* 5pm-midnight Mon, Tue; 5pm-1am Wed-Sat. *Food served* until 10pm Mon, Tue; 11pm Wed-Sat. **Minimum age** 23. **Map** p100 B2 ㊱

One of the few bars on Götgatan that can compete with the clubs around Stureplan, Ljunggren is a darkly sleek place for hip young things. The DJs favour hip hop and electronic music and the small bar area spills into a trendy, miniature shopping mall equipped with an additional bar.

Pelikan

Blekingegatan 40 (55 60 90 90, www.pelikan.se). T-bana Skanstull or bus 55, 59, 66, 76. **Open** *Bar* 5pm-midnight Mon, Tue; 5pm-1am Wed-Sun. *Food served* until 11pm daily. **Map** p100 B4 ㊲

This charming beer hall is well away from the action in a mainly residential area in southern Södermalm. The clientele ranges from ageing regulars to young Southside hipsters in designer clothes. Drop in for a beer or visit the adjoining bar, Kristallen, adorned with oriental rugs and ornate chandeliers. For the restaurant review, *see p104*.

Pet Sounds Bar

Skånegatan 80 (643 82 25, www.petsoundsbar.se). T-bana Medborgarplatsen or bus 59, 66, 96. **Open** *Bar* 5pm-1am Tue-Thur; 2pm-1am Fri, Sat. *Food served* until 10pm Tue-Thur, Sat, Sun; until 11pm Fri. **Minimum age** 20. **Map** p100 C4 ㊳

Home to Söder's large indie-rock crowd, Pet Sounds Bar is an extension of the legendary record store across the street. The Pet Sounds record store (*see p107*) used to host small concerts and was the first to book New Order in the 1980s. Nowadays the bar hosts these concerts in its basement, which features a stage, bar and DJ booth. The ground floor houses a restaurant. Both areas are decorated with concert and film posters on the black- and red-tiled walls.

Snotty

Skånegatan 90 (644 39 10). T-bana Medborgarplatsen or bus 3, 59, 66, 76, 96. **Open** *Bar* 4pm-1am daily. *Food served* 5-10pm daily. **Minimum age** 20. **Map** p100 C4 ㊴

Local hipsters and musicians love this tiny hole-in-the-wall restaurant-bar. It was previously linked to the Pet Sounds music store and the walls are decorated with images of rock and film stars. The bar staff take their music selection seriously.

Shops & Services

Micro-mall **Bruno Götgatsbacken** (Götgatan 36, 442 18 50, www.brunogotgatsbacken.se), sometimes called Galleria Bruno, is home to branches of various mid-range Swedish brands, including Filippa K, Whyred and Hope. Further south, at Medborgarplatsen, is mall-like food hall **Söderhallarna**, with a great selection of fresh produce but a rather soulless atmosphere.

Alvglans

Östgötagatan 19 (642 69 98, www.alvglans.se). T-bana Medborgarplatsen or Skanstull or bus 2,

53, 55, 59, 66. **Open** 11am-6pm Mon-Fri;
11am-4pm Sat. **Map** p100 B2 ❸ **Comics**
The Spawn action figures alone are worth the trip
to the comics heaven of Alvglans. The shop stocks
bestsellers such as *X-Men* and *Spiderman*, as well as
rare anime movies and manga DVDs.

Cajsa Warg
*Renstiernas gata 20 (642 23 50, www.cajsawarg.se).
Bus 2, 3, 55, 59, 66, 71, 76, 96*. **Open** 8am-8pm
Mon-Fri; 10am-7pm Sat, Sun. **Map** p100 D3 ❸
Food & drink
Cajsa Warg was a famous Swedish chef at the begin-
ning of the 20th century. This shop, which has a large
takeaway menu, uses her name to sell everyday gro-
ceries and deli items (Swedish, Mediterranean and
Asian). A great place to stock up for a picnic.
Other location St Eriksplan 2, Vasastan (33 01 20).

Grandpa
*Södermannagatan 21 (08 643 60 80, www.
grandpa.se). T-bana Medborgarplatsen or bus 59,
66*. **Open** 11am-6.30pm Mon-Fri; 11am-5pm Sat;
noon-5pm Sun. **Map** p100 C4 ❸ **Fashion**
One of the best fashion stores in SoFo, Grandpa
is particularly strong in independent menswear
labels, stocking items from British label Folk and
Danish brands Wood Wood and Norse Projects.
Womenswear labels include the likes of minimarket
and Swedish Hasbeens. There's a vintage homewares shop in the basement, and cool accessories
(sunglasses, candles) displayed throughout.
Other location Fridhemsgatan 43,
Kungsholmen (643 60 81).

Granit
*Götgatan 31 (642 10 68, www.granit.com).
T-bana Medborgarplatsen or Slussen or bus 43,
55, 59, 66*. **Open** 10am-7pm Mon-Fri; 10am-
6pm Sat; 11am-5.30pm Sun. **Map** p100 B2 ❸
Homewares & accessories

Sweden's answer to Muji sells lots of temptingly
simple things at low prices: storage boxes, una-
dorned glassware and crockery, notebooks and
photo albums, plus hundreds of other plain but
pleasant items. Be warned: it's almost impossible to
go into Granit without finding something that you
'need' to buy.
Other locations throughout the city.

Konst-ig
*Åsögatan 124 (20 45 20, www.konstig.se). T-bana
Medborgarplatsen or bus 59, 66*. **Open** 11am-
6.30pm Mon-Fri; 11am-5pm Sat; noon-4pm Sun.
Map p100 B4 ❸ **Books**
Stockholm's leading art bookshop, covering design,
architecture, photography, fashion and more.

Ordning & Reda
*Götgatan 32 (714 96 01, www.ordning-reda.com).
T-bana Medborgarplatsen or Slussen or bus 2, 3,
43, 53, 55, 59, 66, 76*. **Open** 10am-7pm Mon-Fri;
10am-5pm Sat; noon-4pm Sun. **Map** p100 A2
❸ **Stationery**
A heaven for stationery addicts, Ordning & Reda
was established by the same family that owns
Bookbinders, and sells all sorts of fun and brightly
coloured notebooks, diaries, photo albums and
desktop accessories.

Pet Sounds
*Skånegatan 53 (702 97 98, www.petsounds.se).
T-bana Medborgarplatsen or bus 2, 55, 59,
66, 76*. **Open** 2-6pm Mon-Fri; 11am-3pm Sat.
Map p100 C4 ❸ **Music**
Pet Sounds is the oldest indie record shop in
Stockholm, with a well-stocked range of new and
second-hand vinyl and CDs. There's a lot of 1960s
music and soundtracks, plus a decent range of rock,
soul, jazz, country, reggae and world music. The
shop also owns a bar, opposite, which hosts regular
gigs (*see p106*).

EXPLORE

Granit.

Sneakersnstuff

Åsögatan 124 (743 03 22, www.sneakersnstuff.
com). T-bana Medborgarplatsen or bus 59, 66.
Open 11am-6.30pm Mon-Fri; 11am-5pm Sat;
12.30-4.30pm Sun. **Map** p100 C4 ⑰ **Accessories**
Focusing on style rather than running, Sneakersnstuff
is frequented by trend-conscious twentysomethings,
who come here to pick up the latest trainer releases
from Nike, New Balance and Vans. Apparel comes
courtesy of Norse Projects, Adidas, Carhartt and
Danish streetwear label Wood Wood, among others.

Stutterheim

Åsögatan 132 (40 81 03 98, www.stutterheim.
com). T-bana Medborgarplatsen or bus 59, 66.
Open noon-6pm Mon-Fri; noon-4pm Sat, Sun.
Map p100 C3 ㊳ **Fashion**
The phrase 'there's no bad weather, just bad clothes'
is much quoted in Sweden, and this high-end unisex
rainwear shop is the perfect place to indulge it. The
Swedish fisherman-inspired raincoats are hand-
made with top-quality rubberised cotton, and the
simple cuts and tasteful colours make the prospect
of rain seem much more appealing (though the
prices may make you squint a little).

WESTERN SÖDERMALM

Although the residents of Södermalm are today
as well off as other Stockholmers, the district
is traditionally associated with the working
class. Functionalist apartment buildings have
replaced most of the small wooden houses that
once covered the island. However, if you walk
west up Bastugatan from Slussen you pass a
charming neighbourhood on adjoining **Lilla
Skinnarviksgränd**, with its few remaining
17th- and 18th-century wooden houses.
Continue along to the cliffside boardwalk of
Monteliusvägen for a truly spectacular view of
the bay of Riddarfjärden and Skinnarviksberget,
Stockholm's highest point at 53 metres (174 feet).
Directly below it is **Söder Mälarstrand**; this
quayside road isn't as bustling or picturesque as
its neighbour to the north (Kungsholmen's Norr
Mälarstrand), but it is now home to Stockholm's
most-renowned boat bar, **Patricia**.

South of Monteliusvägen, crossing the busy
thoroughfare of Hornsgatan, is **Mariatorget**,
an enjoyable square that is home to the stylish
Rival hotel complex, which comprises a hotel
(*see p217*), restaurant and café, with original
art deco features. One block to the east of
Mariatorget is **Maria Magdalena Kyrka**,
the oldest church on Söder, while heading south
brings you to some prime shopping streets – head
for Swedensborgsgatan, Wollmar Yxkullsgatan
and, further to the west, Krukmakargatan, if
you're into independent boutiques. Hornsgatan
itself is also great for vintage stores, with
menswear shop **Herr Judit** leading the pack.

The wide street of Ringvägen curves round
the southern border of Södermalm, while the
island's biggest and best park, **Tantolunden**,
sits near the south-western shore. The park is
something of a hipster hangout and is normally
packed on sunny summer days. A waterside
walkway takes you from the park all the way
round the southern side of the island, taking in
the lovely Tanto allotment gardens (*see p112*)
on the way, as well as some popular wild
swimming spots, including a wooden diving
pier. From here you can see the shiny new
residential developments across the water,
on **Liljeholmen**.

North of Tantolunden, on the other side of
Hornsgatan, is the large red-brick church of
Högalidskyrkan, designed by Ivar Tengbom
in the National Romantic style and completed
in 1923. Its octagonal twin towers are a striking
landmark visible from many parts of the city.

At the very western end of Södermalm is
the residential neighbourhood of **Hornstull**,
thoroughly enjoying its continuing hipster status.
The area's cafés, restaurants and shops now count
Swedish indie/rock stars and high-profile artists
as customers, while waterside promenade
Hornstulls Strand is now home to rock club
Debaser Huvudkontor (previously located
at Slussen; *see p163*) and its Mexican-themed
restaurant-bar Calexico's and Brooklyn Brewery-
sponsored bar. Also here is the small local
Biografteatern Rio cinema (*see p156*), rescued
by the Swedish Church a few years' back when the
city snubbed the one-man show and refused
to continue to subsidise its rent. Residents of
Hornstull are proud of their left-leaning
neighbourhood, despite the new signs of affluence
– most obvious in the subterranean shopping
centre next to the Hornstull metro station, offering
a range of Swedish and international fashion
chains, as well as a *systembolaget* (alcohol store)
and a branch of **Akki Sushi**. Next to the station
is the new three-storey **Hornhuset** building,
housing a bistro, bar and arthouse cinema.

Continue north from here and you'll reach the
charming old **Lasse i Parken** café – a lovely
spot for an alfresco lunch or *fika*, which also
sometimes hosts live music in the evenings –
and then the huge **Västerbron** bridge that
connects the island with Kungsholmen, offering
wonderful views of Långholmen and Gamla
Stan en route.

Sights & Museums

▣FREE Maria Magdalena Församling

St Paulsgatan 10 (462 29 40, www.svenskakyrkan.
se/mariaagdalena). T-bana Slussen or bus 2, 3,
53, 71, 76, 96. **Open** 11am-5pm Mon, Tue, Thur,
Fri, Sat; 11am-7.30pm Wed. *Sunday communion*
11am. **Admission** free. **Map** p100 A1 ㊴

IN THE SWIM

Summer in Stockholm means refreshing dips in the city's clear waters.

Stockholm is built on 14 islands sprinkled across the crisp blue water of Lake Mälaren and, despite the climate, locals are proud of the fact that, thanks to a successful purification treatment in the 1960s, you can take a dip in the waters around the city centre.

At this latitude, summer is often more a state of mind than a certain temperature. On sunny days, local swimmers and sunbathers are quick to stake out their territories on one of the many beaches, grassy waterside spaces or outdoor pool areas the city offers. You can swim almost everywhere, but avoid dirty Karlbergskanalen (between Kungsholmen and Vasastaden) and leave the waves and very strong currents in Strömmen (east of Gamla Stan) to the fishermen. On Djurgården, try the small spit Waldemarsudde (bus 44 or tram 7 to Ryssviken and follow the path south to the water's edge) on the southern shore. Or get to one of these popular summer spots fast:

LÅNGHOLMSBADET
Långholmen. T-bana Hornstull or bus 4, 40.
Map p249 K2.
Situated on green Långholmen, Stockholm's seventh largest island, this popular beach is surrounded by inviting green areas and gets crowded during weekends and holidays, so arrive early. Due to the proximity to trendy Hornstull, the chances of spotting a Swedish indie rock star in a bathing suit are good. For those who didn't bring a picnic, there's a lovely café, Stora Henriksvik (*see p117*).

SMEDSUDDSBADET
Kungsholmen. T-bana Fridhemsplan.
The largest of the city beaches is located opposite Långholmsbadet, in sprawling

Rålambshovsparken on Kungsholmen. Smedsuddsbadet is popular with families, so if you can handle the risk of getting hit by a beach ball, then this is a nice place to soak up the sun and cool off with a swim. Facilities include changing rooms, toilets and showers.

FREDHÄLLBADET
Kungsholmen. T-bana Kristineberg.
Despite its tucked-away location at the south-western tip of Kungsholmen, these bare 'cliffs' are a popular destination for sunbathers, swimmers and lovebirds. The water can't be approached slowly as there is no 'shallow end'; instead, you have to climb down from Snoilskyvägen or Atterbomsvägen on to the rocks, and shock your body by jumping straight in. There are no toilets or cafés – just trees, rocks and water.

ERIKSDALSBADET
Hammarby Slussväg 20 (508 40 258, www. eriksdalsbadet.se). T-bana Skanstull or bus 4.
Map p250 O8.
This Olympic-size pool was built for the 1962 European Aquatics Championships and is a classic summer destination for those who require a certain water temperature, or who aren't thrilled at the prospect of swimming with live fish. Facilities include saunas, barbecue grills, a volleyball court and a café.

FJÄDERHOLMARNAS BAD
Ferry from Slussen.
The cluster of ultra-scenic islands called Fjäderholmarna (*see p180*), at the start of the archipelago, can be reached in just 25 minutes by ferry from Slussen. The beaches are sandy and clean, and the water is crisp blue... and cold.

EXPLORE

Långholmsbadet.

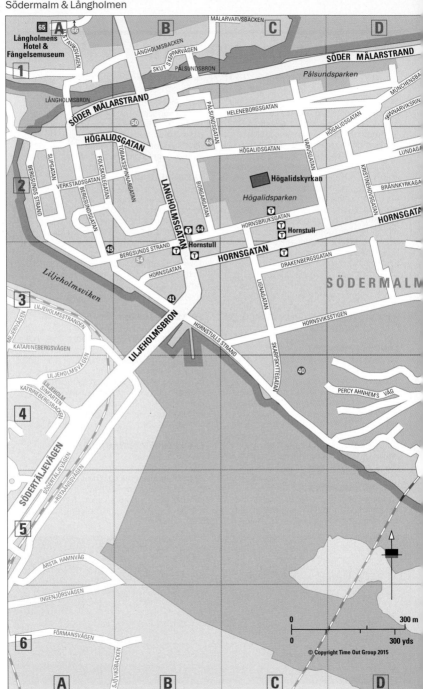

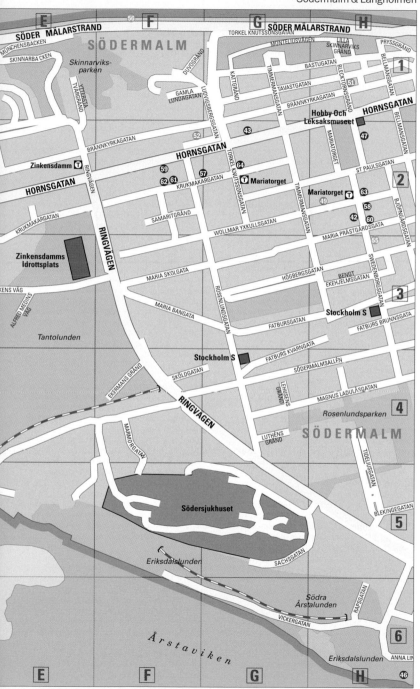

During his church-destroying spree after the Reformation in 1527, Gustav Vasa tore down the chapel that had stood on this site since the 1300s. His son, Johan III, methodically rebuilt most of the churches in the late 1500s. Construction on this yellowish-orange church with white corners began in 1580, but was not completed for about 40 years. It's Söder's oldest church and the first in Stockholm to be built with a central plan rather than a cross plan. Tessin the Elder designed the transept in the late 17th century and his son, the Younger, created the French-inspired stonework of the entrance portal in 1716. The church's rococo interior – with its depiction of Maria Magdalena on the golden pulpit and Carl Fredrik Adelcrantz's elaborate organ screen – was created after a fire in 1759. Several of Sweden's eminent poets are buried here, including beloved troubadour Evert Taube.

FREE Tantolunden
Map p110 C4 ⑩

Södermalm's largest public park is situated close to the restaurants and cafés of Hornstull, and is a popular spot in summer for picnicking and bathing at the adjoining beach area. During the winter, it makes for an excellent sledding spot too. There's a playground, a beach volleyball court, minigolf and an open-air theatre. Stroll up the hill for the lovely Tanto allotment gardens, which were established here nearly a century ago; the waiting list for a plot is unsurprisingly lengthy.

Restaurants

The three-storey asymmetrical **Hornhuset** (Långholmsgatan 15B, 52 52 02 60, www. hornhuset.se) building next to Hornstull metro station houses a Mediterranean restaurant on the second floor and a football-inspired pizza parlour on the third, as well as several bars and a rooftop terrace.

Bistro Barbro
Hornstulls Strand 13 (55 06 02 66, www.bar-bro. se). T-bana Hornstull or bus 4. **Open** 5-11pm Tue-Thur, Sun; 5pm-12.30am Fri, Sat. **Main courses** 95kr-210kr. **Map** p110 B3 ⓬ **Japanese fusion**

Located just below Liljeholmsbron (hence the name, 'bridge bar'), next to the water, this Japanese-inspired bistro with contemporary decor is part of the new wave of venues that make up gentrified Hornstull. There's a large number of fusion-style dishes on the menu, taking in everything from fried dumplings, sushi and sashimi to seared tuna with sesame dressing and sirloin steak with udon noodles. The building also houses a cinema-lounge bar, hosting, in collaboration with Biografteatern Rio (*see p156*), film screenings, film quizzes and live music. It's a very popular spot during the summer months, when stylish regulars hang out on the outdoor bench seating.

Bistro Süd
Swedenborgsgatan 8A (640 41 11, www.bistro sud.se). T-bana Mariatorget or bus 4, 43, 55, 66, 74. **Open** 5pm-midnight daily. *Kitchen closes* at 11pm. **Main courses** 165kr-345kr. **Map** p111 H2 ⓬ **Contemporary**

This is a friendly neighbourhood place for the Mariatorget crowd of well-to-do journalists and artists. Food is straightforward and usually very good, and it's a pleasant place to have a bite to eat and rub shoulders in the crowded but relaxed bar. The same owners are behind the PA & Co restaurant (*see p125*), a second home for many of Stockholm's celebrities.

Folkbaren
Hornsgatan 72 (658 51 80, www.folkbaren.se). T-bana Mariatorget or bus 4, 43, 55, 66, 74. **Open** 4pm-1am Tue-Thur; 11.30am-1am Fri, Sat; 4-10pm Sun. **Main courses** 115kr-255kr. **Map** p111 G2 ⓭ **Contemporary**

This might be the culinary annexe to the city's alternative opera scene (*see p166*), but most of the clientele aren't just in for a pre-show drink. The restaurant is an attraction in its own right – there's a bar downstairs, a cosy lounge with a good menu upstairs, and a main dining room dishing up ambitious modern food at reasonable prices. The generous T-bone steak is served with deep-fried new potatoes, while the poached cod with horseradish is a more subtle creation. The bars can get rather crowded later on.

Linje Tio
Hornsbruksgatan 24 (22 00 21, www.linjetio.com). T-bana Hornstull or bus 4. **Open** 5pm-1am Mon-Thur; 4pm-2am Fri; noon-2am Sat; noon-1am Sun. **Main courses** 185kr-265kr. **Map** p110 B2 ⓬ **Mediterranean**

Named after an old local tram line, this southern European restaurant and brunch spot offers a contemporary take on classic Mediterranean cuisine, with burrata taking the place of mozzarella in the caprese starter, and mains such as sausage, cauliflower, kale and browned crème fraiche or grilled and braised pork ribs with balsamic and polenta. There's a good range of wines by the glass and a well thought-out cocktail list, while the interior mixes rustic with modern, largely successfully.

Moldau
Bergsunds Strand 33 (84 75 48). T-bana Hornstull. **Open** 4-11pm Mon-Fri; 2-11pm Sat, Sun. **Main courses** 88kr-175kr. **Map** p110 A3 ⓯ **Austrian**

This Austrian schnitzel restaurant, housed in an unassuming building at the western tip of Söder, has been around for years, but has regained popularity with the twenty- and thirtysomethings of Hornstull in recent times, who love it for its unpretentious dishes and affordable prices. The Alpine-style interior gives a rustic atmosphere, while the schnitzel menu includes six meat options and two vegetarian.

Lasse i Parken.

Nyfiken Gul

Hammarby Slussväg 15 (642 52 02, www.
nyfikengul.se). T-bana Skanstull or bus 3,4. **Open**
11am-midnight daily. Closed Oct-Apr. **Main**
courses 120kr-155kr. **Map** p111 H6  **Grill**
This open-air grill, located next to the Årstaviken
waterfront, is a popular summer spot. Customers
can participate in the cooking of their food – which
consists of barbecued meat, fish or vegetable
wraps, with a healthy dose of sides, sauces, salads
and the ubiquitous potatoes. It's a busy spot, but
the staff work hard to get you a table quickly if you
have to wait at the bar.
► *This is a good place to head to after a swim*
in the Olympic-sized open-air pool at nearby
Eriksdalsbadet. See also p111.

Rival

Mariatorget 3 (54 57 89 15, www.rival.se).
T-bana Mariatorget or bus 43, 55, 66, 74.
Open 5pm-midnight Mon-Sat; 6-11pm Sun.
Main courses 205kr-625kr. **Map** p111 H2
Contemporary
Benny of ABBA fame is part-owner of this food
and hotel emporium, which has all the components
for a complete date under one roof: get some dinner,
catch a movie, grab a late-night cocktail and, if you
get lucky, go to bed in one of the boutique hotel
rooms. The food menu is mainly run-of-the-mill
Swedish staples, with dishes such as *toast skagen*
(shrimp salad on toast), meatballs and *svampfyllda*
kroppkakor (mushroom-filled potato dumplings
served with lingonberries). For a review of the hotel,
see p217.

Cafés

Café dello Sport

Pålsundsgatan 8 (668 74 88, www.cafedello
sport.se). T-bana Hornstull or bus 4, 40, 66, 94.
Open 8am-8pm Mon-Fri; 10am-8pm Sat, Sun.
Map p110 B2

This soccer-mad café is fairly famous during cup
matches, when enthusiastic crowds assemble to
watch the game. The staff are an incredibly jolly
bunch and the café is situated at the foot of Högalids
Kyrka, opposite a pleasant play park, so it really is
worth a visit even if you have absolutely no interest
in sport. The focaccias, cappuccinos and Italian soft
drinks are all delicious.

★ Drop Coffee Roasters

Wollmar Yxkullsgatan 10 (410 233 63, www.
dropcoffee.com). T-bana Mariatorget or bus 43,
55, 66. **Open** 7.30am-6pm Mon-Fri; 10am-5pm
Sat, Sun. **Map** p111 H2
This micro-roastery and café near Mariatorget is
one for the true coffee geeks. Drop Coffee Roasters'
baristas take their trade seriously, making every
effort to ensure that temperature, equipment and
operation are all exactly right, and favouring man-
ual and filter methods. And then, of course, there's
the coffee itself – the establishment uses top-quality,
fairly traded and sustainably grown beans, available
to buy. The rustic café itself smells divine, and is a
popular spot for *fika* and lunch (grilled sandwiches
and soup are the mainstays).

★ Lasse i Parken

Högalidsgatan 56 (658 33 95, www.lasseiparken.
se). T-bana Hornstull or bus 4, 40. **Open** 11am-
11pm Mon-Sat; 11am-5pm Sun. Closed Oct-Apr.
Map p110 B1
This charming café is set in an 18th-century house,
with many original features. Outside is a large
seating area complete with a stage, used for musical and theatrical performances in the summer. As
this is a popular place at weekends, it can take time
to queue up and get your refreshments – however,
it's such a lovely location that it's worth the minor
aggravation. To get there, take bus 4 or 40 over
Västerbron to Högalidsgatan for an amazing view of
Långholmen. The place sometimes stays open late
in good weather.

Brandstationen.

Magnolia Café, Gallery & Flowers

Blecktornsgränd 9 (641 33 81, www.magnolia cafe.se). T-bana Mariatorget or bus 43, 55. **Open** 11.30am-10pm daily. **Map** p111 H1 ⑤

This artsy venue is situated halfway up the steps from Hornsgatan to Monteliusvägen. It's worth the climb for the delicious food and excellent coffee and cava, as well as the colourful atmosphere provided by the in-house florist. Frequent exhibition openings and wine-tasting events create a sociable vibe in the evenings, when you can enjoy a range of *pintxos*.

Mellqvist Café & Bar

Hornsgatan 78 (768 75 29 92). T-bana Zinkensdamm or bus 4, 43, 55, 66, 94. **Open** 7am-6pm Mon-Fri; 9am-6pm Sat, Sun. **Map** p111 F2 ⑤

This much-loved espresso bar continues to draw an engaged crowd, who hang at the outside tables on sunny days. The coffee is very much the focus here, perfect with a cinnamon and cardamom bun, but the place also offers a selection of tasty sandwiches and fruit juices. Author Stieg Larsson was a former regular and the place appears in several of his novels.

Bars

The **Rival Hotel** (*see p217*) on Mariatorget has a cosy, art deco cocktail bar that's open to

---

IN THE KNOW
SOURDOUGH HOTEL

Stockholmers are crazy for sourdough bread – so much so that there's now what's known as a 'sourdough hotel' in Södermalm. This novel concept, run by the **Urban Deli** (see *p104*), is a kind of nursery for sourdough. Customers bring in their fermenting dough before they head off on holiday and the shop gives it the required love it needs while they're away, so that they can come back to a well-nourished dough that's ready for the oven.

---

non-guests. And Asian bistro **Barbro** (*see p112*) also houses a popular lounge bar with an arthouse cinema. *See also pp160-165* **Nightlife**.

Akkurat

Hornsgatan 18 (644 00 15, www.akkurat.se). T-bana Slussen or bus 43, 55, 66. **Open** *Bar* 11am-midnight Mon; 11am-1am Tue-Fri; 3pm-1am Sat; 6pm-1am Sun. *Food served* until 11pm Mon, Tue; midnight Wed-Sun. **Minimum age** 23. **Map** p100 A1 ⑤

Beer lovers frustrated with Stockholm's lack of good ale should head straight to Akkurat. Don't be put off by the run-of-the-mill pub interior – this bar offers no fewer than 28 varieties of beer on tap, from fermented Belgian lambics to British cask-conditioned ale. There are 600 varieties of bottled beer and 400 whiskies too. True connoisseurs can book taste tests. Music every Sunday at 9pm includes anything from covers groups to indie rock. Some of the more exotic beers are quite pricey.

★ Judit & Bertil

Bergsundsstrand 38 (669 31 31, www.juditbertil.se). T-bana Hornstull or bus 4, 40. **Open** 5pm-1am daily. *Food served* until closing. **Map** p110 B3 ⑤

This Hornstull favourite is named after, and dedicated to, a couple who lived nearby in the 1930s and were related to one of the owners. It was the scene of a political scandal a few years ago, when then Secretary of State Ulrika Schenström got drunk and was photographed kissing a journalist while on duty. The downstairs is dominated by a beautiful blue-tiled bar, and up a spiral staircase there's a parlour-style lounge. The furniture is comfy, the menu and drinks list humorous (how about a bottle of 'make-out wine'?), and the vibe homely and welcoming.

Morfar Ginko & Papa Ray Ray

Swedenborgsgatan 13 (641 13 40, www.morfar ginko.se). T-bana Mariatorget or bus 43, 55, 66. **Open** 5pm-1am Mon-Thur; 4pm-1am Fri; noon-1am Sat, Sun. *Food served* until 10pm Mon-Thur, Sun; 11pm Fri, Sat. **Minimum age** 23 (flexible on weekends). **Map** p111 H3 ⑤

Morfar Ginko is a two-room industrial-style bar with enough 'edge' to attract the cool crowd. But its hedonistic vibe means partygoers are welcome too. In the summer, punters sup beers at the outside tables or the back courtyard (complete with ping pong) until around 11pm, at which point the terrace closes and the place becomes more of a cocktail-fuelled DJ bar. Pappa Ray Ray is the bar next door, run by the same owners and offering well-priced cava and tapas.

Patricia
Söder Mälarstrand, Kajplats 19 (743 05 70, www.patricia.st). T-bana Mariatorget or bus 4, 66, 94. **Open** 5pm-midnight Wed, Thur; 6pm-5am Fri, Sat; 6pm-5am Sun (gay night). **Minimum age** 18. **Admission** (after 9pm) 120kr; (after midnight) 150kr. **Map** p111 F1 ⓖ
Now in a new mooring on Södermalm's northern quayside, this well-established boat venue is a gay-friendly soul bar, restaurant and nightclub rolled into one. *See also p138* **Summer Watering Holes.**

Shops & Services

★ Brandstationen
Krukmakargatan 22 (658 30 10, www.herrjudit.se). T-bana Zinkensdamm, or bus 4, 191, 192. **Open** 11am-6pm Mon-Fri; 11am-4pm Sat; noon-3pm Sun. **Map** p111 F2 ⓖ **Vintage homewares**
This antiques shop, run by vintage menswear store Herr Judit (*see right*), plays to contemporary tastes, with a cherry-picked selection of retro maps, globes, midcentury furniture and lighting. There's also a cabinet full of costume-style jewellery. Prices are fairly high, but a browse here is always a pleasure.
▶ *The owners of Brandstationen announced as this guide went to press that the shop is moving to Hornsgatan 64, just round the corner.*

Bric-a-Brac
Swedenborgsgatan 5A (www.bric-a-brac.se). T-bana Mariatorget or bus 43, 55, 66. **Open** 11am-6pm Mon-Fri; 11am-4pm Sat; noon-4pm Sun. **Map** p111 H2 ⓖ **Fashion**
This boutique stocks a well-selected range of mid- to high-end Scandinavian and European labels, including Ally Capellino, Ganni and Marimekko, for men and women. Look out for the seasonal sales, when there are often huge discounts.

★ Herr Judit
Hornsgatan 65 (658 30 37, www.herrjudit.se). T-bana Zinkensdamm or bus 4, 191, 192. **Open** 11am-6pm Mon-Fri; 11am-5pm Sat; noon-3pm Sun. **Map** p111 F2 ⓖ **Vintage**
This high-end vintage menswear shop is a great source of good-quality blazers and jackets by the likes of Edwin, Acne and Burberry, as well as collectible vintage watches, classic leather satchels and designer luggage.
Other location Sibyllegatan 29, Östermalm.
▶ *Vintage homewares shop Brandstationen (see left), situated a ten-minute walk away, is run by the same team.*

Johan & Nyström
Swedenborgsgatan 7, Södermalm (702 20 40, www.johanochnystrom.se). T-bana Mariatorget or bus 43 55, 66. **Open** 7.30am-6pm Mon-Fri; 10am-4pm Sat; 11am-4pm Sun. **Map** p111 H2 ⓖ **Food & drink**
The café wing of the local coffee bean roaster reflects the ethos of the brand well – the beans are roasted by hand in small batches, and this personal approach is translated into this space, which is filled from floor to ceiling with coffee and tea, and related equipment. If you want to extend your coffee knowledge, there are courses held here regularly.

Our Legacy
Krukmakargatan 24-26 (668 20 60, www.ourlegacy.se). T-bana Zinkensdamm or bus 4, 66, 74, 94. **Open** noon-6.30pm Mon-Fri; 11am-5pm Sat; noon-4pm Sun. **Map** p111 F2 ⓖ **Fashion**
This contemporary Swedish menswear label, the brainchild of Christopher Nying and Jockum Hallin, is all about high-quality wardrobe staples – simply cut plain shirts, T-shirts, sweaters and jackets dominate.
Other location Jakobsbergsgatan 11, Norrmalm.
▶ *Next door, fashion boutique Nitty Gritty (658 24 40, www.nittygrittystore.com) stocks a range of high-fashion brands for men and women, such as APC, Helmut Lang and Isabel Marant Étoile.*

★ Papercut
Krukmakargatan 24-26, Södermalm (13 35 74, www.papercutshop.se). T-bana Zinkensdamm or bus 4, 66, 74, 94. **Open** 11am-6.30pm Mon-Fri; 11am-5pm Sat; noon-4pm Sun (July 11am-4pm Mon-Sat, closed Sun). **Map** p111 F2 ⓖ **Books**

EXPLORE

Papercut, in the same building as menswear label Our Legacy (*see p115*), stocks an impressive range of international art magazines, coffee-table books and arthouse DVDs.

Sandqvist
Swedenborgsgatan 3 (21 04 75, www.sandqvist. net). T-bana Mariatorget or bus 43, 55, 66. **Open** 11am-6.30pm Mon-Fri; 11am-5pm Sat; noon-6pm Sun. **Map** p111 H2 ⑥ **Luggage**
Head here for messenger bags, laptop cases, leather satchels, rucksacks, weekend bags and wallets, all made from quality leather and/or canvas, in a range of tasteful tones. This Swedish brand has grown rapidly over the past few years, and these bags are now seen on the back of many a stylish Stockholmer.

Wigerdals Värld
Krukmakargatan 14, Södermalm (31 64 04, www.wigerdal.com). T-bana Mariatorget or bus 4, 66, 74, 94. **Open** noon-6pm Mon-Fri; 11am-3pm Sat. **Map** p111 G2 ⑥ **Homewares**
Wigerdals Värld is a delightful little shop selling a well-edited range of 20th-century homewares, furniture and knick-knacks.

EXPLORE

Stora Henriksvik.

LÅNGHOLMEN

Off the north-west tip of Söder, near Hornstull, lies the long, narrow island of Långholmen (Long Island). For 250 years (1724-1975) this beautiful green island, almost a mile long, was home to a prison. Thanks largely to the presence of the jail, Långholmen has remained undeveloped and, as a result, is something of a green retreat, complete with tree-shaded paths, allotment gardens, cliffs dotted with nest-like nooks and two sandy beaches perfect for swimming. Today, the remaining part of the prison is run as the **Långholmen Hotel**, a very pleasant budget hotel/hostel (*see p218*), with a café, conference centre and museum (**Långholmens Fängelsemusuem**). You can walk to the island across Långholmsbron (which provides closest access to the former prison from Hornstull), or via Pålsundsbron to the east, located near a shipyard dating back to the 1680s. To access the middle of the island directly, walk across the enormous Västerbron bridge (worth crossing to take in the view of the city) and then take the newly renovated ramp or stairs down.

A walking/cycling path leads from the south of the island to the cliffs and beach in the north. The lovely **Stora Henriksvik**, a 17th-century house with a delightful café and garden, lies behind the beach, **Långholmsbadet**. The beach itself is one of the most popular swimming spots in the city (*see p109* **In the Swim**). For outdoor swimming without the hordes, head east to **Klippbadet**, a tiny, sandy cove. To the west of the prison stands **Karlshäll**, the previous residence of the prison warden, now a conference centre and restaurant. Curving back round to the south, take in the grace of the lovingly cared-for wooden sailboats lining the picture-perfect canal. Prisoners used to walk across a bridge to work at the factories on **Reimersholme**, a tiny island. Best known historically for the production of aquavit, the island is now residential.

Sights & Museums

Långholmens Fängelsemuseum
Långholmen Hotel, Långholmsmuren 20 (720 85 00, www.langholmen.com). T-bana Hornstull or bus 4, 40, 77. **Open** 11am-4pm daily. **Admission** 25kr; 10kr reductions; free for hotel & hostel guests. *Guided tours* (July, Aug) 65kr; 2pm Sun. **Map** p110 A1 ⑥
This small museum describes the history of the Swedish penal system and gives a flavour of life inside Kronohäktet prison before it was turned into a hotel/hostel. You can visit a typical cell used between 1845 and 1930, read about Sweden's last executioner, Anders Gustaf Dalman, and see a scale model of the guillotine imported from France and used only once, in 1910 (the actual guillotine used is stored at the Nordiska Museet, though not on display). Visitors can view an assortment of prison paraphernalia,

including the sinister hoods worn to hide an accused person's identity until sentenced (used until 1935). Nowadays, the Swedish government tries to avoid incarceration and a quarter of the 12,000 criminals sentenced each year are tagged rather than imprisoned. Book in advance if you want a tour in English.

Cafés

★ Stora Henriksvik

Långholmsmuren 21 (669 69 69, www.stora henriksvik.se). T-bana Hornstull or bus 4, 40,

77, 94. **Open** 11am-5pm daily. Closed Oct-Mar. **Map** p110 A1 ⑥⑥
The oldest part of this attractive two-storey house was built in the late 17th century as the toll office for boats travelling into Stockholm. The Bellmanmuseet (Bellman Museum) that was until recently on the ground floor – devoted to celebrated troubadour/songwriter Carl Michael Bellman – is now just a small exhibition, but the pleasant café remains, offering own-made pastries, good coffee and simple dishes. The café is popular with bathers who use the beach in front of the house (*see p109* **In the Swim**).

STIEG LARSSON
The man behind the Millennium Trilogy.

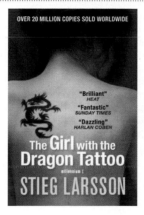

Stieg Larsson.

Only someone who's been hiding under a rock for the past few years can have failed to hear about the literary phenomenon that has become the Millennium Trilogy, Swedish author Stieg Larsson's series of crime novels published posthumously after the author died in 2004. The novels have become a worldwide success story (27 million copies had been sold in 40 countries by spring 2010), spawning a series of blockbuster feature film adaptations. The books are also arguably responsible for an increase in tourism to Sweden over the past few years.

Born in Skelleftehamn, near Skellefteå in the north of Sweden, in 1954, Larsson's official full name was Karl Stig-Erland Larsson. His writing career began in his late teens, when Larsson became heavily involved in science fiction. During the 1970s, '80s and '90s, he also worked successfully as a graphic designer and journalist in Stockholm, developing his interest in, and knowledge of, left-wing political ideologies, which he actively defended both at home and abroad.

Upon his death from a heart attack at the age of 50 (he was a famously heavy smoker), Larsson left behind three manuscripts for crime novels. Planned as a series of ten books, Larsson had made few attempts to get the completed works published, but had secured a deal shortly before he died. The first – *Män som Hatar Kvinnor* ('Men who hate women'), published in English as

The Girl with the Dragon Tattoo – went on sale in 2005 (2008 in English) and was an immediate success. *Flickan som Lekte med Elden* (*The Girl Who Played with Fire*) followed in 2006 (2009 in English), winning the Best Swedish Crime Novel award for that year. *Luftslottet som Sprängdes* ('The Air Castle that was Blown Up') was published in Sweden in 2007, appearing in English as *The Girl Who Kicked the Hornets' Nest* in 2009.

Violence against women, incompetence in investigative journalism and right-wing extremism are recurring themes in Larsson's novels. Much of the intrigue in the stories takes place in Södermalm; journalist Mikael Blomkvist, a central character, has his office on Götgatan, and the favourite drinking spot (Kvarnen; see *p106*) of his other protagonist, hacker/researcher Lisbeth Salander, is also on the island. The Millennium walking tours run by the Stockholms Stadsmuseum (see *p103*) follow the paths of these characters, and are the perfect way for Larsson fans to get their fix and discover a different side to Södermalm at the same time.

Östermalm & Gärdet

This urban playground for the rich, beautiful and, often, famous is a shopper's paradise by day and a clubber's paradise by night. The main focus is the bustling square of Stureplan, at the centre of which stands the concrete rain shelter known as Svampen (the Mushroom). Formerly a rather run-down area, Stureplan was revamped at the end of the 1980s and is now party central for glamour-seeking, fashion-conscious Stockholmers.

The whole area to the east of Norrmalm was previously called Ladugårdsgärdet, which roughly translates as 'the field of barns'. As more affluent people moved in, the association with cattle became less desirable, and in 1885 the name was changed to Östermalm. Today, the district north of Valhallavägen and the open parkland to its south-east are known as Gärdet, although the undeveloped grassy area is still officially called Ladugårdsgärdet.

Östermalms Saluhall.

Don't Miss

1 **Gastrologik** Top-notch New Nordic nosh (p124).

2 **Östermalms Saluhall** Epicurean delights at this posh food hall (p130).

3 **Svenskt Tenn** Classic textiles and Josef Frank homewares (p131).

4 **Hallwylska Museet** The eccentric home of Count and Countess von Hallwyl (p121).

5 **Historiska Museet** From the Stone Age to the 16th century (p121).

EXPLORE

ÖSTERMALM

Aside from the nightlife, Stureplan is the city's most upmarket shopping area. The ultra-posh **Sturegallerian** shopping mall borders the square; as well as designer boutiques, it also houses the exclusive art nouveau **Sturebadet** bathhouse. Shopaholics can spend a few happy hours trawling the surrounding streets, notably the lower end of Birger Jarlsgatan (which extends from the north of the city all the way to the water at Nybroviken). This is where you'll find international designer fashion boutiques, classy jewellery, fancy cosmetics and posh chocolates galore.

At the bottom end of Birger Jarlsgatan is Nybroviken, where Cinderella and Strömma Kanalbolaget ferries depart for destinations in Lake Mälaren and the archipelago. Classics by Strindberg and Shakespeare are performed in the ornate white marble building facing Nybroplan square, the **Kungliga Dramatiska Teatern** (*see p169*) – one of Stockholm's leading theatres. Nearby is the idiosyncratic **Hallwylska Museet**.

If you walk up Sibyllegatan to the right of the theatre, you'll pass three buildings constructed by royal commission. Bread for the soldiers of the royal army was baked at the Kronobageriet, which today houses the child-friendly former **Musikmuseet** – it's currently closed and is due to reopen as the Scenkonst Museet (Swedish Museum of Performing Arts) in 2016. The royal family's horses and cars are still kept in the **Kungliga Hovstallet**, the huge brick building to the right of the bakery. Further up is the unusual **Armémuseum**, where the royal arsenal used to be stored. Behind this lies 17th-century **Hedvig Eleonora Kyrka**, the former place of worship for the royal navy, which now holds regular classical music concerts.

To catch a glimpse of the Östermalm upper classes, head to Östermalmstorg opposite the church. When the first plans for Östermalm were drawn up back in the 1640s, sailors and craftsmen lived around this square. Nowadays, expensive boutiques sell clothes and home accessories, and the pavements are teeming with mink-clad elderly women walking small dogs. On the corner of the square is **Östermalms Saluhall**, a dark red-brick building constructed in 1888 and the flagship of the city's market halls. You can buy all sorts of gourmet delicacies, from fresh Baltic fish to wild rabbit – but it's pricey, so you could just stroll around the magnificent interior.

Östermalm's main green space is the **Humlegården**, the site of the king's hop gardens back in the 16th century and today a pleasant and very popular park, with the **Kungliga Bibliotek** (Royal Library) on its southern bank. Theatre performances are held in the park in summer. Further up Karlavägen, on a hill overlooking

the city, looms the tall brick tower of **Engelbrektskyrkan**. Designed by leading Jugendstil architect Lars Israel Wahlman and opened in 1914, the church has an amazingly high nave – supposedly the tallest in Scandinavia.

For another kind of high life, follow the water's edge from Nybroplan along grand Strandvägen, lined with luxurious late 19th-century residences, as well as two classic interiors shops – **Svenskt Tenn** and **Malmstenbutiken** – from which to kit them out. Until the 1940s, sailing boats carrying firewood from the archipelago islands used to dock on the quayside at Strandvägen; some of these vintage boats – with labels by each one – are now docked on its southern edge.

At the end of Strandvägen is the bridge leading over to leafy Djurgården, and north from there, on Narvavägen, is the imposing **Historiska Museet**; it's Sweden's largest archaeological museum, with an exceptional collection of Viking artefacts.

Strandvägen is part of an esplanade system mapped out for Östermalm in the late 1800s by city planner Albert Lindhagen. The project was only partially implemented, but includes the broad boulevards of Valhallavägen, Narvavägen and Karlavägen – the latter two radiating out from the fountain and circular pond (added in 1929) at Karlaplan. The central section of Karlavägen is dotted with sculptures by various international artists, and at its eastern end are the headquarters of Swedish radio and television. The buildings were designed by Erik Ahnborg and Sune Lindström, who were also responsible for the **Berwaldhallen** concert hall (*see p166*) next door, home of the Swedish Radio Symphony Orchestra and Radio Choir.

Engelbrektskyrkan.

IN THE KNOW
LATE-NIGHT ÖSTERMALM

The clubs near here close around 5am at the weekend – later than the capital's other party spots – so you'll often see hordes of clubbers queuing in the small hours, in all weathers, to get into the most fashionable places.

Beyond the TV and radio buildings, on the border with Gärdet, is **Diplomatstaden**, a complex of grand mansions that houses most of the city's foreign embassies, including those of the UK and US. The adjacent park next to the water is named after Alfred Nobel, scientist, inventor and founder of the famous prizes.

Sights & Museums

Armémuseum

Riddargatan 13 (51 95 63 00, www.armemuseum. org). T-bana Östermalmstorg or bus 52, 62, 69, 76, 91. **Open** *Sept-May* 11am-8pm Tue; 11am-5pm Wed-Sun. *June-Aug* 10am-5pm daily. **Admission** 80kr; 50kr reductions; free under-19s. Free with SC. **Map** p122 C5 ❶

The story of Sweden at war, rather than its military infrastructure, is the museum's dominant theme, which may seem odd since Sweden has avoided conflict for the last 200 years. But with 1,000 years of history on show, you soon learn that the Swedes were once a bloody and gruesome lot. The Army Museum – housed since 1879 in the former arsenal, an impressive white pile built in the 18th century – reopened in May 2000 after a seven-year revamp. Exhibited over three floors, it's not all uniforms and gleaming weaponry. Life-size (and lifelike) tableaux, such as a woman scavenging meat from a dead horse and doctors performing an amputation, show the horrific effects of war on both soldiers and civilians. The main exhibition begins on the top floor with the Viking age and the Thirty Years War, and continues below with the 20th century. The ground-floor area houses an artillery exhibit and a restaurant. If you miss the highly recommended guided tour in English, the front desk provides a detailed pamphlet, also in English. The Royal Guard marches off from the museum (summer only) for the changing of the guard (*see p44*) at the Kungliga Slottet.

★ Hallwylska Museet

Hamngatan 4 (402 30 99, www.hallwylskamuseet. se). T-bana Östermalmstorg or Kungsträdgården or bus 2, 52, 55, 62, 69, 76, 96. **Open** *Jan-May, Sept-Dec* noon-4pm Tue, Thur-Sun; noon-7pm Wed. *June-Aug* 10am-4pm Tue-Sun. *Guided tours* see website for details. **Admission** 80kr; free under-18s. Free with SC. **Map** p122 B5 ❷

Enter the opulent world of Count and Countess Walther and Wilhelmina von Hallwyl in one of Stockholm's most eccentric and engaging museums. This palatial residence was built as a winter home for the immensely rich couple in 1898. Designed by Isak Gustav Clason (architect of the Nordiska Museet), it was very modern for its time, with electricity, central heating, lifts, bathrooms and phones. The Countess was an avid collector of almost everything, from paintings and furniture to silverware and armoury that she picked up on her travels around Europe, the Middle East and Africa. She always planned that the house should become a museum, and donated the building and its collections to the Swedish state in 1920. Her vision became a reality in 1938 when the Hallwyl Museum was opened to the public, eight years after her death. The house has been preserved exactly as it was left, and situated among the objets d'art are personal peculiarities, including a chunk of the Count's beard and a slice of their wedding cake. For a taste of how the other half used to live, the guided tour takes you through an assortment of 40 incredibly lavish rooms and is led by extremely well-spoken guides dressed up as butlers and maids.

★ Historiska Museet

Narvavägen 13-17 (51 95 56 00, www.historiska. se). T-bana Karlaplan or bus 44, 56, 69, 76. **Open** *June-Aug* 10am-6pm daily. *Sept-May* 11am-5pm Tue-Sun; 11am-8pm Wed. *Guided tours* (English) June-Aug 1pm daily; check website for further details. **Admission** 100kr; 80kr reductions; free under-18s & all 4-8pm Wed, all day Fri. Free with SC. **Map** p123 F5 ❸

Objects from the Stone Age to the 16th century are displayed in the Museum of National Antiquities, Sweden's largest archaeological museum. The plain design of this 1940 building – the façade looks like a tall brick wall with a door – gives no indication of the treasures within. To see the best exhibits, enter the darkened hall on the ground floor, where an impressive collection of Viking rune stones, swords, skeletons and jewellery is displayed. Detailed texts (in English) and maps describe the Vikings' economy, class structure, travels and methods of punishment. In the large halls upstairs, you'll find beautiful wooden church altarpieces, textiles and other medieval ecclesiastical artworks. Don't miss the basement, where the circular Guldrummet (Gold Room) displays more than 3,000 artefacts in gold and silver, from the Bronze to the Middle Ages. This collection was made possible by a unique Swedish law, more than 300 years old, which entitles the finders of such treasures to payment equal to their market value. In the foyer there's a copy of an Athenian marble lion statue – check out the Viking graffiti on its side. In 2004, the Historiska Museet hit the headlines in connection with an installation about suicide bombers by an Israeli-born artist. On a visit to the museum, the Israeli ambassador to Sweden intentionally

EXPLORE

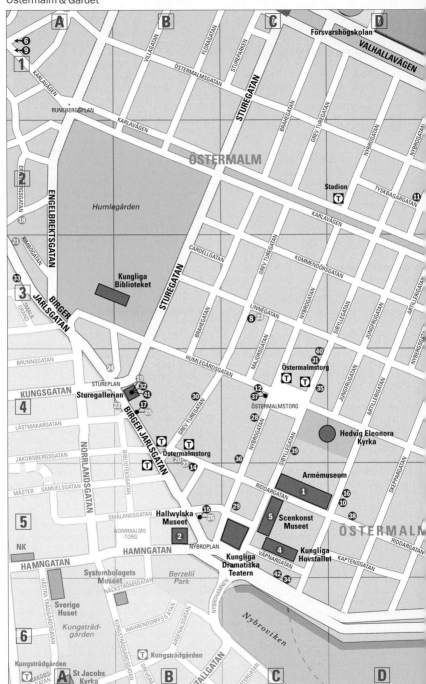

EXPLORE

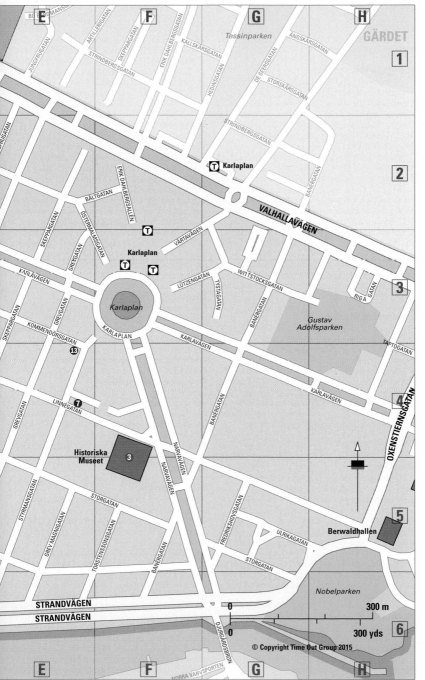

GÄRDET

Tessinparken

Karlaplan

VALHALLAVÄGEN

Karlaplan

Karlaplan

Gustav
Adolfsparken

KARLAVÄGEN

LINNEGATAN

Historiska
Museet

Berwaldhallen

Nobelparken

STRANDVÄGEN

STRANDVÄGEN

300 m

300 yds

© Copyright Time Out Group 2015

EXPLORE

knocked over a lighting stand into the red pool designed to represent blood, shorting the electricity and causing a huge stir.

Kungliga Hovstallet

Väpnargatan 1 (402 61 06, www.royalcourt.se). T-bana Östermalmstorg or bus 2, 55, 62, 69, 71. **Open** (guided tours only, in Swedish & English) *Mid Aug-mid Dec, mid Jan-May* 2pm Fri-Sun. *June-mid Aug* 1pm, 3pm Mon-Fri; 5pm, 7pm Wed. **Admission** 100kr; 50kr reductions. **Map** p122 C5 ❹

The royal family's own horses, carriages and cars are taken care of in this late 19th-century striped brick building designed by architect Fritz Eckert. The building is so vast that it occupies almost the entire block next to the Kungliga Dramatiska Teatern (*see p169*). A collection of 40 carriages from the 19th and 20th centuries (some still used for ceremonial occasions) stands in a long hall above the garage. Inside the garage are 11 cars, including a 1950 Daimler and a 1969 Cadillac Fleetwood. The stalls and riding arena may be empty if you visit in summer, as this is when the horses are 'on vacation'. This place may well be a big hit for equestrian enthusiasts, but otherwise the tour is not particularly thrilling.

Scenkonst Museet

Sibyllegatan 2 (51 95 54 90, www.musikverket.se/ scenkonstmuseet). T-bana Östermalmstorg or bus 2, 55, 62, 69, 71. **Closed** until 2016. **Map** p122 C5 ❺

The former Musikmuseet, which housed some 6,000 musical instruments, closed in 2014, and is expected to reopen in early 2016 as Scenkonst Museet – the Swedish Museum of Performing Arts. It will receive a full makeover, though details of the new concept were not available as this guide went to press.

Restaurants

Bon Bon

Kungstensgatan 9 (20 17 10, www.restaurang bonbon.se). T-bana Rådmansgatan or bus 2, 43, 96. **Open** 6pm-midnight Mon-Thur; 5pm-midnight Fri, Sat. **Tapas** 55kr. **Map** p122 A1 ❻ **Swedish/French**

Bon Bon offers a fun, unpredictable dining experience, with a selection of tapas-style dishes. If this sounds fussy, it really isn't – the kitchen and staff are well prepared. For every dish, most of which are Swedish and French bistro classics, you're given a marble, and these are then counted up when it comes to settling the bill.

Brasserie Elverket

Linnégatan 69 (661 25 62, www.brasserie elverket.se). T-bana Karlaplan or bus 42, 44, 56. **Open** 11am-2pm, 5-10pm Mon-Fri; noon-11pm Sat. **Main courses** 145kr-295kr. **Map** p123 E4 ❼ **Contemporary**

This busy bar-restaurant is in an old electricity plant, together with the more experimental stage of the Dramaten theatre (*see p169*). The food served is modern crossover and moderately priced, with a pre-theatre menu and a selection of tapas, as well as a popular weekend brunch. It's closed for a month after Midsummer, when the owners retreat to the island of Gotland to run their restaurant there.

Brasserie Godot

Grevturegatan 36 (660 06 14, www.godot.se). T-bana Östermalmstorg or bus 56, 62, 91. **Open** 5-11pm Mon, Tue; 5pm-midnight Wed, Thur; 5pm-1am Fri, Sat. **Main courses** 205kr-395kr. **Set menu** 495kr-625kr. **Map** p122 C3 ❽ **French/Swedish**

The bar is busy during weekends with rich youngsters showing off designer bags and parental credit cards, but walk beyond that area and you come to a formal but intimate dining room where superb food – a mix of French brasserie classics and modern Swedish cuisine – is served. Both the seafood (lobster, smoked shrimps) and meat dishes (veal, spring lamb) are excellent. The steak tartare is a highlight.

Esperanto/Råkultur

Kungstensgatan 2 (693 23 23, www.esperanto restaurant.se/696 23 25, www.rakultur.se). T-Bana Rådmansgatan or bus 2, 42, 43, 96. **Open** *Esperanto* 6.30pm-midnight Wed-Sat. *Råkultur* 11.30am-3.30pm, 5-10pm Mon-Fri. **Råkultur sushi** 65kr-195kr. **Esperanto set menu** 1,250kr 6 courses, 1,650kr 10 courses. **Map** p122 A1 ❾ **Contemporary/Japanese**

Esperanto serves two set menus (1,250kr/1,650kr), one combining the culinary cultures of Sweden and Japan, and the other slightly more Swedish. It's wonderfully elegant, and the Michelin star is well deserved. Its sister restaurant on the first floor, Råkultur, serves Stockholm's best sushi, as well as other Japanese dishes. Both places are always full of foodies.

★ Gastrologik

Artillerigatan 14 (662 30 60, www.gastrologik.se). T-bana Östermalmstorg or bus 52, 62, 69, 76, 91. **Open** 7pm-1am Tue-Sat. **Tasting menu** 1,295kr (six courses). **Wine menu** 995kr. **Map** p122 D5 ❿ **New Nordic**

Gastrologik, housed in a minimalist space with white tablecloths and hanging brass lamps, is among the wave of Noma-influenced restaurants that have been popping up around Scandinavia in recent years. However, it's much more than an imitation Noma. An emphasis on seasonal ingredients is expected in a New Nordic restaurant, but this place – run by chefs Jacob Holmström and Anton Bjuhr – takes this focus to the extreme. There is no written menu, as the produce (and thus the dishes) is chosen on the day, depending on what's available and what's freshest. This will rule the place out for fussy

Gastrologik.

eaters (though vegetarians and allergy sufferers can normally be catered for) but adds sensory engagement and a real element of surprise to those open to the experience. And with vegetables provided by Rosendals Trädgård (*see p92*), imaginative fish, seafood and meat dishes, and expert wine pairing, the culinary quality is always high and the creativity impressive. So much so that the place now has a Michelin star.

▶ *The owners of Gastrologik opened a bakficka ('back pocket') in the same building a few months after opening; the more affordable Speceriet has been just as successful. See right and p79* **Staying in Pocket** *for more information.*

Halv Grek plus Turk

Jungfrugatan 33 (665 94 22, www.halvgrekplus turk.se). T-bana Karlaplan or Stadion or bus 1, 42, 44, 62, 91. **Open** 11.30am-2pm, 5pm-midnight Mon-Fri; 5pm-midnight Sat; 6pm-midnight Sun. **Meze** 44kr-99kr each. **Map** p122 D2 ⓫ **Middle Eastern**
Slightly off the beaten track and with an entrance marked by an easy-to-miss sign, it's worth the extra effort to find this gem of a restaurant. Born of a friendship between Greek and Turkish restaurateurs, the decor at Halv Grek plus Turk is modern Middle Eastern, accented with elegant lounge sofas, bright colours and soft lighting. The clientele is a mixed urban set and the menu features small meze, and an assortment of cold and hot dishes. Aside from the traditional classics (houmous, meatballs, baba ganoush), you'll find inspired creations such as chicken liver terrine with metaxa. The 'Manti' dumplings (yoghurt and spiced lamb) are a particular delight. Service is attentive, friendly and efficient.

Lisa Elmqvist

Östermalms Saluhall (55 34 04 10, www.lisa elmqvist.se). T-bana Östermalmstorg or bus 56, 62, 91. **Open** 9.30am-6pm Mon-Thur; 9.30am-7pm Fri; 9.30am-4pm Sat. **Main courses** 155kr-315kr. **Map** p122 C4 ⓬ **Seafood**
Lisa Elmqvist is one of three sister restaurants. The main one, located inside the fabulous red-brick indoor food market Östermalms Saluhall, is a wonderful place to sit and enjoy classic Swedish fish

dishes surrounded by the bustle of the market shoppers. Outside on Östermalmstorg is an outdoor café, Lisa på Torget.
▶ *For more on Östermalms Saluhall, see p130.*

★ Lo Scudetto

Kommendörsgatan 46 (640 42 15, www. loscudetto.se). T-bana Karlaplan or bus 42, 44, 56. **Open** 5-11pm Mon-Sat. **Main courses** 187kr-297kr. **Map** p123 E4 ⓭ **Italian**
A culinary pioneer, this local Italian spot used to be situated on Åsögatan, where it was also about rustic charm. Now located in Östermalm, the place has smartened up its image with white tablecloths and a stylish bar. The food remains marvellously subtle, with the bresaola, ravioli and tiramisu all prepared with a loving and skilful hand. One of the city's few genuinely top-class Italians. Reservations essential.

★ PA & Co

Riddargatan 8 (611 08 45, www.paco.se). T-bana Östermalmstorg or bus 2, 55, 56, 62, 91, 96. **Open** 5pm-midnight daily. **Main courses** 160kr-400kr. **Map** p122 B5 ⓮ **Contemporary**
This small restaurant has long been a favourite hangout for Stockholmers. And no wonder. The food – Swedish classic and international fare – is superb, and the service splendid: swift and friendly but with personality. Tables fill up fast so you can have a hard time getting in, but waiting at the bar is pleasant.

Riche

Birger Jarlsgatan 4 (54 50 35 60, www.riche.se). T-bana Östermalmstorg or bus 2, 55, 96. **Open** 7.30am-midnight Mon; 7.30am-2am Tue-Fri; noon-2am Sat; noon-midnight Sun. **Main courses** 185kr-385kr. **Map** p122 B5 ⓯ **Contemporary**
Riche is one of the most popular places in town for an afterwork drink, especially among the media set, but the menu – a fairly ambitious mix of traditional Swedish dishes with international classics – doesn't always succeed. For a more intimate and reliable experience, you may want to opt for adjacent Teatergrillen (Nybrogatan 3, 54 50 35 65).

Speceriet

Artillerigatan 14 (662 30 60, www.speceriet.se). T-bana Östermalmstorg or bus 52, 62, 69, 76, 91. **Open** 5-10pm Mon, Sat; 11.30am-2pm, 5-10pm Tue-Fri. Closed late July-mid Aug. **Small plates** 125kr-165kr. **Map** p122 D5 ⓰ **New Nordic**
Though it has the same focus on seasonal produce and exciting flavour combinations as its big sister, Gastrologik (*see p124*), Speceriet offers a more spontaneous and laid-back approach to New Nordic cooking. The restaurant doesn't take reservations, and the minimalist space is unfussy and contains an in-house deli. The place is especially good for lunch, with creative yet simple dishes such as beets with grilled lamb brisket and goat's cheese or roasted cauliflower with mussels, fennel, hazelnuts and parsley.

EXPLORE

FISH, FORAGING & FIKA: A GUIDE TO SWEDISH GASTRONOMY

Swedish cuisine is much more than just meatballs.

EXPLORE

EATING OUT

Choices for a night out in Stockholm range from traditional places serving classic Swedish dishes – herring or meatballs, with lots of potatoes, dill and lingonberries – up to the handful of world-class restaurants that offer extraordinarily innovative cuisine in ultra-hip surroundings. There are also more non-Swedish options than ever before. Swedes as a nation travel a great deal, and all those trips abroad have broadened their horizons and raised their expectations, so that you can now find everything from Mexican street food (**La Neta**; www.laneta.se) to vegetarian Chinese (**Lao Wai**; see p75). Conversely, a cuisine based on Scandinavian culinary heritage and produce – known as New Nordic – has also been making its mark on the city over the past few years. The New Nordic focus may still be on Copenhagen, thanks to Rene Redzepi's Noma, but Stockholm restaurants such as **Frantzén** (see p52), **Gastrologik** (see p124) and **Smörgåstårteriet** (see p78), which all focus on local ingredients, are gaining local and international attention.

Note that the restaurants of the moment are often packed, so it can sometimes be a battle to find a free table, even on weekdays. For popular places, you should always book in advance, especially for Fridays and Saturdays. Be aware, too, that many restaurants close in July (and sometimes the first half of August) for summer holidays. Children are welcome everywhere, even in the smartest restaurants, and many places provide high chairs and kids' menus. All restaurants are smoke-free. Many restaurants will have a version of the menu in English, but at the ones that don't, staff are normally happy to translate. For food terms, see p229 **Vocabulary**.

Whether you're eating in traditional food trucks or upmarket restaurants, you'll almost certainly encounter several of the following ingredients and dishes during your trip. Here's a rundown of what to expect.

FISH

Herring – called **sill** on the west coast and **strömming** in Stockholm – used to be the staple food of the Swedish diet. Today, this little fish is still much loved and always on the menu, from the cheapest lunch restaurant to the poshest luxury establishment. For lunch, it's often blackened (*sotare*) and served with mashed potatoes, melted butter and perhaps lingonberry sauce. Don't be put off by the sweet lingonberries: all savoury traditional foods are served with sweet preserves – and it tastes great.

Inlagd strömming (pickled herring) is prepared in lots of different ways. If you manage to find a traditional Swedish *smorgasbord* (available in every restaurant around Christmas), this is what you should start with, before moving on to the meats. A plate of pickled herring and new potatoes with special soured cream (**gräddfil**) will make any Swede foggy-eyed, while **gravad strömming** (pickled herring cured with a mustard sauce) is indispensable for celebrating Midsummer. It's served with some beer and aquavit, a liqueur distilled from potato or grain mash and flavoured with caraway seeds (*kalled snaps*).

Red kräftor (crayfish) are eaten everywhere when the season starts in August, with crayfish parties galore (preferably outside under a full moon). Cooked with huge amounts of dill, they're an unmissable treat.

A common starter in Stockholm restaurants is **toast Skagen**, a delicious dish consisting of prawns with mayonnaise, lemon and dill, served on toasted rye bread. **Lax** (salmon) needs no introduction: just remember that *gravlax* means cured with sugar and salt, not to be confused with the smoked variety.

Fish from inland lakes and the Baltic are quite rare, the most delicious being the **gös** (pike-perch). However, plenty of fish from the west coast lands on the plates of Stockholm's restaurants, and **torsk** (cod), though more and more scarce, is a vital part of Swedish culinary tradition and served in any different ways. The most interesting is **tfisk**, which is only available at Christmas. ne cod is salted and air-dried, then soaked lye, which transforms it into something that oks and tastes nothing like fish. It's served ith peas, butter and a béchamel sauce.

IEAT

wedish **köttbullar** (meatballs) 're, of course, a speciality, nmortalised not least by the wedish chef in the *The Muppet how*. They're traditionally eaten ith pickled cucumber, a cream auce and lingonberries.

Pytt i panna is regularly found most restaurants: it consists of ced and fried meat and potatoes, dorned with a fried egg and pickled eetroots. **Rimmad oxbringa** (lightly salted 'isket of beef) is beautifully tender. Anything ith 'rimmad' attached to it means that it's 'st salted and then boiled.

Kåldolmar (stuffed cabbage rolls) are made wedish by wrapping cabbage leaves rather than ne leaves around minced pork. The concept as introduced when King Karl XII was stranded Turkey after attempting, and failing, to invade ussia in 1708.

Game, such as **älg** (elk) and **rådjur** (roe deer), popular in the autumn. It's mainly roasted nd served with potatoes, lingonberries and cream sauce.

EGETABLES, BREAD AND DAIRY

s well as lingonberries and dill, you'll find at many Swedish dishes feature foraged ild mushrooms – especially chanterelle **antarell**), which can be foraged all over weden. Vegetarians, in particular, nould look out for mushroom **roppkakor**. These old-school otato dumplings, which hail om southern Sweden, are aditionally made with pork nd onions, but the tasty ushroom-filled variety ometimes appears as a egetarian option in restaurants ot least in new restaurant **Nalle & roppkakan**, which seems to be part f a revival of the dish; *see p147*). Both eat and vegetarian *kroppkakor* are served ith butter, cream and lingonberry jam.

Bread in Sweden is normally excellent, and anges from dark, dense rye breads, buttery ake-like bread, the ever-popular sourdough, s well, of course, as lots of different varieties f crispbread (**knäckebröd**).

Fermented milk products, such as yoghurt and soured milk, are traditional breakfast foods in Sweden, and often appear in hotel breakfast buffets, as do hard-boiled eggs, linseeds, cereals and breads, smoked salmon and gravlax, pastries – and, if you're lucky, fried cinnamon bread.

SCHNAPPS

Stockholmers use pretty much every excuse to drink a glass or more of **brännvin** (schnapps). It comes in many varieties, highly flavoured with native herbs and spices such as caraway, aniseed, coriander and fennel. The traditional way to drink it is to fill the first glass to the brim, the second only halfway. Before downing the glasses, it's customary to sing a *snapsvisa* ('schnapps ditty').

CAFÉS & FIKA

Café culture in Sweden is as rich as the coffee the natives consume by the gallon. As the pub is to the Brits, so the café is to the Swedes. Apart from the Finns, the Swedes drink more coffee per capita than any other nation, on average downing 4.5 cups each per day – and, unlike the take-out cup culture prevalent elsewhere, Swedes like to sit down with a classic white porcelain cup and saucer for their cup of java. This laid-back and sociable tradition, known as '*fika*', probably goes a long way to explaining why Stockholm is mercifully free from US-style coffee chains.

Most cafés serve the usual range of lattes and cappuccinos. The exception to this is the more traditional style of *konditori*, which may be restricted to the filtered variety. Decaffeinated coffee is generally regarded with both suspicion and derision, and you'll also find it hard to get a cup of tea that the British would recognise as such. Strong coffee, weak tea sort of sums it up.

All cafés serve a selection of biscuits, cakes and sandwiches. The **kanelbulle** (cinnamon and cardamom bun) is a typical treat to have alongside your coffee, as is the **chokladboll** (a golf ball-sized concoction made of oatmeal, sugar, coffee, cocoa and butter, and normally covered in coconut flakes). Many cafés also served delicious Swedish cheesecakes (**ostkaka**). Watch out, too, for seasonal favourites – at Christmas time it's the **lussekatt** (a saffron-flavoured bun), and at Easter it's the magnificent **semla**, a truly epic creation of pastry, almond paste and whipped cream.

KANEL-BULLE 22

EXPLORE

Sturehof

Stureplan 2 (440 57 30, www.sturehof.com).
T-bana Östermalmstorg or bus 2, 55, 96. **Open**
11am-2am Mon-Fri; noon-2am Sat; 1pm-2am Sun.
Main courses 155kr-495kr. **Map** p122 B4
Mediterranean/seafood
Long opening hours make it possible to get a meal in
this classic Stockholm brasserie at almost any time
of day, a rare thing in this city. The massive dining
room is elegant, with white linen tablecloths, uni-
formed waiters and nicely designed furniture, but
the atmosphere stays lively and cheerful. Service is
attentive, and the menu follows classic French bistro tradition, with seafood and shellfish a speciality.
Among the starters are a few Swedish classics such
as smoked Baltic herring and *toast skagen* (shrimp
and other ingredients, on sautéed bread). After dinner, step into the lively O-baren (*see p129*).

Cafés

For gourmet food hall **Östermalms Saluhall**,
see p130.

Café Saturnus

Eriksbergsgatan 6 (611 77 00, www.cafesaturnus.
se). T-bana Östermalmstorg or bus 2, 42, 44, 96.
Open 8am-8pm Mon-Fri; 9am-7pm Sat, Sun.
Map p122 A2 ⑱
Sweden's Crown Princess Victoria has been known
to frequent this place, although the famous cinnamon buns hardly need the royal seal of approval;
these gigantic pastries are out of this world. You
might have problems finding Saturnus, though –
there isn't a proper sign, just a model of the planet
hanging above the entrance. It's close to independent
cinema Zita (*see p156*), so it's packed with cinephiles
during evenings and weekends.

Gateau

Sturegallerian, Stureplan (519 791 01, www.
gateau.se). T-bana Östermalmstorg or bus 1, 2, 55,
56, 96. **Open** 7.30am-7pm Mon-Fri; 9am-6pm Sat;
11am-5pm Sun. **Map** p122 B4 ⑲
Hold on to your purse strings – sweet-toothed tourists could blow their holiday budget at Gateau,
purveyor of amazingly good cakes and pastries.
Spaciously spread out across the first floor of luxurious shopping centre Sturegallerian, Gateau has
several award-winning chefs on board. Prices are
deservedly high but the afternoon tea special (warm
scones, jam, marmalade and tea) won't break the
bank. There's also a small shop in the mall, on the
floor below, selling cakes and bread.
Other locations throughout the city.

Sturekatten

Riddargatan 4 (611 16 12, www.sturekatten.se).
T-bana Östermalmstorg or bus 2, 55, 96. **Open**
8am-7pm Mon-Fri; 8am-6pm Sat; 10am-6pm
Sun. **Map** p122 B4 ⑳

Riche.

If it ever stops serving fine coffee and cakes,
Sturekatten should be delicately preserved forever.
With two storeys of lace and antiques it's like an
18th-century doll's house. The house speciality is
apple pie with meringue, but it also serves delicious
semlor (whipped cream and almond-paste buns).
The waitresses don old-style black-and-whites and,
though it may sound like a pensioner's pleasure-
dome, it's actually just as popular with teenagers.
During the summer months, there's a pleasant little
courtyard terrace.
► *Free tables don't come easy here. If the queue*
is too unbearable, sister café Vete-Katten
(Kungsgatan 55, 20 84 05) in nearby Norrmalm
is worth a try to experience a similar taste of
old-fashioned hospitality.

Vurma

Birger Jarlsgatan 36 (611 00 45, www.vurma.se).
T-bana Östermalmstorg or bus 2, 43, 96. **Open**
11am-10pm Mon, Tue; 11am-11pm Wed-Fri;
11am-midnight Sat. **Map** p122 A3 ㉑
The lengthy menu here adds an exotic twist to the
usual sandwiches and snacks, catering imagina-
tively for both veggies and carnivores. The decor is a
1970s kaleidoscope of colour, with swirls of orange,
brown and green. The service is good, as is the grub,
and the soothing tunes tone down the brash interior.
Vurma's Kungsholmen branch has its own bakery,
while the Södermalm venue is a popular hangout for
local hipsters. Recommended.
Other locations Polhemsgatan 15-17,
Kungsholmen (08 650 93 50); Gästrikegatan 2,
Vasastan (08 30 62 30); Bergsundsstrand 31,
Södermalm (08 669 09 60).

Bars

East

Stureplan 13 (611 49 59, www.east.se). T-bana
Östermalmstorg or bus 1, 2, 55, 56, 96. **Open**
Bar 11.30am-3am Mon-Fri; 5pm-3am Sat, Sun.
Food served until 1am daily. **Minimum age** 23.
Map p122 B4 ㉒

A sushi restaurant by day, East turns into Stockholm's foremost hip hop and soul hangout by night. Two bars serve beer and cocktails, while a DJ plays hard-hitting beats for one of the most ethnically diverse crowds in the city. A small section of the first bar doubles as a dancefloor later. In summer, East offers an outdoor bar-terrace area with a lovely view of Stureplan. It can be difficult to get past the bouncers, so dress to impress and arrive before 10.30pm to avoid the hassle and the long wait.

Hotellet

Linnégatan 18 (442 89 00, www.hotelletsthlm.se). T-bana Östermalmstorg or bus 1, 55, 56, 62, 91. **Open** *Bar* 5pm-midnight Tue; 5pm-1am Wed, Thur; 11.30am-2am Fri; 5pm-2am Sat. *Food served* until 11pm. **Minimum age** 25. **Map** p122 C3 ㉓
Featured in international design magazines such as *Wallpaper**, Hotellet has become a hotspot for young urban professionals and posh partygoers alike. Its two storeys, plus an extra level upstairs, contain a total of four bars, plus a restaurant. The downstairs lounge heats up at night as the DJ sorts out pop and house music. In summer, Hotellet opens its Miami-style outside patio, with a handsome lawn and two bars (May-Sept). Queues lengthen around 11pm.

Laroy

Biblioteksgatan 23 (54 50 76 00, www.stureplansgruppen.se). T-bana Östermalmstorg or bus 1, 2, 55, 56, 96. **Open** *Bar* 10pm-3am Fri, Sat. **Minimum age** 20. **Map** p122 A4 ㉔
Rich kids in designer shirts flash platinum cards and order bottles of champagne at this posh, two-storey bar and restaurant. Although there's no dancefloor, people let loose on all available floor space as pop tunes pump through the speakers. Dress smart and arrive before 10.30pm to get in.

★ O-baren

Stureplan 2 (440 57 30, www.obaren.se). T-bana Östermalmstorg or bus 1, 2, 55, 56, 96. **Open** 7pm-2am Mon-Thur, Sat, Sun; 5pm-2am Fri. **Minimum age** 21. **Map** p122 B4 ㉕
A dark rock, hip hop and soul den in a back room of the exclusive Sturehof restaurant (*see p128*), Walking past the older restaurant crowd sat down for a classy dinner can feel awkward, but it adds to the thrill when you step into the dark rock, hip hop and soul den hidden in the back. O-baren has a bar and dancefloor bounded by bleacher-like seats but the place is small and can get overcrowded. Tuesday nights are a bit of a novelty here as the resident DJ hits the old 90s and 00s hip-hop like nobody in town. Although spontaneous dancing is commonplace, the clientele never loses its cool.

★ Riche

Birger Jarlsgatan 4 (54 50 35 60, www.riche.se). T-bana Östermalmstorg or bus 2, 55, 96. **Open** 11.30am-midnight Mon; 11.30am-2am Tue-Fri; noon-2am Sat; noon-midnight Sun. *Food served* until 11pm Sun, Mon; until midnight Tue-Sat. **Minimum age** 23. **Map** p122 B5 ㉖
A favourite with Stockholm's business, media and advertising professionals, Riche is more atmospheric than most Stureplan bars. Twenty- and thirty-somethings hang out in the smaller bar (Lilla Baren) with loud DJ music and spontaneous dancing. The larger bar-dining area features an older crowd who remember when Riche was the coolest place in town in the 1980s. The two queues get bad around 11pm at weekends.

Story Hotel

Riddargatan 6 (545 039 40, www.storyhotels.com). T-bana Östermalmstorg or bus 1, 2, 55, 56, 96. **Open** 6-11pm Mon, Sun; 6pm-midnight Tue; 6pm-1am Wed-Sat. *Food served* until 10pm daily. **Minimum age** 22. **Map** p122 B4 ㉗
This is far from your average hotel lobby bar. Past the discreet and purposely scruffy entrance is a spacious Parisian-style lounge framed by raw concrete walls hung with art. During the week, when the bar isn't so crowded and the DJ isn't pumping up the volume, this is a place for real conversations, about art, life and love. Head up the stairs beyond the lobby for a lovely terrace area. Story Hotel attracts a slightly edgier crowd than neighbouring bars.

Shops & Services

Östermalm is best for luxury goods and posh delis. **Birger Jarlsgatan** is home to some of the big names of the fashion world. **Sibyllegatan** and **Nybrogatan** are key streets for interior design, while down on **Strandvägen** there are two legendary Swedish design stores: **Svenskt Tenn** and **Carl Malmstenbutiken**.

Afro Art

Nybrogatan 29 (667 26 58, www.afroart.se). T-bana Östermalmstorg or bus 56, 62, 91. **Open** 10.30am-6pm Mon-Fri; 11am-4pm Sat; noon-4pm Sun. **Map** p122 C4 ㉘ **Homewares & accessories**
A colourful collection of good-quality textiles, kitchenware, jewellery, ornaments, wash bags, masks, musical instruments and toys from all over Africa, as well as Asia and Latin America. Local craftsmen also work with textile designers from Stockholm to produce modern handicrafts.
Other location Hornsgatan 58, Södermalm (642 50 95).

Androuët Östermalmsgatan

Nybrogatan 6 (660 58 33, www.androuet.nu). T-bana Östermalmstorg or bus 62, 69, 91. **Open** 10am-6pm Mon-Fri; 10am-4pm Sat. **Map** p122 C5 ㉙ **Food & drink**
In 1909, Henri Androuët set up his first cheese store in Paris; the Stockholm outlet opened in 1997. In this excellent shop you'll find more than 100 different

EXPLORE

cheeses from all over France. Many are quite obscure, but all are outstanding.
Other location Götgatan 39, Södermalm (641 90 78).

Anna Holtblad

Grev Turegatan 13 (54 50 22 20, www.anna holtblad.com). T-bana Östermalmstorg or bus 1, 2, 55, 56. **Open** 10.30am-6.30pm Mon-Fri; 10.30am-4pm Sat. **Map** p122 B4 ⏢ **Fashion**
Anna Holtblad has been one of Sweden's top designers for the past 20 years. She's best known for her folklore-inspired knitwear.
Other location Kungstensgatan 20, Vasastan (458 93 00).

Asplund

Sibyllegatan 31 (662 52 84, www.asplund.org). T-bana Östermalmstorg or bus 56, 62, 91. **Open** 11am-6pm Mon-Fri; 11am-4pm Sat. **Map** p122 C4 ⏢ **Interiors**
The airy Asplund showroom is a good source of newly produced design classics, including furniture, rugs, glasswares and lighting, by Scandinavian and international designers. New for 2014 is a kitchens department.

Hedengrens Bokhandel

Sturegallerian, Stureplan 4 (611 51 28, www. hedengrens.se). T-bana Östermalmstorg or bus 1, 2, 55, 56, 96. **Open** 10am-7pm Mon-Fri; 10am-5pm Sat; noon-5pm Sun. **Map** p122 B4 ⏢ **Books**
Opened in 1898, Hedengrens is one of Stockholm's most famous bookshops. It specialises in novels and the arts, and half the stock is in English. Check out the English translations of Swedish authors such as Selma Lagerlöf, Torgny Lindgren and Astrid Lindgren. The fiction section also includes titles in Spanish, Italian, German, French, Danish and Norwegian. Ideal for browsing.
▶ *Sturegallerian (www.sturegallerian.se) houses a good range of upmarket stores, including branches of Björn Borg (for underwear, bags and shoes), J Lindeberg and Bang & Olufsen. The renowned Sturehof restaurant (see p128) is also here.*

Kurt Ribbhagen

Birger Jarlsgatan 2 (54 50 78 60, www.kurt ribbhagen.com). T-bana Östermalmstorg or bus 2, 55, 96. **Open** 9am-6pm Mon-Fri. **Map** p122 A3 ⏢ **Antiques**
Kurt Ribbhagen is the best antique silver shop in the city and is also handily located next door to the Stockholm branch of renowned Danish silversmith Georg Jensen.

Malmstenbutiken

Strandvägen 5B (23 33 80, www.malmsten.se). T-bana Östermalmstorg or bus 69, 76. **Open** 10am-6pm Mon-Fri; 10am-4pm Sat; noon-4pm Sun. **Map** p122 C5/6 ⏢ **Interiors**

High-quality furniture, textiles and light fittings by legendary Swedish designer Carl Malmsten. The shop, which is now run by his grandson Jerk Malmsten, sells classics from the 1950s and 1960s, as well as rugs and books.

★ Modernity

Sibyllegatan 6 (20 80 25, www.modernity.se). T-bana Östermalmstorg or bus 56, 62, 91. **Open** noon-6pm Mon-Fri; noon-3pm Sat. **Map** p122 C4 ⏢ **Interiors**
Scotsman Andrew Duncanson specialises in 20th-century Scandinavian design, including furniture, ceramics, glass and jewellery. If you're a fan of Alvar Aalto and Arne Jacobsen, then this place is a must.

Nordiska Galleriet

Nybrogatan 11 (442 83 60, www.nordiskagalleriet. se). T-bana Östermalmstorg or bus 52, 55, 62, 91, 96. **Open** 10am-6pm Mon-Fri; 10am-5pm Sat; noon-4pm Sun. **Map** p122 C4 ⏢ **Interiors**
In its large, fashionable home on Nybrogatan, Nordiska Galleriet stocks furniture, lights and gifts from Nordic and international designers. Both past masters (Alvar Aalto, Arne Jacobsen) and big contemporary names (Philippe Starck, Jonas Bohlin) feature.

Östermalms Saluhall

Östermalmstorg (www.ostermalmshallen.se). T-bana Östermalmstorg or bus 1, 2, 56, 62, 91. **Open** 9.30am-6pm Mon-Thur; 9.30am-7pm Fri; 9.30am-4pm Sat. **Map** p122 C4 ⏢ **Food & drink**
See p131 **Historical Hall of Plenty.**

★ Riddarbageriet

Riddargatan 15 (660 33 75). T-bana Östermalmstorg or bus 62, 91. **Open** 8am-6pm Mon-Fri; 9am-3pm Sat. **Map** p122 D5 ⏢ **Food & drink**
The best bread in Stockholm. The cakes are outstanding, too, but it's Johan Sörberg's sourdough loaves that the locals love. There are a handful of small tables inside and it's one of the few places in town that serves tea in a pot.

Scampi

Nybrogatan 20 (663 14 44, http://scampi.se). T-bana Östermalmstorg or bus 1, 42, 44, 56, 62, 91. **Open** 11am-6pm Mon-Fri; 11am-3pm Sat. **Map** p122 C4 ⏢ **Accessories**
The name of this Swedish swimwear label may not give an upmarket ring in English, but the colourful bikinis and swimming costumes are top quality (with prices to match), made with long-lasting materials and great attention to detail. There are shapes and sizes to suit a wide range of figures.

Sibyllans Kaffe & Tehandel

Sibyllegatan 35 (662 06 63, www.sibyllans.se). T-bana Östermalmstorg or bus 1, 42, 44, 56, 62, 91. **Open** 10am-6pm Mon-Thur; 10am-7pm Fri; 10am-4pm Sat. **Map** p122 C4 ⏢ **Food & drink**

When the wind comes from the south you can smell the heady fragrance of Sibyllans ten blocks away. This family-run shop dates back to World War I and the lovely interior hasn't changed much since. There's a vast range of teas from all over the world. Sibyllans' own blend, Sir Williams, is a mix of Chinese green teas.

Sturebadet
Sturegallerian 36, Stureplan (54 50 15 00, www.sturebadet.se). T-bana Östermalmstorg or bus 1, 2, 55, 56, 62. **Open** 6.30am-10pm Mon-Fri; 9am-7pm Sat, Sun. **Admission** annual membership from 15,000kr; day membership from 495kr. **Minimum age** 18. **Map** p122 B4 ⓵ **Spa**

Dating from 1885, swanky Sturebadet is the traditional upper-class and celeb favourite, next to the hub of their universe, Stureplan. It offers a gym with personal trainers, assorted massages, treatments and cures, a beautiful art nouveau pool, plus an extraordinary Turkish bath that can be rented for meetings with up to 20 people.

★ Svenskt Tenn
Strandvägen 5 (670 16 00, www.svenskttenn.se). T-bana Östermalmstorg or bus 69, 76. **Open** 10am-6pm Mon-Fri; 10am-4pm Sat. **Map** p122 C5 ⓸ **Interiors**
A Stockholm classic that should not be missed. Founded by Estrid Ericson in 1924, Svenskt Tenn is best known for the furniture and, in particular,

HISTORICAL HALL OF PLENTY
Östermalm's gourmet food hall has an illustrious past.

This gastronomic temple, referred to as both Östermalms Saluhall and Östermalmshallen, has been serving the city's gourmets since the 19th century. Located on the western side of Östermalmstorg, the food hall was set up by three bankers, and took just six months to construct. It had its own steam power station (providing electricity), sophisticated lighting and ventilation, and wonderfully decorative produce displays. However, despite the magnificence of the building, many stalls remained empty at first due to the high rents, leading to the food hall being bought up by the city government. The city's sly bureaucrats then introduced new hygiene laws to impose a ban on open-air trade on Östermalmstorg, meaning that there was little choice for the outdoor traders but to move into the hall. A stall, restaurant or café in Östermalms Saluhall soon became much sought after, and the place was frequented by chefs to the royal household, as well as ordinary folk.

Highlights from the 20 or so stalls, restaurants, wine bars and cafés include a wide variety of fresh bread from **Amandas Brödbod** (783 05 91), delicious chocolate treats from **Betsy Sandbergs Choklad** (663 63 05, www.betsysandberg.se), vegetables from **JE Olsson & Söner** (661 31 42), coffee and teas from Finnish brand **Robert's Coffee** (662 51 06, www.robertscoffee.com), top-notch Danish *smørrebrød* (open sandwiches) from **Nybroe Smørrebrød** (662 23 20, www.nybroe.se), and excellent fish and seafood (including restaurant meals) at **Melanders Fisk** (662 45 79, www.melanders.se), classic meeting place **Gerdas Fisk & Skaldjursrestaurang** (553 404 40, www.gerdas.se), and the highly acclaimed **Lisa Elmqvist Fisk** (see p125). The square outside has a handsome flower stall and an open-air café, **Lisapåtorget** (www.lisapatorget.se).

For the food hall's address and opening hours, see p130.

EXPLORE

the textiles created by Josef Frank, who worked for the company for 30 years after joining in 1934. His designs are still the mainstay of the shop's products, which are expensive but exquisite. *See also pp200-205* **Swedish Design**.

GÄRDET

Functionalist apartment complexes were built for working people in Gärdet and its northern neighbour, **Hjorthagen**, in the 1930s. The apartments are now mainly inhabited by middle-class residents and students. The stately complexes of the **Försvarshögskolan** (Swedish National Defence College) and the **Kungliga Musikhögskolan** (Royal College of Music) are located next to each other on the northern side of Valhallavägen. Just across Lidingövägen (the main road north-east to the island of Lidingö) stands historic **Stockholms Stadion**, built for the 1912 Olympic Games. It was designed by architect Torben Grut in National Romantic style to resemble the walls surrounding a medieval city, and its twin brick towers are a striking landmark.

Ladugårdsgärdet is part of **Ekoparken** (58 71 40 41, www.ekoparken.com), the world's first National City Park, which also includes Djurgården, Hagaparken, Norra Djurgården and the Fjäderholmarna islands. Mainly open grassland and woods, with a few scattered buildings, this portion of the park stretches for about two and a half kilometres (four miles) to the waters of Lilla Värtan, on the other side of which lies the island of **Lidingö**. Stockholmers come here to picnic, jog, ride horses or just get a taste of the countryside.

Nearer Östermalm is the 'Museum Park', a cluster of three museums: the **Sjöhistoriska Museet**, **Etnografiska Museet** and **Tekniska Museet**. Keen sightseers could try to visit the lot in one day.

Further east is the **Kaknästornet** broadcasting tower, rising up from the forest like a giant concrete spear. Ascend to the observation deck at the top of the tower for a fantastic view right across the city; high-altitude refreshments are available in the tower's restaurant and café.

If you follow Kaknäsvägen, the road that runs past the Kaknäs tower, north-east towards the water, you will come to a dirt trail in the forest to your right that winds around the scenic shoreline of **Lilla Värtan**. A 100-year-old pet cemetery with dogs, cats and a circus horse lies to the right of the trail.

Sights & Museums

Etnografiska Museet

Djurgårdsbrunnsvägen 34 (10 456 12 00, www. etnografiska.se). Bus 69. **Open** 11am-5pm Tue,

Thur-Sun; 11am-8pm Wed. *Guided tours & workshops* call or check the website for details. **Admission** 80kr; free under-19s. **Map** p133 D3 ㊳
The dimly lit ground floor of the exotic-looking National Museum of Ethnography features masks, musical instruments and religious objects from seven holy cities (Auroville, Benin, Benares, Jerusalem, Yogyakarta, Beijing and Teotihuacan). Traveller's Trunk is a collection of artefacts brought home by Swedish explorers, the oldest of which were seized by the pupils of Swedish botanist Carl Linnaeus on their travels with Captain Cook. There's a wide variety of colourful exhibits, beautifully displayed. When you're tired of feeling thoughtful, beers and teas of the world are served at the mellow Babjan restaurant. In the summer, the restaurant lends bamboo mats for sitting outside. You can also reserve a place for a tea ceremony in the authentic Japanese tea house situated in the garden. There's also a small museum shop selling ethnic toys, trinkets and books. There are lots of family-oriented workshops on offer, with activities ranging from recycled sculpture-making to African dance.

Kaknästornet

Mörka kroken 28 (667 21 80, www.kaknastornet. se). Bus 69. **Open** *Lift & shop* Feb-Mar 10am-5pm Mon; 10am-9pm Tue-Sat; 10am-6pm Sun. Apr-May, Sept-Dec 10am-9pm Mon-Sat; 10am-6pm Sun. June-Aug 9am-10pm Mon-Sat; 9am-7pm Sun. *Café & Skybar* Feb-May, Sept-Dec 10am-5pm Mon-Thur; 10am-9pm Fri, Sat; 10am-6pm Sun. June-Aug 9am-10pm Mon-Sat; 9am-7pm Sun. *Restaurant* times vary; check website. **Admission** 55kr; 20kr reductions; free under-7s & with restaurant reservation. Free with SC. **Map** p133 D3 ㊴
For an utterly spectacular aerial view of Stockholm and its surroundings, visit this 155m (510ft) tower – one of Scandinavia's tallest buildings. On a clear day you can see up to 60km (37 miles) from its observation points up on the 30th and 31st floors. Nearer to hand are the island of Djurgården to the south, Gamla Stan and downtown to the west, and the beginning of the archipelago out to the east. Designed by Bengt Lindroos and Hans Borgström, the rather ugly concrete structure was completed in 1967 and still transmits radio and TV broadcasts. On the ground floor, the Stockholm Information Service operates a visitor centre and gift shop. Lunch and dinner are served on the 28th floor.

Sjöhistoriska Museet

Djurgårdsbrunnsvägen 24 (51 95 49 20, www. sjohistoriska.se). Bus 69. **Open** 10am-5pm Tue-Sun. *Guided tours* 2pm daily. **Admission** free. **Map** p133 C3 ㊵
Hundreds of model ships are displayed within the long, curved National Maritime Museum, designed in 1936 by Ragnar Östberg, the architect behind Stockholm's famous Stadshuset (*see p138*). It's an extensive survey – as it should be, considering

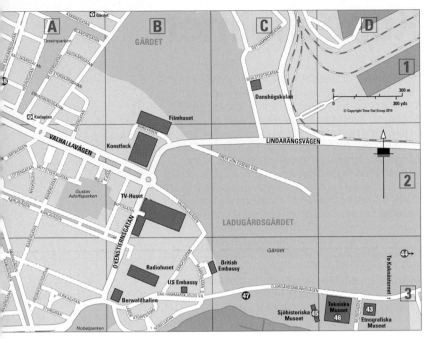

Sweden's long and dramatic maritime history. Two floors of minutely detailed models are grouped in permanent exhibitions on merchant shipping, battleships and ocean liners. Ship figureheads depicting monsters and bare-breasted women decorate the museum walls, and the upper floor displays two ships' cabins from the 1870s and 1970s. In the basement, the children's room Saltkråkan offers ships and a lighthouse to play in and, aside from a short summer break, a kids' workshop runs on Saturdays (11.30am-4pm; 30kr per child).

Tekniska Museet

Museivägen 7 (450 56 00, www.tekniskamuseet.se). Bus 69. **Open** 10am-5pm Mon, Tue, Thur, Fri; 10am-8pm Wed; 11am-5pm Sat, Sun. *Miniature railway* 11am, 2pm Mon-Fri; noon, 3pm Sat, Sun. **Admission** (incl Telemuseum) 120kr; 40kr reductions; free under-7s. *Cino 4* 80kr; 40kr reductions; free 5-8pm Wed. Free with SC (museum only). **Map** p133 D3 **46**

Inquisitive kids and adults can roam for hours at the Museum of Science and Technology, which has exhibits and activities intended to entertain and educate – and they do. Sweden's oldest steam engine, built in 1832, dominates the large Machine Hall, where aeroplanes – including one of Sweden's first commercial aircraft from 1924 – hang from the ceiling above bicycles, engines and cars. Cino 4 (Sweden's only 4-D movie theatre) has daily shows in English.

Restaurants

★ Villa Källhagen

Djurgårdsbrunnsvagen 10 (665 03 00, www. kallhagen.se). Bus 69. **Open** 11.30am-2pm, 5-10pm Mon-Fri; 7am-10.30am, 11.30am-2pm, 5-10pm Sat; *Brunch* noon-2pm, 2.30-4.30pm Sun. **Main courses** 180kr-260kr. **Brunch** 225kr. **Map** p133 C3 **47 Traditional Swedish**

A dining experience of the first order, where typical Swedish dishes, with a European twist, are transformed into works of art at this house set in beautiful parkland. In summer you can sit outdoors to eat and then stroll along the water. In autumn and winter there's a fire blazing in the hearth. The popular brunch blends Asian treats with a typical Swedish *smörgåsbord*. For the hotel of the same name on the premises, *see p219*.

Shops & Services

Ejes Chokladfabrik

Erik Dahlbergsgatan 25 (664 27 09, www. ejeschoklad.se). T-bana Karlaplan or bus 1, 4, 62, 72, 91, 94. **Open** 10am-6pm Mon-Fri; 10am-3pm Sat. **Map** p133 A1 **48 Food & drink**

The mocha nougat and Irish coffee truffles alone are worth the trip to this traditional chocolatier, which was established in 1923. Everything is made by hand without preservatives. Call to book a tasting.

Kungsholmen

The majestic Stadshuset (City Hall), an architectural gem visible from far and wide, faces visitors as they cross Stadshusbron from Norrmalm, and the city's famous landmark tends to leave the rest of the island in its shadow. It's most famous for hosting the 1,300 or so guests who are lucky enough to be invited along to the annual Nobel Prize banquet, held on 10 December after the prizes have been awarded at Konserthuset.

While what lies beyond Stadshuset is a fairly nondescript mix of apartments, shops and offices, Kungsholmen does also have a sprinkling of tranquil parks and some good neighbourhood restaurants, plus a few hip outposts worth the trek. The island is within a whisker of a Swedish mile (6.2 miles/ten kilometres) in circumference, and the island's waterside walkways are popular with joggers seeking a run with a view.

EXPLORE

Rålambshovparken.

Don't Miss

1 Stadshuset The majestic City Hall is Stockholm's most prominent landmark (p138).

2 Mälarpaviljongen Idyllic waterside views and a floating bar (p141).

3 AG Restaurang Nose-to-tail eating in an industrial space (p139).

4 Rålambshovparken This waterside park is a hive of activity in summer (p136).

5 Mäster Anders Classic brasserie with a cool neighbourhood vibe (p139).

Golden Hall, Stadshuset. *See p138.*

KUNGSHOLMEN

The quickest way to get to **Stadshuset** is to walk across Stadshusbron bridge from Norrmalm – though navigating the roads and railway lines leading from Central Station can be a bit of a nightmare. The Stadshuset is on your left – it's gigantic and hard to miss – and the former Serafimerlasarettet hospital is on your right. Continue on down Hantverkargatan and you'll reach **Kungsholms Kyrka**, a 17th-century church with a Greek cross plan and a park-like cemetery. Two blocks further on, a right on to Scheelegatan puts you on one of Kungsholmen's major thoroughfares, packed with restaurants and bars.

Further down Scheelegatan, at the corner of Bergsgatan, squats the city's gigantic, majestic **Rådhuset** (courthouse), designed by Carl Westman (1866-1936), a leading architect of the National Romantic School. Completed in 1915, it was designed to look like 16th-century Vadstena castle in southern Sweden, but also has art nouveau touches. There are no guided tours, but you can take a look around the public areas, including the lovely cloister-like garden.

Continuing west on Bergsgatan, you arrive at **Kronobergsparken**, a pleasant hillside park with Stockholm's oldest Jewish cemetery in its north-west corner. To the north of the island the **Tullmuseet** (Customs Museum) is inside the Customs Office on Alströmergatan. Nearby is one of Stockholm's trendiest interior design shops, **R.O.O.M.**.

Kungsholmen's shops tend to offer a fairly bland retail diet, but an increasing number of individual treats have popped up of late. Kungsholmen's main shopping streets are **St Eriksgatan** and **Fleminggatan**, at their most plentiful around the Fridhemsplan Tunnelbana station. Music lovers head to the former for its second-hand CD and vinyl shops. If you work up an appetite, stop for coffee and cakes at **Thelins**, an excellent *konditori*. Alternatively, the bright and airy **Västermalmsgallerian** shopping mall, on the corner of St Eriksgatan and Fleminggatan, offers a decent array of Sweden's favourite brand names.

The huge but strangely elegant double-spanned **Västerbron** bridge (1935) connects Kungsholmen with Södermalm across the expanse of Lake Mälaren. It's heavily trafficked, but you'll get a spectacular view of Stockholm from the centre of the bridge.

Marieberg, the area on Kungsholmen just to the north of the bridge, once contained military installations and a porcelain factory, but is now the city's newspaper district. Two of the four Stockholm dailies – *Dagens Nyheter* and *Expressen* – have offices here. The *Expressen* building, designed by Paul Hedqvist, is prominent, soaring to 82 metres (270 feet).

The flat green lawns of adjoining **Rålambshovparken** were created in 1935, at the same time as Västerbron; the sculpture-studded park is popular with runners, picnickers and hipsters, and there's a small sandy beach just along the shore at Smedsuddsbadet.

Walking and cycling paths line the northern and southern shores of Kungsholmen. For a beautiful view across the water, stroll from the Stadshuset along tree-lined **Mälarpromenaden**. Vintage boats and yachts moor here, and there are a couple of well-placed cafés en route. **Norr Mälarstrand**, the road that runs alongside the promenade, is lined with grand apartment blocks, built in the early 20th century when the factories had finally departed. Look out particularly for No.76, which was designed by Ragnar Östberg, architect of Stadshuset.

Sights & Museums

FREE Rålambshovparken
West of Västerbron bridge. T-bana Thorildsplan or Fridhelmsplan. **Map** p137 D2 **❶**

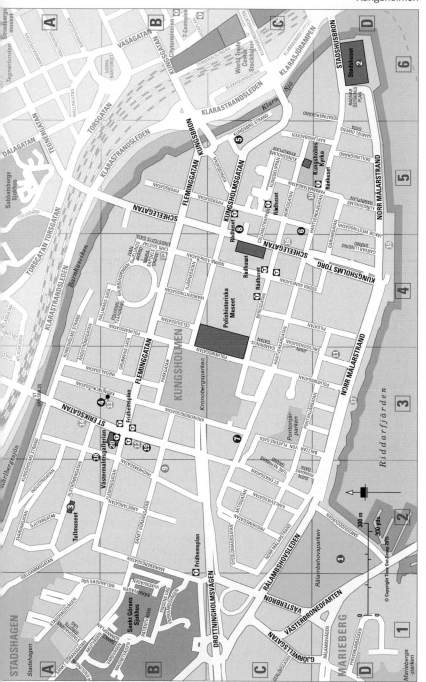

Kungsholmen

EXPLORE

© Copyright Time Out Group 2013

Time Out Stockholm **137**

This well-used lakeside park comes alive in summer – a popular boules bar opens, and the climbing walls and skate park under Västerbron bridge are at their busiest. The plentiful trails around the park are popular with joggers, and there's also an amphitheatre on the eastern side, built in the 1950s and used for open-air concerts, theatre and children's shows.

★ Stadshuset

Hantverkargatan 1 (50 82 90 58, www.stockholm. se/stadshuset). T-bana Rådhuset or T-Centralen or bus 3, 62. **Open** *Stadshuset* (guided tours only; tours are in English) Apr-Sept 10am, 11am, noon (and Swedish), 1pm, 2pm (and Swedish), 3pm daily. June-Aug every half hour 9.30-4pm. No prior booking. *Tower* May-Sept 9.15am-3.55pm daily; 9.15am-5.15pm June-Aug. Closed Oct-Apr. **Admission** *Guided tour* Jan-Mar, Nov-Dec 70kr. Apr-Oct 100kr. *Tower* 40kr; free under-11s. Free with SC. **Map** p137 D6 ❷

The City Hall (1923), Stockholm's most prominent landmark, stands imposingly on the northern shore of the bay of Riddarfjärden. A massive red-brick building, it was designed by Ragnar Östberg (1866-1945) in the National Romantic style, with two inner courtyards and a 106m (348ft) tower. It's most famous for hosting the annual Nobel Prize banquet, an event held in the Blue Hall on 10 December. The hall – which is designed to look like an Italian Renaissance piazza – was meant to be painted blue, but Östberg liked the way the sun hit the red bricks and changed his mind. The hall is also the home of an immense organ, with more than 10,000 pipes and 138 stops.

In the astonishing Golden Hall upstairs, scenes from Swedish history are depicted on the walls in 18 million mosaic pieces in gold leaf. The artist, Einar Forseth (1892-1988), covered the northern wall with a mosaic known as the 'Queen of Lake Mälaren', representing Stockholm being honoured from all sides. The beamed ceiling of the Council Chamber,

---

SUMMER WATERING HOLES

Stockholm's boat and pontoon bars come alive with the sunshine.

EXPLORE

The southern edge of Kungsholmen is home to several boat bars and restaurants, the full opening of which is a clear signal that the summer season is under way. **Flyt** (*see* *p141*), previously located near the Slussen locks at the edge of Gamla Stan, is now docked at Norr Mälarstrand, a ten-minute walk west from Stadshuset, and often packed to the gills in summer. Nearby is **Pontonen**, the floating bar and lounge of quayside Italian restaurant Trattorian (Kajplats 464, 50 52, 44, 54, www.trattorian.se).

Mälarpaviljongen (*see p141*), slightly further west on the same stretch, was once a simple summer restaurant, but has branched out with a vast pontoon with a hugely popular bar. The designer furniture, elevated sofa deck, flowers and olive trees bring together the best Scandinavian design has to offer. It's Miami Stockholm-style, with heated floors to boot. The view of Riddarfjärden is great. On the downside, drinks are steep. But if you're only going to try one floating bar in Stockholm, make this the one.

Though not as busy as its northern equivalent, Söder Mälarstrand, across the water, is home to one of Stockholm's most famous boat bars. **Patricia** (*see p159*), best known for its gay nights on Sundays, serves up a major party on summer nights and winter weekends. The boat was launched in 1938 from Smith's Shipyard in Middlesbrough, and once worked as a lightship in the English

Channel. Winston Churchill spent time on the ship during the war and the 35-seat private room has been named in his honour. In its current state, *Patricia* is a restaurant, bar and sleezy but fun nightclub all fused into one. It features four dancefloors and as many as seven bars on four levels in summer.

On Södermalm's hip south-eastern edge is **Restaurang Loopen** (Hornstulls Strand 6, 84 42 85, www.loopen.se), a Caribbean-influenced summer pontoon bar and restaurant in Hornstulls Strand, with a Swedish food menu, a long list of cocktails and a party-focused vibe. For a more grown-up and moneyed crowd, meanwhile, head east for **Strandbryggan** (Strandvägskajen 27, 660 37 14, www.strandvagen.se), located right beside the bridge for Djurgården. It offers coffee, salads, a bistro-style à la carte menu, and low-key DJs on some evenings.

Mälarpaviljongen.

where the city council meets every other Monday, resembles the open roof of a Viking longhouse. The furniture was designed by Carl Malmsten. The opulent Oval Room, which is part of the guided tour, is a popular place for Swedish nuptials. Such is the demand, it's a speedy marriage merry-go-round as couples tie the knot in a no-frills 40-second ceremony. The extended version is three minutes.

You can only visit the interior of the Stadshuset by guided tour, but you can climb the tower independently. Follow a series of winding red-brick slopes then wooden stairs for a fantastic view over Gamla Stan. Three gold crowns – the Tre Kronor, Sweden's heraldic symbol – top the tower. At the edge of the outdoor terrace below the tower, by the waters of Riddarfjärden, are two statues by famous Swedish sculptor Carl Eldh (1873-1954): the female *Dansen* (Dance) and the male *Sången* (Song). For refreshments, a cafeteria-style restaurant serves up classic Swedish dishes at lunchtime, while the Stadshuskällaren cellar restaurant offers the previous year's menu from the Nobel banquet. *Photo p136.*

FREE Tullmuseet

Alströmergatan 39 (653 05 03, www.tullverket.se/ museum). T-bana Fridhemsplan or bus 1, 3, 4, 77. **Open** 11am-4pm Tue, Wed, Sun. **Admission** free. **Evening tours** (pre-booked; 50kr, 40kr reductions) 6-8pm Tue, Wed, Sun. **Map** p137 A2 ❸

The most interesting part of the Customs Museum is its section on smuggling. The oldest exhibits date from the 1920s and '30s when alcohol was smuggled in from Estonia and Finland. One of the oldest pieces is a pair of XXL knickers dating from the 1920s, with secret pockets to conceal canisters filled with 96% proof spirit, home-made by a lady caught by Swedish customs (a gurgling noise was heard by officers). Other methods for concealing contraband included bread, sofas and teddy bears. In 1622, a fence and tollbooths (*tull*) were built around Stockholm to raise money for the wars of King Gustav II Adolf, and the museum displays a copy of one of these, as well as an early 20th-century customs office.

Restaurants

★ AG Restaurang

2nd floor, Kronobergsgatan 37 (41 06 81 00, www.restaurangag.se). T-bana Fridhemsplan or bus 1, 3, 4, 56, 77, 91, 94. **Open** 5pm-1am Mon-Sat. **Main courses** 195kr-625kr. **Map** p137 B3 ❹ **Contemporary**

This is a place for meat lovers – the first thing you see upon entering the industrial-style space are large fridges filled with chunks of cured produce. Head chef Johan Jureskog, something of a celebrity in Stockholm, is known as a keen follower of nose-to-tail eating. The menu also includes classics from the French and Swedish kitchens, with full flavours to the fore. The tapas bar is a good spot for some appetisers before being seated. For a review of the bar, *see p140.*

AG Restaurang.

Hong Kong

Kungsbro Strand 23 (653 77 20, www.restaurang hongkong.com). T-bana Rådhuset or bus 1, 40, 52, 56, 91. **Open** 11am-10pm Mon-Fri; 1-10pm Sat, Sun. **Main courses** 145kr-268kr. **Map** p137 C5 ❺ **Asian**

This is one of only a few places in Stockholm serving authentic Chinese food. Owner Sonny Li delivers spicy Cantonese and Sichuanese dishes from the giant gas stove. Apart from the stir-fry dishes, there's an ambitious array of steam-cooked choices. The speciality is Peking duck – Chinese business folk (and the King, no less) all come here for the red-glazed bird, which must be ordered two days in advance.

Mäster Anders

Pipersgatan 1 (654 20 01, www.masteranders.se). T-bana Rådhuset or bus 3, 40, 52, 62. **Open** 11.15am-midnight Mon-Fri; 1pm-midnight Sat; 5-11pm Sun. **Main courses** 192kr-489kr. **Map** p137 C5 ❻ **Brasserie/Grill**

With traditional decor (black-and-white floor tiles, big mirrors, round tables and globe hanging lights) and well-executed dishes, Mäster Anders is very much the classic brasserie. As good for a quick bite as it is for a full dinner, it's a popular spot. Highlights are the seafood and chargrilled dishes.

Roppongi

Hantverkargatan 76 (650 17 72, www.roppongi.se).
T-bana Fridhemsplan or bus 3, 40, 49, 62. **Open**
11am-10pm Mon-Fri; 5-10pm Sat, Sun. **Main**
courses 120kr-245kr. **Map** p137 C3 **7 Asian**
Roppongi serves the best sushi in this part of town,
plus decent tempura and *gyoza*. It's always crowded,
especially the few tables outside in the summer. You
can always order takeaway sushi and walk down to
the water at nearby Rålambshovsparken.

Spisa Hos Helena

Scheelegatan 18 (654 49 26, www.spisahoshelena.
se). T-bana Rådhuset or bus 1, 3, 40, 52, 56, 62, 91.
Open 11am-midnight Mon-Fri; 4pm-midnight
Sat; 4-11pm Sun. **Main courses** 185kr-270kr.
Map p137 C5 **8 Contemporary**
A home from home for many locals, serving straightforward, delicious, meat-focused Modern European
cuisine. *Toast skagen* is on the shortlist of starters,
while mains feature the likes of grilled rack of lamb
with fresh herbs, served with rocket and feta salad,
and grilled entrecôte with spinach and fennel salad.

Cafés

Bagel Deli

St Göransgatan 67 (716 11 40, www.bageldeli.se).
T-bana Fridhemsplan or bus 1, 3, 4, 40, 49, 62.
Open 7am-9pm Mon-Thur; 7am-8pm Fri, Sat;
9am-8pm Sun. **Map** p137 B2 **9**
This school of bagel wizardry wouldn't look out of
place in New York. They're keen on cream cheese
here, but there's a feast of other fillings on the menu.
Otherwise, the salads are stomach-stuffing, there's
always something typically Swedish and seasonal
on the menu, and the lattes and freshly baked cakes
are some of the best in town.

IN THE KNOW
STARVATION ISLAND

During the 1640s, craftsmen, labourers and
factory owners were lured to Kungsholmen,
then mostly fields, by the promise of a ten-
year tax break. The island soon became
home to all of the smelly, fire-prone and
dangerous businesses that nobody else
wanted. Unsurprisingly, given the conditions,
many residents became ill, and Sweden's
first hospital, the Serafimerlasarettet,
was built here in the 1750s. During the
Industrial Revolution, conditions hit an
all-time low – its diseased, starving
inhabitants earned Kungsholmen the
nickname 'Starvation Island'. The factories
finally left the island in the early 1900s,
to be replaced by government agencies,
offices and apartment buildings.

Bageriet Bulleboden

Parmmätargatan 7 (653 05 42). T-bana Rådhuset
or bus 3, 62. **Open** 7.30am-5pm Tue-Fri; 10am-4pm
Sat. **Map** p137 C5 **10**
This gorgeous little café is conveniently situated
right beside the Tunnelbana exit. The entrance is a
slightly perilous set of steps down into a cosy little
cavern. Boasting the best carrot cake in Stockholm,
this is the perfect place to hole up on a winter's day.

Petite France

John Ericssonsgatan 6 (618 28 00). T-bana
Rådhuset or bus 3, 62. **Open** *Bakery/café* 8am-
6pm Mon-Fri; 9am-5pm Sat, Sun. *Bistro* 6-11pm
Tue-Sat. **Map** p137 D3 **11**
This bakery, café and bistro is known for its mouthwatering array of both French and Swedish breads,
buns and cakes, but it also offers classic French lunch
dishes (croque monsieur or madame, quiche lorraine,
omelettes), and bistro classics in the evening.

Thelins

St Eriksgatan 43 (651 19 00, www.thelinskonditori.
se). T-bana Fridhemsplan or bus 1, 3, 4, 49. **Open**
7am-8pm Mon-Thur; 7am-7pm Fri; 8am-6pm Sat,
Sun. **Map** p137 B3 **12**
This traditional *konditori* is the place to sample the
finest sweet Swedish delicacies. Thelins sells the
very best *semlor* in Stockholm. Pick up a numbered
ticket on your way in, and don't be afraid to ask the
staff for advice on what to order.
Other locations throughout the city.

Bars

AG Bar

2nd floor, Kronobergsgatan 37 (410 68 100,
www.restaurangag.se). T-bana Fridhemsplan
or bus 1, 3, 4, 56, 77, 91, 94. **Open** 5pm-1am
Mon-Sat. **Map** p137 B3 **13**
AG doesn't have its own street entrance. Instead,
patrons must pass through the door of a seedy office
building (next to a porn shop) and climb two flights
of stairs to reach the entrance. Inside, the look is very
cool – tiled white walls offset by brown Chippendale
couches and dark designer furniture. The clientele is
a mix of trendy artist types and designer suits.

Dovas

St Eriksgatan 53A (650 80 49). T-bana Fridhemsplan
or bus 1, 3, 4, 56, 77, 91, 94. **Open** *Bar* 11am-1am
daily. *Food served* until 10am. **Map** p137 A3 **14**
Dovas is easily one of the most unsettling dives in
Fridhemsplan. Its darkened interior with wooden
booths houses a bizarre mix of local drunks and others too young to get into trendier places with higher
minimum ages. Tattoos and shaved heads are commonplace, as are random conversations that start
with an accusation and end with some inebriated
barfly putting his arm round your shoulder. The
beer is dirt cheap at around 40kr for a half-litre glass.

Flyt

Norrmälarstrand Kajplats 464 (21 37 29, www.flyt. se). T-bana Rådhuset or bus 3, 40, 52, 62. **Open** 3pm-1am Mon-Thur; noon-1am Fri-Sun. *Food served* until 10pm. **Minimum age** 18. **Map** p137 D4
This restaurant-bar, previously moored in Gamla Stan, is made to look like an old steamboat, but is in fact nothing more than a decked-out pontoon. *See also p138* **Summer Watering Holes**.

Lokal

Scheelegatan 8 (650 98 09, www.lokallemon.se). T-bana Rådhuset or bus 3, 40, 52, 62. **Open** *Bar* 4pm-1am Mon, Tue; 4pm-2am Wed, Thur; 4pm-3am Fri, Sat. *Food served* until closing time. **Minimum age** 23. **Map** p137 C4
When Lokal first opened a few years back, everyone compared it to Storstad (www.storstad.se) in Vasastan. Both have similarly stylish modern interiors, enormous shopfront windows, L-shaped bars and guest DJs playing soul and house. However, Lokal is (as the name implies) more of a local venue.

★ Mälarpaviljongen

Norr Mälarstrand 64 (650 87 01, www. malarpaviljongen.se). T-bana Frihemsplan or Rådhuset or bus 3, 40, 52, 62. **Open** *Apr-June, Sept-Oct* 11am-midnight daily. *July, Aug* 11am-1am daily (weather permitting). *Food served* until 11pm daily. **Map** p137 D3
This hugely popular alfresco bistro-bar on the shore of Lake Mälaren is one of the prettiest spots in Stockholm to enjoy a latte, beer, glass of wine or even a full meal, with a waterside setting that takes in a gazebo, a floating bar and fabulous views of Södermalm and Långholmen. *See also pp157-159* and *p138* **Summer Watering Holes**.

Shops & Services

★ Grandpa

Fridhemsgatan 43 (643 60 81, www.grandpa.se). T-bana Fridhemsplan or bus 1, 3, 4, 40, 49, 62. **Open** 11am-7pm Mon-Fri; 11am-5pm Sat; noon-4pm Sun. **Map** p137 A3 **Fashion**
The sister shop to the Södermalm fashion-forward favourite (*see p107*) has the same range of trendy menswear and womenswear labels, plus retro knickknacks and homewares. But this branch trumps the other by housing a lovely café, Sixten & Frans (www.sixtenfrans.se), serving breakfast and lunch dishes, plus decent coffee.

Hugo

St Eriksgatan 39 (652 49 90, www.hugo-sthlm. com). T-bana Fridhemsplan or bus 1, 3, 4, 40, 49, 62. **Open** 10.30am-7pm Mon-Fri; 11am-4pm Sat; noon-4pm Sun. *July* 10.30am-6pm Tue-Fri; 11am-4pm Sat. **Map** p137 B3 **Fashion**
Fashion-conscious men who don't worry about paying a little extra to look a little extra get everything from underwear to suits at Hugo. Staff hand-pick a few garments from international labels every season, so this is the place to find something exclusive. Swedish designer label Tiger is also sold here.

Västermalmsgallerian

St Eriksgatan 44 (696 32 00, www.vastermalms gallerian.se). T-bana Fridhemsplan or bus 1, 3, 4, 49. **Open** 10am-7pm Mon-Fri; 10am-5pm Sat; 11am-5pm Sun. **Map** p137 B3 **Mall**
This pleasant mall includes an ICA Supermarket, Björn Borg, FACE Stockholm, Granit, DesignTorget and many others. Café Dubbel W in the entrance is busy all day long.

EXPLORE

Grandpa.

Further Afield

Though Stockholm's central districts contain enough diversions to entertain visitors for weeks, there are several attractions further out of town. The first of these is Hagaparken, just north of Vasastan – a popular outdoor destination with lawns, woodlands and 18th-century buildings. Moving east from here, you'll know you're in Frescati – a cluster of scientific and academic institutions on the eastern shore of Brunnsviken – by the sound of Roslagsvägen, a thoroughfare that cuts through its northern side. The lovely Bergianska Trädgården, north-west of here, is an idyllic horticultural retreat.

Lidingö, north-east of the city centre, is an island of suburban tranquillity, largely populated by Stockholm's wealthier classes. Several of the city's southern districts, including Liljeholmen, Midsommarkransen and Hammarby Sjöstad, have been the focus of gentrification in recent years.

Lux Dag för Dag

Don't Miss

1 **Bergianska Trädgården** Fantastic flora at this botanical garden (p145).

2 **Lux Dag för Dag** Creative cooking and laid-back lounging (p147).

3 **Naturhistoriska Riksmuseet** Dinosaurs and more (p145).

4 **Millesgården** Bronze statues in a brilliant setting (p146).

5 **Nalle & Kroppkakan** Dumpling delight (p147).

Bergianska Trädgården.

HAGA & AROUND

The legacy of King Gustav III and architect Fredrik Magnus Piper, the romantic English-style **Hagaparken** features meandering paths, scenic views and assorted pavilions. It forms part of a broader Stockholm national park, christened **Ekoparken** (www.ekoparken.org) in 1995 by the Swedish parliament. Tagged as the world's first national park within a city, Ekoparken consists of 27 square kilometres (ten square miles) of land and water, cutting a diagonal green swathe across the city from the island of Djurgården in the south-east to Ulriksdals Palace in the north-west.

In Haga's northern section, the **Fjärilshuset** conservatory is full of exotic butterflies and tropical rainforest vegetation. To the south, three colourful copper tents form **Koppartälten**. Built as Gustav III's stables and guards' quarters, it now houses a restaurant, café and the **Haga Park Museum** (27 42 52, www.visithaga.se, free admission), which contains an interesting pictorial history (all text is in Swedish) of the park and its buildings. The 'ruins' of a palace left incomplete after Gustav III's assassination in 1792 are east of the tents. Sweden's current king, Carl XVI Gustaf, was born in nearby **Haga Slott** (0171 41 47 00, www.sejour.se), a castle now converted into a hotel and conference centre. Other buildings include the waterfront **Gustav III's Paviljong** (402 61 30, www.royalcourt.se), with Pompeii-style interiors by 18th-century interior decorator Louis Masreliéz. It's only

open for guided tours in summer (June-Aug noon, 1pm, 2pm, 3pm Tue-Sun, 100kr). You can also test the acoustics in the outdoor **Ekotemplet**, which was originally used as a summer dining room. The 18th-century obsession with the exotic is evident in the Chinese pagoda and Turkish pavilion in the south of the park. A small island nearby (May 1-3pm Sun, June-Aug 9am-3pm Thur) has been the burial place of Swedish royalty since the 1910s.

On the southern tip of Hagaparken, enjoy a meal or brunch at **Haga Forum** (Annerovägen 4, 833 48 44, www.viljagruppen.se/hagaforum), a bus terminal turned modern restaurant with a terrace overlooking the park and water.

Sculptures by Swedish artists stand in **Norra begravningsplats** (Northern Cemetery), an elaborate 19th-century cemetery to the west across the E4 highway and north of Karolinska Sjukhuset hospital. Alfred Nobel, August Strindberg and Ingrid Bergman lie amid its hedges and landscaped hills.

Bus 3 or 59 will take you to Karolinska Sjukhuset from where you can walk to southern Hagaparken. For northern Haga, take the T-bana to Odenplan then bus 515 to the Haga Norra stop.

NORTHERN FRESCATI

On the west side of the highway (cross under the viaduct) is the **Royal Swedish Academy of Sciences**, and beyond that, the lovely gardens and conservatories of **Bergianska Trädgården**, which borders Brunnsviken.

On the east side stands the **Naturhistoriska Riksmuseet**, while to the south, in Frescati, lies the sprawling campus of **Stockholm University**, relocated from cramped city quarters to this site in 1970. From the campus, head east to Ekoparken's **Norra Djurgården** for hiking, horse riding or bird watching, or take a ten-minute walk west to **Brunnsviksbadet**, a local beach, where you can swim or rent canoes.

You can get to northern Frescati on the T-bana to Universitetet, then walk north for about seven minutes. Alternatively, take the Roslagsbanan commuter train, which leaves from Stockholm's Östra station near the Tekniska Högskolan. Get off at Frescati station: the gardens and museum are directly to the west and east, respectively.

Sights & Museums

Bergianska Trädgården
Gustafsborgsvägen 4, Frescati (545 917 00, www.bergianska.se). T-bana Universitetet or bus 40, 540. **Open** *Gardens* 24hrs daily. *Edvard Andersons Växthus* Apr-Sept 11am-5pm daily; Oct-Mar 11am-4pm Mon-Fri, 11am-5pm Sat, Sun. *Victoriahuset* May-Sept 11am-4pm Mon-Fri; 11am-5pm Sat, Sun (June-Aug open Thur until 8pm). Closed Oct-Apr. **Admission** *Gardens* free. *Edvard Andersons Växthus* 60kr. *Victoriahuset* 20kr. Free under-15s. Free with SC.
Botanists and picnickers will love this botanical garden on a hilly peninsula by Brunnsviken. The Royal Swedish Academy of Sciences, which still conducts research here, moved the garden from Vasastan to this waterfront area in 1885. Orchids and vines fill Victoriahuset, a small conservatory (1900); its pond contains giant water lilies, measuring up to 2.5m (8ft) across. The more recent Edvard Andersons Växthus, an all-glass conservatory, contains Mediterranean plants and trees in its central room, and flora from Australia, South Africa and California.

Naturhistoriska Riksmuseet
Frescativägen 40 (51 95 40 00, www.nrm.se). T-bana Universitetet or bus 40, 540. **Open** 10am-6pm Tue-Fri; 11am-6pm Sat, Sun (June-Aug 10am-6pm Mon). **Admission** *Museum* 100kr; 70kr reductions; free under-18s. *IMAX* 100kr; 70kr reductions; 50kr 5-18s. *Museum & IMAX* 150kr; 105kr reductions. Museum free with SC.
Founded in 1739, the National Museum of Natural History is the largest museum complex in Sweden. More than nine million biological and mineral samples are stored in this monolithic brick building designed in 1907 by Axel Anderberg, architect of the Royal Opera. Beneath the black-shingled roof and light-filled cupola stands an exceptionally well-made tableau of extinct creatures, prehistoric man and Swedish wildlife. Visitors enter the dinosaur exhibit through a dark volcanic room. The hands-on exhibits about space include a red Martian landscape and a

spaceship's cockpit. Sweden's only IMAX cinema, the Cosmonova (*see p156*), is also here, showing movies about the natural world on its huge screen.

LIDINGÖ

The main attraction here is **Millesgården**, the former home and studio of sculptor Carl Milles. Lidingö is also the birthplace of Raoul Wallenberg, the World War II diplomat who disappeared mysteriously in 1945 while in Soviet custody. Sculptures around the island have been erected in his honour. Lidingö is popular with outdoor enthusiasts: there's golf near Sticklinge and at Ekholmsnäs; cycling and jogging paths, which become cross-country ski trails in winter, at Stockby Motionsgård; and one of the nearest downhill ski slopes to Stockholm at the 70-metre high (230-foot) Ekholmsnäsbacken, south of

Naturhistoriska Riksmuseet.

the Hustegafjärden inlet. The beach at Fågelöuddebadet, in Lidingö's north-east corner, has a café and miniature golf course, as do the Breviksbadet outdoor pools in the south.

Sights & Museums

Millesgården

Heserudsvägen 32 (446 75 90, www.millesgarden. se). T-bana Ropsten then bus 207 or bus 201, 202, 204, 205, 206, to Torsvik Torg then walk. **Open** *May-Sept* 11am-5pm daily. *Oct-Apr* 11am-5pm Tue-Sun. **Tours** (in English) *June-Aug* 1.15pm Tue, Thur; price included in entrance fee. **Admission** 100kr; 80kr reductions; free under-19s. Exhibition prices vary; check website for details. Free with SC. Works by sculptor Carl Milles are displayed at his home, which he donated to the state in 1936. His bronze statues stand alongside works by other artists on wide stone terraces, and the hilltop setting provides a dramatic backdrop of sky, land and water. The house is decorated with paintings and antiques purchased by Milles on his travels – the largest private collection of Greek and Roman statues in Sweden.

THE SOUTHERN SUBURBS

Directly south of Södermalm, and attached by the Skanstullsbron bridge, is the district of Johanneshov, which is home to one of Stockholm's landmarks, the Ericsson Globe (popularly known as **Globen**). The sports arena is apparently the world's largest hemispherical building.

The areas to the west, south and east of Södermalm are home to a large number of high-density suburbs that have been growing in popularity in recent years, partly due to residents being financially squeezed out of Stockholm's centre. The districts closest to the centre are Liljeholmen, Midsommarkransen and Hammarby Sjöstad, and the islands Lilla Essingen and Stora Essingen. The latter two, which sit below western Kungsholmen, are former industrial zones that house many apartment blocks, as well as Henrik Norström's lovely restaurant **Lux Dag för Dag**. The streets around nearby Liljeholmen and Midsommarkransen, meanwhile, are now home to an increasingly youthful and creative crowd, many of whom call *kroppkakor* restaurant **Nalle & Kroppkakan** their local. Over on the south-eastern side is Hammarby Sjöstad, a modern, harbourside residential district.

Sights & Museums

Färgfabriken

Lövholmsbrinken 1, Liljeholmen (645 07 07, www.fargfabriken.se). T-bana Liljeholmen or bus 133, 152, 161. **Open** *Exhibition Hall* 11am-7pm Thur; 11am-4pm Fri, Sat. *Café* 11am-4pm Wed-Sun. **Admission** 60kr; 50kr reductions; free under-18s. Free with SC.

Globen.

The Centre for Contemporary Art and Architecture occupies an important position on the Stockholm art scene. Founded in 1995, it is housed in an old factory, with one main exhibition space, plus three smaller rooms. Recent projects have included a music installation by Talking Head David Byrne, and exhibitions by Liz Cohen, Peter Geschwind and Natalie Djurberg. Its outdoor space puts on weekly music and food events in the summer.

Globen
Arenavägen, Johanneshov (600 91 00, box office 077 131 00 00, www.globearenas.se). T-bana Globen. **Box office** 9.30am-6pm Mon-Fri; 9.30am-5pm Sat, Sun (hours vary during hols). *By phone* 9am-6pm Mon-Fri; 10am-2pm Sat, Sun.
With a capacity of just under 14,000, the futuristic Globen hosts major competitions in tennis, ice hockey, handball, showjumping and floorball (*innebandy*), as well as concerts and other big events. It's also home to the Djurgården ice hockey team. Globen's Skyview attraction (*see p50*) is a new way to see the city from above.

Restaurants

★ Lux Dag för Dag
Primusgatan 116, Lilla Essingen (619 01 90, www.luxdagfordag.se). T-bana Liljeholmen or bus 133, 152, 161. **Open** 11.30am-2pm, 5-11pm Tue-Fri; 5-11pm Sat. **Main courses** 215kr-295kr.
Modern Scandinavian
Celebrity chef Henrik Norström boldly changed his Michelin-starred Lux Stockholm restaurant into the more laid-back and budget-friendly Lux Dag för Dag in 2013, and its focus on the freshest ingredients and a creative, daily-changing menu has been drawing in Stockholm's foodies. At the back of the beautiful red-brick building is the restaurant's 'Lux Walk Through' mini-market area (11.30am-7pm Tue-Fri), where you can buy fruit and vegetables, dishes from the menu, meat and fish, flowers, cakes and takeaway coffees.

Nalle & Kroppkakan
Svandammsvägen 41, Midsommarkransen (752 99 33, www.nalleokroppkakan.se). T-bana Midsommarkransen. **Open** 11am-2.30pm, 4.30-10pm Tue-Thur; 11am-2.30pm, 4.30-10.30pm Fri; 1-10.30pm Sat; 1-9pm Sun. **Main courses** 139kr. **Swedish**
This relaxed restaurant specialises in *kroppkakor* – traditional Swedish potato dumplings served with melted butter and lingonberry jam. The pork varieties are the most popular, but the vegetarian wild mushroom-filled versions are also delicious. You can elect to have your dumplings steamed or fried; the former is more traditional, but the latter gives a richer taste. The interior is nicely decked out with black tables, chequered floors and a huge landscape photo, though the outside tables are the place to be in summer.

Nalle & Kroppkakan.

Arts & Entertainment

Children

Children – and parents – will find themselves very well looked after in Stockholm, one of the most child-friendly cities in the world. Thanks to a healthy attitude towards children and an extensive social welfare policy, the young are generally taken care of and respected within Swedish society. If your family likes to spend time outdoors, as the Swedes do, Stockholm offers wide pavements, plenty of open green spaces and a beautiful location on the water. In winter, when the lakes are frozen, you'll even see parents skating across the ice pushing prams. In the warmer months, head out to the island of Djurgården, an urban national park. As well as acres of grass to run around on, it contains most of the city's best kids' attractions. It's also mostly traffic-free, and there are ample opportunities for exploring on foot or by bike, bus or tram.

ATTRACTIONS

Fjärilshuset & Haga Ocean

Haga Trädgård, Hagaparken (730 39 81, www.fjarilshuset.se). T-bana Odenplan then bus 515. **Open** 10am-5pm daily. **Admission** 135kr; 70kr-100kr reductions; free under-4s. Free with SC. In a beautiful setting at the northern end of historic Hagaparken (*see p144*), the fantastic Butterfly House – all 850sq m (3,050sq ft) of it – is the closest you'll get to a tropical rainforest in Stockholm. Mingle with free-flying exotic butterflies and birds, or check out the pond full of koi carp and the Asian garden. A new attraction, Haga Ocean, opened within the complex in 2013; this 30m (98ft) shark tank is the largest of its kind in Scandinavia, housing large and small reef sharks as well as colourful fish. There's also a child-friendly café in the adjacent greenhouse offering an extensive menu for children.

★ Gröna Lund

Allmänna Gränd, Djurgården (708 70 00, www.gronalund.se). Bus 44, or tram 7, or ferry from Slussen or Nybroplan. **Open** *May-late Sept* days & times vary; call or check website for details. *Late June-mid Aug* typically 10am-11pm Mon-Thur, Sat; 10am-10pm Sun. Closed end Sept-end Apr. **Admission** 110kr; free under-6s

& over-65s; one-day bracelet (all rides) 310kr. Free with SC. **Map** p242 J11.
Perched on the edge of Djurgården with fantastic views across the water, Gröna Lund is Sweden's oldest amusement park. Built in 1883 and owned by the same family ever since, its historic buildings and well-preserved rides retain an old-world charm. Older (and tamer) favourites such as carousels, bumper cars, Ferris wheels and a funhouse are on offer alongside more modern (and daring) rides such as Europe's highest free-fall 'power tower'. *Harry Potter* fans will appreciate the park's Kvasten (Broomstick) ride, a family rollercoaster that carries riders on suspended carriages beneath the tracks, feet dangling in the air, giving them the sensation of flying on a magic broomstick. New rides over the past few years include the Twister, a classic wooden rollercoaster, and the Blå Tåget (Blue Train) ghost train. The park is also a baby-friendly place, with pram ramps on all the stairs and a Happy Baby Centre for feeding and soothing tots. Note that on concert nights it costs 220kr to get in.

★ Junibacken

Galärvarvsvägen, Djurgården (58 72 30 00, www.junibacken.se). Bus 44, 69, or tram 7, or ferry from Slussen or Nybroplan. **Open** *Jan-Apr* 10am-5pm Tue-Sun; *May, June* 10am-5pm daily;

July, Aug 10am-6pm daily. **Admission** 145kr; 125kr reductions; free under-2s. Free with SC. **Map** p242 G10.

A favourite haunt of local kids and a top tourist attraction, Junibacken is a mini indoor theme park devoted to wild-child storybook character Pippi Longstocking and other characters created by Swedish author Astrid Lindgren. Lindgren, who died in 2002, was the country's most famous and beloved children's author, whose daughter Karin inspired the idea for Pippi when she asked her mother to tell her a story when she was ill. Lindgren published the first Pippi Longstocking book in 1945, and in 1946 became the children's books editor at Rabén & Sjögren, where she worked until her retirement. A prolific, multi-faceted and radical author, she wrote some 80 books, including children's and young adult fiction, detective novels, fairytales, TV scripts, and fiction that blended a variety of genres. She was also a fierce and outspoken campaigner, and fought for, among other causes, a more child-centred educational system.

Junibacken is formed around a fairytale train ride (ask for narration in English) that crosses miniature fictional landscapes, flies over rooftops and passes through quaint Swedish houses (the last train departs 45 minutes before the park closes). On the upper floor, kids are welcome inside Pippi's house, Villa Villekulla, where they can dress up like Pippi, slide down the roof and wreak general havoc. Stories by other writers feature, too, and activities include storytelling and visits from some of the storybook characters. For those who are unfamiliar with Swedish children's books, there's a very good shop that carries many of the better-known titles in translation.

IN THE KNOW OUT AND ABOUT

The city is ideal for parents of babies and younger kids. All new buses graciously bow to street level, giving parents with prams easy access; bus travel is also free for one adult with a child in a pram. Under-sevens travel free on buses, the Tunnelbana and commuter trains, and at weekends (noon on Friday to midnight on Sunday) up to six children under the age of 12 ride for free with an accompanying adult. Although there are no restaurants specifically aimed at kids, most cafés and restaurants provide highchairs, children's menus and help with warming baby food. If you're planning to visit a lot of museums, it might be worthwhile investing in a **Stockholm Card** (www.visit stockholm.com); you can buy a maximum of three child cards per adult card.

★ Skansen & Skansen Akvariet

Djurgårdsslätten 49-51, Djurgården. Bus 44, or tram 7, or ferry from Slussen or Nybroplan. **Map** p243 H12-J12.
Skansen *(442 80 00, www.skansen.se).* **Open** *Jan, Feb, Nov, Dec* 10am-3pm Mon-Fri; 10am-4pm Sat, Sun. *Mar, Apr, Oct* 10am-4pm daily. *May-mid June* 10am-7pm daily. *Mid June-Aug* 10am-10pm daily. *Sept* 10am-6pm daily. **Admission** 65kr-170kr; 25kr-60kr reductions; free under-6s. Free with SC.
Skansen Akvariet *(666 10 00, www.skansen-akvariet.se).* **Open** *May* 10am-5pm Mon-Fri; 10am-6pm Sat, Sun. *1st 3wks June* 10am-6pm

Gröna Lund.

Mon-Fri; 10am-7pm Sat, Sun. *Midsummer-end July* 10am-8pm daily. *Aug* 10am-6pm Mon-Fri; 10am-7pm Sat, Sun. *Sept-Dec* 10am-4pm Mon-Fri; 10am-5pm Sat, Sun. *Christmas* 10am-4pm Sat, Sun. **Admission** 120kr; 60kr reductions; free under-6s. Free with SC.

Skansen is a zoo, aquarium, amusement park and museum rolled into one. Young children might find the old buildings a bit dull, but the animals are always a hit. The regular zoo specialises in Nordic animals, among them brown bears and wolves. At the children's zoo, Lill-Skansen, kids can pet Swedish farm animals. Adventurous kids can also pet snakes and spiders in the small aquarium (Akvariet; separate entrance fee). The charming Galejan amusement park has rides dating back to the 19th century. Every Wednesday from May to September is children's day, and kids can find a host of activities laid on for their amusement. Other diversions include Jazz on Mondays (from 6pm), 'sing-a-long Tuesdays' (10am-8pm), guided pony rides, horse and carriage rides and a mini-train ride. Some sights are only open during the summer.

▶ *The Skansenshop, located just outside Skansen, sells a lovely range of hand-crafted traditional Swedish products, including kitchen and garden tools, pottery, jewellery, clothing and foodstuffs.*

MUSEUMS

The **Vasamuseet** (*see p90*) on Djurgården, with its amazingly preserved 17th-century warship, is a surefire hit for children over six who like (very) big boats. For a more hands-on experience, take the kids on board the two museum ships moored outside – the ice-breaker *St Erik* (summer months only) and the light ship *Finngrundet*, which has recently reopened after a three-year restoration; entrance to these is included in the Vasamuseet fee. Also nearby is the free-to-enter **Båthall 2** (Boat Hall 2), displaying a collection of boats from the 18th to the 20th centuries.

Kids who love anything on wheels will enjoy the **Spårvägsmuseet** (Transport Museum; *see p102*) on Södermalm, where they can clamber into many of the vintage buses, train cars and trolleys, and play at driving a tram. A good option for older kids is **Naturhistoriska Riksmuseet** (Swedish Museum of Natural History; *see p145*) just north of Stockholm; as well as a Martian landscape and the regulation dinosaurs, the museum also houses an IMAX cinema.

The child-friendly former Musikmuseet (Music Museum) is now closed and will reopen in 2016 as the **Scenkonst Museet** (Swedish Museum of Performing Arts). In the 17th-century vaulted cellar of **Lilla Posten** (the 'Little Post Office' at the Postmuseum; *see p48*), children can load a postal van with packages or create and post their own postcards in a replica 1920s post office scaled down to child size. Any budding artists in the

Eriksdalsbadet.

family can drop into the **Moderna Museet** (*see p94*) for a creative crafts/building session for 7-14s led by museum staff (1pm Sundays; kids free on an adult ticket).

Nordiska Museet

Djurgårdsvägen 6-16, Djurgården (51 95 46 00, www.nordiskamuseet.se). Bus 44, 69, 76, or tram 7, or ferry from Slussen or Nybroplan (only in summer). **Open** 10am-5pm daily. **Admission** 100kr; free under-18s. Free with SC. **Map** p242 G11.

In the Lekstugan ('Playhouse') at Sweden's museum of cultural history, you can travel back in time to 1895 through the museum's vivid recreation of life in the Swedish countryside. Kids over five can try their hand at different occupations at the farm cottage, the mill, the stable and the general store. They can touch and use all the exhibits, including antique objects. The museum is recommended for children aged five to 12 (must be accompanied by an adult). *See also p88.*

Tekniska Museet

Museivägen 7, Gärdet (450 56 00, www.tekniska museet.se). Bus 69. **Open** 10am-5pm Mon, Tue, Thur, Fri; 10am-8pm Wed; 11am-5pm Sat, Sun. **Admission** 120kr; 40kr-125kr reductions; free under-7s & before 5pm Wed. *Cino4* (cinema) 80kr; 40kr reductions. Free with SC. **Map** p243 G14.

Sprawling across three floors, the Museum of Science and Technology is sure to keep inquisitive minds busy for hours. Although highly pedagogical, it's more like a funhouse than a museum, and a great place for babies, kids and adults alike. The Minirama room will have babies cooing at special mirrors, blocks and assorted toys; in the Teknorama area, small kids can discover how machines work by using their own bodies (such as running in a huge wheel to generate electricity). For older children the machinery hall has aeroplanes suspended from the ceiling, steam-driven cars and a 1927 Harley-Davidson. The museum is also home to Sweden's first multi-sensory cinema, Cino4 (separate admission), unveiled a few years ago; kids sit in special seats that shake, rattle and roll, and are equipped with 3D glasses and a personal remote control for a joltingly interactive learning experience.

OUTDOORS

Stockholm has plenty of open spaces for active kids. The waterside **Djurgårdsbrons Sjöcafé** (www.sjocafeet.se), just across the bridge on Djurgården, doubles as a boat and bike rental company. You can hire paddleboats, rowing boats, canoes, kayaks, bicycles or in-line skates for a practical and fun way to explore the island and its various waterways. Heading further into the island, at **Rosendals Trädgård**, you'll find a small but charming playground built from logs and natural materials. You can eat at the outdoor café (see p92) or bring along a picnic. Further afield, there's glorious Hagaparken, whose delights include the butterfly house and shark aquarium **Fjärilshuset & Haga Ocean** (see p150).

If you want to experience the Stockholm archipelago, but don't have the time to explore it properly, tiny **Fjäderholmarna** island (see p180) is just a 20-minute boat ride away. Kids can visit an aquarium, explore a wooden playground in the form of a ship, and pet bunnies in the Trädgården. Lifejackets for your kids can be borrowed here if they want to play on the rocky shores. Boats to Fjäderholmarna are operated by **Strömma Kanalbolaget** (12 00 40 00, www.stromma.se, daily May-Sept, Tue-Fri Oct) from Nybroplan, and **Stockholms Ström** (611 40 00, www.stockholmsstrom.se, daily May-Sept), from Slussen.

In winter, head for the free outdoor ice-skating rinks (skates for hire) at **Kungsträdgården** (skates 60kr/hr adults, 30kr/hr under-20s) and **Medborgarplatsen** (see p98).

SWIMMING

If you're visiting Stockholm during a warm summer, forget the swimming pools – you can dive straight into the surprisingly clean water around the city (see p111 **In the Swim**). Note that lifeguards are definitely not a Swedish concept. If that sounds a little too chilly, try the beautiful Jugendstil **Centralbadet** bathhouse (see p70), or **Eriksdalsbadet** on the southern tip of Södermalm (see p99), which has indoor and outdoor pools, including a dedicated outdoor children's pool.

THEATRE, FILM & MUSIC

Children's theatre is hugely popular in Stockholm, and there are regular performances (mostly in Swedish) at **Dramaten, Stockholms Stadsteatern, Strindbergs Intima, Dockteatern Tittut** and **Marionetteatern** (for all, see pp166-171 **Performing Arts**).

If you're planning a trip to the cinema, remember that children's films are usually dubbed. The **Cosmonova IMAX** cinema (see p156) at the Naturhistoriska Riksmuseet offers earphones with English translation at screenings (usually documentaries; under-5s not admitted). Södermalm's arty **Bio Rio** cinema (see p156) puts on Babybio ('baby cinema') sessions.

The **Konserthuset** (see p167), one of Stockholm's main venues for classical music, features lots of child-focused events, including a Family Saturday series (normally at 2pm) during the school year, when Stockholm's Royal Philharmonic plays to a boisterous crowd of toddlers and kids. Expect classical and Swedish favourites, singalongs and guest appearances by clowns, magicians and other characters.

BABYSITTING

Hemfrid i Sverige

Rosenlundsgatan 13, Södermalm (02 00 11 45 50, www.hemfrid.se). **Open** 8am-5pm Mon-Fri.
This outfit offers an array of services, including babysitting, cleaning, laundry and cooking.

RESOURCES & ACTIVITIES

Rum för Barn, Kulturhuset

4th floor, Kulturhuset, Sergels Torg (information 50 62 02 73, library 50 83 14 16, www. kulturhusetstadsteatern.se/bibliotek/rum-for-barn). T-bana T-Centralen or Hötorget or bus 52, 56, 59, 65. **Open** 11am-5pm Mon-Fri; 11am-4pm Sat, Sun. Workshop closes 30mins before Rum för Barn. **Admission** *library* free; *workshop* 30kr. **Map** p241 G7.
The 'Room for Kids' on the fourth floor of Kulturhuset (see p168), the city's main cultural centre, is dedicated to activities for children aged up to 12. The beautifully renovated children's library is the main attraction; its carefully designed reading areas each cater to children of different ages and abilities, and contain hundreds of books in English and other languages. There's an arts and crafts workshop and internet access just for kids in the library. Daily events (in Swedish), such as film screenings, storytelling and poetry readings, are tailored to different age groups. Before you even step into the building, a traffic light – visible in the library window from Sergels Torg outside – warns visitors of potential queues: red means full, yellow means queuing, and green means no waiting.

ARTS & ENTERTAINMENT

Film

Swedes have a real passion for the silver screen, with a healthy home-grown market and a long and varied filmmaking history. Which makes it all the more sad that several arthouse treasures – including Biblioteksgatan's Röda Kvarn (now an Urban Outfitters) and Nybrogatan's Astoria – have been forced to close their doors in the past few years, partly as a result of the recent monopoly by production/distribution house and cinema operator SF (Svensk Filmindustri). Several gems still remain, though.

In the sphere of film production, things look brighter. New funding initiatives have meant that much of the work has moved to production centres outside Stockholm – especially Film i Väst outside Gothenburg, now Scandinavia's major regional film organisation – and the number of films made per year is on the increase.

SWEDEN'S CINEMA HISTORY

In the 1920s, Sweden was among the world's leading filmmaking nations. Directors such as Victor Sjöström and Mauritz Stiller made an impact with films that were widely regarded as masterpieces at the time, and which are now considered to be classics. Several of these were based on books by Selma Lagerlöf (Nobel Prize laureate, 1909), including *The Phantom Carriage* (1921) and *The Treasure of Arne* (1919) by Sjöström, and *The Story of Gösta Berling* (1924) by Stiller (the film that catapulted Greta Garbo to fame). These films were groundbreaking as they were shot on location using nature as a key element, at a time when most films were still shot in studios.

The golden age of Swedish film was brief, though, as some of the industry's biggest stars were lured abroad – Sjöström, Stiller and Garbo all emigrated to Hollywood. The 1930s and '40s were characterised by rather provincial and burlesque comedies, and it wasn't until the early '50s that Swedish film again attracted the world's attention. Alf Sjöberg's version of Strindberg's play *Miss Julie* (1951) and Arne Mattsson's *One Summer of Happiness* (1952) stunned audiences in Venice and Berlin. At Cannes in 1956, Ingmar Bergman won international fame with *Smiles of a Summer Night*, and he remained in the spotlight throughout his filmmaking career (*see p155* **Death, Religion and Wild Strawberries**). But with the exception of Bergman, Swedish film wasn't especially fertile until the late 1960s, when government funding helped a new generation of talent to emerge. Directors such as Jan Troell, Bo Widerberg and Viglot Sjöman became big names in an increasingly politicised era of filmmaking.

In the 1980s, Stockholm-born Lasse Hallström drew the attention of the film world with his 1987 hit *My Life as a Dog*, which earned two Oscar

IN THE KNOW
TIMES AND TICKETS

Cinemas open one hour before the first screening (usually around 11am or 5pm). Most films are shown in their original language with Swedish subtitles. Tickets usually cost between 100kr and 120kr. Listings and information can be found in the daily papers or online.

DEATH, RELIGION AND WILD STRAWBERRIES

Ingmar Bergman is still the most prolific Swedish filmmaker of all time.

Ingmar Bergman began his creative life in the theatre, following the Scandinavian traditions of Ibsen and Stockholm's own August Strindberg. But Sweden's other great dramatist was always destined for the cinema. Bergman recalled 'listening' to the light falling through a window of his grandmother's house in Uppsala, and lovingly described the rickety film projector that he was given at the age of ten as 'my first conjuring set'.

The would-be conjurer grew up in the privileged district of Östermalm, the son of a pastor. A childhood spent amid the angels and devils of his father's sermons provided Bergman with a tangible sense of the spiritual 'to revolt against', and a fascination with morality and mortality that would remain a theme throughout his career. Perhaps the director's most recognisable image is that of the medieval knight playing chess with Death in *The Seventh Seal* (1956), iconic long before being parodied by Woody Allen and later in *Bill and Ted's Bogus Journey*.

Many of Bergman's early films take place in a medieval world defined by the uneasy co-existence of paganism and religion, culminating in *The Virgin Spring*, which won the Academy Award for Best Foreign Language Film in 1961. From then on, Bergman's thematic eye shifted from the allegorical past and ventured internally, with films like *Through a Glass Darkly* and *Persona* examining human faith and sexuality with an unflinching psychological honesty that has informed cinema ever since.

Though never a box-office draw in his homeland, Bergman famously despised Hollywood, calling it a 'ruthlessly efficient sausage machine'. Indeed, it was only his self-imposed exile from Sweden in 1976 over charges of tax evasion that saw him leave his beloved country (somewhat ironically he will feature on the new 200kr notes, which will be issued in 2015). Bergman returned in 1982 to direct *Fanny och Alexander* – which he said at the time would be his last film. He kept that promise for 20 years, then made *Saraband* (2003), a follow-up to his internationally successful TV series *Scenes from a Marriage*. He spent the last years of his life in Fårö, remaining active in the theatre until his death in 2007.

Visitors to Stockholm, and Bergman initiates, should watch *Wild Strawberries* (1957), one of his more accessible films, and a comedic love letter to the director's own teenage years spent in the archipelago.

ARTS & ENTERTAINMENT

IN THE KNOW BLUE MOVIES

Sweden has the largely undeserved reputation as the birthplace of pornographic film. Titles often referred to are: *Do You Believe in Angels?* (1961), *Dear John* (1964) and *I Am Curious: Yellow* (1967). These films were seen as extremely daring in their time, but by today's standards they are far from pornographic. Paradoxically, along with being the first makers of 'porn', Swedes have the oldest system of film censorship in the world, established in 1911.

nominations and a Golden Globe for best foreign-language film. US studios came calling, and the results have included *What's Eating Gilbert Grape*, *The Shipping News*, *Chocolat* and *Salmon Fishing in the Yemen*. Like so many foreign-language filmmakers before and after him – including Victor Sjöström and Lucas Moodysson – Hallström answered Hollywood's siren call and proved that Swedish filmmakers are able to adapt to the very different rules of US cinema.

An exciting new era in Swedish filmmaking began with Lukas Moodysson's excellent *Fucking Åmål* (also known as *Show Me Love*; 1998). He was the first to challenge the norm by making a very different film, one that took teenagers seriously. Moreover, Moodysson showed that such filmmaking was possible on quite a small budget. He has gone on to make several critically acclaimed films, including *Together* (2000) and, more recently, *We are the Best* (2013).

Tomas Alfredson, director of romantic-horror vampire movie *Let the Right One In* (2008), is another pioneer in contemporary Swedish filmmaking, while other notable names include Mikael Håfström, Daniel Espinosa, Teresa Fabik, Jesper Ganslandt, Reza Parsa and Josef Fares. The last two are among several young immigrant filmmakers to have gained recent international recognition, with *Before the Storm* (2000) and *Jalla! Jalla!* (2000) respectively. And in September 2014, Roy Andersson won the Golden Lion award at the Venice Film Festival for offbeat comedy *A Pigeon Sat on a Branch Reflecting on Existence*.

On a sadder note, Swedish documentary filmmaker Malik Bendjelloul, who shot to fame after winning a BAFTA and an Academy Award in 2013 for *Searching for Sugarman* (2012), died in 2014 at the tender age of 36.

CINEMAS

Biografteatern Rio

Hornstulls Strand 3, Södermalm (669 95 00, www.biorio.se). T-bana Hornstull or bus 4, 40. Map p249 L2.

Biografteatern Rio, formerly Kvartersbion, looks the same as it did in the 1940s. The cinema was extensively refurbished a few years ago, and now shows an eclectic range of indie and arthouse films.

Filmhuset

Borgvägen 1-5, Gärdet (665 11 00, www.sfi.se/filmhuset). T-bana Karlaplan or bus 56, 72, 76. Map p247 E12.
The Filmhuset, one of the city's largest cinemas, houses the Swedish Film Institute.

Filmstaden Sergel

Hötorget, Norrmalm (56 26 00 00, www.sf.se). T-bana Hötorget or bus 1, 56, 59. Map p241 F6.
With no fewer than 14 screens to choose from, this cinema, run by Svenska Bio Cinemas, is the place to go for a bustling multiplex atmosphere.

Skandia

Drottninggatan 82, Norrmalm (56 26 00 00, www.sf.se). T-bana Hötorget or bus 1, 53, 65, 69. Map p241 F6.
This eccentric cinema opened in 1923. Most of the interior, designed by architect Gunnar Asplund, is still intact. It's now run by Svenska Bio Cinemas and shows mainstream fare.

Sture

Birger Jarlsgatan 41A, Östermalm (56 29 48 80, www.biosture.se). T-bana Östermalmstorg or bus 2, 43, 96. Map p245 E7.
This three-screen cinema shows arthouse films, as well as more commercial fare. The curtain in Cinema One was made by Ernst Billgren, one of Sweden's most famous contemporary artists.

Zita Folkets Bio

Birger Jarlsgatan 37, Östermalm (23 20 20, www.zita.se). T-bana Östermalmstorg or bus 2, 43, 55, 56, 96. Map p245 E7.
One of the only cinemas in town with a bar, Zita screens films from all over of the world. It frequently shows documentaries and short films, and runs a 'people's choice' programme whereby customers can choose films they'd like to be screened (a minimum of ten tickets need to be sold).

IMAX

Cosmonova

Naturhistoriska Riksmuseet, Frescativägen 40, Northern Frescati (51 95 40 00, www.nrm.se/cosmonova). T-bana Universitetet or bus 40, 540. No under-5s admitted unless otherwise stated; check website for details.
This IMAX cinema is a paradise for families. Films shown on its 11m-tall (36ft) dome-shaped screen are usually nature-based, and worth seeing. Screenings are in Swedish only, so don't forget to buy an earphone for translation with your tickets.

Gay & Lesbian

In comparison with other European capitals, Stockholm's gay scene can seem underwhelming. There's no gay neighbourhood and few specific bars, and if you spend just a few days out and about you'll soon start to see the same faces. One reason for this lack of exuberance is that Stockholm is a thoroughly enlightened city. You'll see old married couples visiting gay cafés, while gay people take their straight mates out for a night of clubbing (and vice versa). There is less of a sense of a distinct gay life here, because if a bar or café or club is any good, everyone wants to go there. The trick with Stockholm is not to judge it on what it lacks, but to appreciate that what it offers is unique and wonderful. When the weather is good, the place can be magical. Standing on the deck of *Patricia* and watching the sun set (or rise) or going for a post-club swim in the centre of town – these are the sort of experiences that only Stockholm can deliver.

HOTELS

Two men or two women checking in to a Stockholm hotel together won't cause so much as a raised eyebrow. There are, however, a handful of hotels that actively court gay visitors. The **Lord Nelson** (*see p209*), **Lady Hamilton** (*see p208*) and **Victory** (Lilla Nygatan 5, 506 400 00,

www.thecollectorshotels.se) are a trio of upmarket properties with a historic maritime theme in Gamla Stan. Also in Gamla Stan is the five-star **First Hotel Reisen** (*see p209*). The **Rival** (*see p217*), on Södermalm, is stylish and handily located for Pride events. The lovely island of Skeppsholmen, meanwhile, is home to the very gay-friendly **Hotel Skeppsholmen** (*see p213*), a member of the Stockholm Gay & Lesbian Network. Other central design hotels that belong to this network include **Berns Hotel** (*see p211*), also home to Saturday gay club night Polari, the beautiful **Ett Hem** (*see p218*), **Hotel Hellsten** (*see p212*), **Lydmar Hotel** (*see p209*) and **Nobis Hotel** (*see p209*).

CAFÉS, RESTAURANTS & BARS

In addition to the venues listed here, **Magnolia** (*see p114*) is a gay-friendly café in Södermalm.

Bistro by Adam

Norrtullsgatan 43, Vasastan (89 74 51, www.byadam.se). T-bana Odenplan. **Open** 11am-10pm Mon-Thur; 11am-1am Fri; 11am-3am Sat. **Map** p245 C5.

IN THE KNOW GAY MEDIA

To find out what's happening, pick up **QX**, the excellent free gay newspaper. It's in Swedish but the listings are easy to follow. *QX* also produces an invaluable map of gay Stockholm, which is widely available at gay and gay-friendly bars and cafés. The *QX* website, www.qx.se, has a guide to the city in English (and also serves as the Swedish equivalent of Gaydar). You can also listen to Radio QX online. Other popular websites include **Sylvia** (www.sylvia.se) for women, and **Sylvester** (www.sylvester.se) for men. Both are in Swedish.

Pride

This popular, LGBT-friendly café-restaurant-bar has club-style modern decor (think black furniture, leather stool seating, chequerboard floors and bright coloured lights), a friendly vibe and a menu that includes a good number of Italian-inspired meat and pasta dishes.

★ Chokladkoppen

Stortorget 18, Gamla Stan (20 31 70, www.chokladkoppen.com). T-bana Gamla Stan or bus 2, 3, 43, 53, 55, 76, 96. **Open** *Winter* 10am-10pm Mon-Thur; 10am-11pm Fri; 9am-11pm Sat; 9am-10pm Sun. *Summer* 9am-11pm daily. **Map** p241 J7.
There's something wonderful about the fact that the world's best gay hot chocolate café (a narrow field, admittedly) is housed in one of Stockholm's most photographed buildings in the heart of Gamla Stan. As well as rich hot chocolate, there's also superb chocolate cake, white chocolate cheesecake to die for and huge sandwiches. Service can be slow and erratic, but it's generally worth the wait.

★ Mälarpaviljongen

Norr Mälarstrand 64, Kungsholmen (650 87 01, www.malarpaviljongen.se). T-bana Rådhuset or Fridhemsplan or bus 3, 40, 52, 62. **Open** *Apr-Oct* 11am-1am daily, weather permitting. Closed winter. *Food served* 11am-11pm daily. **Map** p240 H3.
This wonderful alfresco bistro-bar opened in 2004 and was an instant hit. The waterfront setting is lovely: a gazebo juts over the water and there's a floating bar. The crowd gets gayer as the hour gets later.

Naglo

Regeringsgatan 4, Norrmalm (10 27 57, www.naglo.com). T-bana Kungsträdgården or bus 2, 43, 55, 62, 65, 91. **Open** 9pm-3am Mon-Sat. **Map** p241 G7.
This tiny vodka bar is one of those places that falls into the blurry gay-straight category that's so common in Stockholm; the crowd tends to become gayer as the night wears on. It's known for playing schlager music, so on a good night it can be a great final destination.

Side Track

Wollmar Yxkullsgatan 7, Södermalm (641 16 88, www.sidetrack.nu). T-bana Mariatorget or bus 43, 55, 66. **Open** 6pm-1am Wed-Sat. **Map** p250 L7.
This subterranean bar and restaurant is a very popular choice with the T-shirt and jeans set. Side Track is not the least bit fashionable, and that suits the mostly male crowd just fine. It isn't for the claustrophobic, but if you're ready and willing to elbow your way to the bar and order a *stor stark* ('big, strong beer'), you'll enjoy yourself here.

Torget

Mälartorget 13, Gamla Stan (20 55 60, www.torgetbaren.com). T-bana Gamla Stan or bus 3, 53. **Open** *Bar* 5pm-1am daily (DJ sets Fri, Sat). *Kitchen* closes 10pm daily. **Map** p241 J7.
Torget remains the most popular gay bar in town and also the most cosmopolitan. For many gay visitors, it's their first port of call. It has a great location close to the T-bana station on Gamla Stan, friendly staff and excellent food – in the early evening or weekend lunchtime, it's one of the nicest places to dine in the Old Town. The bar has been resting on its laurels for

---

IN THE KNOW TAKING PRIDE

Stockholm's annual **Pride** celebration (see p32) is the largest in Scandinavia and usually takes place in late July or early August. The focus of activity is Pride Park, an enclosure set up in one of Stockholm's parks. Inside are a number of stalls set up by gay cafés and bars, plus a stage for pop concerts. To get in you need to buy a pass, known locally as a dog-tag. Other highlights of the event include a gay film festival, the coronation of the new Mr Gay Sweden and a parade through the city. For a full programme of events, see www.stockholmpride.org.

some time, but until a serious rival emerges it's still the best bet to start your weekend.

Whakapapa

Maskinistgatan 1, Gröndal (744 24 84), www.kafewhakapapa.se). T-bana Liljeholmen or bus 133, 152, 161. **Open** 9am-7pm Mon-Fri; 10am-6pm Sat, Sun. **Map** p249 M3.

The little sister venue of now-defunct lesbian café Copacabana (which closed in 2014) is just as laid-back and friendly, with 1970s-style decor, decent coffee, a sunny terrace and a menu serving scrumptious salads and sourdough bread.

CLUBS & CLUB NIGHTS

Stockholm's gay clubbing scene is pretty small, and different clubs dominate different nights. But one thing's for sure – everyone, absolutely everyone, goes to boat bar **Patricia** on a Sunday (which has now moved). At times it can seem as though Stockholm's entire gay population is on board. As a patron was once heard to remark: 'If this ship were to sink, you'd never be able to get a haircut in this town.'

As well as the clubs mentioned below, popular gay club nights include **Candy** at Le Bon Palais on Fridays (Barnhusgatan 12, Norrmalm, 10 09 32, www.lebonpalais.se, 11pm-4am, 140kr-160kr, over-20s), known for its stage shows; and **Honey** at Magenta on Saturdays (Regeringsgatan 61, Norrmalm, www.clubmagenta.se, midnight-5am, 140kr, 23 and over).

★ Patricia

Söder Mälarstrand, Berth 19, Södermalm (743 05 70, www.patricia.st). T-bana Mariatorget or bus 4, 66, 94. **Open** 5pm-midnight Wed, Thur; 6pm-5am Fri, Sat; 6pm-5am Sun (gay night). **Admission** 120kr after 9pm; 150kr after midnight. **Map** p241 K7.

The *Patricia* was built in Middlesbrough, and once served a stint as the royal yacht of Queen Elizabeth, the Queen Mother, but now it's established as one of the crown jewels of gay life in Stockholm. Every Sunday for the past 15 or so years, gays and lesbians have gathered here to eat, drink and dance on this three-level party boat, now moored at Söder Mälarstrand (due to construction works at Slussen). On Sundays food is heavily discounted, so book ahead to enjoy a delicious dinner that constitutes one of the best deals in town. The mood, food and crowd are all excellent; the views from the decks are the icing on the cake.

SLM

Wollmar Yxkullsgatan 18, Södermalm (643 31 00, www.slmstockholm.se). T-bana Mariatorget or bus 43, 55, 66. **Open** 7-11pm Wed; 10pm-2am Fri, Sat. **Admission** *membership* 400kr per yr; *non-members* 50kr after 11pm Sat. **Map** p250 L6.

Scandinavian Leather Men (SLM) is a basement leather bar that brings a little corner of Berlin to Stockholm. A heavy door and flight of stairs lead down to a labyrinth of darkrooms, bars and a dancefloor. To get in, you'll have to respect the international dress code of skinhead, military, leather, denim or construction style. Expect a cool, raw atmosphere – not for the limp of wrist or the faint of heart. Men only.

WONK

Kungsgatan 15, Norrmalm (no phone, www.wonk.se). T-bana Östermalmstog or Hötorget. **Open** 11pm-4am Wed; 11pm-5am Fri, Sat. **Admission** 60kr-140kr. **Map** p241 F7.

Wonk, the established Malmö gay club, opened a Stockholm venue not far from Stureplan in 2014. Known for its buffed-up barmen and mixed crowd, Wonk has two dancefloors with DJs playing pop, house and disco.

Patricia.

ARTS & ENTERTAINMENT

Nightlife

Thanks to Sweden's rather byzantine laws and regulations, you have to have a dance licence to have people dancing; in order to receive that, you have to have a drinking licence; in order to have that, you have to serve food. As a result, small and intimate music bars still rule the city's nightlife. But a few larger venues, with professional DJs, lavish visuals and proper dancefloors, have now established themselves on the scene.

Stockholm's music scene, meanwhile, is bigger than ever and, despite its out-of-the-way location, the city is a fertile ground for visiting bands from the UK and US. Then, of course, there are all the home-grown stars and wannabes. Although second-generation immigrants are making themselves heard more and more, when it comes to music you'll notice that Sweden is still very much a rock and pop country at heart.

CLUBS

Stockholm's nightlife is concentrated in the inner city, split between Stureplan, the hub of the town's VIP world of limos and neon, and Södermalm, the hip district where the former working-class inhabitants have been replaced by designers, DJs and musicians. Norrmalm sits in the middle for immortals. By contrast, Vasastan and Kungsholmen have mostly bars and cafés, while nightlife in Gamla Stan is a combination of the touristy and the gay scene. Note that there is some crossover between the nightclubs and music venues featured here.

Norrmalm

★ Berns Gallery 2.35:1

Berzelii Park (56 63 22 00, Ticnet 077 170 70 70, www.berns.se). T-bana Kungsträdgården or bus 2, 52, 55, 62, 69, 76, 96. **Open** 11pm-3am Wed; 11pm-4.30am Thur-Sat. **Minimum age** 20. **Admission** 225kr (in advance via Ticnet, only 50 tickets released per night). **Map** p241 G8.
This eccentric nightclub is located in the landmark Berns Hotel, one of the longest-running entertainment venues in the city. The club is a perfect mix of lavish and grunge, with a red carpet leading to the downstairs space. The music is mainly electronic, with gigs from both resident and guest DJs, while the door policy is strict – limited tickets are sold beforehand and if you're not on the guest list or in possession of a ticket, it's unlikely you'll get in. For restaurants Berns Asia and Berns Bistro, in the same complex, *see p66*.

★ Café Opera

Kungliga Operan, Karl XIIs Torg (676 58 07, www.cafeopera.se). T-bana Kungsträdgården or bus 2, 43, 52, 62, 76, 96. **Open** *Bar* 10pm-3am Wed-Sun. **Minimum age** 20. **Admission** (after 10pm) 220kr. **Map** p241 G8.
After a decade in the shadow of the places around Stureplan, Café Opera, which first opened in 1980, recently started to take back the crown as one of the party kings of Stockholm. The businessmen with ties round their foreheads and girls in tiny dresses are now outnumbered once more by music people, media folk, celebs and even the odd royal rumbling about. VIP tables take up much of the space, but the interior is grander than ever after a recent restoration. Costumed dancers add a special-occasion feel. Note that the entry queue can become unbearable in the small hours, so try to arrive before midnight.

Club Ambassadeur

Kungsgatan 18 (54 50 76 00, www.amba.se).
Open 10am-4pm Fri, Sat. **Minimum age** 21.
Admission varies. **Map** p241 F7.

Famous for its moshpit-style queue, Ambassadeur is a stone's throw from Stureplan and is a hotspot for house music fanatics. The club welcomes a typical Östermalm clientele and some of the world's most famous DJs – dress to impress. Once inside, the interior has an international club feel but falls short of the Ibiza lifestyle it's constantly trying to mimic.

★ Fasching

Kungsgatan 63 (53 18 29 60, www.fasching.se).
T-bana T-Centralen or bus 1, 53, 65, 69. **Open**
6pm-1am Mon-Wed; 6pm-3am Thur; 6pm-4am Fri,
Sat; 5pm-1am Sun (check website for concert times).
Minimum age 20 (18 for concerts). **Admission**
100kr-450kr. **Map** p240 F6.

There are gigs and jam sessions at this legendary jazz hangout six nights a week, but it's the late-night club nights at the weekend that really lift the roof. On Fridays, it's old and new R 'n' B, soul, boogie and house at Club Devotion. On Saturday it's Club Soul, a clubbing institution that packs the dancefloor with the best in funk, northern soul and disco. Tickets are also available from www.tickster.com. *See also p163.*

Kristall

Kungsgatan 56 (545 121 45, www.kristall stockholm.se). T-bana T-Centralen or bus 1, 53, 65, 69. **Admission** varies. **Map** p241 F6.

This huge three-storey nightclub is all about mainstream pop and house tunes. The main attraction is the upstairs terrace, offering a bar with comfortable seating and outdoor heaters. It's easy to get on to the

Café Opera.

club's guest list, and you'll be guaranteed entry as long as you're dressed reasonably smartly.

Södermalm

Debaser Medis (*see p164*) has daily club nights. For the **Kägelbanan** nightclub at cultural centre Södra Teatern, *see p164*.

F1-6 @ Fotografiska

Stadsgårdshamnen 22 (www.fotografiska.eu).
T-bana Slussen or bus 2, 3, 43, 53, 55, 71, 76.
Open 10pm-late 6 times a year; see website for upcoming dates. **Minimum age** 23. **Admission**
200kr-300kr. **Map** p251 L9.

The huge photography museum is a Stockholm mustsee, but what many don't know is that Fotografiska (*see p99*) is also home to one of the coolest club nights in the city. F1-6 (pronounced 'F one to six') is a six-sessions-a-year nightclub that brings in DJs and artists from around the world. Situated around the back of the museum, the industrial space has the sort of Berlin club vibe that Stockholm usually lacks. Tickets (from www.billetto.se/f1-fotografiska) tend to sell out quickly.

★ Marie Laveau: XXX Klubben

Hornsgatan 66 (668 85 00, www.marielaveau.se).
T-bana Mariatorget or bus 43, 55, 66. **Open**
9pm-3am Fri; 10pm-3am Sat. **Minimum age**
23. **Admission** 120kr after 11pm. Closed July.
Map p250 K6.

One of Södermalm's best club/bar venues, Marie Laveau – named after a New Orleans voodoo queen – is a packed basement where the sweat drips from the ceiling every Friday and Saturday. It has moved away from harder electronic beats to a friendlier house, soul and Britpop vibe in recent times; however, it's more about the buzzing atmosphere than the music here. Upstairs is a popular bar with decent happy hour prices and a short but sweet bar menu.

Trädgården

Hammarby Slüssvag 2 (644 20 23, www.
tradgarden.com). T-bana Skanstull or bus 55,
74, 94, 96. **Open** 5pm-1am Mon, Tue; 5pm-
3am Wed, Thur; 5pm-3am Fri; noon-3am Sat.
Admission free-170kr. **Map** p251 O8.

ARTS & ENTERTAINMENT

Trädgården means 'the garden', and that's pretty much what this is: an outdoor yard where you hang out playing games and sipping cold beer, grabbing some barbecue food before dancing under the stars (or the ceiling, if it rains). Needless to say, this is more of a summer hangout; after the summer season, the place closes for a month, then moves inside and opens weekends only as Under the Bridge (Underbron).

Östermalm

Hell's Kitchen

Sturegatan 4 (54 50 76 00, www.stureplans gruppen.se). T-bana Östermalmstorg or bus 1, 2, 55, 56, 96. **Open** midnight-5am Thur-Sat. **Minimum age** 21. **Admission** 250kr. **Map** p241 F8.

Formerly called Neu, this bar is a bit of a novelty for Stureplan as it's not just for posh brats and pretty girls, but also for music aficionados in their thirties who just don't want to go to bed (after 3am). The philosophy is 'rampant maximalism', hence the individual waitress service at every table.

Solidaritet

Lästmakargatan 3 (678 10 50, www.sldrtt.se). T-bana Östermalmstorg or bus 1, 2, 55, 56, 96. **Open** 11pm-5am Thur-Sat. **Minimum age** 25. **Admission** varies; check website for details. **Map** p241 F8.

Don't let the name fool you. Solidaritet (Solidarity) is the quintessential Stureplan bar/club with a long queue, steep cover charge, sleek *Miami Vice*-inspired interior and plenty of reserved tables – not to mention the best-looking people in town and the largest range of electronic and house DJs. The venue has two spacious levels and four bars. Dress to kill and arrive before 11pm to avoid the queue, and get your name on the guest list in advance to avoid the admission fee (see website for details).

Spy Bar

Birger Jarlsgatan 20 (54 50 76 00, www.stureplans gruppen.se). T-bana Östermalmstorg or bus 2, 55, 56, 91, 96. **Open** 11pm-5am Wed-Sat. **Minimum age** 23. **Admission** 90kr-120kr. **Map** p241 E8.

IN THE KNOW CLUBBING RADAR

The best club nights tend to be slightly secretive one-offs, but you can find out what, when and where in the Friday editions of *Aftonbladet*, *Expressen* or *Metro*. Or you can check out the monthly *Nöjesguiden*, *Rodeo* or *Paus*, or visit www.kalendarium.se, www.alltomstockholm.se or the English-language www.totallystockholm.se. Another good way to learn about the hottest nights is to pick up flyers in the clothing shops and cafés around Stureplan or on Södermalm.

A former favourite of B-list celebrities and wannabe stars, the Spy Bar has undergone a makeover and now draws a trendy crowd of fashionistas, musicians and hipsters. Upstairs is a veritable labyrinth of bars and VIP rooms with plush carpets and chandeliers; outside is a very long queue of people trying to convince the bouncers that they really do know the right people.

★ Sturecompagniet

Sturegatan 4 (54 50 76 00, www.stureplansgruppen. se). T-bana Östermalmstorg or bus 1, 2, 55, 56, 96. **Open** midnight-5am Thur-Sat. **Minimum age** 23. **Admission** 180kr-250kr. **Map** p241 F8.

This beautiful three-storey, five-dancefloor party palace with an elaborate interior of marble, roses and purple is where the rich and famous play at the weekends. It can make for a great (if rather expensive) night out. However, only the prettiest things will make it through the doors.

Kungsholmen

La Isla

St Eriksgatan 51 (654 60 43, www.isla.se). T-bana Fridhemsplan or bus 1, 3, 4, 49, 77, 94. **Open** 11pm-4am Fri; 11pm-5am Sat. **Minimum age** varies. **Admission** 120kr. **Map** p239 F3.

The city's largest and longest-running Latin disco, playing Afro-Caribbean sounds for a predominantly Latin crowd from the northern suburbs. There are also salsa courses and an excellent restaurant.

Further Afield

★ Färgfabriken

Lövholmsbrinken 1, Liljeholmen (645 07 07, www. fargfabrikenskafe.se). T-bana Liljeholmen or bus 133, 152, 161. **Open** times vary; see website for details. **Admisssion** 110kr-160kr. **Map** p249 L1.

The Centre for Contemporary Art and Architecture, housed in an old factory in the southern suburb of Liljeholmen (across the bridge from Hornstull), occupies an important position on the Stockholm art scene. But it's more than just a gallery, as the arts space turns into a glowing electro club, concert hall and/or party venue on specific weekends.

Slakthuset

Slakthusgatan 6 (39 51 50, www.slakthuset.nu). T-bana Globen or bus 21, 168. **Open** 10pm-3am Fri, Sat. **Minimum age** 21. **Admission** varies.

This latest mega-club is a far cry from the Stureplan glitz. It's far out, in the meatpacking district south of Södermalm. The name translates to Slaughterhouse, and that's exactly what the space was previously used as – there are still traces of its former incarnation, in the form of rusty meat hooks and refrigerators. These raw and gritty details from the past are mixed up with heavy velvet drapes and designer furniture. The programme focuses on club nights, with some rocking live music thrown into the mix.

ESSENTIAL STOCKHOLM MUSIC
Sounds of the city.

**MUSIK VI MINNS:
EVERT TAUBE
EVERT TAUBE (2003)**
The top troubadour of the
20th-century Swedish
ballad tradition was born in
Gothenburg in 1890 and died
in 1976 as the country's best-
loved poet. The former sailor,
also credited with bringing the
tango to Sweden, is buried in
Maria Magdalena church and
his portrait will appear on the
new 50kr banknote.

**VENI VIDI VICIOUS
THE HIVES (2000)**
The garage/punk rock band
from Fagersta became
internationally known in the
early 2000s, but started
recording on home turf a
decade earlier. The band,
known for their black-and-
white suits and high-energy
live shows, played a series
of secret gigs at small
Stockholm venues, including
Debaser Medis, in 2012.

**YOUTH NOVELS
LYKKE LI (2008)**
This well-travelled young
Swedish singer-songwriter,
who blends indie/pop and
electronic sounds with
instrumentals, released her
debut album, *Youth Novels*,
in 2008. It was praised by
critics for its tenderness and
maturity. Li also appeared on
the eponymous debut album
of Swedish producer Kleerup
– another name to watch.

**ABBA GOLD
ABBA (1992)**
This legendary pop act
needs little introduction.
The foursome formed in
Stockholm in 1970 and won
the Eurovision Song Contest
in 1974 with 'Waterloo'. The
band topped the charts for
the following decade, and
their greatest hits album
ABBA Gold is one of the
world's most popular, with
sales topping 28 million.

**BODY TALK PT 1
ROBYN (2010)**
Sweden's electropop queen
was born in Stockholm in
1979 (as Robin Miriam
Carlsson), and released her
debut album *Robyn is Here*
in 1997. Her third album,
Body Talk Pt 1 – the first in a
trilogy – features the single
'Dancing on My Own', which
became a number one hit
in Sweden and gained her
worldwide recognition.

**THE LION'S ROAR
FIRST AID KIT (2012)**
This indie/folk duo is
made up of Stockholm-born
sisters Johanna and Klara
Söderberg, who began
composing songs in the mid
2000s, becoming a MySpace
success within a year. Their
debut album, *The Big Black
& the Blue*, was released
in 2010, followed by the
critically acclaimed *The
Lion's Roar* two years later.

MUSIC VENUES

The majority of the smaller live music venues for rock, pop and jazz are in Södermalm. This is also the home of the city's best record shops, among them the legendary **Pet Sounds** (*see p107*) on Skånegatan, which also runs a popular bar (*see p165*) opposite the store with live gigs.

As well as the venues listed here, it's also worth keeping an eye out for concerts at cultural centre **Dieselverkstaden** (Markusplatsen 17, Sickla, 718 82 90, www.dieselverkstaden.se), just southeast of Södermalm. Arts space **Färgfabriken** (*see p162*) sometimes hosts indie bands.

Gamla Stan

Stampen
Stora Nygatan 5 (20 57 93, www.stampen.se). *T-bana Gamla Stan or bus 2, 3, 43, 53, 55, 76, 96.* **Open** 5pm-1am Mon-Thur; 8pm-2am Fri, Sat; 1pm-2am Sun. **Admission** free-160kr. **Map** p241 H7.
Once a pawnshop, tiny Stampen is Stockholm's best-known jazz pub. It might have passed its heyday, but interesting live acts still appear every night, playing swing, dixie, trad jazz, blues, rockabilly and country. The crowd is more mature (and touristy) these days.

Norrmalm

★ Fasching
Kungsgatan 63 (tickets 1-5pm Mon-Fri 53 48 29 60, club & restaurant 53 48 29 60, www.fasching. se). T-bana T-Centralen or bus 1, 53, 69. **Open** 6pm-1am Mon-Thur; 6pm-4am Fri, Sat; 6pm-1am Sun. **Admission** 100kr-300kr. **Map** p240 F6.
As the fading photos on the walls attest, many of the greats have performed at this classic jazz club (capacity 600). Gigs and jam sessions are held every night, and you'll hear jazz, Latin and even some hip hop. Advance tickets are available from www.tickster.com, and it's also possible to reserve a restaurant table for a jazz show over dinner. For the club nights, *see p161*.

Glenn Miller Café
Brunnsgatan 21 (10 03 22, www.glennmillercafe. com). T-bana Hötorget or bus 1, 43, 56. **Open** 5pm-1am Mon-Thur; 5pm-2am Fri, Sat; 6pm-1am Sun. **Admission** free (reserve in advance to get a table). **Map** p241 E7.
This simple, cosy jazz pub has live music several nights a week. The intimate space is often packed with a mix of older fans and thirtysomethings who are mates with the band. If you love jazz, and aren't claustrophobic, this is a great choice.

Nalen
Regeringsgatan 74 (50 52 92 00, www.nalen.com). T-bana Hötorget or bus 1, 2, 43, 56, 96. **Open** varies; see website for details. **Admission** 150kr-550kr. **Map** p241 E7.

Built in 1888, Nalen was famous as a jazz mecca from the 1930s until the end of the '60s, when a church took over and got rid of all that sinful noise. Thoroughly renovated, Nalen now caters for all kinds of music, from jazz and folk to pop and hip hop. There are two auditoriums, plus a restaurant, bar and club, Alcazar.

Djurgården

Cirkus
Djurgårdsslätten 43-45 (box office 660 10 20, Ticnet 077 170 70 70, www.cirkus.se). Bus 44 or tram 7 or ferry from Nybroplan or Slussen. **Open** varies; see website for details. **Admission** 400kr-745kr. **Map** p243 J11.
Cirkus is housed in a cylindrical wooden building built in 1892 for circus troupes, with seating for 1,700, plus a bar and restaurant. It's an awe-inspiring place and attracts some big names, but concerts can lack atmosphere due to it being an all-seated venue. Comedy acts and shows also perform here.

Södermalm

Debaser Huvudkontor
Hornstulls Strand 9 (462 98 60, www.debaser.se). T-bana Hornstull or bus 4, 40, 77, 94. **Open** times vary. **Admission** varies. **Map** p249 L2.
Name after a Pixies song, Debaser quickly became one of the leading live rock venues in the city when it opened in an old distillery in Slussen in 2002. The venue moved to the site of the former Strand club, in Hornstull, in late 2013, and has retained the industrial feel, with dark walls and red accents. Bands play here seven nights a week, and there's DJ action on club nights. The Debaser-run Mexican restaurant Calexico's is next door, alongside Bar Brooklyn.

★ Debaser Medis
Medborgarplatsen 8 (694 79 00, www.debaser.se). T-bana Medborgarplatsen or bus 59, 66. **Open** 7pm-1am Mon-Thur; 7pm-3am Fri, Sat. **Admission** varies. **Map** p250 L8.
The former Mondo has been part of the Debaser empire for a few years now (and it's also opened up in Malmö), but it's practically the same set-up as before: at least ten concerts a week (country, pop, rock, indie, hip hop and reggae) in three spaces (the largest holds 1,200), as well as five bars, four dance-floors, a cinema and a decent restaurant. Located in the square that sits just off Götgatan, it's a hard-to-miss venue with a grand staircase leading up to the entrance. A safe bet.

Fylkingen
Munchenbryggeriet, Torkel Knutssonsgatan 2 (84 54 43, www.fylkingen.se). T-bana Mariatorget or bus 4, 3, 55, 56. **Open** times vary; see website for details. Closed July. **Admission** 100kr. **No credit cards.** **Map** p250 L6.

Södra Teatern.

This long-running concert hall and arts space in a converted brewery is the best place to hear alternative, DIY and experimental, electro-acoustic music. There's always something interesting going on, though the music might not be to everyone's taste.

Göta Källare

Folkungagatan 45 (642 09 57, www.gotakallare. com). T-bana Medborgarplatsen or bus 59, 66. **Open** *Club* 7pm-1am Wed; 10pm-3am Fri, Sat. *Concerts* call for details. **Admission** *Club* free-130kr. *Concerts* 100kr-355kr. **Map** p250 L8.
If you aren't into Swedish 'dance bands' (oompah bands with men in golden suits playing for five hours straight), then Göta Källare is not the best bet for a night out. It works more as a plan B for gig promoters when other places are already booked.

Kafé 44

Tjärhovsgatan 46 (644 53 12, www.kafe44.org). T-bana Medborgarplatsen or bus 59, 66. **Open** concerts usually Tue, Thur; call or see website for details. Closed July. **Admission** free-100kr. **No credit cards. Map** p251 L9.
This hangout for Södermalm's anarchists hosts a lot of punk and rock concerts, as well as an alternative, righteous brand of hip hop. There's no minimum age limit and no alcohol is served, but with the sort of bands that play here, you won't need a drink to get a kick. Music nights (usually on Tuesdays and Thursdays) aren't normally held during the summer months; visit the Facebook page for updates.

Pet Sounds Bar

Skånegatan 80 (643 82 25, www.petsoundsbar.se). T-bana Medborgarplatsen or bus 59, 66, 96. **Open** 5pm-1am Tue-Thur; 2pm-1am Fri, Sat. **Minimum age** 20. **Admission** usually free. **Map** p251 M9.
Home to Söder's large indie-rock crowd, Pet Sounds Bar is an extension of the legendary record store across the street. The Pet Sounds record store (*see p107*) used to host small concerts and was the first to book New Order in the 1980s. Nowadays the bar hosts these concerts in its basement, which features

a stage, bar and DJ booth. The ground floor houses a restaurant. Both areas are decorated with concert and film posters on the black- and red-tiled walls.

★ Södra Teatern

Mosebacketorg 1-3 (53 19 94 00, www.sodrateatern. com). T-bana Slussen or bus 2, 3, 43, 53, 55, 71, 76, 96. **Box office** 9am-8pm Mon-Fri. **Admission** varies. **Map** p250 K8.
This cultural centre has always got something interesting going on. Built in 1859, the main auditorium, Stora Scenen (capacity 400), has red velvet chairs and puts on pop, electronic, jazz and folk concerts. The basement, Kägelbanan (capacity 700), hosts more sing-along pop, plus electronic nights in its club area and indie pop concerts. Otherwise there's world music, plus poetry readings and spoken word. Touring theatre companies perform here occasionally. There are also outdoor terraces in summer.

Further Afield

Allhuset

Frescativägen 9, Frescati (16 20 00, www.sus.su.se). T-bana Universitetet or bus 40, 70. **Open** times vary; see website for details. Closed July. **Admission** prices vary.
At this modern venue (capacity 500) on the Stockholm University campus, students wearing T-shirts adorned with their favourite band's name talk about music and drink cheap beer in a relaxed atmosphere. There are gigs from interesting Swedish and international acts, as well as plenty of up-and-coming bands.

Globen

Globentorget 2, Johanneshov (information 600 91 00, box office 077 131 00 00, www.globearenas.se). T-bana Globen. **Box office** 9am-6pm Mon-Fri; 10am-2pm Sat, Sun. **Admission** varies.
Like it or not (and many don't), you can't deny that Globen – still the world's largest spherical building – is one of Stockholm's most recognisable structures. It's also an arena for everything from sports events to gala events and, of course, big-name concerts (Dolly Parton played here in summer 2014). If you're seated up high, you should probably bring binoculars or watch the TV screens instead. The atmosphere in the large stadium is almost non-existent, but the venue does house smaller, more personal venues such as Annexet. *See also p147.*

Landet

LM Ericssons väg 27 (41 01 93 20, www.landet. nu). T-bana Telefonplan or bus 141, 142, 161, 190. **Open** 4pm-midnight Mon-Thur; 4pm-1am Fri, Sat. In the vibrant suburb of Midsommarkransen lies art school Konstfack and Designens Hus, and the area attracts lots of trendy young people. It's also the home of Landet (Countryside), a laid-back restaurant and bar with an upstairs ballroom hosting clubs and concerts from local bands (usually Wed-Sat).

ARTS & ENTERTAINMENT

Performing Arts

Stockholm has far more ensembles and performing arts venues than most cities of a similar size, boasting two full-strength symphony orchestras that can compete with the best in Europe, two permanent opera houses, three major theatres and a healthy chamber music scene. Such riches are partly down to the fact that the old Swedish social democratic cultural policy prevails when it comes to the arts, with the State subsidising many cultural institutions.

Whereas the theatre scene tends to be a rather stagnant and serious world of mostly national interest (unless you have a strong grasp of Swedish), the Stockholm dance scene is considerably more vibrant and international in outlook. The innovative modern dance scene – led by Dansens Hus – is particularly fascinating, while dance theatre is also big in the city.

CLASSICAL MUSIC & OPERA

The music and opera calendar is seasonal, running from August to June, with concerts held primarily on weekdays. In the summer, the focus moves to the court theatres and parks around town. One exception is the **Stockholm Konserthuset**, which stays open in July for a four-week festival. Two other important dates are the five-day **Stockholm Early Music Festival** (www.semf.se) in June, and the **Baltic Sea Festival** (www.sverigesradio.se/berwaldhallen). The monthly English-language tourist magazine *Totally Stockholm* (www.totallystockholm.se) lists the main concerts, and the Thursday entertainment section of daily newspaper *Dagens Nyheter* has extensive listings. Also check out the free daily *Metro* paper, available from metro stations around town. You can buy tickets by phone or online from most venues. For major venues, try **Ticnet** (077 170 70 70, www.ticnet.se).

Venues

★ Berwaldhallen
Dag Hammarskjölds väg 3, Östermalm (box office 784 18 00, www.sverigesradio.se/berwaldhallen).
Bus 4, 42, 56, 76, 69. **Box office** noon-6pm Mon-Fri & 2hrs before show. *By phone* 9am-6pm Mon-Fri; 10am-3pm Sat. Closed July. **Tickets** 85kr-475kr. **Map** p243 F11.
The Berwaldhallen was built in 1979 for the Sveriges Radio Symfoniorkester (Swedish Radio Symphony Orchestra) and the Radiokören (Radio Choir). The acclaimed modernist hall, surrounded by parkland, is mainly underground. The Symfoniorkester, established in 1967, enjoyed a particularly successful period under the direction of Finn Esa-Pekka Salonen during the second half of the 1980s. The orchestra has a more contemporary touch than other Swedish orchestras, commissioning a significant amount of new music from home-grown and international composers. The Radiokören is considered to be one of the best choirs in the world.

Folkoperan
Hornsgatan 72, Södermalm (box office 616 07 50, www.folkoperan.se). T-bana Mariatorget or bus 4, 43, 55, 74. **Box office** 2-6pm Wed-Sat (depending on programme). Closed July. **Tickets** 250kr-450kr. **Map** p250 K6.
Folkoperan has been a healthy rival to Kungliga Operan (*see p167*) since its founding in 1976. Its modern stagings of classic operas sung in Swedish,

its unconventional and often controversial productions and the intimacy of the auditorium are among Folkoperan's distinctive features. The main season runs from September to May, when there are performances most nights of the week. The bar and restaurant are popular with a trendy young crowd.

Konserthuset

Hötorget 8, Norrmalm (box office 50 66 77 88, www.konserthuset.se). T-bana Hötorget or bus 1, 56, 59. **Box office** 11am-6pm Mon-Fri; 11am-3pm Sat; 2hrs before show. **Tickets** 55kr-410kr. **Map** p241 F7.

Konserthuset has been the home of the Kungliga Filharmonikerna (Royal Stockholm Philharmonic Orchestra) since its inauguration in 1926, and Sakari Oramo has been principal conductor since 2008. Architect Ivar Tengbom wanted to 'raise a musical temple not far from the Arctic Circle', and the bright blue structure is one of the foremost examples of early 20th-century Swedish neoclassical design. The 1,800-seat Main Hall is used for major concerts, while the beautiful Grünewald Hall (capacity 460), decorated by painter Isaac Grunewald, handles smaller chamber music concerts. Konserthuset's repertoire is based solidly in the classical and romantic periods, but it also hosts the renowned and well-established Stockholm International Composer Festival each autumn, focusing on living composers.

★ Kungliga Operan

Gustav Adolfs Torg 2, Norrmalm (box office 791 44 00, www.operan.se). T-bana Kungsträdgården or bus 2, 43, 55, 62, 65, 71, 76, 96. **Box office** 10am-4pm Tue, Sat; 10am-7pm Wed-Fri. **Tickets** 50kr-890kr; half-price under-26s. **Map** p241 G7.

Konserthuset.

When it opened in 1782, the Royal Opera House was considered to be the height of modern design. Just 100 years later it was demolished to make way for the current opera house, which was inaugurated by King Oscar II in 1898. While the building's exterior is neo-Renaissance in style, its interior staircase, foyer and auditorium have a Baroque design. The most lavish room is the first-floor Golden Foyer (Guldfoajén), with murals by Carl Larsson, gold stucco walls and ceiling, and crystal chandeliers. The room was painstakingly restored to its original condition in 1989. Contemporary art exhibitions are displayed here when the opera is dark during the summer months.

The Royal Opera has sent a string of great singers on to the international stage – among them Jenny Lind, Jussi Björling, Birgit Nilsson and Elisabeth Söderström – but, as is the case with Swedish footballers and hockey players, the most talented leave the country at a young age and rarely return to the Kungliga. It's also home to the Swedish Royal Ballet. There are guided tours of the opera house in Swedish and English, costing 120kr (50kr 7-18s); for times, call the main box office. For details of the opera house's restaurants, *see pp58-81. Photo p168.*

Ensembles

Kroumata – Capitol

St Eriksgatan 82, Vasastan (54 54 15 80, 72 33 86 033, www.kroumata.se). T-bana St Erikspan or bus 3, 4, 42, 72, 77, 94. **Tickets** 120kr-150kr. **Map** p244 D3.

Swedish percussion ensemble Kroumata was formed in 1978 and has since developed something of a cult status, touring widely. Since 1997, Kroumata's rehearsal space, Capitol, has served as an intimate concert hall for a few performances a year.

Stockholm Sinfonietta

Riddarhuset, Riddarhustorget 10, Gamla Stan (www.sinfonietta.se). T-bana Gamla Stan or bus 3, 53. **Tickets** approx 250kr-800kr (www. ticnet.se, or 1hr before concert at Riddarhuset or Hedvig Eleonora Church, Main Street 2). **Map** p241 H7.

The Stockholm Sinfonietta has worked with a host of venerable names, including conductors Sixten Ehrling and Okko Kamu, and soloists such as Catalan soprano Montserrat Caballé and Swedish cellist Frans Helmerson. The repertoire stretches all the way from baroque to contemporary, and the Stockholm Sinfonietta has the sole right to perform at the marvellous Riddarhuset.

THEATRE

Jugendstil building **Kungliga Dramatiska Teatern**, or Dramaten, is Sweden's national theatre, established in 1788. Over the years it has played host to a large number of superb actors

ARTS & ENTERTAINMENT

Kungliga Operan. *See p167.*

and directors (most famous, of course, being Ingmar Bergman). Dramaten has several stages for its productions, which range from traditional plays to more modern offerings. The city's other key theatre, **Stockholms Stadsteatern**, located in the Kulturhuset, also has numerous stages and has a wider repertoire than Dramaten.

The largest commercial theatre, showing large-scale musicals and comedies (in Swedish), is **Oscarsteatern** (Kungsgatan 63, box office 20 50 00, www.oscarsteatern.se). Other commercial theatres include **Göta Lejon** (Götgatan 55, box office 505 29 00, www.gotalegon.se), **Maximteatern** (Karlaplan 4, Ticket Forum 30 11 00, www.maximteatern.com), **Intiman** (Odengatan 81, box office 30 24 50, www.intiman.nu) and **China Teatern** (Berzelii Park 9, box office 56 28 92 00, www.chinateatern.se). **Cirkus** (Djurgårdsslätten 43, next to Skansen, box office 660 10 20, www.cirkus.se) also presents large-scale shows. **Södra Teatern** (*see p164*) is mainly a music venue, but occasionally puts on good theatre shows.

Major venues

★ Kulturhuset

Sergels Torg, Norrmalm (box office 50 83 15 08, www.kulturhusetstadsteatern.se). T-bana T-Centralen or Hörtorget or bus 52, 56, 59, 65. **Box office** noon-6pm Mon-Fri; 11am-4pm Sat, Sun. **Tickets** vary. **Map** p241 G7.
Kulturhuset, or the House of Culture – designed by Peter Celsing – is one of the most prominent modern buildings in Stockholm. The building certainly lives up to its name: there are three galleries, a library (with a wide selection of foreign newspapers),

activities for children, cafés, the city's main tourist information centre, and a terrace with an impressive view. There are two stages in the building – Kilen and Hörsalen – showing a wide spectrum of theatre, dance and music, with Kilen showing the more experimental work. The International Writers' Stage has hosted guests such as Sara Waters and Robert Fisk. The building also houses the Kulturhuset Stadsteatern (*see below*), with its six stages.

Kulturhuset Stadsteatern

Sergels Torg, Norrmalm (box office 50 62 02 00, www.stadsteatern.stockholm.se). T-bana T-Centralen or bus 52, 56, 59, 69. **Box office** noon-6pm Mon; noon-7pm Tue-Sun. **Tickets** 60kr-300kr. **Map** p241 G7.
With six stages in all, plus its successful summer Parkteatern programme, Stadsteatern is one of Scandinavia's largest theatrical institutions. Like Dramaten, it has a mainly conventional repertoire. There are exceptions, though – *Det allra viktigaste* was an extraordinary four-hour play with a gay theme, directed by Suzanne Osten. The smaller stages offer more experimental drama, often for a younger audience. The Marionetteatern puppet theatre, created in the 1950s by puppet master Michael Meschke, also has its home at Stadsteatern. The adjacent puppet museum, Marionettmuseet (www.marionettmuseet.se), contains puppets from all around the world. Stadsteatern also puts on an ambitious children's programme, and lately it has been hosting more innovative theatre. During the summer, Stadsteatern organises Parkteatern, with home-grown and international theatre and dance in parks all over the city.

▶ *Stadsteatern is now also home to dance company K Kvarnström & Co (see p171).*

★ Kungliga Dramatiska Teatern

Nybroplan, Östermalm (box office 667 06 80,
www.dramaten.se). T-bana Östermalmstorg
or Kungsträdgården or bus 2, 52, 55, 62, 69.
Box office noon-7pm Tue-Sat; noon-4pm Sun.
Tickets 100kr-390kr. **Map** p241 F8.

The Royal Dramatic Theatre, known as Dramaten,
is Sweden's finest theatre, and some of the country's
best actors tread its boards. Ingmar Bergman was
the driving force behind Dramaten from the early
1960s, directing a colossal number of productions,
and the place also played host to a pre-Hollywood
Greta Garbo. The main stage mounts plenty of
Shakespeare and Strindberg, mixed with avant-
garde dramatic works. The lavish structure was
built between 1902 and 1908 in Jugendstil style, with
a white marble façade and gilded bronzework. The
interior is glorious, and features paintings and sculptures by Sweden's most famous artists; Theodor
Lundberg created the golden statues of Poetry and
Drama at the front; Carl Milles was responsible for
the large sculptural group below the raised central
section of the façade; and Carl Larsson painted
the foyer ceiling. The theatre's architect, Fredrik
Liljekvist, wanted to create a grand and imposing
structure, and added the domed attic to give the
building more prominence. It worked – it's one of
Stockholm's most striking structures, particularly
when the setting sun hits the golden lampposts and
statues. The auditorium is equally stunning.

A red light outside means the main stage is sold
out. Dramaten's other stage, Elverket (Linnégatan
69) – a converted power station – has a younger
profile, producing modern drama, often with dance
or nouveau cirque elements. A guided tour (in both
Swedish and English) covers the main stage, smaller
stages and rehearsal rooms. Tours in English take
place at 4pm or 5pm (Tue-Sat). For a wonderful view
over Nybroviken, visit the outdoor café.
▶ *For more on Ingmar Bergman, see pp154-156.*

Fringe venues

Since the 1970s, several experimental theatre
groups working with new forms and expressions
have sprung up. As Stockholm is relatively small,
this type of theatre can be a bit of a risk-taking
exercise, but **Galeasen** and **Moment** are two
prominent groups that seldom disappoint. Non-
Swedish speaking visitors will be pleased to hear
that Stockholm is also home to well-respected
English-language theatre company **SEST**
(Stockholm English Speaking Theatre).

Aliasteatern

Hälsingegatan 3, Vasastan (box office 32 82
90, www.aliasteatern.com). T-bana Odenplan
or St Eriksplan or bus 4, 42, 47, 53, 69, 70,
72. **Box office** 1-5pm Mon-Fri (until 7pm
performance nights). Closed July. **Tickets**
150kr-250kr. **No credit cards. Map** p244 D4.

Kungliga Dramatiska Teatern.

This small theatre has been Stockholm's link to Spanish-language drama since 1978. During the past decade, however, it has mainly performed the works of Spanish-speaking dramatists in Swedish. The programme includes music and children's plays.

Dockteatern Tittut

Lundagatan 33, Södermalm (box office 720 75 99, www.dockteatern-tittut.com). T-bana Zinkensdamm or bus 4, 66, 94. **Box office** 9am-noon Mon-Fri; 9am-1pm Sat, Sun. Closed June-Aug. **Tickets** 80kr Mon-Fri; 60kr Sat, Sun. **No credit cards.** **Map** p249 K4.

This puppet theatre in Södermalm has been making high-quality shows for children (aged from two) for more than 25 years, combining puppet and shadow play. Performances are during the daytime.

Fylkingen

Münchenbryggeriet, Torkel Knutssonsgatan 2, Södermalm (84 54 43, www.fylkingen.se). T-bana Mariatorget or bus 4, 43, 55, 66. **Box office** 10am-5pm Mon-Fri. **Tickets** 100kr; 80kr reductions. **No credit cards.** **Map** p240 K6.

Founded way back in 1933, Fylkingen is the place to be if you're into new music and intermedia art. It's always been committed to new and experimental forms: 'happenings', musical theatre and text-sound compositions were prominent during the 1960s. In recent years, an increasing amount of ambitious performance art and dance has been staged. Fylkingen holds several festivals each year; check the website for details of forthcoming events.

Moment

Gubbängstorget 117, Gubbängen (box office 50 85 01 28, www.moment.org.se). T-bana Gubbängen. **Tickets** 160kr.

This cultural centre, housed in a converted 1940s cinema in the suburb of Gubbängen, is run by a group of young artists and directors. The programme includes new drama, music, art exhibitions and cinema. It's 20 minutes by T-bana from the city centre.

Orionteatern

Katarina Bangata 77, Södermalm (box office 643 88 80, www.orionteatern.se, ticnet.se). T-bana Skanstull or bus 3, 59, 76, 96. **Box office** 1hr before small stage performances; 2hrs before main stage performances. Closed Midsummer-Aug. **Tickets** 290kr-375kr. **Map** p251 N10.

The Orion Theatre, Stockholm's largest avant-garde company, was formed in 1983, and has since collaborated with the likes of Peking Opera from Shanghai and Complicité from London. The building, once a factory, makes an effective theatre space.

Playhouse Teater

Sibyllegatan 29, Östermalmstorg (654 40 30, www.playhouseteater.se). T-bana Östermalmtorg or bus 1, 2, 56. **Tickets** vary. **Map** p242 F9.

Sweden's only 'off-Broadway' theatre (meaning it's between the size of a main theatre and a fringe one) mainly shows plays from New York – both classics and award-winning new productions – translated into Swedish.

Strindbergs Intima Teater

Barnhusgatan 20, Norrmalm (box office 20 08 43, www.strindbergsintimateater.se). T-bana T-Centralen or Hötorget or bus 53, 65, 69. **Box office** 2hrs before performance. **No credit cards.** **Map** p240 F5.

Founded by August Strindberg back in 1907, this small theatre used to show the dramatist's plays exclusively. Nowadays the programme, co-ordinated by Strindbergsmuseet, is more varied and includes guest performances and theatre for children.

Teater Galeasen

Slupskjulsvägen 30, Skeppsholmen (box office 611 00 30, City Theatre 076 026 20 70, www.galeasen. se). Bus 65. **Box office** Tickets from website or City Theatre desk in Kulturhuset (11am-6pm Mon-Fri; 11am-4pm Sat, Sun). **Tickets** vary. **Map** p242 H9.

In the 1980s and early 1990s this was the hip spot for theatregoers. Nowadays, things have changed and actors of that generation are now household names. But Galeasen has continued to be a breeding ground for young actors and directors, and the work on show here is still high quality.

Teater Pero

Sveavägen 114, Vasastaden (box office 612 99 00, www.pero.se). T-bana Rådmansgatan or bus 2, 4, 42, 53, 70, 72. **Box office** 1hr before performance. Closed summer. **Map** p245 C6.

Teater Pero has a strong tradition of mime, and has been producing shows for children and adults for more than 20 years.

English-language

★ SEST (Stockholm English Speaking Theatre)

www.sestcompany.com

The Stockholm English Speaking Theatre (SEST) was founded in 2010 by Samuele Caldognetto, Kristina Leon and Ingela Lundh with the aim of producing distinguished, thought-provoking plays in English. The first production was the critically acclaimed *4.48 Psychosis* by Sarah Kane, which was followed up by David Mamet's *Boston Marriage*. In the summer, the company shows Shakespeare plays at outdoor venues, such as Djurgården's Parkteatern and Drottningholm Palace.

DANCE

Stockholm's dance audience has grown steadily during the last decade. **Moderna Dansteatern,** in Skeppsholmen, has been the home base for many freelance dancers and choreographers for more than 20 years; renowned dance company **K Kvarnström & Co** is now in residence at the Stadsteatern; and the **WELD** studio focuses on more conceptual work. The **Cullbergbaletten** (www.cullbergbaletten.se), a truly international company with a solid reputation, is also based in Stockholm. Mats Ek, founder Birgit Cullberg's son, no longer leads the company, but he's still active as a freelance choreographer.

The most significant modern dance scene, though, is at **Dansens Hus** (House of Dance), which opened in 1990. Its extensive programme includes visiting companies from around the world, and the quality is consistently high. Dansens Hus plays host to some of the most creative local choreographers, including Cristina Caprioli, Örjan Andersson, Virpi Pahkinen and Helena Franzén.

Dance theatre also has a strong showing in Sweden – award-winning Birgitta Egerbladh, with her Pina Bausch-inspired, humorous choreography, now has her base at Stockholms Stadsteatern. For dance listings, check the Swedish-language magazine *Danstidningen* (www.danstidningen.se) or 'På Stan', the Thursday supplement of *Dagens Nyheter*.

For traditional ballet and classic performances, head to **Kungliga Operan** for the Kungliga Baletten (Royal Ballet).

Venues

★ Dansens Hus
Barnhusgatan 12-14, Norrmalm (box office 50 89 90 90, www.dansenshus.se). T-bana Hötorget or T-Centralen/bus 1, 53, 59, 65, 69.

Box office 2-6pm Tue-Sat; noon-2pm Sun (performance days). Closed Midsummer-mid Aug. **Tickets** 157kr-490kr. **Map** p241 E6.

The two-stage House of Dance is the major venue for Swedish dance, with around 35 performances a year. This is where you'll find the Cullberg Ballet when they're in town, and the guest list might include the likes of Anna Teresa de Keersmaeker's Rosas company, Nederlands Dans Theater and Akram Khan. Swedish dance group Bounce! has also been a huge success here, with its funny, street dance-inspired shows drawing large audiences.

Kungliga Operan
For listings information, see p167.

The Royal Opera, which was founded in 1733 and is one of Europe's grandest opera houses (the current building opened in 1898), is home to Sweden's finest classical company, the Royal Ballet. The dancers are outstanding and, though the repertoire is largely traditional, there is occasionally some modern work on show. The interior, as you would expect, is totally over the top – the chandelier weighs two tons and the Golden Room is simply stunning. Note that the building closes for performances between June and the end of August.

Moderna Dansteatern (MDT)
Slupskjulsvägen 30, Skeppsholmen (box office 611 14 56, www.mdtsthlm.se). Bus 65. **Box office** tickets available from www.ticnet.se or 30mins before performance. **Tickets** 180kr; 90kr reductions. **Map** p242 H9.

The small Modern Dance Theatre was founded by Margaretha Åsberg, the grande dame of Swedish dance, and single-handedly provides a space for postmodern and avant-garde dance in Stockholm. Performance art has also found a refuge here.

Dansens Hus.

Escapes & Excursions

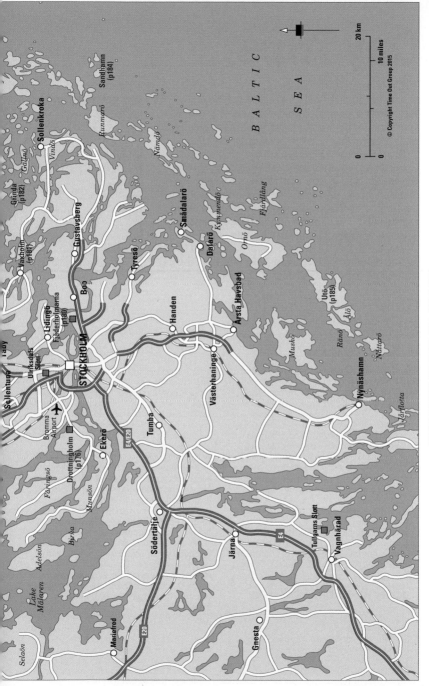

ESCAPES & EXCURSIONS

Sollenkroka

Sandhamn (p184)

Ginda (p182)

Gustavsberg

Vaxholm (p181)

Boo

Smådalarö

Tyresö

Dalarö

Lidingö

Fjäderholmarna (p180)

Handen

Åsta Havsbad

STOCKHOLM

Utö (p185)

Ulriksdals Slott

Nynäshamn

Täby

Sollentuna

Bromma Airport

Västerhaninge

Drottningholm (p176)

Ekerö

Tumbra

Faringsö

Munsön

Södertälje

Järna

Tullgarns Slott

Vagnhärad

Adelsön

Björkö

E20

Mariefred

Gnesta

Selaön

Lake Mälaren

BALTIC

SEA

Rumarö

Nämdö

Krusmundö

Ornö

Flärdfäng

Ränö

Muskö

Nåttarö

Ålö

Järnflotta

Vindö

Gålnö

0   20 km
0   10 miles

© Copyright Time Out Group 2015

Day Trips

Lovely though Stockholm is, it would be a great shame not to head out of the city during your visit. There are some fantastic places within easy reach, many of them perfect for day trips.

The region's rich history means that the area to the west is stuffed with castles and palaces, the grandest being the royal family's home of Drottningholm – an hour's trip by boat from the city centre. North of Stockholm lies the former Viking stronghold of Sigtuna, one of the oldest towns in Sweden, and beyond that is charming and historic Uppsala – Sweden's answer to Cambridge or Oxford. Situated at the northern tip of Lake Mälaren, the city is dominated by its university and grand cathedral.

ESCAPES & EXCURSIONS

DROTTNINGHOLM

The grand palatial estate of Drottningholm – the permanent residence of the Swedish royal family since 1981 – attracts more than 100,000 visitors annually. Located just ten kilometres (six miles) to the west of central Stockholm, on the sparsely populated island of Lovön, it's an essential excursion from the city. The very well-preserved grounds – 300-year-old trees frame the statues and fountains of the French garden behind the palace – and some excellent 17th- and 18th-century architecture, including a still-functioning theatre from 1766 and the exotic Kina Slott at the western end, led UNESCO to add the site to its World Heritage List back in 1991.

Constructed at the very height of Sweden's power in Europe during the mid 17th century, **Drottningholms Slott** was built to impress – and impress it certainly does. Wealthy dowager

IN THE KNOW DEAD FAMOUS

Uppsala's **Domkyrkan** (see p179) is the last resting place of several famous Swedes. Carl Linnaeus and Emanuel Swedenborg are buried here, and Gustav Vasa is entombed beneath a monument depicting him and his two queens.

Queen Hedvig Eleonora financed the initial phase of the palace's construction, which lasted from 1662 to 1686. The royal architect Nicodemus Tessin the Elder modelled the waterfront residence on the Palace of Versailles. Don't-miss highlights include the monumental staircase, the Ehrenstrahl drawing room and Hedvig Eleonora's state bedchamber.

The palace's second period of growth began after Lovisa Ulrika married Crown Prince Adolf Fredrik in 1744. She was a great lover of the arts and it was at her commission that architect Carl Fredrik Adelcrantz constructed **Drottningholms Slottsteater**. With its original stage sets and hand-driven machinery in place, this is the world's oldest working theatre – concerts, ballets and operas are still held here in the summer.

Behind the palace is the long, rectangular **French Baroque Garden**, laid out in five stages separated by lateral paths. Its bronze statues are copies of early 17th-century works by the Dutch sculptor Adriaen de Vries. The originals were moved across the street to the **Museum de Vries**, which opened in 2001. The statues – spoils of war from Denmark's Fredriksborg Palace and Prague – are arranged in the former royal stable in the same pattern as those in the garden.

North of the baroque garden is the beautiful, lake-studded **English Park**, so named because it followed the English style of naturalistic landscaping that was fashionable at the time. It was added by Gustav III after he took over the palace in 1777.

Kina Slott stands near the end of the garden down a tree-lined avenue. As a surprise for Lovisa Ulrika's 33rd birthday in 1753, Adolf Fredrik had a Chinese-inspired wooden pavilion built here. Ten years later it was replaced by this rococo pleasure palace, also designed by CF Adelcrantz. The palace, which was extensively renovated between 1989 and 1996, has been repainted in its original red colour with yellow trim and light-green roofs; tours are available.

Across from Kina Slott is the small **Confidencen** pavilion. When the royal family wanted to dine in complete privacy, they sat in the top room and servants hoisted up a fully set table from below. Down the road behind the palace is the former studio of the 20th-century Swedish artist **Evert Lundquist** (402 62 70, www. evertlundquistsateljemuseum.se, guided tours in Swedish 4pm Sun during May-Aug, 70kr).

Drottningholms Slott

402 62 80, www.royalcourt.se. **Open** *Jan-Mar, Nov-Dec* noon-3.30pm Sat, Sun. *Apr, Oct* 11am-3.30pm Fri-Sun. *May-Sept* 10am-4.30pm daily. Closed mid Dec-early Jan. Guided tours in English every Sat, Sun (check website for times). **Admission** 120kr; 60kr reductions; free under-7s. Free with SC.
A combined ticket to Kina Slott and Drottningholms Slott costs 180kr.

Kina Slott

402 62 70. **Open** *May-Aug* 11am-4.30pm daily. *Sept* noon-3.30pm daily. Closed Oct-Apr. Guided tours weekends May-June; daily mid June-Sept. **Admission** (incl tour) 100kr; 50kr reductions; free under-7s.

Museum de Vries

402 62 80. **Open** by guided tour only (call for times). Closed Sept-mid May. **Admission** 100kr; free under-17s.

Slottsteater

Administrative office (May-Sept 759 04 06, Oct-Apr 55 69 31 00, www.dtm.se). **Open** *Apr, Oct* noon-3.30pm Fri-Sun. *May-Aug* 11am-4.30pm daily. *Sept* noon-3.30pm daily. Closed Nov-Apr. **Admission** 100kr; 70kr-80kr reductions; free under-17s. Free with SC.

Where to eat & drink

Kina Slotts Servering (759 03 96, www. serveringenkinaslott.se, closed dinner & Nov-Mar) is located near Kina Slott and serves coffee, sandwiches and waffles. Alternatively, take a picnic to eat on the lawns.

Getting there

By metro/bus

T-bana to Brommaplan, then bus 176, 177 or 311.

By boat

Between May and early September you can travel by steamboat from Stadshusbron near Stadshuset on Kungsholmen (195kr return); the journey takes 1hr, though the company organises various cruise packages. Contact **Strömma Kanalbolaget** (www.stromma.se) for information.

By car

From Kungsholmen take Drottningholmsvägen west towards Vällingby, then at Brommaplan follow signs to Drottningholm. It's a 15min drive.

By bicycle

There is a cycle path from Stadshuset in Stockholm to Drottningholm; the ride takes about 50mins.

SIGTUNA

A thousand years ago, this small town by Lake Mälaren was the most important in Sweden. Founded around 980 by King Erik Segersäll, Sigtuna was a major port during Viking times.

Later, the town became the centre of activity for Christian missionaries. After King Gustav Vasa's Reformation, when he demolished many churches and monasteries, Sigtuna fell into ruin. Virtually all that is left from its great period are the remains of three 12th-century granite churches (from an original seven) bordering the town centre, and a collection of artefacts in the Sigtuna Museum.

Sigtuna.

Many of the buildings date back to the 18th and 19th centuries. The **Rådhus**, in the central square, was built in 1744 and is the smallest town hall in Sweden. The **Sigtuna Museum** is built on the site of a former king's residence and has an excellent exhibition on the Vikings. It also runs the Rådhus and **Lundströmska Gården**, a middle-class house where a merchant lived with his family. Stop by the tourist office to book a tour of the town. Off the main street, you can take a stroll through the church ruins and cemeteries of **St Lars**, **St Per** and **St Olof**. The church of **St Maria**, which looks quite new compared to the others, was actually built by the Dominicans in the 13th century. Down by the water, you can rent canoes and bicycles. Summer is the ideal time to visit Sigtuna, but frozen Lake Mälaren during winter is breathtaking.

Lundströmska Gården
Stora Gatan 39. **Open** *June-Aug* noon-4pm daily. **Admission** free with museum entry.

Rådhus
Stora Torget. **Open** *June-Aug* noon-4pm daily. **Admission** free.

Sigtuna Museum
Stora Gatan 55 (59 12 66 70, www.sigtuna museum.se). **Open** *June-Aug* noon-4pm daily. *Sept-May* noon-4pm Tue-Sun. **Admission** 20kr; 10kr reductions.

Where to eat & drink

The **Båthuset Krog & Bar** (Hamngatan 2, 59 25 67 80, www.bathuset.com, main courses 200kr-300kr, closed Mon, dinner only) is located out on the water; a wooden dock leads to the restaurant, which serves portions of fresh mussels and cod. For one of the best waterfront views, visit the terrace at the **Sigtuna Stads Hotell**'s restaurant (Stora Nygatan 3, 59 25 01 00, www.sigtunastadshotell.se, mains 295kr-350kr, closed Sun, July & 1st wk Aug).

Resources

Sigtuna Turism
Stora Gatan 33 (59 48 06 50, www.sigtunaturism. se). **Open** *1st 3wks June* 10am-5pm daily. *End June-Aug* 10am-6pm Mon-Sat; 11am-5pm Sun. *Sept* 10am-5pm Mon-Sat; 11am-4pm Sun. *Oct-May* 10am-5pm Mon-Fri; 11am-4pm Sat; noon-4pm Sun.

Getting there

By train/bus
The no.36 train to Märsta (www.sl.se) takes 40mins (72kr-80kr depending on whether you buy it in advance or on the train). From Märsta,

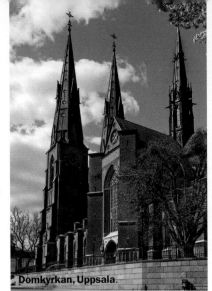
Domkyrkan, Uppsala.

take bus 570 or 575 to Sigtuna bus station, near the town centre. From Stockholm Central Station the trip takes 1hr in total.

By car
Head north on the E4 for about 30km (18 miles), then exit on the 263 and follow signs to Sigtuna. Drive about 10km (six miles) west until you come to a roundabout, where you turn towards Sigtuna Centrum. The journey takes about 50mins.

UPPSALA

The historic city of Uppsala is home to the oldest university in Scandinavia – dating back to 1477 – and some 30,000 students. It's a bustling, charming city, situated at the northern tip of Lake Mälaren, about 70 kilometres (40 miles) north of Stockholm, with ancient buildings, plenty of cafés and beautiful parks.

The city's magnificent Domkyrkan, Scandinavia's largest cathedral, stands on a ridge to the west of the downtown area beside a 16th-century brick castle. The small Fyrisån river runs through the centre of town. One block to the east is a pedestrian shopping street and the busy main square of **Stora Torget**. The former home and garden of the famous botanist Carl Linnaeus (whose face adorns the Swedish 100kr note) are located nearby, along with several other university museums.

The red-brick Gothic **Domkyrkan**, completed in 1435, was built on a cross plan. The building is as tall as it is long, with two western towers rising up to a neck-craning 118.7 metres (389 feet). Inside there's an enormous vaulted ceiling, a floor covered with gravestones and Sweden's largest Baroque pulpit.

The buildings of Uppsala University are scattered throughout the city. Across from the cathedral stands the **Gustavianum**, formerly the university's main building, now a museum. Beneath its dome are exhibits on the history of science, an old anatomical theatre, some Nordic, classical and Egyptian antiquities, and the curiosities of the Augsburg Art Cabinet.

Up the hill from the cathedral is the huge, earth-red **Uppsala Slott**, built by Gustav Vasa in the late 1540s as a fortress. His sons later added to the building, although much of it was destroyed in the city fire of 1702. It houses an art gallery and the county governor's residence, Vasaborgen, but is not as spectacular as you might expect. The castle's freestanding bell tower, Gunillaklockan, has become a symbol of Uppsala; it strikes at 6am and 9pm.

The university's grand **Botaniska Trädgården** (Villavägen 8, 018 471 28 38, www.botan.uu.se), west of the castle, includes a tropical greenhouse, Baroque formal garden and 11,000 species of plants. To see where the university's first botanical garden stood, visit **Linnéträdgården**, situated one block north of pedestrianised Gågatan. Carl von Linné (1707-78), better known as Linnaeus, restored the garden in 1741 soon after taking up a professorship at the university. One of the world's most famous scientists, Linnaeus developed a method of classifying and naming plants and animals that was adopted by scientists around the world and is still in use today. He lived in the small house on the corner of the property, now the **Linnémuseet**, which has a permanent exhibition on his life and work.

Gamla Uppsala (Old Uppsala), two kilometres (1.2 miles) to the north of Uppsala, is the site of the original settlement. The Gamla Uppsala museum opened in 2000, and features exhibits about Viking history and myths.

Domkyrkan

Domkyrkoplan (018 430 36 30, www.uppsala domkyrka.se). **Open** *Cathedral* 8am-6pm daily. *Treasury* May-Sept 10am-5pm Mon-Sat; 12.30-5pm Sun. Oct-Apr 10am-4pm Mon-Sat; 12.30-4pm Sun. **Admission** *Cathedral* free. *Treasury* 40kr.

Gamla Uppsala

Disavägen (018 23 93 12, www.raa.se/ gamlauppsala). Bus 2 or 110 from central Uppsala. **Open** *Jan-Mar, Sept-Dec* noon-4pm Mon, Wed, Sat, Sun. *Apr-Aug* 11am-5pm daily. **Admission** 70kr; 50kr reductions; free under-18s.

Gustavianum

Akademigatan 3 (01 84 71 75 71, www. gustavianum.uu.se). **Open** *June-Aug* 10am-6pm Tue-Sun. **Admission** 50kr; 40kr reductions; free under-12s.

Linnéträdgården & Linnémuseet

Svartbäcksgatan 27 (018 13 65 40, 018 471 28 38, www.linnaeus.uu.se). **Open** *Garden* May-Sept 11am-5pm daily (gates close at 8pm). Closed Oct-Apr. *Museum* May-end Sept 11am-5pm Tue-Sun. Group bookings all year. **Admission** *Garden & Museum* 60kr; free under-16s.

Uppsala Slott

018 54 48 11, www.uppsalaslott.com. **Open** *Castle* (guided tours only) June-Sept (English) 1pm, 3pm Tue-Sun. Closed Sept-May. *Art gallery* noon-4pm Tue, Thur, Fri; noon-8pm Wed; noon-4.30pm Sat, Sun. **Admission** *Castle* 90kr; 15kr under-20s (includes art gallery). *Art gallery* 40kr; free under-20s, students & all 4-8pm Wed.

Where to eat & drink

The city's finest dining can be found at **Domtrappkällaren** (St Eriksgränd 15, 018 13 09 55, www.domtrappkallaren.se, main courses 245kr-310kr, closed Sun), which serves excellent Swedish and French cuisine in a 13th-century vault near the cathedral steps. One block east is **Hambergs Fisk** (Fyristorg 8, 018 71 21 50, www.hambergs.se, main courses 110kr-305kr, closed Mon, Sun), specialising in seafood.

For an excellent vegetarian lunch, try **Fröjas Sal Vegetarisk Restaurang** (Bäverns Gränd 24, 018 10 13 10, www.frojassal.se, set menus 80kr Mon-Fri, closed Sat, Sun). One of Uppsala's most famous cafés is **Ofvandahls Hovkonditori** (Sysslomansgatan 5, www.ofvandahls.se, 018 13 42 04), founded in the 19th century.

Resources

Uppsala Tourism

Kungsgatan 50 (01 87 27 48 00, www.destination uppsala.se). **Open** 10am-6pm Mon-Fri; 10am-3pm Sat (July, Aug 11am-3pm Sun).

Getting there

By train

Several trains a day leave for Uppsala from Stockholm's Central Station (www.sj.se). Journey time is around 40mins.

By bus

Swebus Express's (www.swebus.se) buses 801 and 899 depart for Uppsala several times a day from Stockholm's Cityterminalen. The journey takes about 1hr and costs 59kr-89kr one-way.

By car

Follow the E4 north from Stockholm for about 50mins. The highway passes through the eastern half of Uppsala, from where you follow signs to Uppsala Centrum to the west.

The Archipelago

The Stockholm archipelago begins just a few miles east of the capital, covering about 140 kilometres (90 miles) from north to south. Only 150 of the 30,000 islands and islets are inhabited, but many Stockholmers have summer houses in the archipelago and visitor numbers swell in the warmer months, especially July. Fjäderholmarna, Vaxholm, Grinda, Sandhamn, Utö and Finnhamn are the most popular islands, with the first two the easiest to reach for day trips. The landscape varies hugely, from the more populated, thickly wooded inner archipelago to the bare, flat rocks of the central and outer islands. The boat trip to the islands is part of the fun, but those who'd rather travel by road than sea can still enjoy the archipelago by heading to Värmdö, part of which is attached to the mainland. Vaxholm can also be reached by road.

WHEN TO GO

The archipelago is best visited from mid June to mid August – during the rest of the year many of the hotels, restaurants and other facilities are closed, ferries are more limited, and some of the islands pretty much shut down to visitors. Always book ahead to ensure there will be accommodation available.

During the summer months the archipelago often gets more sunshine than the mainland, but it's still a good idea to pack a raincoat and sweater. Sunscreen and mosquito repellent are also recommended. Take provisions as shops are not always open, and remember that cashpoints are scarce.

FJÄDERHOLMARNA

The four islands that make up Fjäderholmarna are the closest archipelago islands to Stockholm – situated just six kilometres (four miles) east of downtown. Ferries drop visitors off at the main island of **Stora Fjärderholmen**. A paved walking path circles the island, passing the restaurants, small museums and handicraft boutiques on the northern and eastern shores, and the forested area and flat rocks to the west. About a dozen people live on **Ängsholmen**

and **Stora Fjäderholmen**. The smaller islands of **Libertas** and **Rövarns Holme** provide sanctuary for birds, but there's no way to get to them unless you happen to have your own boat. The shops and boat museum usually close around 5-5.30pm, while the restaurants are often open until midnight, leaving time to catch the last boat back to Stockholm.

When the weather is good, the southern cliffs of Stora Fjärderholmen are flooded with sunbathing Stockholmers and tourists, and the place can feel a bit cramped. Swimming options are limited, with no easily accessible beaches. The ferries from Stockholm dock on the northern shore next to the guest harbour. Traditional wooden boats called *allmogebåtar* are displayed nearby. Further round, a small street contains an art gallery and studios where artists make and sell pottery, linen goods and wooden handicrafts. At **Åtta Glas** (716 11 24, www.atta-glas.se) you can watch glass being blown and then buy the finished article in the little shop next door.

Where to eat & drink

As you step off the ferry on the northern side, **Restaurang Rökeriet** (716 50 88, www. rokeriet.nu, main courses 165kr-358kr) is on

IN THE KNOW
WILD CAMPING AND FORAGING

The law in Sweden grants public access to private land for hiking and camping – the right to roam. This right also applies in the Stockholm archipelago, though with some caveats. In archipelago nature reserves, campers are permitted to stay for two nights in a row in the same place. Open fires are only allowed in designated areas, though barbecues are allowed. When it comes to foraging, it's fine to pick some berries and mushrooms (and many Swedes do), but visitors are forbidden from cutting down branches.

your left along the water's edge. The restaurant has a beautiful view over the neighbouring islands. The nearby **Fjäderholmarnas Krog** (718 33 55, www.fjaderholmarnaskrog.se, main courses 185kr-395kr) offers an upmarket menu, and has a harbour view. For dessert, **Systrarna Degens Glasstuga** (716 78 01, closed Oct-Apr) specialises in ice-cream and smoothies.

Resources

The island doesn't have a tourist office that you can visit in person, but online information is available at www.fjaderholmarna.se.

Getting there

By boat
Strömma Kanalbolaget (*see p223*) ferries leave from Nybroplan (every 30mins 10am-8.30pm, then 9.30pm, 10.30pm, 11.30pm mid May-mid Aug; every hr 10am-8pm, then 9.30pm, 11.30pm

end Apr-mid May, mid Aug-early Sept; return 130kr). **Fjäderholmslinjen** boats (21 55 00, www.fjaderholmslinjen.se) depart every hour from Slussen 10am-11pm daily May-early Sept; return 120kr.

VAXHOLM

The island of Vaxholm, just 3.5 kilometres (two miles) long, is by far the most populated and easily accessible island in the archipelago. It is located about 17 kilometres (11 miles) north-east of Stockholm and is connected to the mainland by highway 274. The place is overrun in summer, when roughly a million visitors come for Vaxholm's waterfront restaurants, handicraft shops and art galleries. Ferries from Stockholm dock at Vaxholm's historic downtown, located on the island's south-east corner. The town has a lively, beach-side feel and frequent outdoor events in the summer. On the main street of Hamngatan, to the north, you'll find all the conveniences you might expect in a small town.

Gustav Vasa founded the city of Vaxholm in the 1540s after winning Sweden's war with Denmark. The city supplied food and water to the newly constructed fortress and tower located on the small island to the east. Several additions were made to the fortress during the 19th century, and today it contains the **Vaxholms Fästnings Museum** (54 13 33 61, www.vaxholmsfastning. sc). The museum is easily reached by a two-minute boat trip from Vaxholm wharf.

West of Hamngatan is **Vaxholm Kyrka**, designed in the 1760s. The church hosts concerts in the summer. The city's old **Rådhuset** (Town Hall) is home to the tourist office, and the cobbled square outside has stalls selling handicrafts in summer. Every year Vaxholm harbour hosts a steamboat festival, **Skärgårdsbåtens Dag** (*see p30*), on the second Wednesday in June.

ESCAPES & EXCURSIONS

Vaxholm.

Grinda.

island (Waxholm Strand). It has a camping site and around 20 cabins, and its sandy beach is a good spot for families.

Resources

Vaxholms Turistbyrå & Visit Vaxholm AB
Rådhuset (54 13 14 80, www.vaxholm.se).
Open *Oct-Apr* 10am-3pm daily. *May, Sept* 10am-3pm Mon-Fri. *June-Aug* 10am-6pm Mon-Fri; 10am-4pm Sat, Sun.
Stop by the tourist office to get hold of island maps, fishing licences and an events schedule. The website gives general information on facilities and attractions.

Getting there

By metro & bus
T-bana Tekniska Högskolan, then bus 670 to Vaxholm. The journey takes about 1hr.

By boat
Waxholmsbolaget boats (*see p223*) from Strömkajen are the best option; they run several times a day all year (60kr-75kr each way) and take around an hour. **Cinderellabåtarna** (now owned by Strömma Skärgård) boats (*see p221*) from Strandvägen are less frequent, running up to three times a day late Apr-end Aug (60-90mins, 110kr each way).

By car
Head north on the E18 for 15km (9 miles) then exit at the Arninge Trafikplats on to highway 274. Follow signs to Vaxholm, which will lead you through Stockholmsvägen and Kungsgatan to downtown.

GRINDA

Grinda, which is just over an hour by boat from Stockholm and accessible year round, is one of the archipelago's most popular islands. Visitors come for the peaceful surroundings, swimming, good restaurants, pine forests and wildlife.

In 1906, Henrik Santesson, the first director of the Nobel Foundation, bought the island and commissioned architect Ernst Stenhammar to design a summer residence. The result was a beautiful art nouveau stone house, the present-day **Grinda Wärdshus**.

Grinda Gård is the starting point for a path through the forest to Grinda's highest point, Klubbudden, 35 metres (115 feet) above sea level.

Grinda has plenty of good swimming spots; **Källviken**, along the path to the guest harbour and the inn, has a shallow sandy beach, ideal for children. There are also some popular spots between Källviken and the guest harbour, and by the northern and southern piers.

Where to eat & drink

There's a good choice of restaurants along the wharf, including seafood, Italian and Chinese. For fine dining with a view of the water, try **Waxholms Hotell** (*see below*; main courses 159kr-355kr), serving dishes such as turbot stuffed with truffles and lobster. For more down-to-earth fare, take a seat on the patio of popular **Hamnkrogen** (Söderhamnen 10, 54 13 20 39, www.hamnkrogenvaxholm.com, main courses 125kr-315kr). You'll also find pizzas and hamburgers in abundance.

Located just around the corner from the harbour, on the eastern end of the island and opposite the Kastellet (castle), is **Restaurang Magasinet** (Fiskaregatan 1, 541 325 00, www.magasinetvaxholm.se, main courses 120kr-200kr), hidden away up a flight of steps. The popular restaurant, complete with terrace, serves up modern Swedish dishes, while the attached shop is the Swedish equivalent of the UK's Cath Kidston.

Where to stay

Waxholms Hotell (Hamngatan 2, 54 13 01 50, www.waxholmshotell.se, 1,135kr-1,750kr double), built in 1901, has light, tastefully decorated rooms and satellite TV. Alternatively, you can book a B&B (around 300kr per person per night) through the Vaxholm tourist office (*see right*). There's even a B&B situated on the Kastellet – a 16th-century castle on its own tiny island – called **Kastellet B&B** (768 555 444, www.kastelletbnb.se), the 27-room B&B has shabby-chic rooms that cost between 1,000kr and 2,000kr per night. **Eriksö Cabins & Camping** (981 16 68) is located at the western end of the

WHERE CREATIVITY COMES NATURALLY

The archipelago's new space for art and architecture.

Not many people associate the Stockholm archipelago with contemporary art and architecture; indeed, the islands are really a place to escape modernity and stimulation and get back to nature. However, since 2012, visitors have been able to mix both interests through the opening of **Artipelag** (www.artipelag.se), an exhibition space housed in a wonderfully innovative coastal building at Baggensfjärden, in the municipality of Värmdö.

The privately owned space, reached from Stockholm by bus in just 20 minutes, is the manifested vision of BabyBjörn founder Björn Jakobson, an art lover and lifetime visitor to the archipelago. Visitors who have been to Denmark's outstandingly beautiful Louisiana Museum of Modern Art, which is said to have influenced the creation of Artipelag, will be familiar with the idea: modern art exhibitions skillfully blended with the Scandinavian love of nature through innovative architecture, water and a stunning natural setting. Throw in two high-quality restaurants and a design shop, and you have a perfect day out for those who want to satisfy all the senses.

There's an overriding sense of space here: the site covers 22 hectares and includes 1,800 square metres (19,000 square feet)

of exhibition space and a concert/conference hall. But it's not just about the geographical stats – the far-reaching sea views, minimalist rooftop terrace, large windows and restaurant terrace give a sensation of space and nature that's both calming and stimulating.

Architect Johan Nyrén, who died shortly after the building's completion, designed the three-storey building to be in harmony with the surrounding cliffs and pines, with moulded concrete walls, wooden walkways, a plant-covered roof and a huge rock in the lower restaurant.

That Artipelag doesn't have a permanent art collection is perhaps it's only downfall. The temporary art exhibitions on display here are an ambitious but still evolving mix of contemporary and classical, loosely held together by the organisation's aim to 'explore the borderland between fine art, crafts and design.' The shop, meanwhile, sells custom-made design products, as well as a range of BabyBjörn accessories.

A special bus service runs from Vasagatan in Stockholm directly to Artipelag, or you can take an SL bus from Slussen to Värmdö Marknad. It can also be reached via a 90-minute boat service (*M/S Nämdöfjärd* from Nybroviken) in summer.

ESCAPES & EXCURSIONS

Sandhamn.

Where to eat & drink

The island's best restaurant is the award-winning **Grinda Wärdshus** (*see below*; mains 190kr-330kr). It's open all year round and booking is essential; try the poached catfish. **Framfickan** (54 24 94 91, closed Sept-mid June, mains 130kr-230kr), by the guest harbour, serves pasta dishes.

Where to stay

Grinda Wärdshus (54 24 94 91, www.grinda.se, 995kr per person) has 30 double rooms in red wooden houses beside the restaurant. The rooms have no telephone or TV, but are light and stylish. **Grinda Stugby & Vandrarhem** (54 24 94 91, www.grindawardshus.se/en/vandrarhem-stugby, closed mid Oct-Apr, cottages 570kr-1,200kr, hostel 600kr, campsite 80kr) has 30 basic cottages, as well as a 44-bed hostel and campsite. Camping is only allowed in the designated area.

Getting there

Cinderellabåtarna (*see p221*) boats depart twice a day from Strandvägen (late Apr-end Aug, single 145kr) and stop at the south pier. **Waxholmsbolaget** (*see p223*) boats run all year round (single 90kr) to both piers. There are several crossings a day during the summer, and the journey normally takes around 90mins.

SANDHAMN

For archipelago beauty without total isolation, opt for Sandhamn. The island (officially named Sandön, but known as Sandhamn) boasts a hotel and conference centre, various restaurants and bars, bustling nightlife and a long, sandy beach. Pine forests cover most of the island, but the village, which dates back to the 1600s, has a few shops, a post office and a small museum.

Many of the island's points of interest are near the ferry dock. The **Hembygdsmuseum** (closed Sept-Midsummer) stands by the water in a red 18th-century storehouse, containing equipment from the toll station and an exhibition on alcohol smuggling. The **Tullhuset** (Toll House) is nearby; it operated until 1965 but is now leased out to private residents. In the 1870s, August Strindberg lived with his wife in a building, now called **Strindbergsgården**, overlooking the harbour.

There are beaches at **Fläskberget**, to the west of the village, and at **Dansberget** to the east, but you should really take the 20-minute walk through the forest to the beautiful sandy beach at **Trouville** in the south. Bikes can be rented at the **Viamare Sea Club** (50 61 21 18, www.viamare. se), which also has an outdoor pool, bar and café.

Where to eat & drink

For an upmarket dinner choice, try the **Seglarrestaurangen** at the Sandhamn Hotell & Konferens (*see below*), with its veranda and views of the harbour. The historic **Sandhamns Värdshus** (57 15 30 51, www.sandhamns-vardshus.se, mains 128kr-297kr) serves fish and wild game in a cosy environment. A livelier time can be had at **Dykarbaren** (57 15 35 54, www. dykarbaren.se), a popular bar with a restaurant upstairs. The **Sands Hotell** (*see below*) also has a restaurant.

Where to stay

The **Sandhamn Hotell & Konferens** (57 45 04 00, www.sandhamn.com, 2,590kr double), overlooking the guest harbour, has 79 luxurious rooms, plus a pool, fitness centre and sauna. The **Sands Hotell** (57 15 30 20, www.sandshotell.se, 1,900kr double) enjoys splendid views, and is smartly decorated within. For **B&Bs**, visit www.destinationsandhamn.se.

Getting there

By boat

Catch bus 434 from Slussen to Stavsnäs Brygga (1hr), which arrives in time for the ferry to Sandhamn (25mins, single 75kr). Alternatively, **Waxholmsbolaget** (*see p223*) and **Cinderellabåtarna** (*see p221*) boats depart several times a day from Strandvägen or Strömkajen in Stockholm during the summer. They take 120-180mins, and cost around 165kr for a single journey.

UTÖ

Utö is one of the largest islands in the archipelago, and over the summer it receives about 300,000 visitors. The main harbour is **Gruvbryggan**, where ferries from Stockholm arrive and most of the island's facilities can be found, including the tourist office, the only hotel, restaurants, shops and guest harbour. Ferries also stop at **Spränga** and on the adjoining island, **Ålö**, connected to Utö by road.

Utö is ideal for swimming and some of the best beaches can be found on the southern shore. Families should head for **Barnesbad**,

Utö.

a child-friendly beach 1.5 kilometres (one mile) north of Gruvbryggan harbour. The best way to get around Utö is by bike, which you can rent at Gruvbryggan during high season. The tourist office also rents out bikes and these can be booked in advance. Alternatively, hire a kayak or rowing boat to explore the coast.

Where to eat & drink

Gourmet cooking is served up at the beautiful **Utö Värdshus** (50 42 03 00, www.utovardshus. se, mains 245kr-395kr), frequently voted the best restaurant in the archipelago. A short stroll after dinner will bring you to **Bakfickan** (closed mid Aug-May), a popular cellar bar.

In summer, you can eat at **Seglarbaren** (50 42 03 00, open May-Sept, mains 100kr-200kr), on the waterfront by the main harbour. The island's bakery, **Utö Bageri** (700 15 19 00, closed Sept-May), near the harbour, sells great pastries, sandwiches and coffee, as well as its own special sailors' bread, Utölimpa.

Where to stay

A five-minute walk uphill from Gruvbryggan is **Utö Värdshus** (*see above*), the island's only hotel. It offers a variety of accommodation in scattered historic buildings, including four-person wooden cottages. Utö Värdshus also runs the **STF Youth Hostel** (50 42 03 00, www. svenskaturistforeningen.se, 350kr-400kr per person, closed Oct-Apr), with 72 beds. You can also rent basic cottages through the tourist office (*see below*). Camping is available near the harbour (contact the marina office).

Resources

Utö Turistbyrå
Gruvbryggan (50 15 74 10, www.utoturistbyra.se). **Open** 11am-3pm daily (July, Aug 10am-5pm daily).

Getting there

By boat
Waxholmsbolaget boats (*see p223*) run from Strömkajen several times a day between May and Aug (2.5-3hrs, single 130kr). Boats also stop at the next-door island of Ålö, so if you phone ahead you can arrange for a bike to be waiting there and cycle north to Uto.

By train, bus & boat
From Central Station take a pendeltåg train to Västerhaninge (about 35mins), then bus 846 to Årsta Brygga (SL passes valid on the train and bus), then a boat (single 75kr-80kr) to Utö. The journey takes about 40mins to Gruvbryggan, and another 10mins to Spränga.

In Context

History

Blond ambition.

Compared with many European capitals, Stockholm is a relative newcomer. While human activity in the region around Lake Mälaren dates back thousands of years, the city itself wasn't founded until the 13th century, when Birger Jarl came to power, following 300 years of Viking culture. The population of the island now known as Gamla Stan steadily grew, but it took until the 14th and 15th centuries for Stockholm to be recognised as Sweden's political and economic centre. It was during these centuries that the city started to expand, with the mainland area of Norrmalm and the large island of Södermalm forming new urban areas. Construction was, from here, unstoppable. The Royal Palace and Opera House were constructed in the 17th century, cementing Stockholm's place as one of Europe's cultural centres, while sea trading in the centuries that followed led to further growth and the city's increasing importance in the region.

IN CONTEXT

FIRST TRACKS

The earliest evidence of human habitation in Sweden is of nomadic reindeer hunters from continental Europe, who seem to have followed the receding glaciers north into Scandinavia at the end of the last Ice Age in approximately 11,000 BC. By about 7500 BC, Mesolithic hunter-gatherers had migrated to the coastal areas of central and northern Sweden. Between 4000 and 2800 BC, villages dotted the southern half of the country and people eked out a living as farmers. Sweden's inhabitants began establishing trading links with the wider world during the Bronze Age (1500 to 500 BC). They had access to large supplies of fur and amber, which they traded for raw metals, weapons and decorative objects.

Between AD 550 and 1000 two main rival groups emerged – the Svear, who were based in the Lake Mälaren region, and the Götar, who controlled a swathe of territory to the west and south. The geographical terms Svealand and Götaland are still in use today, and Sverige, Sweden's modern name in Swedish, comes from *Svea rike* – the Svea kingdom.

VIKING SPIRIT

The Viking culture emerged in various parts of Scandinavia in the early ninth century. The word 'Viking' is thought to come from the *viks* (Old Norse for 'inlets') in which they harboured their long ships. Extremely capable mariners, by the mid ninth century they had reached both the Black and Caspian Seas, where they launched attacks on Byzantium and north-east Iran. While often violent, the Vikings of Sweden were somewhat more business-minded than those of Denmark and Norway, and they successfully developed lucrative trading contacts with Byzantium.

Taken as a group, the Vikings effectively dominated the political and economic life of Europe until the mid 11th century. Remnants of their civilisation have been uncovered at a number of sites not far from Stockholm's city limits, most notably at Birka, a town founded in about AD 700 that was Sweden's leading trading centre in the early tenth century. Gamla Uppsala is even older than Birka, with some of its royal graves dating back to the sixth century. The Historiska Museet has an excellent exhibition introducing visitors to a wealth of information and artefacts that cast light on Viking culture.

The Swedes were among the last Europeans to abandon paganism. In spite of the efforts of a number of crusading monks and priests, and the baptism of King Olof Skötkonung in 1008 (and all his successors after him), many Swedes stubbornly remained true to the old Norse gods until the end of the 11th century. By the middle of the 12th century, the Church had finally gained a foothold and Sweden's first archbishopric was established in Uppsala. The first Swedish archbishop, appointed in 1164, was an English monk called Stephen. King Erik Jedvardsson (1156-60), who had led a crusade to christianise the Finns, was chosen to become Sweden's patron saint. He is commemorated in place names such as St Eriksplan and St Eriksgatan; his remains are entombed at Uppsala Cathedral.

BIRTH OF A CITY

The foundation of Stockholm is intimately connected to the power struggles between the monarchy and the nobility that characterised Swedish history after the collapse of Viking culture. The physical city and its name can be traced to 13th-century ruler Birger Jarl.

Birger Jarl came to power in 1229, after the then king, Erik Erikssen, had been deposed. He is remembered for two main accomplishments: the long and turbulent process he initiated to centralise political power in Sweden, and the founding of the city of Stockholm. In 1247-51, he made great progress towards achieving his first goal by using German money and soldiers to successfully defeat a rebellion led by noblemen in the area around Lake Mälaren. Shortly after this victory he offered good trading terms to German merchants, especially those from Lübeck, which led to Sweden's long-lasting ties to the Hanseatic League.

The 13th-century Swedish kingdom consisted of the area around Lake Mälaren, the Stockholm and Åland archipelagos, and the Gulf of Finland all the way to Viborg (now part of Russia). Low sea levels meant that the passage from the Baltic Sea into Lake Mälaren was restricted to a narrow channel now known as Norrström. This passage became a vital trade route and a key defensive position, and in 1252 Birger Jarl constructed a mighty fortress on the site: the Tre Kronor (on the site of the present Kungliga Slottet). It would grow to become the city of Stockholm.

In that same year, Birger Jarl wrote two letters in which the name 'Stockholm' is mentioned for the first time. The origin of the name is unclear, but it may be derived from from the fact that logs (*stockar*) were used to build up the small island (*holme*) upon which the fortress was built.

The settlement at Tre Kronor soon became one of Sweden's most important economic centres. Ships from Lübeck and other Hanseatic towns traded enthusiastically with the expatriate Germans who were setting up copper and iron-ore mines in Sweden, while products from the interior of the country (fur, grain and iron) were traded with merchants from across northern Europe.

Birger Jarl's son Magnus took power in 1275. A renewed repression of the country's unruly nobles concentrated power in his hands, and the various edicts and rulings with which he limited the power of the nobility are credited with forestalling the development of feudalism in Sweden. After his death in 1290, power shifted briefly back to the nobility before Magnus's son Birger assumed the throne in 1302, but his rule was blighted by a power struggle with his brothers, who demanded that he divide the kingdom between them. In 1317, he had them arrested, thrown in prison and starved to death. The horrified nobility deposed him, forcing him to flee the country.

Magnus, the child of a Swedish duke and, at the age of three, already king of Norway, was to be his successor. Upon reaching adulthood Magnus assumed the throne and set about making changes to the Swedish social order. He abolished *träldom*, a form of slavery, in 1335, and established Sweden's first national legal code in 1350. His dual kingdom was huge – after the signing of the treaty of Novgorod in 1323 Finland had officially become part of the Swedish realm – but the majority of his subjects lived in abject poverty. During the mid 14th century the kingdom was hit by the bubonic plague, and approximately a third of the population was killed.

By the mid 1300s, King Magnus was in serious trouble. Long-running disputes about the then Danish provinces of Skåne and Blekinge resulted in devastating Danish attacks on Swedish targets. In the 1360s, the nobility lost all patience with Magnus and enlisted the help of Duke Albrecht of Mecklenburg (1364-88) to unseat him.

Albrecht and his forces quickly conquered Stockholm and the nobles carved up the country for themselves.

NORDIC ALLIANCE

Upon the death in 1386 of Bo Jonsson Grip – chief of Sweden's ruling nobles – the nobility turned to Margaret, daughter of Danish King Valdemar and wife of Magnus's son King Håkon of Norway. Since the deaths of her father and husband she had already been made regent in both Denmark and Norway for her son Olof. Though Olof died in 1387, she retained her hold on power in the three kingdoms. In 1389, she was proclaimed ruler of Sweden and in return she confirmed all the privileges of the Swedish nobility. When they asked her to choose a king she nominated 14-year-old Erik VII of Pomerania. As he was already king of Norway and Denmark, Scandinavia now had just one ruler. However, Margaret was the real power behind the throne and remained so until her death in 1412.

In 1397, she formalised a Nordic alliance called the Kalmar Union to limit the commercial and political influence of the Hanseatic League. By the start of the 15th century the union encompassed Norway, Sweden, Finland, Iceland and Greenland, making it the largest kingdom in Europe. The union was threatened many times over the next 125 years by Swedish rebellion against Danish forces.

Christopher of Bavaria ruled the union from 1439 to 1448. Upon his death, the noble families of Norway, Sweden and Denmark could not agree on a single candidate to fill the kingship. Sweden's nationalists, led by the Sture family, seized this opportunity to attempt to free Sweden from the union. This led to vicious fighting with Sweden's unionist faction, which was led by the Oxenstierna family. Finally, in 1470, the nationalists had the upper hand and Sten Sture the Elder (1471-97, 1501-3) was appointed the 'Guardian of the Realm'. A year later the Battle of Brunkeberg broke out in what is now the centre of Stockholm, resulting in the decimation of the unionist forces. The statue of St George and the Dragon in Storkyrkan was donated by Sture to commemorate the victory.

STOCKHOLM BLOODBATH

Aside from his crucial military victories, Sten Sture the Elder is remembered for the many

IN CONTEXT

technological, cultural and educational steps forward that Sweden made under his leadership. He established Sweden's first university in Uppsala in 1477, and in 1483 Sweden's first printing press was set up. Decorative arts became more sophisticated, as shown by the many fine German- and Dutch-style paintings that adorn Swedish churches of this period. Stockholm continued to grow throughout the 15th century, and by the early 16th century the city had between 6,000 and 7,000 inhabitants, most of them living in present-day Gamla Stan. Though these numbers made Stockholm Sweden's largest town, by continental standards it was tiny. In 1500, Lübeck had 25,000 inhabitants and Paris more than 100,000.

From the start, the population of Stockholm was a mix of people from different parts of Sweden and other areas of Europe. The largest 'foreign' contingent – between 10 and 20 per cent of the population – was made up of Finns, largely a result of Finland's status, since the mid 12th century, as a Swedish province. The Germans comprised a smaller, but much more powerful, proportion; since the city had been founded with Hanseatic support, wealthy German merchants had been living in Stockholm from its beginnings. Dutch, Scottish, French, English, Italian, Danish, Russian and Polish merchants and traders also became increasingly significant in Stockholm during the 15th century.

By the late 15th century, most Swedes thought the Kalmar Union was a thing of the past, but the alliance was still popular in Denmark and Sweden's rulers had to deal with numerous Danish attacks. When Christian II assumed the Danish throne in 1513, the unionist movement rejoiced, thinking it had now finally found a leader who would be able to crush the Swedish nationalists.

Sure enough, Christian attacked Sweden and killed the then ruler, Sten Sture the Younger (1512-20). After Sture's death, Christian gathered leading members of the Swedish nobility together at Tre Kronor castle under the guise of granting them amnesty for their opposition to the union. After three days of feasting and celebrating, he locked the doors to the castle and arrested his guests.

Around 90 men were sentenced to death and taken to Stortorget, outside the castle, where they were killed one by one. The event

Stockholm Bloodbath.

came to be known as the Stockholm Bloodbath, and it earned Christian II the name Christian the Tyrant. After the killings, Sture's followers were ruthlessly persecuted. This proved counter-productive, as it provoked widespread opposition to Danish rule and finally resulted in the complete breakdown of the union in 1521-23. Sweden then became a totally independent country under the leadership of Gustav Eriksson, who was crowned King Gustav Vasa (1523-60).

AGE OF EMPIRE

During Gustav Vasa's long reign Sweden was changed in two fundamental ways: it was unified under a strong hereditary monarch, and it became a Protestant country. Gustav Vasa was never a particularly religious man, and his Reformation had more to do with politics and economics than theology. Lacking the wealth he required to fulfil his ambitions, he confiscated Church property, reassigned it to the Crown, and began a propaganda campaign that stressed the negative role the Church's leadership had played in the past – in particular, Archbishop Gustav Trolle's support for Christian the Tyrant. These measures resulted in the eventual adoption of the Lutheran faith as the state religion.

The Reformation led to the state-sanctioned destruction of scores of Swedish monasteries, convents and churches, their riches going to an increasingly wealthy and powerful king. Gustav Vasa even had plans to tear down Storkyrkan because he felt it was situated too close to the royal residence at Tre Kronor castle, thereby complicating its defence. But public opinion was strongly opposed to the destruction of Stockholm's spiritual heart, so the King relented and decided only to make minor alterations. (Gustav Vasa's son Johan was more interested in both architecture and religion than his father, and in the 1580s he had a number of Stockholm's demolished churches rebuilt.)

His larder full and his domestic goals largely accomplished, Gustav Vasa launched a campaign to weaken Russia, Poland and Denmark and thereby make Sweden the dominant Baltic power, beginning with a modestly successful war against Russia in 1555-57. After his death in 1560, his sons, King Erik XIV, King Johan III and King Karl IX, took up the mission. Gustav Vasa is seen as the monarch who was most responsible for turning Sweden into a nation. He created a modern army, navy and civil service, and the intellectual figures he brought to his court connected Sweden with the Renaissance in the arts and sciences.

In 1570-95, Sweden fought another war against Russia, with some success. But Denmark was harder to beat – in spite of the break-up of the Kalmar Union, it had remained the most powerful country in the region, as Sweden learned to its cost in the expensive wars of 1563-70 and 1611-13. It was not until the Thirty Years War, which began in Germany in 1618, that the tide finally turned decisively in Sweden's favour in its rivalry with the Danes. After suffering a devastating defeat at the hands of the Swedes in the Battle of Lutter-am-Barenburg in 1626, Denmark was forced to pull out of the war. In 1630, Sweden officially entered the war on the side of the Protestants. The resulting peace treaty of 1648 gave Sweden new provinces in northern Germany, and by 1658 a severely weakened Denmark had been forced to surrender parts of Norway plus all Danish provinces east of Öresund. As a result, by the end of the 17th century Sweden had become the most powerful nation in northern Europe.

Gustav II Adolf and his chancellor, Axel Oxenstierna, were eager to develop Stockholm and make it the political and administrative centre of the growing Swedish empire. They strengthened Stockholm's position as a centre of foreign trade, founded Sweden's Supreme Court in the city and reorganised the national assembly into four estates; nobility, clergy, burghers and farmers. The medieval wall was torn down so that the city could expand to the north and south and the old wooden buildings that dominated Södermalm and Norrmalm were replaced by straight streets lined with stone buildings.

After Gustav II Adolf's death his young daughter, Christina, became queen, with Oxenstierna as regent until 1644. In 1654, Christina converted to Catholicism, renounced the throne and moved to Rome, where she lived out her life building up one of the finest art and book collections in Europe. She left the throne to Karl X Gustav (1654-60), who is remembered best for his invasion and defeat of Denmark in 1657, creating the largest Swedish empire ever. He was succeeded by his son, Karl XI (1660-97), who in 1682 pronounced himself to be Sweden's first absolute monarch, answerable only to God.

Stockholm's population grew rapidly during Sweden's age of empire; by the 1670s the city had between 50,000 and 55,000 citizens. Literacy rates were rising, grammar schools were established, and creativity flourished under the likes of George Stiernhielm (1598-1672), the father of modern Swedish poetry. Architecturally this was the age of the Tessins, who completed the fabulous Drottningholms Slott in 1686. It was a golden age for Swedish history, in military, cultural, economic and social terms.

RISE OF THE ARISTOCRACY

It was during the reign of Karl XII (1697-1718) – who assumed the throne at the tender age of 15 – that Sweden lost her empire. Between 1700 and 1721 Sweden fought the Great Northern War against a number of opponents, notably the defensive alliance of Saxony-Poland, Russia and Denmark. The young King fought valiantly against the odds to hold on to all of Sweden's far-flung possessions, but suffered a terrible loss to Russia's Peter the Great at the Battle of Poltava in 1709. His bravery in battle is still revered in Sweden's

IN CONTEXT

far-right circles to this day. He was finally killed in Norway by a sniper's bullet in 1718. Since he had no heir, the period after Karl's death was marked by a weakening of the monarchy and the rise of the aristocracy.

In 1719, the role of the monarch was reduced to that of nominal head of state, and with the government dominated by cabals of squabbling noblemen, the economy was left to stagnate, and political and social reforms were slow in coming.

By the end of the Great Northern War in 1721, Sweden had lost parts of Pomerania in Germany, as well as its strongholds in modern-day Estonia, Latvia, north-west Russia and Finland. Disastrous attempts were made to reconquer some of these territories by fighting wars with Russia in 1741-43 and 1788-90. Participation in the Seven Years War (1756-63) resulted in the loss of Swedish territory to Prussia. Sweden was no longer the great power it had been.

This was also a trying time for the citizens of Stockholm – on top of coping with their country's political and military difficulties, their city was ravaged by fire and disease. In 1697, it was devastated by a fire that destroyed Tre Kronor, the royal palace and pride of Stockholm. In 1710, plague swept through, killing about a third of the population.

Later in the century Stockholm suffered three more devastating fires, which resulted in a municipal ban on wood as a material for new houses. Over the course of the 18th century the population stayed static at about 70,000 inhabitants. Unsanitary conditions, overcrowding, cold and disease all contributed to the fact that Stockholm's death rate was among the highest of all European cities.

But there was a brighter side. In the decades leading up to 1754, Stockholm buzzed with the building of the new Kungliga Slottet to replace Tre Kronor. The construction work was a huge stimulus for the city's artisans, and for Stockholm's economy overall. There was an influx of skilled workers from overseas and new industries began to grow up in Stockholm. The city's foreign trade was also developing rapidly – not only with Europe but also with the Far East and the Americas.

Many of Stockholm's burghers used their increasing wealth to build larger houses, especially along Skeppsbron in Gamla Stan. New residential neighbourhoods sprang up on Södermalm and Norrmalm, and many of the houses on Gamla Stan were renovated.

SCIENTIFIC PROGRESS

The 18th century was also an age of scientific and intellectual advance in Stockholm, and throughout Sweden. Key figures included the famous botanist Carl von Linné (aka Linnaeus; 1707-78); Anders Celsius (1701-44), inventor of the centigrade temperature scale; and mystical philosopher Emanuel Swedenborg (1688-1772). Sweden's best-loved poet, Carl Michael Bellman (1740-95), did much to encourage Swedish nationalism. Religious life became less strictly constrained; Jews were allowed to settle in Sweden in 1744, and in 1781 Catholics were permitted to establish a church in Stockholm for the first time since the Reformation.

The monarchy regained some of its old power under Gustav III (1771-92). Seeing that the Riksdag (Parliament) was divided, the King seized the opportunity to force through a new constitution that would make the nobility share power with the Crown. Gustav III was initially popular with his subjects because he built hospitals, allowed freedom of worship and lessened economic controls. He was also a man of culture who imported French opera, theatre and literature to Sweden, and in 1782 he founded Stockholm's first opera house. During his reign, several newspapers were established, and political and cultural debate flourished. The nobility were not so happy with his tyrannical behaviour, however, especially after the start of the French Revolution. In 1792, Gustav III was shot by an assassin at a masked ball at the Kungliga Operan; he died two weeks later.

In 1805 Gustav III's successor, Gustav IV Adolf (1792-1809), was drawn into the Napoleonic Wars on the British side. This resulted in a number of gains and losses; most significantly, Sweden lost Finland to Russia and gained Norway from Denmark. All this upheaval resulted in political changes, notably the constitution of 1809, which established a system whereby a liberal monarchy would be responsible to an elected Riksdag.

The union with Norway was established in 1814, and was formalised in the 1815 Act of Union. The settlement took account of the Norwegian desire for self-government, declaring Norway a separate nation from

Gustav III.

Sweden. However, King Karl XIII (1748-1818) was now sovereign over Norway. The tension between the Swedish desire to strengthen the union, and the Norwegian wish for further autonomy, was set to increase over the century that followed.

Following the death of Karl XIII in 1818, one of Napoleon's generals, Jean-Baptiste Bernadotte, was invited to assume the Swedish throne. He accepted and took the name Karl XIV Johan (1818-44). In spite of the fact that he spoke no Swedish and had never visited Scandinavia prior to accepting the kingship, Sweden prospered under his rule.

His successor, Oscar I (1844-59), gave women inheritance rights equal to those of their brothers in 1845, passed an Education Act (1842) and a Poor Care law (1855), and reformed the restrictive craftsmen's guilds. The reign of his son, Karl XV (1859-72), is remembered for the reformation of the Riksdag in 1866 – the old four estates were replaced with a dual-chamber representative parliament. This act marked the beginning of the end for the monarch's role in politics, essentially reducing the role to a figurehead.

INDUSTRIAL REVOLUTION

Industrialisation arrived late to Sweden, and the mechanisation of what little industry did exist (mining, forestry and the like) was half-hearted – hardly what you would call a revolution. Meanwhile, the rural population had grown steadily through the first half of the 19th century. There was neither enough land, nor jobs in the cities, to support everyone. A severe famine during 1867-68 tipped the scales, and over one million Swedes emigrated to North America between 1860 and 1910 – a traumatic event for a country whose population in 1860 was only four million.

In the 1860s, Sweden's first railway lines finally opened reliable communications between Stockholm and the country's southern regions; by 1871 the railway to the north was complete. The railways were a boon for nascent industry. High-quality, efficiently made steel and safety matches (a Swedish invention) were to become the two most notable Swedish manufactured products. By the late 19th century, a number of large industries had been established in Stockholm; for example, a shoe factory on Södermalm, and a huge Bolinders factory on Kungsholmen producing steam engines, cast-iron stoves, and other household items. In 1876, Lars Magnus Ericsson opened his Ericsson telephone company in Stockholm, and soon the city had more phones per capita than any other city in Europe.

By 1900, one in four Swedes lived in a city, and industrialisation was finally in full swing. Stockholm's factories attracted workers from all over the country, causing the population to grow from 100,000 in 1856 to 300,000 in 1900. Conditions in many factories were appalling, and unions emerged to fight for the rights of workers. The unions formed a confederation in 1898 but found it difficult to make progress under harsh laws on picketing.

Living conditions in the city were nearly as bad as working conditions. In response to Stockholm's growing housing crisis, the city planners – led by Claes Albert Lindhagen – put forward a proposal in 1866 to build wide boulevards and esplanades similar to those in Paris, which would create some green space within the city as well as allowing traffic to move freely. The plan resulted in the construction of some of the city's key arteries, such as Birger Jarlsgatan, Ringvägen, Karlavägen and Strandvägen. In just one decade, the 1880s, Stockholm's population increased by 46 per cent – more buildings were constructed in the 1880s than during the previous 70 years; neighbourhoods such as Östermalm, Vasastaden, Kungsholmen, Hornstull and Skanstull were created.

IN CONTEXT

The late 19th century also saw the arrival of Stockholm's first continental-style hotels, cafés, restaurants, shopping galleries and department stores, to serve the city's upper classes, and the beginnings of a tourist industry. The arts and academies also prospered. Swedish dramatist August Strindberg achieved critical success across Europe, and folk historian Artur Hazelius founded the Nordiska Museet and open-air Skansen museum. The Academy of Stockholm (now the University of Stockholm) was founded in 1878, and in 1896 Alfred Nobel donated his fortune to fund the Nobel Prizes.

'During the 1880s, Stockholm's population increased by 46 per cent.'

SOCIAL DEMOCRACY TO THE FORE

In 1905, the union between Sweden and Norway finally dissolved. Norway took full control of its own affairs, and the Swedish state assumed its current shape.

At the outbreak of World War I Sweden declared itself neutral, in spite of its German sympathies. The British demanded that Sweden enforce a blockade against Germany. When Sweden refused to co-operate, the British blacklisted Swedish goods and interfered with Swedish commercial shipping, going so far as to seize ships' cargoes. The economy suffered dramatically and inflation shot through the roof. The British tactics led to rationing, as well as severe food shortages. Demonstrations broke out in 1917-18, partly inspired by the Russian Revolution. The demonstrators focused on food shortages and demands for democratic reforms, particularly the extension of voting rights to women.

The privations of the war helped social democracy make its breakthrough. By the end of the war, the Social Democrat Party had been active for some time – its first member had been elected to the Riksdag in 1902 – though it remained marginal. After the Russian Revolution, it presented a less extreme alternative to communism in Sweden, and gained popularity. In 1920, Hjalmar Branting became Sweden's first Social Democrat prime minister, and reforms quickly followed: women

were awarded the vote; the state-controlled alcohol-selling system was established; and the working day was limited to eight hours.

The Social Democrats' dominance of political affairs began in earnest in the 1930s. From 1932, the party enjoyed an unbroken 40 years in power. This made it possible to take the first steps towards building the notion of a People's Home (Folkhemmet), in which higher taxes would finance a decent standard of living for all. The first components of the welfare system were unemployment benefits, paid holidays, family allowances and increased old-age pensions.

At the outbreak of World War II there was little sympathy in Sweden for the Germans – unlike in 1914. Sweden declared neutrality but was in a difficult position. Germany was allied with Finland against the Soviet Union, and the relationship between Sweden and Finland was traditionally close – with Russia the age-old enemy. But when the Soviets invaded Finland in 1939, Sweden was only drawn in to a certain degree, providing weapons, volunteers and refuge to the Finns, but refusing to send regular troops. Sweden's position became even more uncomfortable in 1940, when Germany invaded Denmark and Norway, thus isolating Sweden and compelling it to supply the Nazis with iron ore and to allow them to transport their troops across Swedish territory and in Swedish waters. In 1942, the Swedish navy fought an undeclared war against Soviet submarines.

On the other hand, western allied airmen were rescued in Sweden and often sent back to Britain, and Danish and Norwegian armed resistance groups were organised on Swedish soil in 1942-43. Jewish lives were also saved, notably by Swedish businessman Raoul Wallenberg, who managed to prevent about 100,000 Hungarian Jews from being deported by the SS. After the Soviet conquest of Budapest in January 1945, Wallenberg was arrested as a suspected spy and disappeared. For years, rumours flew about whether or not he had died in a Moscow prison in 1947; Soviet documents unearthed in 1989 indicated this was what had most likely happened.

The main goal for the Swedish government during the war was not strict neutrality but rather to avoid Sweden being dragged into the conflict – this was accomplished at high diplomatic and moral cost.

IN CONTEXT

At the start of the Cold War, in 1948-49, Sweden tried to form a defensive alliance with Denmark and Norway, but the plans failed partly because the other two countries wanted close links with the western allies. When the Danes and Norwegians became members of NATO in 1949, Sweden remained outside, ostensibly to prevent Finland becoming isolated in the face of the Soviet Union. In recent years it has emerged that Sweden was, in fact, in secret co-operation with NATO from as far back as the early 1950s.

A CHANGING SKYLINE

After the end of World War II, a large-scale transformation of Stockholm's city centre began, despite the fact that Stockholm was one of the few European capitals to survive the war unscathed. Once the rebuilding process on the Continent was in full swing, with American-style skyscrapers rising from the ashes of all the bombed-out cities, Sweden felt left out. The city government began to tear down many of its decaying old buildings and construct anew. As more and more people moved to Stockholm in the post-war period (the capital's population more than doubled in the 20th century), the city once again developed a severe housing crisis. Stockholm's Tunnelbana system was inaugurated in 1950 and new suburbs were built along it, to the south and north-west.

Under the leadership of Tage Erlander (1946-69), the Social Democrats introduced models for industrial bargaining and full employment that were successful in boosting the economy. At the same time, the country created a national health service and a

Gamla Stan, 1897.

IN CONTEXT

disability benefits system, improved the quality of its schools and instituted free university education. Sweden established itself as a leading industrial country and was proud of its 'Third Way', a blending of corporate capitalism with a cradle-to-grave social safety net for all.

In 1953, Swedish diplomat Dag Hammarskjöld was appointed secretary-general of the United Nations. A controversial figure who tried to use his position to broker peace in the conflicts of the period, he became a thorn in the side of the superpowers. He died in 1961 in a mysterious plane crash over northern Rhodesia while on a mission to try to solve the Congo crisis. News of his death caused profound sadness across Sweden, as he personified the Swedes' perception of themselves as the world's conscience.

Sweden's booming post-war economy produced a demand for labour that the national workforce could not meet. From about 1950, Sweden began to import skilled labour, primarily from the Nordic countries but also from Italy, Greece and Yugoslavia. This immigration continued unrestricted until the mid 1960s, reaching its peak in 1969-70, when more than 75,000 immigrants were entering Sweden each year. Thereafter numbers fell significantly, although Sweden continued to welcome political refugees from around the globe. By the mid 1990s, 11 per cent of Sweden's population were foreign-born.

In the 1970s, international economic pressures began to put the squeeze on Sweden's social goals, and it was under Olof Palme's leadership (1982-86) that the Third Way began to falter. Palme spent a lot of time and energy building up Sweden's international image, while Sweden's high-tax economy was sliding into stagnation. When an unknown assailant murdered Palme on a Stockholm street in 1986 it created a national trauma.

The end of the Cold War in the late 1980s led to a serious re-evaluation of Sweden's position in international politics. The early 1990s saw the Social Democrats replaced by a centre-right coalition. This coincided with an economic crisis; long-term economic stagnation and budgetary problems led to a huge devaluation of the krona. A programme of austerity measures was then implemented, but it wasn't enough. Sweden suffered its worst recession since the 1930s and

unemployment soared to a record 14 per cent. In 1994, the Social Democrats were returned to power. With its economy and confidence severely shaken, Sweden voted (by a very narrow margin) to join the European Union, its membership taking effect on 1 January 1995.

Since then, the economy has improved considerably, with both unemployment and inflation falling greatly, particularly during the IT boom of the 1990s. The bursting of the IT bubble seemed to threaten this renewed prosperity, but the industry picked itself up, growing steadily over the past decade.

Sweden's relationship with the EU remained controversial, with many on the left fearing that closer co-operation with other European countries threatened to undermine the tenets of the welfare state. These arguments were given a good airing in the referendum in 2003 on the euro. Despite support for membership from almost all the major parties, voters chose to stay outside the single currency zone. After the vote, the prime minister, Göran Persson, declared that Sweden would not hold another referendum on the issue for at least ten years.

The 2003 referendum came two days after the murder of Anna Lindh, the popular foreign minister, in a Stockholm department store. A young Swede of Serbian origin, Mijailo Mijailovic, was convicted of her killing. A motive was never established, but Mijailovic was later ruled to have been suffering from a mental illness at the time of the attack.

The killing came as a huge shock to Swedes, and to the Social Democrat Party. It was to be the first of a number of blows to Prime Minister Göran Persson that would culminate in his defeat in the 2006 general election.

TSUNAMI TRAGEDY

A tragedy of much greater proportions befell Sweden on 26 December 2004, when 543 Swedes were killed in the Asian tsunami. The number of Swedes killed was greater even than in the 1994 Estonia ferry disaster, in which 501 Swedes died. With most ministers and civil servants at home for Christmas, it took a whole day for the government to realise that thousands of Swedes were holidaying in the area. The episode dented the government's reputation, and the next two years were dominated by inquiries into the handling of Sweden's response to the disaster.

The opposition found themselves in a good position to capitalise on the Social Democrats' discomfort. The four centre-right parties – the Moderate Party, the Liberal People's Party, the Centre Party and the Christian Democrats – agreed to campaign on a joint manifesto. Calling themselves the Alliance for Sweden, they went on to win the election in September 2006, promising modest tax cuts and cuts to some benefits. The aim, they said, was to reduce Sweden's hidden unemployment, which by some measures was between 15 and 20 per cent.

Moderate leader Fredrik Reinfeldt was the first non-Social Democrat prime minister for 12 years. He was also a rarity from the longer-term perspective – the Social Democrats had ruled Sweden for 67 of the previous 76 years. He was the youngest prime minister for 80 years, and his cabinet included the first Swedish minister of African descent and the first gay minister (same sex marriage was legalised in Sweden in 2009). While his tax cuts and benefit cuts were small, he also put into action plans to privatise state industries such as Vin&Sprit, maker of Absolut Vodka, which was bought by Pernod Ricard in 2008.

THE LEFT STRIKES BACK

Reinfeldt was re-elected in 2010, after a closely fought campaign. However, the Alliance for Sweden fell short of an overall majority by two seats, forcing it to form a minority coalition government. It was in this election that the far-right, anti-immigration Sweden Democrats Party gained ground, winning 20 parliamentary seats – the first seats it had ever won. A December 2010 suicide bombing in Stockholm, the first terrorist attack in the Nordic countries to be linked to Islamic terrorism, is thought to have fuelled far-right, anti-immigration sentiment further, after two people were injured.

Two royal weddings in five years have, however, helped to lighten the public mood. Sweden's Crown Princess Victoria walked down the aisle with Daniel Westling, her former personal trainer, in June 2010. The royal wedding was watched on television by around three million Swedes. In 2012, Victoria gave birth to Princess Estelle, who became second in line to the Swedish throne. In June 2013, Victoria's young sister, Princess Madeleine, followed suit, marrying British-American investment banker Christopher O'Neill, and giving birth to Princess Leonore in New York City in February 2014. Madeleine's wedding took place only a month after riots had erupted in the Stockholm immigrant suburb of Husby, following the fatal shooting of an elderly Portuguese expat by local police. Some 150 vehicles were set on fire during the seven-day riots, which spread to several other suburbs and unleashed a vast amount of discontent.

The increased concern over Sweden's high unemployment, mounting inequality and declining welfare state led to the comeback of the Social Democrats, under Stefan Lofven, in the September 2014 general election, when the party won 43.7 per cent of seats – enough to end the centre-right Alliance's rule, though not enough to form a clear parliamentary majority. The Sweden Democrats won 13 per cent of seats, making it the country's third biggest party, though Lofven has vowed not to work with the anti-immigration party. Time will tell whether the Social Democrats' minority government will be strong enough to roll back the welfare cuts of recent years and return Sweden to its public-private glory days. A new consumer class and high immigration are two potential obstacles that remain in its path.

Crown Princess Victoria with Princess Estelle.

IN CONTEXT

Swedish Design

Never forget the three Fs: form, function and flat-packing.

IN CONTEXT

In the world of furniture, glassware, industrial and fashion design, Swedes have carved out a profitable niche, creating products that are functional and effortlessly stylish. The result is big business around the world, with Swedish design flying off the shelves from Tallinn to Tokyo. The roots of Swedish design are everywhere to be seen. Ikea, the biggest exporter of the Swedish functionalist concept, still furnishes the majority of Sweden's homes. Alternatively, walk around the boutiques of Östermalm or the fashionable SoFo district of Södermalm, and you'll find achingly simple furniture, homewares and fashion at achingly high prices. But while sleek and functional is still the order of the day in most Stockholm studios, a new generation of designers is less bound to the philosophy that underpins the minimalist tradition. Today, designers of glassware, furniture, wallpaper and industrial products are looking abroad to the rest of Europe, the Middle East, Africa and Asia for inspiration.

DEVELOPMENT

Though modern Swedish design dates back roughly 100 years, its aesthetic roots can be traced further back. The highly influential Gustavian style, which came about during the reign of King Gustav III in the 18th century, marked a move away from elaborate Baroque to a more classical, restrained elegance characterised by white wood and simple curves. Then, in the late 1800s, the Swedish elite was exposed to German art nouveau, a new style that changed the way well-to-do Swedes thought about their homes. It marked a further shift towards organic forms and sinewy curves, inspired by nature, and led to even less fancy and more ergonomic furniture and household accessories.

The paintings of late 19th-century artist **Carl Larsson** (1853-1919) played a significant role in the development of Swedish interior design. In 1899, he created a widely reproduced series of watercolours called *Ett Hem* ('A Home'), featuring the simple furniture and pale-coloured textiles created by his wife Karin, who was inspired by local design traditions, the English Arts and Crafts movement and art nouveau trends on the Continent. In Larsson's paintings, it is easy to recognise the rural wooden floors and rectangular woven rag rugs that are still common in Swedish homes. The striped patterns on the simple white-painted chairs are also strikingly similar to those sold today by Swedish interior decorating monolith Ikea.

In an essay entitled 'Skönhet för Alla' ('Beauty for All'; 1899), which was inspired by the Larssons' aesthetics, Swedish social critic Ellen Key defined the democratic ideals embodied in the Larssons' rustic home: 'Not until nothing ugly can be bought, when the beautiful is as cheap as the ugly, only then can beauty for all become a reality.' These democratic principles, as well as those expressed by Gregor Paulsson in 1919 in his book *More Beautiful Things for Everyday Use*, still inform much of Swedish society and influence new design.

Many of the classics of Swedish design came out during the creatively fertile 1930s, as modernism blossomed throughout northern Europe. The movement made its breakthrough in Sweden at the Stockholm Exhibition in 1930, organised by influential Swedish architect **Gunnar Asplund**

Svenskt Tenn.

(1885-1940), and the Swedish offshoot came to be known as functionalism. Some speculate that Sweden was especially receptive to the gospel of functionalism – and later to minimalist severity – because of sober Swedish Lutheranism, as well as a national penchant for social engineering.

The fresh air, natural light and access to greenery extolled by Asplund's functionalism quickly became the defining characteristics of Swedish home design and urban planning. During the next two decades, as news of the practical and beautiful designs coming out of the Nordic region spread to other parts of Europe, as well as to North America, the reputation of Scandinavian style became firmly established.

DESIGN ICONS

The demigods of Swedish furniture design – Carl Malmsten and Bruno Mathsson both flourished during the dynamic pre-war period. **Carl Malmsten** (1888-1972) sought forms that some described as 'rural rococo', and aspired to a craft-oriented and functional approach to furniture design. The company/ shop that he founded 60 years ago – **Malmstenbutiken** (see p130) – is still in the same family. His counterpart, **Bruno Mathsson** (1907-88), is famous for his groundbreaking work with bentwood. Mathsson's light and simple modernistic designs can be seen in Stockholm at **Studio B3**'s permanent showroom (Barnhusgatan 3, Norrmalm, 08 21 42 31, www.scandinaviandesign.com/b3).

A third giant of the pre-war design era was modernist architect and designer **Josef Frank** (1885-1967), an Austrian exile in Sweden, who created elegant furniture and vibrant floral textiles. Frank was so ahead of his time that his brilliant patterns look like they could have been created yesterday, and are still very popular. Frank's colourful fabrics can be seen at **Svenskt Tenn** (see p131), a well-loved design shop in Östermalm.

The term 'Scandinavian design' was coined in the 1950s when the exhibition 'Design in Scandinavia' toured northern America, and Nordic design, with its clean lines, high-level functionality and accessibility, became the most internationally influential design movement of the time. The latter half of the 20th century inevitably brought some variance from the founding facets of Swedish design,

with designers responding to the times and experimenting. For instance, in the 1960s an 'anti-functional' movement took root as Swedish designers looked to their Italian counterparts for inspiration. Free from the rules of functionalism, they began to produce chairs, lamps and sofas in all sizes, shapes and colours, and in a variety of new and unusual materials, notably plastic.

During the economic boom of the 1980s, eclecticism and postmodernism took over as designers such as **Jonas Bohlin** (born 1953) and **Mats Theselius** (born 1956) began creating 'work of art' furniture in limited editions for sale to collectors. Bohlin's breakthrough came in 1980 with 'Concrete', a chair made out of, yes, concrete.

A kind of neo-functionalist minimalism had taken over by the 1990s. Suddenly every bar and restaurant in the city, it seemed, was painted white, with unobtrusive furniture and almost no decoration on the walls or tables. This Scandinavian ultra-simplicity quickly spread to the rest of the world, in no small part owing to the praise it earned from international style magazines such as *Wallpaper**.

FRESH FACES

These days, a fresh generation of creators, inspired by everything from baroque furniture to Japanese cartoons, is bringing a playful and often witty twist to the local design scene.

Designers Anna Holmquist and Chandra Ahlsell of industrial design firm **FolkForm** (www.folkform.se) are good examples of this. Their masonite tabletop embedded with a real butterfly won them the prestigious main prize at Future Design Days (www.future designdays.com), a cutting-edge international design festival.

Established and up-and-coming designers are showcased at Stockholm Design Week in February every year, which centres around the **Stockholm Furniture Fair** and the **Northern Light Fair** (for both, visit www.stockholm furniturelightfair.se). Recent Stockholm designers to have made waves include furniture designer **Thomas Bernstrand** (of design company Bernstrand); furniture and lighting designer **Alexander Lervik**, whose Light Bar, made up of LED-lit coloured plastic heads, dazzled visitors to the 2011 Stockholm Furniture Fair; and furniture and industrial designer **Monica Forster**.

IN CONTEXT

> *'The design scene, while loyal in many ways to its minimalist heritage, is daring to think outside the monochrome box.'*

Swedish fashion, meanwhile, continues to go from strength to strength, with big-name labels such as **Acne** (*see p69*), **Filippa K** (*see p71*) and **WhyRed** (*see p73*) leading to the emergence of a new wave of successful fashion designers, including **Ann-Sofie Back**, and **Ann Ringstrand** and **Stefan Söderberg**, the duo behind fashion-forward Swedish label **Hope** (www.hope-sthlm.com).

MINIMALIST NO MORE?

The *International Herald Tribune* declared in 2007 that Swedish design was 'minimalist no more'. This assertion hasn't really been borne out, and Swedish designers such as Thomas Bernstrand, **Anna von Schewen** and Jonas Bohlin remain keen disciples of the clean lines and functionalism that have characterised the country's fashion, furniture and industrial design. However, a new generation of creative talent is breaking out of the mould, creating in the process a more opulent, witty Swedish style. The result of all this is a design scene in Stockholm that, while loyal in many ways to its minimalist heritage, is daring to think outside the monochrome box.

PRODUCT PLACEMENT

Many young Swedish designers' cool creations – ranging from ceramics and jewellery to wine carriers and axes – can be found in Stockholm's seven **DesignTorget** stores (*see p70*), the largest of which is located in Kulturhuset at Sergels Torg. Other upscale design outlets include the **NK** department store (*see p72*), **R.O.O.M** (www.room.se) and **Asplund** (*see p130*).

If money's no issue, head for high-profile **Svenskt Tenn** (*see p131*). The company was founded in 1924 by art teacher Estrid Ericson and pewter artist Nils Fougstedt. The name

means 'Swedish Pewter', and it still produces exquisite objects made from the alloy. Today, however, it is perhaps best known for Josef Frank's textile designs, with rich nature-inspired patterns. The store underwent a huge refurbishment in early 2011.

To get a taste of the alternative side of Stockholm's design culture, it's definitely worth taking a safari around **SoFo**, located on the hip south side of town. SoFo comprises the area south of Folkungagatan and east of Götgatan on Södermalm – hence, SoFo – and is chock-full of cute cafés and postage stamp-sized fashion and design boutiques, often started by recent graduates of Beckmans School of Design.

If that sounds a little too bijou, then do as many locals do and hop on the free shuttle bus from Regeringsgatan 13 to **Ikea**'s gigantic warehouse store at Kungens Kurva (*see p71*). Ikea's products, though mass-produced and restricted at times by the flat-packing system, are design-savvy, and well-known designers work on its collections. Beware though: this mega home-furnishing palace is so vast that once you enter, you may never find your way out.

IN CONTEXT

A good place to get a sense of Swedish design through the years would normally be the **Nationalmuseum** (see *p64*), which features a permanent exhibition on Scandinavian design from 1900 to 2000, as well as an impressive collection of applied art, design and industrial design from the 14th century to the present day – but the museum is currently undergoing a major renovation, and is closed until 2017. However, during its closure, the museum is collaborating with **Kulturhuset** (see *p168*) to produce a temporary design collection, which will be displayed in a new 850-square-metre (9,150-square-foot) space in the latter's main building until the Nationalmuseum reopens its doors.

The partnership is the initiative of National Museum director Berndt Arell, partly in response to an intense ongoing debate about the lack of a dedicated and innovative Swedish design museum in Stockholm. This debate surfaced strongly in the mid noughties, leading to government proposals for a new design museum that would sit next to the National Museum, as well as for a new design centre adjacent to the Konstfack college of art and design at Telefonplan. Both plans were eventually abandoned, however, when the authorities decided instead to focus on the expansion of the Museum of Architecture (Arkitekturmuseet) – which was renamed **ArkDes** (see *p94*) a couple of years back – to encompass a wider field of design. However, this is deemed by critics to have been something of a failure, leading to employee resignations and the eventual dismissal of ArkDes's director in 2014. Writing in daily newspaper *Svenska Dagbolet* in August 2014, Ewa Kumlin, CEO of long-established design organisation Svensk Form (Swedish Society of Crafts and Design), stated that ArkDes's recent mission has failed to elicit engaged public debate on design, and that she sees the merging of ArkDes with its more visionary and self-confident neighbour, the **Moderna Museet** (Museum of Modern Art; see *p94*), as a potential way forward. To follow the debate, pick up a copy of Svensk Form's magazine, **Form** (www.formmagazine.com), a comprehensive publication for Nordic design and architecture.

Ikea.

IN CONTEXT

Essential Information

Hotels

No wonder Stockholm is a major conference destination: it's a compact city full of effortlessly multilingual people and lots of mid-range hotels. However, several world-class design hotels – including the Lydmar, Hotel Skeppsholmen, Nobis Hotel and Ett Hemm – have opened over the past few years, raising the bar at the upper end of the spectrum with inspiring contemporary Swedish interiors. Standards in general are high, though, and wherever you stay staff will almost certainly speak excellent English. Breakfast is typically a buffet of cereals, fruit, cold cuts, fish, cheese, hot dishes, crispbread, juice, tea and coffee. Swedes value the quality of beds and bedding; note that double beds tend to come with two single duvets rather than one double. Stockholm is not cheap, but it does have several youth hostels. These aren't just scuzzy pads for backpackers, but clean lodgings ideal for a family stay.

PRICES AND RESERVATIONS

Stockholm is a business hub and hotel rates can drop by as much as half on weekends. This means you can often enjoy deluxe surroundings for much less than you might expect. Always ask about packages and special deals (you may have to book two nights to get a discounted rate). Rates in July, when most Swedes take the month off, are often cheaper too.

We've divided the hotels by area and then by price category, according to a standard double room in high season, normally with breakfast included. The categories are: deluxe (around 2,000kr); expensive (around 1,300kr-2,000kr); moderate (800kr-1,300kr); and budget (under 800kr), which also includes youth hostels. Rates can vary wildly according to season or room category within a single property, so these categories should only be used as a rough guide.

The tourist office produces a free hotel brochure and runs a reservations service in conjunction with **Nordic Travel**: book online with its comprehensive accommodation search-and-book facility (stockholm.visit.com), by phone (50 82 85 08 or 40 90 64 00) or in person at the Kulturhuset office in Sergels Torg. There are also free-to-use computers so you can book online yourself. You could also try **Destination Stockholm** (663 00 80, www.destination-stockholm.com), which offers various hotel and sightseeing packages.

GAMLA STAN
Deluxe

Lady Hamilton Hotel
Storkyrkobrinken 5, 111 28 (50 64 01 00, www.thecollectorshotels.se). T-bana Gamla Stan or bus 2, 3, 43, 53, 55, 59, 71, 76, 96. **Rooms** 35. **Map** p241 H7.

The Lady Hamilton is perhaps the nicest of the three small hotels owned by the Bengtsson family – the others are the Lord Nelson (*see p209*) and the Victory (see website). As the names suggest, all have some connection with the British naval hero. A ship's figurehead and a portrait of Nelson's mistress dominate the lobby at the four-star Lady Hamilton, but the rest of this warren-like building (dating from 1470) is stuffed with antiques. The 35 rooms are each named after a regional wildflower, and there are four

ESSENTIAL INFORMATION

apartments for rent. The mix of colourful cupboards, wall paintings, grandfather clocks and old-fashioned fabrics is charming. A 14th-century well in the basement is now a plunge pool for the sauna.

Expensive

First Hotel Reisen

Skeppsbron 12, 111 30 (22 32 60, www.firsthotels. com). T-bana Gamla Stan or bus 2, 43, 55, 71, 76, 96. **Rooms** 144. **Map** p241 H8.

This 17th-century former coffee house became a hotel in 1819. Now run by the First Hotel chain, it fully exploits its harbourside location, with each of the 144 handsome rooms enjoying some sort of view of the water. There's a spa with a pool in the vaulted cellar, while the deluxe rooms have either a sauna or jacuzzi en suite. A good restaurant adjoins the lobby, but sadly the five-star Reisen hasn't quite shaken off its chain-hotel feel.

Lord Nelson Hotel

Västerlånggatan 22, 111 29 (50 64 01 20, www.thecollectorshotels.se). T-bana Gamla Stan or bus 2, 3, 43, 53, 55, 59, 71, 76, 96. **Rooms** 29. **Map** p241 J7.

The smallest and cheapest option in the Bengtsson family's hotel group, the three-star Nelson must also be Sweden's narrowest hotel, only 5m (16ft) wide. Located right on Gamla Stan's tourist strip, this tall, 17th-century building with its glass-and-brass entrance is pretty ship-shape itself. Add in the long mahogany reception desk, the portraits of Nelson, the names of the floors (Gun Deck, Quarter Deck) and naval antiques and you could be forgiven for thinking you were sailing the ocean blue. The 29 rooms are pleasant but, as on a ship, quite snug – lots are singles. A snack bar serves breakfast and light meals.

Scandic Gamla Stan

Lilla Nygatan 25, 111 28 (723 72 50, www. scandichotels.com). T-bana Gamla Stan or bus 3, 53. **Rooms** 52. **Map** p241 J7.

This 52-room hotel in a 17th-century building is steps from the waterfront, but none of the rooms has a view. For 65 years it was owned by the Salvation Army, which used it as a hostel until it was purchased by Norwegian hotel chain Rica in 1998, which transformed it into a first-class property. It's been a Scandic hotel since 2014. Rooms are elegant, in an understated way, but they aren't very large. If you want to steep yourself in the Old Town, and if location matters more than space, this is the place.

NORRMALM

Deluxe

★ Grand Hôtel

Södra Blasieholmshamnen 8, 103 27 (679 35 60, www.grandhotel.se). T-bana Kungsträdgården

or bus 2, 43, 55, 62, 65, 76, 96. **Rooms** 278. **Map** p241 G8.

See p216 **Grand Slam**.

Lydmar Hotel

Södra Blasieholmshamnen 2, 103 24 (22 31 60, www.lydmar.com). T-bana Kungsträdgården or Östermalmstorg or bus 2, 43, 55, 62, 65, 76, 96. **Rooms** 46. **Map** p241 G8.

While the closure of the old Lydmar Hotel was a sad affair, the new Lydmar, located next to the Grand Hôtel, is an inspiring proposition. Guest rooms in the luxury boutique hotel are some of the most spacious in the city, and all are individually furnished with a mix of contemporary and classic furniture and textiles, as well as works of art. Ask for a room with a view of the harbour.

★ Nobis Hotel

Norrmalmstorg 2-4, 111 86 (614 10 00, www. nobishotel.se). T-bana Kungsträdgården or Östermalmstorg or bus 2, 43, 52, 55, 62, 69, 76, 96. **Rooms** 201. **Map** p241 F8.

The Nobis group's flagship hotel is also its most stylish, with a minimalist Swedish interior that's all about neutral tones and comfortable, top-quality textiles. Lighting here is a big thing, with a range of designer lamps creating a lovely atmosphere in the guest rooms (of which there are 201) and the public areas. The hotel's glamorous Gold Bar (*see p69*) is a popular spot with Stockholm's fashionistas, while its restaurant, Caina, offers top-notch Italian cuisine. Breakfast here is also a real treat. The central lounge area, with its interesting mix of lamps, textiles and cacti, is an inspiring place to hang out, day and night.

Nobis Hotel.

A BOUTIQUE HOTEL EXPERIENCE AT AN AFFORDABLE PRICE

HTL is your home in the heart of the city.
We've only included the essentials, and only the best in
our rooms. Welcome to save money and collect memories.

Welcome

HTL

HTLHOTELS.COM

Radisson Blu Strand Hotel

Nybrokajen 9, 103 27 (50 66 40 00, www. radissonblu.com/strandhotel-stockholm). T-bana Kungsträdgården or Östermalmstorg or bus 2, 62, 65, 76, 96. **Rooms** 152. **Map** p241 G8.

Knockout views of the boats and ferries moored along Nybrokajen and Strandvägen give this excellent business hotel something extra. It was built in 1912 for the Stockholm Olympics, and all the 152 rooms are tastefully furnished in classic Swedish style. A real splurge is the Tower Suite, a two-floor apartment with rooftop terrace, dining room, sitting room and spiral staircase leading up to the bedroom.

Expensive

Berns Hotel

Näckströmsgatan 8, 111 47 (56 63 22 00, www.berns.se). T-bana Kungsträdgården or Östermalmstorg or bus 2, 52, 55, 62, 69, 76, 96. **Rooms** 82. **Map** p241 G8.

This boutique hotel is fantastically located near Kungsträdgården, the shops of Hamngatan and the boats of Nybroviken, and is popular with visiting pop stars and business executives. Top-floor rooms have big windows overlooking Berzelii Park. If you really want to push the boat out, consider the Parkview Suite with a private patio overlooking the Dramaten Theatre and the boats of Nybroviken, or the Clock Suite, situated behind the distinctive Berns clock, with a private sauna. The suites were recently updated by Spanish interior designer Lázaro Rosa-Violán. Service is first class, and night owls will be pleased to hear that some rates give guests VIP access to the city's Berns-owned nightclubs and bars, of which there are several.

Clarion Sign

Östra Järnvägsgatan 35, 101 26 (676 98 00, www. clarionsign.com). T-bana T-Centralen or Hötorget or bus 1, 53, 65, 69. **Rooms** 558. **Map** p240 F5.

The Clarion Sign is Stockholm's largest hotel. Located right next to Central Station, it has 558 rooms across 11 floors, a spa, an outdoor pool and a healthy dose of Scandinavian attitude. There are furnishings by Arne Jacobsen, Norway Says, Poul Kjærholm and Alvar Aalto, while Swedish super-chef Marcus Samuelsson returned to Stockholm with his US-inspired American Table restaurant. The Selma Cityspa is on the roof, alongside a heated outdoor pool with fabulous city views.

Freys Hotel

Bryggargatan 12, 101 31 (50 62 13 00, www. freyshotels.com). T-bana T-Centralen or bus 1, 53, 65, 69. **Rooms** 127. **Map** p241 F6.

The Freys Hotel is a likeable, idiosyncratic place, with 127 cheerfully decorated rooms. The location, down a car-free street close to Central Station and the shops on Drottninggatan, is convenient if a little drab. Still, you can always cheer yourself up by

---

IN THE KNOW
APARTMENTS AND B&BS

One of the cheapest ways to stay in Stockholm is in a private home. The following agencies can arrange a room for you (usually 900kr-1,300kr per person): **Stockholm Guesthouse** (www. stockholmguesthouse.com); **Bed and Breakfast Service Stockholm** (www.bed breakfast.a.se); and **Gästrummet** (www. gastrummet.com). The website **airbnb** (www.airbnb.com) also lists properties in Stockholm. For private apartments, try **Checkin** (Oxenstiernsgatan 33, 115 27 Stockholm, 658 50 00, www.checkin.se), which offers several furnished apartments for short-term rental, including in trendy areas such as Södermalm's Hornstull.

---

visiting the adjoining continental-style bar, which stocks more than 400 brands of Belgian beer. Note: smokers can specify a room with a balcony, but they're more expensive.

Nordic Light Hotel

Vasaplan 7, 101 37 (50 56 34 20, www.nordic lighthotel.se). T-bana T-Centralen or bus 1, 53, 65, 69. **Rooms** 175. **Map** p240 G6.

The Nordic Light is stylish in a very Scandinavian way: white walls, wooden floors, absurdly comfortable beds, hearty breakfasts and, the icing on the cake, a 'Light Manager' to oversee hotel illumination. Sophisticated lighting effects are employed throughout, with pretty patterns projected on to the walls of the 175 bedrooms and a chandelier that slowly changes colour in the airy bar-restaurant. The hotel's location near the Arlanda Express means it's only 20 minutes from hotel check-out to airport check-in.

Moderate

Best Western Hotel Bentleys

Drottninggatan 77, 111 60 (14 13 95, www. bentleys.se). T-bana Hötorget or bus 1, 52, 56, 59, 65. **Rooms** 119. **Map** p245 E6.

Now a Best Western, Bentleys is set in a converted townhouse, with a beautiful marble staircase and old-fashioned cage lift. The 119 rooms are simple, clean and pleasant. From the stained-glass panels in the front door to the art nouveau patterns on the hallway ceiling, there's charm to be found here. Choose a room on a higher floor with views over the inner courtyard to avoid being disturbed by street noise.

★ HTL Kungsgatan

Kungsgatan 53, 111 22 (41 08 41 50, www. htlhotels.com). T-bana Hötorget or bus 56. **Rooms** 274. **Map** p241 F6.

HTL Kungsgatan. *See p211.*

This innovative Scandinavian mini-chain has hit on a winning formula that appeals to a wide range of visitors keen not to break the bank when in town, yet who want to stay in a central location. Rooms are smaller than the norm, but well designed, with pleasant decor, basic digital mod cons, under-bed storage and blackout curtains. The spacious communal area is the highlight, with a buzzy vibe, a courtyard bar and a restaurant.

Queen's Hotel
Drottninggatan 71A, 111 36 (24 94 60, www. queenshotel.se). T-bana Hötorget or bus 1, 56, 59. **Rooms** 60. **Map** p241 F6.
On the main pedestrian street in the heart of the shopping district, this hotel is a good bet if you like hustle, bustle and a convenient location. Family-owned, it has 60 clean, plain but stylish enough rooms with private bathrooms. Most of the doubles can accommodate an extra bed or sofa bed.

Budget

City Backpackers Inn
Upplandsgatan 2, 111 23 (20 69 20, www.city backpackers.se). T-bana T-Centralen or Hötorget or bus 1, 53, 65, 69. **Beds** 144. **Map** p240 F5.

Set in a 19th-century building on Norra Bantorget square, this 144-bed hostel is just ten minutes' walk from Central Station, and near Hötorget and the shopping district. Dorm rooms sleep from four to 12. Alternatively, there are private en suite rooms or six-person apartments with private kitchen and bathroom. Facilities include a comfy lounge with a TV, books and games, kitchen, laundry, free internet access, a sauna and no curfew. There's an attached breakfast café or you can always fill up on the free pasta that's provided.

VASASTAN
Expensive

Hotel Birger Jarl
Tulegatan 8, 104 32 (674 18 00, www.birgerjarl.se). T-bana Rådmansgatan or bus 2, 43, 96. **Rooms** 271. **Map** p245 D6.
The Birger Jarl is a design-savvy business hotel that has made innovative use of space by getting renowned Swedish fashion designers (such as Filippa Knutsson of Filippa K) to decorate one wall of each of its dozen or so 'cabin rooms' – small rooms without windows. The rest of the rooms have been designed in a more conventional (but still very attractive) style. Fans of genuine retro should book the Retro Room, which looks just as it did in 1974, having accidentally been overlooked during the hotel's renovation. The location is quiet, but it's only a short walk from the action.

★ Hotel Hellsten
Luntmakargatan 68, 113 51 (661 86 00, www.hellsten.se). T-bana Rådmansgatan or bus 43, 59. **Rooms** 78. **Map** p245 D6.
Located in a late 19th-century building on a quiet residential street, the friendly Hotel Hellsten is an ideal balance of comfort and style. Its 78 individually designed rooms feature a lovely mix of antique furniture from Europe, Asia and Africa, plus strong colour schemes and mod cons such as flatscreen TVs. Bathrooms are huge, with luxurious Karystos stone tiles from Greece and underfloor heating. The public areas are equally inspiring, with the walls in the laid-back bar area featuring black-and-white photographs taken by the charismatic owner, Per, during his travels. Hellsten is well located for restaurants, with several good bets nearby, including excellent Chinese vegetarian restaurant Lao Wai (*see p78*).

Hotell August Strindberg
Tegnérgatan 38, 113 59 (32 50 06, www. hotellstrindberg.se). T-bana Hötorget or Rådmansgatan or bus 40, 53, 65, 69. **Rooms** 26. **Map** p245 E5.
This welcoming hotel stands near a small park containing a startling nude statue of Swedish dramatist August Strindberg, who once lived down the road.

Hotel Hellsten.

It has 26 rooms and a lobby decorated with a mural of Strindberg (cleverly made from the first three chapters of one of his books). Rooms are pleasant, and there's a courtyard garden.

★ Miss Clara Hotel
Sveavägen 48, 111 34 (440 67 00, www.miss clarahotel.com). T-bana Hötorget or bus 59. **Rooms** 92. **Map** p245 E6.
This Nobis group hotel (the company is also behind Nobis Hotel and Hotel Skeppsholmen) opened in 2014, in an art nouveau building that once housed the Ateneum girls' school. Original features, such as the beautiful staircase railings, have been left intact, while signature Nobis touches – design-focused lighting and premium Scandinavian textiles – can be found throughout the hotel. Rooms are large, light and supremely stylish and comfortable, with parquet floors, a neutral colour scheme and deluxe bathrooms. The breakfast buffet isn't included in the rate, but is well worth a splurge.

Miss Clara Hotel.

Moderate

Hotel Oden
Karlbergsvägen 24, 102 34 (457 97 00, www. hoteloden.se). T-bana Odenplan or bus 2, 4, 40, 65. **Rooms** 135. **Map** p244 D4.
Notable mostly for its low prices, the Oden will appeal to budget travellers looking to save money on meals, since doubles are available with a fridge and stove (no frying allowed). There's a basic solarium, sauna and exercise room in the basement.

Budget

Hostel Bed & Breakfast
Rehnsgatan 21, 113 57 (15 28 38, www.hostel bedandbreakfast.com). T-bana Rådmansgatan or bus 2, 42, 43, 59. **Beds** 36. **Map** p245 D6.
A basic, centrally located youth hostel. There are 36 beds in two-, four-, eight- and ten-bed rooms (14 rooms in total), plus a summer-only annexe that sleeps 40 in one dormitory (mostly used for school trips). All showers and toilets are shared, and there's a kitchen and laundry room. It's a basement hostel, so don't expect a room with a window. Do expect a free breakfast, though.

DJURGÅRDEN & SKEPPSHOLMEN
Expensive

★ Hotel Skeppsholmen
Gröna gången 1, Skeppsholmen, 111 86 (407 23 00, www.hotelskeppsholmen.com). Bus 65. **Rooms** 81. **Map** p242 J10.
Hotel Skeppsholmen is the embodiment of the term 'urban oasis'. Located in a former navy barracks that dates back to 1699, on the tiny, cultural island of Skeppsholmen, the hotel has generated

WE HAVE EVERYTHING YOU
FIND IN OTHER HOTELS.
ONLY A LITTLE BETTER.

STOCKHOLM FROM A DIFFERENT POINT OF VIEW.

BYREDO PARFUMS

PAVILLON

BOUGIE PARFUMÉE

9 FL.OZ

Hotel Skeppsholmen
Gröna gången 1, P.O. Box 1616
SE- 111 86 Stockholm
Sweden

www.hotelskeppsholmen.com
Hotel Reservations: +46 8 407 23 00
reservations@hotelskeppsholmen.se

Telephone: +46 8 407 23 00
info@hotelskeppsholmen.se
facebook.com/hotelskeppsholm
twitter.com/#!/LifeStyleHS

well-deserved international acclaim since opening in 2009 for its contemporary interior, superb restaurant and welcoming, distinctly Swedish vibe. Rooms are inspiring and soothing at the same time, featuring unique Boffi basins, stylish furniture, Scandinavian wool blankets, and views of the island and the surrounding water. Staff wear Acne-designed uniforms. The restaurant offers an outstanding breakfast buffet, traditional *fika* (Sweden's version of afternoon tea) and contemporary versions of Swedish classics, often made with organic ingredients. The hotel's green credentials have led to it being awarded the prestigious Nordic Ecolabel. This is without doubt one of the best places to lay your head in Stockholm.

Melody Hotel

Djurgårdsvägen 68, Djurgården, 115 21 (50 25 41 40, www.melody.se). Bus 44 or tram 7. **Rooms** 49. **Map** p242 J11.

ABBA obsessives who have travelled to Stockholm partly to visit the new ABBA The Museum (*see p86*) might want to go the whole hog and stay in the heart of the action, at the museum's official hotel, located right beside it. The modern, minimalist rooms won't appeal to those looking for character, but they're stylish enough, and floor-to-ceiling windows mean plenty of natural light. What's more, you can enter the museum directly from the hotel.

Scandic Hasselbacken

Hazeliusbacken 20, Djurgården, 100 55 (51 73 43 00, www.scandic-hotels.se). Bus 44. **Rooms** 113. **Map** p242 J11.

Flanked by the trees of the Swedish capital's greenest island, its small garden full of peonies, the Scandic Hasselbacken's setting is delightful. Typically Scandinavian in style, its 113 rooms are comfortable and unfussy. The terrace and elegant Restaurang Hasselbacken are busy all weekend. Note that there's no local T-bana, so access is by

Hotel Skeppsholmen. See p213.

bus, tram or the small ferry from Slussen. But the Hasselbacken does place you just a short walk from the Vasamuseet and Skansen.

Budget

★ STF Hostel af Chapman & Skeppsholmen

Flaggmansvägen 8, Skeppsholmen, 111 49 (463 22 66). Bus 65. **Rooms** 77. **Beds** 282. **Map** p242 H9.

You can't miss this youth hostel – the huge white boat, which dates from 1949, is one of Skeppsholmen's most recognisable symbols, and has been a hostel since 1972. Cabins are small but cosy, simply arranged with beds and a sink. There are two single cabins available, the rest are shared (six beds). You'll need to book well ahead to secure a place on deck in the summer months; if it's fully booked, note that there are additional rooms available in an adjacent 19th-century building, which has standard hostel facilities, shared internet access,

IN THE KNOW
STOCKHOLM SYNDROME

The building that houses both the **Nobis Hotel** (see p209) and the **Acne** flagship (see p69) was formerly a bank; the term 'Stockholm Syndrome' was coined here after a robbery in 1973 when some of the bank's employees were held hostage inside the building for six days. The victims became emotionally attached to their captors, defending them after they were freed. If you're staying in the Nobis, ask to see the holes that were drilled by the rescuers to enable them to shoot at the bank robbers – the hotel has kept them for posterity.

GRAND SLAM

The Grand has kept its groove.

The location of the **Grand Hôtel** (*see p209*) could hardly be more perfect – or more symbolic. Built in 1874, it stands by the harbour, with splendid views of the Royal Palace. On one side of the water, a regal building crowned with fluttering flags that's owned by the country's most influential family; on the other side, the King's official residence.

The Grand Hôtel is part of Investor, an investment company reckoned to be worth around €13 billion in 2006, which is controlled by the Wallenberg family. (The most famous member of the family was

Raoul Wallenberg, who saved many Hungarian Jews from the Holocaust.)

Unlike so many classic hotels that simply let themselves go in old age, the Grand has kept up with the times – though the decor is traditional, materials and amenities are top notch, and there's an impressive spa and a world-renowned, Michelin-starred restaurant, the eponymous Mathias Dahlgren (*see p66*).

The stunning, revamped Cadier Bar is one of the hottest places in town on a Friday night, particularly around the time of the Nobel Banquet, when visiting royals and rock stars rub shoulders with newly crowned laureates, who have stayed in the Grand every year since the first prizes were awarded in 1901.

Each of the 345 rooms is decorated differently, and while the cheapest rooms are far from spacious, the 37 suites have real wow factor. The Princess Lilian Suite (named after a Welsh-born member of the Swedish royal family) is perhaps the most sumptuous in the Nordic region. You'll need a king's ransom to check in – around 70,000kr per night – but if quality and class are top of your list, and money is no object, then this is the place to be.

and a TV room with a pool table. Note there's an additional fee of 50kr if you're not a member of Hostelling International (25kr for children).

SÖDERMALM

Deluxe

Hilton Stockholm Slussen

Guldgränd 8, 104 65 (51 73 53 00, www.hilton. com). T-bana Slussen or bus 2, 3, 43, 53, 55, 71, 76, 96. **Rooms** 289. **Map** p250 K7.

Despite Stockholm Slussen's five-star rating, there's something faintly depressing about its lack of personality. Still, it has what you expect from a high-quality chain: a white marble lobby, two executive floors with their own reception area, bar and breakfast room, and a pool, plus the added bonus of sweeping views towards Gamla Stan. If you can't justify the cost of an executive double room, you can still enjoy the same panorama from the Ekens bar and restaurant, the outdoor terrace or the smaller lobby bar (called, appropriately, Views).

Expensive

Clarion Hotel Stockholm

Ringvägen 98, 104 60 (462 10 00, www.clarion stockholm.com). T-bana Skanstull or bus 3, 4, 55, 66, 74, 94. **Rooms** 532. **Map** p250 N8.

Clarion opened this gleaming 532-room property on the southern edge of Södermalm in 2003. Despite its size, it's surprisingly classy. Bedrooms are airy and stylish, bathrooms are smart, the lobby is flooded with light and staff are attentive. Because it's primarily a business hotel, room rates plummet in summer and on weekends. For tourists, the main drawback is the location: it's on the opposite side of town from Arlanda Airport and a bit of a trek from the city centre. However, the lounge bar, Upstairs, has spectacular views towards Globen, and there's also an on-site spa with a rooftop pool.

Columbus Hotell

Tjärhovsgatan 11, 116 21 (50 31 12 00, www. columbus.se). T-bana Medborgarplatsen or bus 2, 3, 53, 59, 66, 76. **Rooms** 70. **Map** p251 L9.

This 18th-century building has been a brewery, a poorhouse and a hospital. It became a hostel in 1976 and then gradually evolved into a charming three-storey hotel, carefully restored with its original polished-wood floors and tasteful Gustavian furnishings. It's now part of the Best Western chain, though many of the original features have been retained. The courtyard is a pleasant place for breakfast or a drink, and there's a guests-only wine cellar.

Hotel Rival

Mariatorget 3, 118 91 (54 57 89 00, www.rival.se). T-bana Mariatorget or bus 43, 55, 66, 74. **Rooms** 99. **Map** p250 K7.

Part-owned by Benny from ABBA, the Rival was created by combining the best parts of the 1930s hotel that once stood here with high-tech comforts: there are flatscreen TVs, DVD players and iPod stereo-connectors in every room. Nintendo Wiis and Sony PlayStations are also available to rent. The old cocktail bar and plush red-velvet cinema are art deco treasures. Small rooms are comfortable and stylish, while the large rooms have great views over Södermalm's rooftops. Weekend rates can be excellent. The next-door Rival café is one of the best in town and the Rival bakery sells superb bread. This is a really good bet if you want to be in the heart of Södermalm.

▶ *For more ABBA antics, you can now book a room at the Melody Hotel (see p215), bang next door to ABBA The Museum.*

Moderate

Ersta Konferens & Hotell

Erstagatan 1K, 116 91 (714 63 41, www.ersta diakoni.se). Bus 2, 3, 53, 59, 66, 71, 76, 96. **Rooms** 22. **Map** p251 L10.

This 22-room hotel is a quiet oasis perched at the tip of Södermalm, where tour buses stop off for one of Stockholm's most phenomenal views. Constructed for the Deacons' Society in 1850, the building is in a square amid beautifully landscaped gardens and across from Ersta Café, overlooking the city. There are small guest kitchens on each floor, and when the weather's good you can eat your Fairtrade breakfast in the garden.

★ Hotel Hellstens Malmgård

Brännkyrkagatan 110, 117 26 (46 50 58 00, www.hellsten.se). T-bana Zinkensdamm or bus 191, 192. **Rooms** 49. **Map** p249 L4.

Housed in a beautiful mansion with a cobbled yard, located towards the Hornstull end of Södermalm, Hellstens Malmgård has as much character as its original sister hotel (*see p212*), with vintage Gustavian-style furniture, four-poster beds and colourful textiles (18th-century porcelain stoves also appear in 12 of the rooms). The complimentary breakfast buffet is a treat.

Hotell Anno 1647

Mariagränd 3, 116 46 (442 16 80, www.anno 1647.se). T-bana Slussen or bus 2, 3, 43, 53, 55, 71, 76, 96. **Rooms** 42. **Map** p250 K8.

As its name suggests, this is an old building dating back to the 17th century, and the interior tries earnestly to stay in sync with the historic exterior. The 42 rooms (including one family room sleeping up to six) are a little faded, but the traditional decor somehow makes this forgivable. Besides, the location is terrific: it's hidden down a cul-de-sac just off Södermalm's most fashionable shopping street, Götgatan, and the cobbled alleys of the Old Town are just minutes away.

ESSENTIAL INFORMATION

Långholmen Hotel & Youth Hostel.

Budget

Hotel Tre Små Rum
Högbergsgatan 81, 118 54 (641 23 71, www.tre smarum.se). T-bana Mariatorget or bus 4, 43, 55, 66, 74, 94. **Rooms 7. Map** p250 L6.

This tiny, likeable hotel in Söder had three small rooms (hence the name) when it opened in 1993 but now there are seven (six doubles and one single), sharing three shower rooms. Clean and simple, it's ideal for budget travellers who plan to spend most of their time out and about. It's run by the very friendly Jakob, and is just a few minutes' walk from Mariatorget T-bana station.

Zinkensdamm Vandrarhem & Hotell
Zinkens väg 20, 117 41 (hotel 616 81 10, hostel 616 81 00, www.zinkensdamm.com). T-bana Hornstull or Zinkensdamm or bus 4, 66, 77, 94. **Rooms 70. Map** p249 L4.

This youth hostel and family-friendly hotel is tucked away in peaceful Tantolunden park, a few minutes from busy Hornsgatan. Nearby are lots of *kolonträdgårdar* – lovely allotment gardens with charming wooden houses where Stockholmers cultivate a bit of countryside in the city. The yellow wooden hostel has a large courtyard and a small pub where guests congregate. Prices are reasonable and include breakfast.

LÅNGHOLMEN
Budget

Långholmen Hotel & Youth Hostel
Långholmsmuren 20, 102 72 (720 85 00, www.langholmen.com). T-bana Hornstull or bus 4, 40, 77. **Hostel beds 26. Hotel rooms 103. Map** p249 K2.

A former prison has been converted into a far from grim property on this small, green island south of Kungsholmen. Run as a hotel in winter and youth hostel in summer, it has a pub (winter only), a café (summer only, in the former exercise yard) and a 17th-century Wärdshus serving Swedish cuisine. The 19th-century building is still quite jail-like, with cells (yes, that's where you sleep) arranged around a light-filled central atrium. There's a prison museum on site (*see p116*). One of Stockholm's most arresting places to stay.

ÖSTERMALM
Deluxe

★ Ett Hem
Sköldungagatan 2, 114 27 (20 05 90, www.ett hem.se). T-bana Stadion or train to Stockholm Östra station. **Rooms 12. Map** p245 C7.

Stockholm's most exciting boutique hotel opening in recent years is set in an Arts and Crafts townhouse on the outskirts of Östermalm. Ett Hem, meaning 'a home', opened in 2012, and is the vision of owner Jeanette Mix, who wanted to create a space defined by luxurious comfort. A dream team of designers has created spectacularly soothing rooms featuring bespoke furniture, high-end Scandinavian materials (oak, sheepskin, stone and brass) and chalky white tones. Suites raise the bar even further, with four-poster beds and marble bathrooms, while the library area has vintage Kaare Klint leather chairs and parquet floors. Top-quality food, made from seasonal ingredients, is served up daily in the homely kitchen area, designed for conversation. There's also a lovely courtyard garden. You'll want to move in.

Ett Hem.

Hotel Diplomat
*Strandvägen 7C, 104 40 (459 68 00, www.
diplomathotel.com). T-bana Östermalmstorg or
bus 52, 62, 69, 76, 91.* **Rooms** 130. **Map** p242 G9.
The Hotel Diplomat is one of Stockholm's best-
preserved art nouveau buildings, and its glamorous
Strandvägen site affords some stunning views. The
hotel oozes old-fashioned charm, with its antique
cage lift, spiral staircase and intricate stained-glass
windows. More modern are the serene first-floor
lounge and the trendy T-Bar restaurant and bar on
the ground floor, which serves excellent brunch and
afternoon tea.

Expensive

Best Western Premier Hotell Kung Carl
*Birger Jarlsgatan 21, 111 87 (463 50 00,
www.hotellkungcarl.se). T-bana Hötorget or
Östermalmstorg or bus 2, 55, 62, 91, 96.*
Rooms 143. **Map** p241 F8.
The Kung Carl has glamorous neighbours – the
Versace store flanks the entrance and it's close to
affluent Östermalm, home to some of the poshest
shops in Stockholm. The hotel is far from cutting-edge
in style, but full of character and neatly located.
Each of the 143 rooms is uniquely decorated, and
there's an oddly shaped central atrium housing a
small bar and pleasant restaurant.

Hotel Esplanade
*Strandvägen 7A, 114 56 (663 07 40, www.hotel
esplanade.se). T-bana Östermalmstorg or bus 69,
76.* **Rooms** 34. **Map** p242 G9.
The Esplanade is next door to the Diplomat, and has
the same stunning water views and four-star rating.
All 34 rooms are different, and even if some of them
are a little frumpy, it's hard not to love this place for
its charming character, especially as it has retained
some of its original art nouveau interior. Considering
its top-class location, prices are reasonable.

GÄRDET
Expensive

Villa Källhagen
*Djurgårdsbrunnsvägen 10, 115 27 (665 03 00,
www.kallhagen.se). Bus 69.* **Rooms** 36. **Map**
p243 F14.
Villa Källhagen is a tranquil waterside retreat surrounded by rolling parkland, yet it's just a short bus
ride from Östermalm. The original Red Cottage inn,
dating from 1810, is now in the garden behind the
new hotel, which was built in 1990. The sunny rooms
feature the best of Scandinavian design, with bright
fabrics, and light fittings designed by Josef Frank
of Svenskt Tenn fame, although the lobby and café
could do with sprucing up. An excellent restaurant
serves classic Swedish food with continental influences. Just 36 rooms, so book well in advance.

KUNGSHOLMEN
Expensive

Hotel Amaranten
*Kungsholmsgatan 31, 104 30 (692 52 00, www.
darionhotel.com). T-bana Rådhuset or bus 1, 40,
52, 56.* **Rooms** 462. **Map** p240 G4.
Thanks to its swish decor and its location around
the corner from Scheelegatan, one of the city's busiest restaurant rows, this hotel has become a hub of
activity. The expansive lobby bar-restaurant has
leather seats in rich, chocolate hues, walnut floors
and low-level lighting. The luxury doesn't quite
carry through upstairs: rooms are more basic, but
good value. The hotel is an easy ten-minute walk
from Central Station.

FURTHER AFIELD
Deluxe

Sigtuna Stads Hotell
*Stora Nygatan 3, 193 30 Sigtuna (www.sigtuna
stadshotell.se). Märsta train station or Arlanda
Airport.* **Rooms** 26.
From the outside, this looks like a fairly ordinary
small-town hotel. But inside, the Sigtuna Stads
Hotell is impeccably stylish and utterly seductive.
It's all very Scandinavian, with modern furniture,
polished wooden floors and pale walls. About 40
kilometres (25 miles) from Stockholm but close to
Arlanda Airport, it's a perfect place to start or end
a Swedish trip.

Expensive

Hasseludden Konferens & Yasuragi
*Hamndalsvägen 6, 132 81 Saltsjö-Boo (747 64 00,
www.yasuragi.se). Bus 417 to Hamndalsvägen
then 10min walk or Waxholmsbolaget boat
from Strömkajen.* **Rooms** 191.
Sweden's only Japanese spa is the place to ease those
travel-weary muscles with a traditional Japanese
bath, a swim or a soak in an outdoor jacuzzi overlooking the sea. Refresh yourself at the fruit and juice
buffet, try a session of qi gong or Zen meditation –
or go to the sushi school. All 162 sparsely furnished
rooms and suites have water views. The hotel is a
30-minute boat ride from central Stockholm.

Hotel J
*Ellensviksvägen 1, 131 28 Nacka Strand (601 30 00,
www.hotelj.com). Boat from Nybrokajen or Slussen
or T-bana to Slussen then bus 443.* **Rooms** 158.
A 20-minute bus, boat or taxi ride from the city,
this hotel is beautifully situated on the coast. A
1912 summer house and two extensions house 158
rooms. Rooms in the old building are smaller and
without balconies. You can rent mini-catamarans.
Restaurant J on the quayside has excellent views.

Getting Around

ARRIVING & LEAVING

By air

Four airports serve Stockholm: Arlanda, Bromma, Skavsta and Västerås.

Arlanda Airport

010 109 10 00, www.arlanda.se.
Stockholm's main airport, the largest in Scandinavia, is 42km (27 miles) north of the city centre and serves more than 16 million passengers a year. International flights arrive and depart from terminals 2 and 5. Domestic flights arrive and depart from terminals 3 and 4.

It's a light, well-designed place, with good facilities. For currency exchange, there's Forex (terminals 2 and 5), X-Change (terminal 5) and SEB exchange (terminal 5), as well as Handelsbanken and SEB banks in the Sky City shopping and eating area (which connects terminal 5 with 3 and 4). There are ATMs at terminals 2, 4, 5 and Sky City. There's a pharmacy (open 7am-7.30pm Mon-Fri, 9am-5pm Sat, 9am-7.30pm Sun) in Sky City. All terminals have cafés and bars, but head for Sky City for more serious eating.

The fastest way to get into Stockholm is on the bright yellow **Arlanda Express** train service (771 72 02 00, www.arlandaexpress. com), which arrives at its own terminal next to Central Station (the main station for trains and the Tunnelbana). Trains depart 4-6 times an hour, from Arlanda 5.05am-1.05am daily, and from Central Station 4.35am-12.35am daily. Journey time is 20mins; single fare is 260kr (130kr under-25s; four under-18s free with each full-price passenger). Buy tickets from the yellow automatic ticket booths at Arlanda or Central Station, or on the train (for 100kr extra). The booths take all major credit cards.

Alternatively, **Flygbussarna** airport buses (0771 51 52 52, www.flygbussarna.se) leave about every 10mins from all terminals to Cityterminalen (the main bus station next to Central Station, *see right*). Buses run from Arlanda 5am-1am daily (between 1am and 5am buses meet connecting flights, leaving half an hour after arrival), and from Cityterminalen 3.45am-10pm daily. The journey takes around 45mins.

A single fare is 119kr (four under-18s free with each full-price passenger).

There are also plenty of **taxis** at the airport – the usual fixed rate to the city is 520kr, but make sure you ask the driver first since many taxi firms set their own prices. Reliable firms include Taxi Stockholm (15 00 00, www.taxistockholm.se) and Taxi Kurir (30 00 00, www.taxikurir. se); note that they can be most easily identified by looking at the phone numbers on the sides of the cars.

Bromma Airport

010 109 40 00, www.swedavia.com/bromma.
Stockholm city airport, Bromma, is 8km (5 miles) west of the city centre. Its location makes it popular, but only 11 airlines operate from it.

You can get into the city centre on **Flygbussarna** airport buses (*see left*). Buses run from Bromma 7.15am-10pm Mon-Fri, 9.35am-4.20pm Sat, 12.20pm-10pm Sun; and to Bromma 5.30am-8.20pm Mon-Fri, 7.20am-3.20pm Sat, 11.30am-8pm Sun. Single fare is 85kr and the journey takes about 20mins to Cityterminalen.

Taking a **taxi** into town will cost you around 250kr.

Skavsta Airport

0155 28 04 00, www.skavsta.se.
Skavsta serves Stockholm, even though it's 100km (62 miles) to the south. It's the airport of choice for budget airlines. Airport facilities include a Forex exchange bureau, restaurant, café, bar, playground and tax-free shops. **Flygbussarna** airport buses (*see left*; single 139kr) take 80mins to reach the centre of Stockholm. Buses leave Skavsta 20mins after each arriving flight, and Cityterminalen about 3hrs before a departing flight. If you can't find a **taxi** at the airport, you can order one, but the trip to Stockholm will set you back about 1,425kr.

Västerås Airport

021 80 56 00, www.vst.nu.
Ryanair flies into Västerås, located 110km (68 miles) north-west of Stockholm. Facilities include a small café (open 6am-6pm daily), bar, tax-free shop and car hire. The **airport bus** (single 139kr, journey 75mins) leaves 20mins after an arriving flight for Cityterminalen in Stockholm; it returns about 2hrs before departing flights. There are **trains** every hour to

the city (but you'll have to take a bus or taxi to the station first). A **taxi** to Stockholm will cost around 1,450kr.

Airlines

Air France 51 99 99 90, www.airfrance.com
Austrian Airlines 07 70 82 73 73, www.aua.com
British Airways 07 70 11 00 20, www.britishairways.com
Finnair 07 71 78 11 00, www.finnair.com
Iberia 07 71 61 60 68, www.iberia.com
KLM 58 79 97 57, www.klm.com
Lufthansa 07 70 11 10 10, www.lufthansa.com
Malmö Aviation 07 71 55 00 10, www.malmoaviation.se
Norwegian 07 70 45 77 00, www.norwegian.com
Ryanair 0900 10 00 550, www.ryanair.com
SAS 07 70 72 77 27, 797 40 00, www.sas.se

By train

The major rail operator in Sweden is **SJ** (www.sj.se). Domestic, commuter and international trains arrive and depart from Stockholm's Central Station. Just below the station is T-Centralen, the main station for the Tunnelbana system, and taxis are available outside.

SJ *Central Station, Vasagatan, Norrmalm (07 71 75 75 75). T-bana T-Centralen or bus 1, 3, 53, 56, 59, 65, 91.* **Open** 6am-10pm daily. **Map** p241 G6.
To book tickets from abroad, call +46 771 75 75 75 (open 8am-5pm Mon-Fri) or visit www.sj.se and print your e-ticket (or collect at any SJ ticket machine with a credit or debit card).

By bus

Most long-distance coaches stop at **Cityterminalen**, Stockholm's main bus station, next to Central Station. T-Centralen is an escalator ride away, and there are always taxis outside.

Swebus Express *Cityterminalen, Klarabergsgatan, Norrmalm (07 71 21 82 18, www.swebusexpress.se). T-bana T-Centralen or bus 1, 3, 53, 56, 59, 65, 91.* **Open** 7am-7pm daily. **Map** p241 G6.

One of the larger Swedish bus companies, Swebus Express covers Sweden's major cities, along with Oslo and Copenhagen. Tickets can be purchased online and by phone up to 1hr before departure and at Cityterminalen until departure.

Eurolines Scandinavia *Big Travel, Sveavägen 131 (30 24 45, timetable service from abroad +46 31 100 240, www.eurolines.dk). T-bana Odenplan or bus 2, 40, 59, 70.* **Open** 9am-6pm Mon-Fri. **Map** p245 B5. Operates buses to more than 500 European cities.

By car

Stockholm's highway links with Europe have been made easier thanks to the Öresund toll bridge (400kr) between Sweden and Denmark, which opened in 2000 and is crossed by more than 19,500 cars daily. It's 615km (382 miles) from Stockholm to Malmö; 475km (295 miles) to Göteborg. Driving in Sweden is relatively safe – roads are in great condition and there are no other tolls.

By sea

If you arrive by sea, you've most likely come from Finland or Estonia. The main companies operating ferries to/from Stockholm are:

Birka Cruises *Stadsgårdsterminalen, Södermalm (702 72 00, www.birka.se). T-bana Slussen or bus 2, 3, 43, 53, 55, 59, 71, 76, 96.* **Open** *phone enquiries* 8.30am-6pm Mon-Fri; 10am-2.30pm Sat, Sun. **Map** p241 K8. Daily cruises in summer to Gotland, Finland, Tallinn, Riga and Poland. The boat terminal, Stadsgårdskajen, is right next to Slussen.

Tallink Silja Line *Sea and Sky Travel, Klarabergsviadukten 72, Norrmalm (440 59 90, reservations 22 21 40, www.tallinksilja.se). T-bana T-Centralen or bus 1, 3, 53, 56, 65, 69, 91.* **Open** 10am-6pm Mon-Fri. *Phone reservations* 8am-8pm Mon-Thur; 8am-7pm Fri; 8am-6pm Sat; 8am-8pm Sun. **Map** p241 F7.
Silja Line operates ferries to/from Finland. Boats dock at Värtahamnen just north-east of the city centre. The terminal has parking, luggage lockers, an ATM, a kiosk and a café. There are taxis at the terminal and Silja Line has its own bus service to Cityterminalen (single 35kr). Signs show you how to walk the 5-10mins to the nearest T-bana station, Gärdet

(and from Gärdet to the terminal).
Tallink operates ferries to/from Estonia. Boats dock at the Frihamnen terminal, north-east of the centre. It's served by taxis and has its own bus connection between the terminal and Cityterminalen (single 60kr).

Viking Line *Cityterminalen, Klarabergsviadukten 72, Norrmalm (452 40 00, www.vikingline.se). T-bana T-Centralen or bus 1, 3, 53, 56, 59, 65, 91.* **Open** 8am-7pm Mon-Fri; 8am-6pm Sat; 11am-6pm Sun. **Map** p241 G6.
Ferries to/from Finland, and from Helsinki to Tallinn. Boats dock at Vikingterminalen on Södermalm. The terminal has parking and luggage lockers. There are taxis at the terminal, but many prefer to walk the 10mins to Slussen. Viking Line has its own bus link to Stadsgården and Cityterminalen (return 70kr).

PUBLIC TRANSPORT

The **Tunnelbana** (abbreviated to T-bana) metro system is the quickest, cheapest and most convenient way to get around the city. The efficient, comprehensive bus network operates around the clock and covers areas not reached by the metro or the commuter trains. Both the T-bana and city buses are run by **Storstockholms Lokaltrafik**, or **SL** (08 600 10 00, www.sl.se).
Construction of the new **Citybanan** (Stockholm City Line) commuter train tunnel is currently underway, expected to be finished in 2017. It will connect Central Station with Odenplan.

SL Center *Central Station, T-Centralen, Norrmalm. T-bana T-Centralen or bus 1, 3, 53, 56, 59, 65, 91.* **Open** 6.30am-11.15pm Mon-Sat; 7am-11.15pm Sun. **Map** p241 G6. This information centre can answer any questions you might have about public transport. It's located on the floor below the main concourse at Central Station. You can pick up maps and timetables here. Another branch is at Sergels Torg.
Other locations Slussen, by Saltsjöbanan (open 7am-6.30pm Mon-Fri, 10am-5pm Sat); Fridhemsplan (open 7am-6.30pm Mon-Fri; 10am-5pm Sat); Tekniska Högskolan (open 7am-6.30pm Mon-Fri, 10am-5pm Sat).

Fares & tickets

Tickets can be purchased in the T-bana but not on buses. Some bus stations have ticket machines. Single

tickets cost 36kr-72kr depending on how many zones you're covering, and are valid for 1hr 15 mins from when the trip starts. However, it's cheaper and easier to buy a blue **SL Access card** (similar to London's Oyster card), available from Pressbyrån kiosks and SL Centers, and valid on all public transport in Stockholm. These initially cost 20kr, and tickets or credit (*reskassa*) are then loaded on to them electronically. You place the card on top of the card reader at automatic barriers. A 24hr travelcard uploaded to an SL Access card costs 115kr; a 72hr pass is 230kr; a 7-day unlimited travel pass is 300kr.
There's also the **Stockholm Card** (www.visitstockholm.com), which includes unlimited travel on public transport, admission to over 70 museums and sights, sightseeing by boat and more.

Tunnelbana

The three metro lines are identified by colour – red, green or blue – on maps and station signs. All three lines intersect at T-Centralen. At interchanges, lines are indicated by the names of the stations at the end of the line, so you should know in which direction you're heading when changing between lines. The T-bana runs from around 5am to 1am Mon-Thur, Sun; 24hrs Fri, Sat.

Buses

Most bus routes operate from 5am to midnight daily. You board at the front, and get off through the middle or rear doors. Single tickets cannot be bought on board. Tickets must be stamped by the driver. Travel passes should also be shown to the driver.
Most **night buses** run from midnight until 5am, when the regular buses take over. The main stations are Slussen, T-Centralen, Odenplan, Fridhemsplan and Gullmarsplan.

Ferries

Many ferry companies operate on Stockholm's waterways. Some routes are used daily by people commuting to work, while others are designed for sightseeing or excursions into the archipelago. SL travel passes are not valid on the archipelago ferries.

Cinderella Båtarna *12 00 40 45, www.stromma.se/skargard.* Ferries to Vaxholm, Grinda, Santahamina, Möja and more, operated by Stromma Skargard (*see p223*). Boats depart from Nybrokajen on Strandvägen. Buy tickets on board.

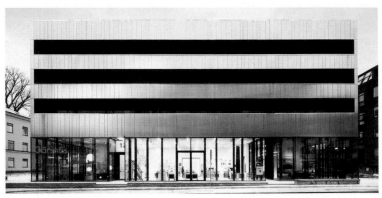

Sven-Harrys Art Museum
Experience art in a new fashion
Art · Living · Food · all in one place

For information about exhibitions and opening hours see www.sven-harrys.se

 Sven-Harrys konstmuseum

Eastmansvägen 10–12 · 113 61 Stockholm
+46 (8) 511 600 60 · www.sven-harrys.se

Djurgårdsfärjan

Year-round ferry service operated by Waxholmsbolaget (*see below*) within Stockholm harbour. It runs between Slussen and Djurgården (stopping at Allmänna Gränd, next to Gröna Lund), Skeppsholmen and Nybroplan. From May to August, it also stops at the Vasamuseet. Buy tickets in ticket booths before boarding; single 44kr. SL travel passes are valid.

Strömma Skärgård *12 00 40 00, www.stromma.se/skargard.*
Departs from Stadshusbron (next to Stadhuset) to Drottningholm and Birka, and from Strandvägen to Fjäderholmarna, Vaxholm and Sandhamn. Tickets can be purchased for some tours on board (cash only) or in the ticket booths by the departure points – check the website for details.

Waxholmsbolaget *679 58 30, www.waxholmsbolaget.se.*
These ferries cover the whole archipelago, from Arholma in the north to Landsort in the south. Boats depart from Strömkajen outside the Grand Hôtel, opposite the Royal Palace. Buy tickets on board.

Local trains

For trips into the suburbs and surrounding towns, there are **commuter trains** run by SL. The same tickets may be used on these trains as on the T-bana. The main commuter train station is Central Station, and trains will take you as far north as Bålsta and Kungsängen, and as far south as Södertälje, Nynäshamn and Gnesta.

The **Citybanan** (Stockholm City Line) is a new railway tunnel currently under construction around the city (hence the building works at Slussen). It will run beneath central Stockholm for 3.7 miles (6km) and be used by the Stockholm Commuter Rail. Its two key stations will be T-Centralen and Odenplan. The line is due to be completed in 2017. The aim of the tunnel is to improve transport links to southern Stockholm and reduce congestion.

TAXIS

Taxis can be ordered by phone, online or hailed on the street, and there are taxi ranks near railway and bus stations. Taxi services offered in private, unmarked cars are illegal in Sweden and should be avoided. Fares (starting at around 30kr) are quite steep; current rates and supplements should be displayed inside each cab.

Taxi companies

The firms listed below take bookings 24hrs a day.

Flygtaxi (airport taxis) 012 09 20 00, www.flygtaxi.se
Taxi Kurir 30 00 00, www.taxikurir.se
Taxi Stockholm 15 00 00, www.taxistockholm.se
Top Cab 33 33 33, www.topcab.com

DRIVING

Driving in Stockholm can be a hassle. There's a lot of traffic, free parking is difficult to find and fuel is expensive. A car is rarely a time-efficient form of transport – it's only out in the country that it becomes an asset. It's wise to familiarise yourself with the dos and don'ts of Swedish road travel; visit the Swedish road administration (www.trafikverket.se) for the lowdown on the driving laws.

Breakdown services

If your car breaks down, look up *Bilreparationer* in the Yellow Pages. If it's a rental car, contact the rental firm direct.

Motormännens Riksförbund
Fridhemsgatan 32, Kungsholmen (690 38 00, www.motormannen.se).
T-bana Fridhemsplan or bus 1, 3, 4, 77, 94. **Open** 8.30am-5pm Mon-Wed; 9am-5pm Thur, Fri. **Map** p239 F2.
Breakdowns (members only) 020 21 11 11. **Open** 9am-4pm Mon-Fri.
The Swedish equivalent of the British AA, with reciprocal arrangements with most European motoring organisations. Call the toll-free number if you have a problem.

Parking

Parking is not easy in the city centre. If you've parked illegally or not paid the right fee, you'll get a hefty fine. *Parkering Förbjuden* means 'parking prohibited'. Car parks (*parkering*), indicated by a white 'P' on a blue sign, charge 60kr-75kr/hr weekdays.

There is also a congestion charge for Swedish-registered vehicles in central Stockholm (6.30am-6.30pm Mon-Fri, 10kr-20kr, maximum 60kr per day). Eco-vehicles and foreign-registered cars are exempt, and rental agencies incorporate the charge into their fees upfront.

Vehicle rental

You have to be 25 years of age to rent a car in Sweden, and you will need a credit card.

Avis *Klarabergsviadukten 86, Norrmalm (010 494 80 50, reservations 07 70 82 00 82, www.avis.se). T-bana T-Centralen or bus 3, 52, 56, 62, 65.* **Open** 7am-6pm Mon-Fri; 8am-1pm Sat; 3pm-8pm Sun. *Phone reservations* 8am-6pm Mon-Fri. **Map** p241 G6.
Other locations Sveavägen 140, Vasastaden (441 89 30); Arlanda Airport (010 494 80 10); Bromma Airport (010 49 48 080).

Europcar *Klarabergsviadukten 49, Norrmalm (21 06 50, customer service 12 07 48 49, www.europcar.se). T-bana T-Centralen or bus 3, 53, 56, 62, 65.* **Open** 7am-8pm Mon-Fri; 10am-6pm Sat, Sun. *Customer service* 9am-4pm Mon-Thur; 9am-3pm Fri. **Map** p241 H6.
Other locations Fiskartorpsvägen 22, Östermalm (20 44 63); Arlanda Airport (55 59 84 00); Bromma Airport (80 08 07).

Hertz *Mäster Samuelsgatan 71, Norrmalm (454 62 50, customer service 96 04 73 30, www.hertz.se). T-bana T-Centralen or bus 3, 53, 59, 62, 65.* **Open** 7am-7pm Mon-Fri; 9am-4pm Sat, Sun. **Map** p241 G6.
Other locations Arlanda Airport (509 90 50); Bromma Airport (629 27 50).

CYCLING

Stockholm is very bike-friendly: not too big or busy, and with plenty of bike lanes. If you're visiting between April and October, try the **Stockholm City Bikes** scheme (www.citybikes.se). Rental cards (3-day 165kr, season 300kr) can be bought directly from the website or from branches of Pressbyrån, 7-Eleven and SL Centers.

The bikes are available 6am-10pm daily (last return 1am), for a 3hr maximum per loan. Some 100 stands are dotted around the city. Hiring a bike for the first time can be confusing – note that the rental card needs to be placed on the card reader located at the end of the stand.

If you're visiting off-season, or simply prefer to have the same bike with you for the whole day, then good rental places include **Visit Djurgården** (*see p84*) and **Gamla Stans Cykel** (Stora Nygatan 44, 411 16 70, www.gamlastanscykel.se).

WALKING

Stockholm is compact, and walking is often the best way to get around. For details of guided Stieg Larsson Millennium Trilogy walks, *see p103*.

ESSENTIAL INFORMATION

Resources A-Z

TRAVEL ADVICE

For up-to-date information on travel to a specific country – including the latest on safety and security, health issues, local laws and customs – contact your home country government's department of foreign affairs. Most have websites with useful advice for would-be travellers.

AUSTRALIA
www.smartraveller.gov.au

CANADA
www.voyage.gc.ca

NEW ZEALAND
www.safetravel.govt.nz

REPUBLIC OF IRELAND
foreignaffairs.gov.ie

UK
www.fco.gov.uk/travel

USA
www.state.gov/travel

ADDRESSES

In Sweden, addresses are written with the building number after the street name. Also, as in the UK, but not the US, the first floor is the floor above street level. The floor at street level is *bottenvåning*, often abbreviated to 'BV'.

AGE RESTRICTIONS

The legal drinking age for bars and restaurants is 18, but you must be 20 years old to buy alcohol at the state-owned monopolistic off-licence Systembolaget. Many clubs also set their own age restrictions – customers typically need to be 20, 21, 23 or over to enter them.

You can smoke and drive at 18. At 15, teens become *byxmyndig*, which, loosely translated, means they are 'in charge of their pants'. In other words, they can legally have sex.

CUSTOMS

You must be at least 18 years old to bring in tobacco products, and 20 to bring in alcohol. Visitors from the EU can bring in alcohol and tobacco for private use without incurring customs duty. Check the Swedish Customs website, www.tullverket.se, for details of the cut-off points between private and commercial use.

DISABLED VISITORS

It is not usually a problem for disabled visitors to get around the city; facilities are good compared to much of Europe, and recent legislation means that all public buildings must be accessible to the disabled and visually impaired.

The streets are in good condition and have wide pavements, and kerbs have ramps for wheelchairs. Wheelchair-adapted toilets are common, and many hotels even have allergy-free rooms. The public transport system is quite wheelchair-accessible, especially the T-bana, which has plenty of elevators, and most buses can 'kneel' at bus stops – although wide gaps between trains and platforms remain a common complaint.

Most taxis are large enough to take wheelchairs, but check before you order a cab. Try **Taxi Stockholm** (15 00 00).

De Handikappades Riksförbund
Storforsplan 44, 123 21 Farsta (685 80 00, www.dhr.se). T-bana Farsta. **Open** *Aug-June* 9am-noon, 1-4pm Mon-Thur; 9am-noon, 1-3pm Fri. Closed July.
Information on facilities for the mobility-impaired. The website has an English version with tips about accessible hotels, restaurants, cinemas, museums and theatres.

DRUGS

Drugs, including cannabis, are nowhere near as widely accepted in Sweden as in some parts of Europe. Possession of any controlled drug, including medicine for which you do not have a prescription, is illegal, and you can be heavily fined for the very smallest amounts.

ELECTRICITY

Sweden, along with most of Europe, has 220-volt AC, 50Hz current and uses two-pin continental plugs. The 220V current works fine with British-bought 240V products with a simple plug adaptor (available at airports or department stores). With US 110V equipment you will need to use a current transformer.

EMBASSIES & CONSULATES

Many foreign embassies are clustered in Diplomatstaden, near Ladugårdsgärdet.

British Embassy
Skarpögatan 6-8, Östermalm (671 30 00, www.ukinsweden.fco. gov.uk). Bus 69. **Open** *Visas* by appointment only, book online. *Consulate and information* 9am-5pm Mon-Fri.* **Map** p243 F12.
Irish Embassy
Hovslagargatan 5, Norrmalm (54 50 40 40, www.embassyofireland.se). T-bana Kungsträdgården, or bus 65. **Open** 9.30am-noon, 2-4.30pm Mon-Fri. **Map** p241 G8.
US Embassy
Dag Hammarskjöldsväg 31, Östermalm (783 53 75, www. stockholm.usembassy.gov). Bus 56, 69, 76. **Open** 8am-8pm Mon-Fri. **Map** p243 F12.

EMERGENCIES

To contact the police, ambulance or fire service in an emergency, call **112** (free of charge, including from public pay phones).

For emergency rooms at hospitals, *see p225* **Accident & emergency**. For central police stations, *see p226* **Police & security**.

GAY & LESBIAN

RFSL
Sveavägen 59, Vasastan (50 16 29 00, www.rfsl.se). T-bana Rådmansgatan or bus 43, 52. **Open** *Phone enquiries* 1-3pm Mon; 10am-noon, 1-3pm Tue-Fri. **Map** p245 D6.
The main office for the National Association for Sexual Equality, Sweden's gay, lesbian and trans rights group.

HEALTH

For advice on minor illnesses or prescription drugs, call the 24-hour **Healthcare Information Service** (1177, www.1177.se); stay on the line when the automatic answering service kicks in and you will be connected to a nurse.

Accident & emergency

The following hospitals have 24-hour emergency rooms:

St Görans Sjukhus
Sanktgöransplan 1, Kungsholmen (58 70 10 00, www.stgoran.se). T-bana Fridhemsplan or bus 49.
Södersjukhuset
Ringvägen 52, Södermalm (616 10 00, www.sodersjukhuset.se). Bus 3, 4, 55, 74, 94. **Map** p250 N6.

Dentists

Afta Akuttandvård
Sergels Torg 12, Norrmalm (20 20 25, www.akuttandvard.se). T-bana T-Centralen or bus 1, 56, 59. **Open** *Drop-in patients* 8am-6pm Mon-Fri; 9am-3pm Sat, Sun. **Map** p241 G7.
City Akuten Tand
Olof Palmes Gata 13A, Norrmalm (20 15 01 50, www.cityakuten.se/tandvard). T-bana Hötorget or bus 1, 56, 59. **Open** 8am-10pm daily. **Map** p241 F6.

Doctors

Sturehälsan
Birger Jarlsgatan 43, Östermalm (20 37 00, www.sturehalsan.se). T-bana Rådmansgatan or bus 2, 43, 96. **Open** 11am-5pm Mon, Wed, Fri; 11am-3pm Sat. Closed Sat July, Aug.
Drop-in GP clinic.

Insurance

EU nationals should obtain a **European Health Insurance Card** (EHIC), which facilitates free medical care under the Swedish national health service. Visitors of other nationalities should arrange insurance prior to their trip.

Opticians

Synsam
Sergelarkaden 12-14, Norrmalm (21 20 44, www.synsam.se). T-bana T-Centralen. **Open** 10am-8pm Mon-Fri; 10am-6pm Sat; 11am-5pm Sun. **Map** p241 G7.

Scandinavia's largest group of opticians has around a dozen branches in Stockholm.

Pharmacies

Pharmacies (*apotek*), identified by a green and white J-shaped sign, can be found all over the city. Most are open 10am-6pm Mon-Fri, and closed at the weekend.

ID

Swedes have national identity cards, but most people use their driving licence as ID. It is a good idea to carry some form of identification when you go to bars and clubs if you're under 25 or look like you could be. Also, ID will be needed if you want to pay the lower price sometimes offered at museums for people under 25 or over 65, as well as when buying alcohol in *systembolagets*.

LIBRARIES

Stockholm's libraries are open to anyone for reference, but if you want to take a book out, you will need ID and an address in Sweden (a hotel address will not do). For a list of public libraries in Stockholm, contact **Stockholms Stadsbiblioteket** (50 83 11 00, www.biblioteket. stockholm.se).

Kungliga Biblioteket

Humlegården, Östermalm (463 40 00, www.kb.se). T-bana Östermalmstorg or bus 1. **Open** 9am-7pm Mon-Thur; 9am-6pm Fri; 11am-3pm Sat. The library closes 1hr earlier mid June-mid Aug and is closed throughout July. **Map** p246 E8.
Mainly oriented towards research.

LOST PROPERTY

Both of Stockholm's two main public transport companies have lost-and-found centres.

SL

Klara Östra Kyrkogata 4, Norrmalm (600 10 00). T-bana T-Centralen or bus 3, 47, 53, 56, 59, 62, 65. **Open** 8am-7pm Mon; 8am-5pm Tue-Fri; 8am-2pm Sat. **Map** p241 G6.
For objects lost on the Tunnelbana, city buses and commuter trains.

SJ

Central Station, Vasagatan, Norrmalm (50 12 55 90). T-bana T-Centralen or bus 1, 3, 53, 56, 59, 65, 91. **Open** 9am-7pm Mon-Fri. **Map** p241 G6.
For long-distance trains.

MEDIA

International newspapers and magazines

Copies of most of the major foreign newspapers and magazines, especially English-language ones, can be found in the press section of **NK** department store (*see p72*) as well as in branches of **Pressbyrån** (www.pressbyran.se), which are all around the city. Gamla Stan's **English Bookshop** (*see p56*) sells the *Guardian Weekly*, while **Papercut** (*see p115*), in Södermalm, is great for English-language arts magazines and journals. One of the best local design and architecture magazines is *FORM* (www.formmagazine.com).

Newspapers

The two main daily papers are **Dagens Nyheter** (738 10 00, www.dn.se), and the right-leaning **Svenska Dagbladet** (618 02 20, www.svd.se). On public transport, you're likely to see people reading **Metro** (402 20 30, www.metro.se), a free daily paper distributed at T-bana stations. **Aftonbladet** (725 20 00, www.aftonbladet.se) and **Expressen** (738 30 00, www.expressen.se) are popular evening tabloids with the latest scandals and gossip, as well as weekly TV guides.

The monthly publication **Nöjesguiden** (www.nojesguiden.se) features stories about the Stockholm scene and events listings. It's available free from shops, cafés and newsstands.

For Swedish news in English, **SR Radio Sweden International** lists brief summaries on its website (www.sverigesradio.se). Alternatively, there is **The Local** (www.thelocal.se), which provides a round-up of Swedish-related news in English, and **Totally Stockholm** (www.totallystockholm.se).

Radio

Radio 107.5 *107.5 MHz*
Contemporary pop and dance music.
NRJ *105.1 MHz*
The latest hits.
Radio Sweden *89.6 MHz*
Check the schedule (www. sverigesradio.se) for English programming during evenings and weekends.
Sveriges Radio P2 *96.2 MHz*
Classical, jazz and opera. Check the schedule (www.sverigesradio.se) for English programming, generally including sport and political topics.

Television

The state channels of **SVT 1** and **SVT 2** were the first to broadcast in Sweden and still earn the highest ratings. Their commercial-free programmes are varied enough to appeal to all ages.

Deregulation during the mid 1980s ended the state's television broadcasting monopoly and allowed for the creation of several private channels. The most successful of these is the terrestrial **TV4**, with news, soap operas, sitcoms and game shows. Similar programming can be found on **TV3** and **Kanal 5**, both of which are broadcast from abroad and – much to the chagrin of the government – do not always adhere to Swedish broadcasting regulations.

Hip youths with carefully dishevelled hair present the music and entertainment programming at popular **ZTV**.

Foreign-made programmes and films are shown in their original language with Swedish subtitles.

MONEY

The Swedish krona (plural kronor, abbreviated to kr or SEK) is divided into 100 öre. It comes in coins of 50 öre, 1kr, 5kr and 10kr, and notes of 20kr, 50kr, 100kr, 500kr and 1,000kr. At the time of going to press: £1 = 11.7kr, $1 (US) = 7.2kr, €1 = 9.1kr.

In 2003 Sweden voted against joining the European Monetary Union (EMU).

ATMs/cash machines

There are two types of ATM: **Bankomat** (the joint system of the business banks) and **Uttag** (which belongs to Swedbank). Don't forget that banks tend to charge commission. You'll find ATMs all over the city, in department stores, shopping centres and at banks.

Banks & bureaux de change

You can change money in the city at banks, many hotels and specialist bureaux de change, such as **Forex** and **X-change**; the latter tend to be best because they often provide a more favourable exchange rate and have numerous offices in the city centre. There are exchange offices in the tourist office, Central Station and at Arlanda Airport (Terminals 2 and 5).

Banks are usually open 9am-3pm Mon-Fri, and some stay open until 6pm at least once a week. All banks are closed at weekends and on public holidays, as well as the day before a public holiday.

Forex
Stureplan, Kungsgatan 2, Norrmalm (611 51 10, www.forex.se). T-bana Hötorget or bus 1, 43, 56. **Open** 9am-7pm Mon-Fri; 10am-4pm Sat. **Map** p241 F8.
Other locations Kungsgatan 2, Östermalm (611 51 10); Central Station, Norrmalm (411 67 34); Cityterminalen, Norrmalm (21 42 80); Vasagatan 16, Norrmalm (10 49 90); Arlanda Airport, Terminal 2, Terminal 5 and Sky City (59 36 22 71).

Credit cards

Major credit and debit cards are widely accepted. Banks will advance cash against a credit card, but prefer you to use an ATM.

Money transfers

Local banks don't do money transfers unless you're a customer of the bank. **Forex** (*see above*), **Western Union** (020 90 10 90, www.westernunion.com) and **MoneyGram** (00 8009 2694 00, www.moneygram.com) are your best bets for money transfers to and from Sweden; all have several branches around Stockholm – see the websites or call for details.

Tax

The sales tax for most commodities is 25 per cent. There is a 12 per cent sales tax on food and hotel bills, and six per cent sales tax on books, movie and concert tickets, and transport (taxis, flights, trains).

The sales tax is always listed separately on the bill but is included in the displayed price.

Non-EU residents can reclaim tax on purchases above 200kr in shops displaying a 'Tax-Free Shopping' sticker. All you have to do is ask for a tax-free receipt when paying for an item. When you leave the EU, show your purchases, receipts and passport to customs officials and have your Global Refund cheques stamped. The refund can be collected from any Global Blue office or credited to your own bank account. Call **Global Blue** (020 74 17 41, 54 52 84 40, www.globalblue.com).

OPENING HOURS

Normal opening hours for shops are 10am-6pm Mon-Fri; 10am-5pm Sat; noon-4pm Sun. Some smaller shops close earlier on Saturdays and do not open on Sundays. All shops used to be closed on public holidays, but this is changing more and more. Many grocery stores are now open 365 days per year.

Restaurant opening hours vary greatly. They are usually open by 11am if they serve lunch; otherwise they'll open some time in the afternoon (usually 4 or 5pm). Closing time is around midnight unless the restaurant has a bar, in which case they may stay open until 1am or even later. Note that many restaurants close in July.

Office hours are generally 8.30am-5pm Mon-Fri. For bank opening hours, *see left* **Banks & bureaux de change**. For post office opening hours, *see below* **Postal services**.

POLICE & SECURITY

The police are not that common a sight in Stockholm, but can always be spotted at concerts or any special events. They speak English and are friendly and helpful. If you're the victim of a crime, call the police on 112, or dial 114 14 in non-emergency situations. But Stockholm is considered a very safe city, so the chances of that happening are small. Still, it's wise to take the usual city precautions: don't openly flaunt money or jewellery, keep a close eye on your surroundings and be careful in dark areas late at night.

Pickpocketing does occur in crowded places. Muggings are rare and there are no particular areas considered dangerous but, as with anywhere, it's best not to walk in dimly lit areas such as parks at night (an increasing number of muggings have taken place in Humlegården, Berzelii Park and Kungsträdgården).

Police HQ
Kungsholmsgatan 43, Kungsholmen (114 14). T-bana Rådhuset or bus 1, 40, 56, 91. **Map** p240 G4.
This is the main police station (it's also the place where people suspected of committing a crime are kept until the trial). Sub-station Torkel is at Knutssonsgatan 20, Södermalm (114 14).

POSTAL SERVICES

Most post offices are open 10am-6pm Mon-Fri, 10am-2pm Sat; they have a yellow sign containing a blue crown and horn symbol. You can also buy stamps at tobacco kiosks, 7-Elevens, and the tourist office (*see p227*).

Posten
Regeringsgatan 65, Norrmalm
(23 22 21, www.posten.se). T-bana
Hötorget. **Open** 8.30am-6pm
Mon-Fri; 9am-6pm Sat, Sun.
Map p241 F7.

RELIGION

Most Swedes are nominally members
of the Church of Sweden, which
is Evangelical Lutheran, but less
than ten per cent of the population
attends church regularly. Many
other Christian sects are represented
in Stockholm, and significant
numbers of Muslims and Jews live
in or near the city.

SMOKING

Sweden passed a law on 1 June
2005 that banned smoking in all
public places where food or drink
is served. You're not allowed to
smoke in most other public places
either, including bus stop cubicles
and all Tunnelbana stations.

STUDY

Many students come from abroad to
study in Sweden.

Universities & colleges

Berghs School of
Communication
PO Box 1380, 111 93 Stockholm
(58 75 50 00, www.berghs.se).
Offers programmes in journalism,
media, advertising and PR.
Handelshögskolan
PO Box 6501, 113 83 Stockholm
(736 90 00, www.hhs.se).
Stockholm's School of Economics,
the city's main business school, was
founded in 1909. The school has an
exchange programme with 155
places each year.
Konstfack
Visiting address: LM Erikssonsväg
14, Hägersten. Postal address:
PO Box 3601, 126 27 Stockholm
(450 41 00, www.konstfack.se).
The University College of Arts,
Crafts and Design.
Kungliga Tekniska
Högskolan
Valhallavägen 79, 100 44 Stockholm
(790 60 00, www.kth.se).
The Institute of Technology is
around 200 years old. It provides one
third of Sweden's technical research
and has established exchanges all
over the world.
Stockholms Filmskola
Karusellplan 13, 126 31
Hägersten (616 00 35, www.
stockholmsfilmskola.com).

A private school offering pre-
university foundation courses
(lasting two years) in film studies.
Stockholms Musikpedagogiska
Institut
Visiting address: Eriksbergsgatan
8B, Östermalm. Postal adress:
PO Box 26164, 100 41 Stockholm
(611 05 02, www.smpi.se).
A small, independent college that
specialises in music and the arts.
Stockholms Universitet
106 91 Stockholm (switchboard
16 20 00, student services 16 28 45,
www.su.se/english/study).
Stockholm University – north of the
city centre, with its own T-bana stop,
Universitetet – has about 35,000
undergraduate students and 2,200
postgraduate students.

TELEPHONES

International & local
dialling codes

To make an international call from
Stockholm, dial 00 and then the
country code, followed by the area
code (omitting the initial 0, if there
is one) and the number. The
international code for the UK is 44;
it's 1 for the US and Canada; 353 for
the Irish Republic; 61 for Australia;
and 64 for New Zealand.
 To call Stockholm from abroad,
dial 00, then 46 for Sweden, then 8
for Stockholm, then the number.
Stockholm phone numbers vary in
the number of digits they contain.
The area code for Stockholm
(including the archipelago) is 08,
but you don't need to dial it if you're
within the area. All phone numbers
in this guide are given as dialled
from within Stockholm. Swedish
mobile phone numbers begin with
07. Numbers beginning 020 are
always toll-free lines.

Public phones

Public phones, operated by partly
state-owned phone company Telia,
are not as widespread as they used
to be. The newest phones accept
coins (both kroner and euro). All
phones accept credit cards and pre-
paid phonecards, which are available
in 30, 60 or 100 units and can be
bought at most newsagents and
tobacconists. One unit buys one
minute of a local call; long-distance
calls cost two units per minute.
 Instructions are given in English.
You can make reverse-charge (collect)
calls from all public phones (key 2,
then enter the number you're calling
including the area code), and call
emergency services (on 112) for free.

Mobile phones

Sweden is on the worldwide GSM
network, so compatible mobile
phones should work fine.

Telia
Sergels Torg 12, Norrmalm (020
40 08 00, www.telia.se). T-bana
Hötorget or bus 1, 56, 59. **Open**
10am-7pm Mon-Fri; 10am-6pm Sat;
11am-5pm Sun.
Sweden's major telephone operator.

TIME

Stockholm is one hour ahead of
GMT, six hours ahead of US Eastern
Standard Time and nine hours ahead
of Pacific Standard Time. Summer
time (an hour later) runs from late
March to late October, with the same
changeover days as the UK.

TIPPING

There are no fixed rules about
tipping in Sweden because the
service charge is almost always
included. In restaurants, most people
leave 5-15 per cent, depending on
how satisfied they are. Rounding
up the bill is usually sufficient when
you pay a bartender (at the bar) or
a taxi driver.

TOILETS

Public toilets (*toalett*; small, green
booths) are usually found near or
in parks. They cost 5kr to use and
are kept clean.
 There are public toilets and
showers at Central Station and at
Sergels Torg by the entrance to the
T-Centralen T-bana station (open
7.15am-10.30pm daily, toilets 5kr,
shower with towel 20kr).

TOURIST
INFORMATION

Stockholm Visitor Centre
Kulturhuset, Sergels Torg 3,
Norrmalm (50 82 85 08, www.
visitstockholm.com). T-bana
T-Centralen or bus 1, 3, 53, 56,
59, 65, 91. **Open** *Mid Sept-*
late Apr 9am-6pm Mon-Fri;
9am-4pm Sat; 10am-4pm Sun.
May-mid Sept 9am-7pm Mon-Fri;
9am-4pm Sat; 10am-4pm Sun.
Map p241 G7.
This is the main tourist office in
Stockholm, with huge amounts of
useful information, plus free books
and maps and the free monthly
magazine *What's On Stockholm*. You
can also buy the Stockholm Card (in
person or online), and theatre and

ESSENTIAL INFORMATION

ESSENTIAL INFORMATION

LOCAL CLIMATE

Average temperatures and monthly rainfall in Stockholm.

	High (°C/°F)	Low (°C/°F)	Rainfall (mm/in)
Jan	0 / 32	-5 / 23	39 / 1.5
Feb	0 / 32	-5 / 23	27 / 1.1
Mar	3 / 37	-3 / 27	26 / 1
Apr	8 / 46	1 / 34	30 / 1.2
May	15 / 59	6 / 43	30 / 1.2
June	21 / 70	11 / 52	45 / 1.8
July	22 / 72	13 / 55	72 / 2.8
Aug	20 / 68	13 / 55	66 / 2.6
Sept	15 / 59	9 / 48	55 / 2.2
Oct	10 / 50	5 / 41	50 / 2
Nov	4 / 39	0 / 32	53 / 2.1
Dec	1 / 34	-3 / 27	46 / 1.8

concert tickets. The hotel booking centre can find and book hotels in all price brackets. Free WiFi is available.

VISAS & PASSPORTS

Sweden is one of the European Union countries covered by the Schengen agreement, meaning many shared visa regulations and reduced border controls (with the exception of the UK and Ireland, the Schengen zone takes in the entire EU, and also extends to Norway and Iceland). To travel to Schengen countries, British and Irish citizens need full passports; most EU nationals usually only need to carry their national identity card when travelling between Nordic countries, but it's wise to carry a passport as well as some airlines require them.

Passports, but not visas, are needed by US, Canadian, Australian and New Zealand citizens for stays of up to three months. Citizens of South Africa and many other countries do need visas, obtainable from Swedish consulates and embassies abroad (or in other Schengen countries that you're planning to visit). Visa requirements can change, so always check the latest information with your country's Swedish embassy.

WEIGHTS & MEASURES

Sweden uses the metric system. Decimal points are indicated by commas, while thousands are defined by full stops. Throughout this guide, we have listed measurements in both metric and imperial.

WHEN TO GO

Most people choose to visit between May and September, which is when most sights and attractions have

extended opening hours. The time around Midsummer (nearest to 24 June) is the big summer holiday weekend, when many people leave town and much of the city is closed. July is the main holiday month for locals, and many restaurants, bars and shops close down for some or all of the month. Mosquitoes can be a nuisance outside the city between June and late September, especially at dusk in the archipelago.

Winter (Nov-Mar) brings short days and cold temperatures, but snow doesn't usually stay on the ground long. The city looks stunning just after a snowfall, especially on clear, crisp, sunny days, which are relatively common.

Public holidays

On public holidays, virtually all shops, banks and offices, and many restaurants and bars, are closed. For a full list of public holidays in Sweden, see p31.

WOMEN

Great measures have been taken in Sweden to guarantee equal opportunities for men and women. Today, women in Sweden can combine having a family and working thanks to the state-sponsored childcare programme; almost 80 per cent of women work and around 75 per cent of children aged one to six use the state childcare system. Swedish women still earn less than men, though, partly because of the professions they choose and the fact that many mothers work part-time.

It's unlikely that female visitors will face any kind of harassment, and Stockholm is a very safe city to walk around, although the normal precautions are recommended.

KvinnorKan (33 52 47, www. kvinnorkan.se) works to enhance the empowerment of women.

WORKING IN STOCKHOLM

If you want to work in Stockholm, but you're not yet in the country, the best way to find a job is to register at some of the many online recruiting companies, such as **Academic Search** (www.academicsearch.se), **Monster** (www.monster.se) and **Stepstone** (www.stepstone.se).

The European Employment Services network, **EURES** (http://ec.europa.eu/eures), provides a comprehensive database of job vacancies throughout the EU and useful information about working conditions.

If you're already living in Sweden, you can start looking for a job by going to the state employment agency, **Arbetsförmedlingen**; it has a lot of information and offers free guidance for people seeking work.

Arbetsförmedlingen
Tunnelgatan 3, Norrmalm (077 160 00 00, www.arbets formedlingen.se). **Open** *Phone enquiries* 8am-4.30pm Mon-Fri. *Office* 10am-4pm Mon-Fri. *Self-service* (use of computers) 8am-4pm Mon-Fri. **Map** p241 E7.

Work permits

All EU nationals can obtain a work permit in Sweden; non-EU citizens must apply for a work permit abroad and hand in the application to a Swedish embassy or consular representative. The rules for obtaining work permits vary for different jobs. EU citizens can stay in Sweden for three months, after which they must apply for a residence permit (which can take a month to process, so it's best to apply as soon as you arrive). Non-EU citizens must apply for a residence permit from outside Sweden. You'll need to produce a valid ID or passport and other documents depending on your status (employee, job-seeker, self-employed, student, etc). Contact the **National Immigration Authority** (Migrationsverket; 0771 23 52 35, www.migrationsverket.se).

Useful organisations

The EU has a website (www.europa. eu) with comprehensive information on your rights, and useful numbers and addresses.

Vocabulary

VOWELS

Swedish vowels include the standard a, e, i, o, u and sometimes y along with three additional vowels: å, ä and ö. Vowels are long when at the end of a word or followed by one consonant, and short when followed by two consonants.

å – as in tore
ä – as in pet
ö – as in fur
y – as in ewe
ej – as in late

CONSONANTS

g (before e, i, y, ä and ö), **j, lj, dj** and **gj** – as in yet
k (before e, i, y, ä and ö), **sj, skj, stj, tj** and **rs** – all more or less like sh, with subtle differences
qu – as kv (though q is hardly ever used in Swedish)
z – as in so

ALPHABETICAL ORDER

Swedish alphabetical order lists **å, ä** and **ö**, in that order, after **z**.

USEFUL WORDS & PHRASES

yes *ja* (yah); **no** *nej* (nay); **please/thank you** *tack*; **hello** *hej* (hay); **goodbye** *hej då* (hay daw); **excuse me** *ursäkta* (ewr-shekta); **I'm sorry** *förlåt* (furr-lawt); **do you speak English?** *talar du engelska?* (tah-lar dew engelska?); **how are you?** *hur är det* (hewr eyre day?)

SIGHTSEEING

entrance *ingång* (in-gawng); **exit** *utgång* (ewt-gawng); **open** *öppen* (ur-pen); **closed** *stängd* (staingd); **toilet (women/men)** *toalett* (too-a-let) *(kvinnor/män)*; **where** *var*; **when** *när* (nair); **near** *nära* (naira); **far** *långt* (lawngt); **(city) square** *torg* (tohrj); **church** *kyrka* (chewr-ka); **art gallery** *konstgalleri*; **town hall** *stadshus*; **street/road** *gata/väg*; **palace** *slott*; **metro** *tunnelbana*; **ticket to…** *biljett till…* (bill-yet till); **how much is this/that?** *hur mycket kostar den/det?* (hewr mewkeh kostar den/det?); **which way to…?** *hur kommer jag till…?* (hewr comer yah til…?)

ACCOMMODATION

hotel *hotell*; **youth hostel** *vandrarhem*; **I have a reservation** *jag har beställt ett rum* (yah har bes-telt ett room); **double room** *dubbelrum*; **single room** *enkelrum*; **double bed** *dubbelsäng*; **twin beds** *två sängar*; **with a bath** *med bad*; **with a shower** *med dusch*

DAYS OF THE WEEK

Monday *måndag*; **Tuesday** *tisdag*; **Wednesday** *onsdag*; **Thursday** *torsdag*; **Friday** *fredag*; **Saturday** *lördag*; **Sunday** *söndag*

NUMBERS

0 *noll*; **1** *ett*; **2** *två* (tvaw); **3** *tre* (trea); **4** *fyra* (few-ra); **5** *fem*; **6** *sex*; **7** *sju* (shew); **8** *åtta* (otta); **9** *nio* (nee-oo) **10** *tio* (tee-oo); **11** *elva*; **12** *tolv*; **13** *tretton*; **14** *fjorton* (fyoor-ton); **15** *femton*; **16** *sexton*; **17** *sjutton* (shew-ton); **18** *arton*; **19** *nitton*; **20** *tjugo* (chew-goo); **21** *tjugoett* (chew-goo-ett); **30** *trettio* (tretti); **40** *fyrtio* (fur-ti); **50** *femtio* (fem-ti); **60** *sextio* (sex-ti); **70** *sjuttio* (shew-ti); **80** *åttio* (otti); **90** *nittio* (nitti); **100** *hundra* (hewndra); **1,000** *tusen* (tews-sen); **1,000,000** *miljon* (milly-oon)

EATING OUT

have you got a table for…? *har ni ett bord för…?* (hahr nee ett boord furr…?); **bill** *notan* (noo-tan); **menu** *meny* (men-ew) **lunch** *lunch* (lewnch); **dinner** *middag* (mid-daag); **main course** *huvudrätt* (hew-vew-dret); **starter** *förrätt* (fur-et); **bottle** *flaska*; **glass** *glas*; **restaurang** *restaurant*

BASIC FOODS & EXTRAS

egg *ägg*; **bread** *bröd*; **cheese** *ost*; **potatoes** *potatis*; **rice** *ris*; **mustard** *senap*; **butter** *smör*; **sandwich** *smörgås*; **sugar** *socker*

SWEDISH SPECIALITIES (HUSMANSKOST)

split pea and pork soup *ärtsoppa*; **steak and mashed potato** *black & white*; **fish soup** *fisksoppa*; **gratin of anchovies and potatoes** *Janssons frestelse*; **stuffed cabbage rolls** *kåldolmar*;

meatballs *köttbullar*; **pork dumpling with smoked salmon** *lufsa*; **potato salad** *potatissallad*; **fried meat and potato hash with a fried egg and pickled beetroot** *pytt i panna*; **lightly salted brisket of beef** *oxbringa*; **assortment of herring dishes** *rimmad sillbricka*; **typical self-service buffet** *smörgåsbord*

FRUIT & VEG (FRUKT & GRÖNSAKER)

orange *apelsin*, **peas** *ärtor*, **lemon** *citron*; **raspberry** *hallon*; **cloudberry** *hjortron*; **strawberries** *jordgubbar*; **cabbage** *kål*; **lingonberry** *lingon*; **onion** *lök*; **carrots** *morötter*; **nuts** *nötter*; **peach** *persika*; **wild strawberries** *smultron*; **mushrooms** *svamp*; **grapes** *vindruvor*; **garlic** *vitlök*

MEAT & GAME (KÖTT & VILT)

elk *älg*; **beef** *biff*; **pork** *fläsk*; **veal** *kalvkött*; **sausage** *korv*; **chicken** *kyckling*; **lamb** *lammkött*; **roe deer** *rådjur*; **reindeer** *ren*; **ham** *skinka*

FISH (FISK)

eel *ål*; **mussels** *blåmusslor*; **trout** *forell*; **pike-perch** *gös*; **lobster** *hummer*; **crayfish** *kräftor*; **salmon** *lax*; **prawns** *räkor*; **sole** *sjötunga*; **herring (pickled/blackened)** *strömming/sill (inlagd/sotare)*; **fermented Baltic herring** *surströmming*; **cod** *torsk*

CAKES/DESSERTS (BAKVERK/DESSERTER)

ice-cream *glass*; **cake** *kaka/tårta*; **saffron bun** *lussekatt*; **Swedish cheesecake** *ostkaka*; **gingerbread biscuits** *pepparkakor*; **miniature pancakes served with jam and cream** *plättar*; **whipped cream and almond paste buns** *semla*

DRINKS (DRYCKER)

schnapps *brännvin*; **fruit juice** *fruktjuice*; **fortified mulled wine** *glögg*; **milk** *mjölk*; **beer** *öl*; **arak-like sweet spirit** *punsch*; **red wine** *rödvin*; **hot chocolate** *varm choklad*; **white wine** *vitt vin*

Further Reference

BOOKS

For books about Sweden in English, visit the Swedish Institute's **English Bookshop** (*see p56*), or the book sections in department stores **NK** (*see p72*) and **Åhlens** (*see p70*).

Architecture, art & design

Claes Caldenby & Olof Hultin *Architecture in Sweden 1995-9* (2001) With text in English and Swedish.
Katrin Cargill *Creating the Look: Swedish Style* (1996) A guide to achieving the Swedish design look.
Courtney Davis *A Treasury of Viking Design* (2000) Scandinavian Viking design in ceramics, textiles, woodwork and so on.
Ralph Skansen Edenheim *Traditional Swedish Style* (2002) Illustrated presentation of the interiors of Skansen's buildings from a cultural and historical perspective.
Charlotte Fiell *Scandinavian Design* (2002) In-depth illustrated guide focusing on 200 designers and design companies.
Groth Hakan & Fritz van der Schulenburg *Neodlassicism in the North: Swedish Furniture and Interiors 1770-1850* (1999) Excellent photographs trace the evolution of the neoclassical style in Sweden.
Susanne Helgeson *Swedish Design* (2002) A survey of Swedish designers. Offers insight into Swedish design philosophies.
Olof Hultin, Bengt Oh Johansson, Johan Mårtelius & Rasmus Waern *The Complete Guide to Architecture in Stockholm* (1999) This guide introduces the reader to 400 of the most notable buildings in the Stockholm area.
Derek E Ostergard & Nina Stritzler-Levine *The Brilliance of Swedish Glass 1918-1939* (1997) Illustrated essays that put Swedish glass production into perspective.
Lars & Ursula Sjöberg *The Swedish Room* (1994) Illustrated guide to interior design.
Michael Snodin & Elisabet Stavenow-Hidemark (eds) *Carl and Karin Larsson: Creators of the Swedish Style* (1998) Numerous essays by experts.
Barbara Stoeltie, René Stoeltie & Angelika Taschen *Country Houses of Sweden* (2001) Coffee-table book with lovely photos of Swedish country houses from various periods.

Biographies

Maaret Koskinen *Ingmar Bergman* (2007) An overview of the late, great filmmaker.
Sharon Linnea *Raoul Wallenberg: The Man who Stopped Death* (1993) Biography of the famous Swedish diplomat who saved the lives of 100,000 Hungarian Jews during World War II and then mysteriously disappeared after going into Soviet custody.
Joe Lovejoy *Sven-Göran Eriksson* (2002) For football lovers only.
Eivor Martinus *Strindberg and Love* (2001) In-depth biography of the dramatist, focusing on the four most important women in his life.
Carl Magnus Palm *From ABBA to Mamma Mia: The Official Book* (2000) The first book published with the co-operation of the band, with lots of good photos.

Fiction & autobiographies

Frans G Bengtsson *The Long Ships* (1945) A true Swedish classic, this novel enchants its readers with the adventures of a fictional Viking.
Ingmar Bergman *The Magic Lantern: An Autobiography* (1989) Memoirs of the film master's career and childhood.
Karin Boye *Kallocain* (1940) A bleak vision of a future totalitarian world state.
Eyvind Johnson *Dreams of Roses and Fire* (1949) Novel by the winner of the 1974 Nobel Prize for Literature.
Selma Lagerlöf *The Wonderful Adventures of Nils* (1906) One of Sweden's best-loved modern folk tales, written to teach Swedish schoolchildren about the geography of their country. Tiny Nils explores the Swedish landscape on the back of a goose and lives through many hair-raising experiences.
Stieg Larsson Larsson, who died in 2004, is best known for his blockbusting Millennium crime trilogy, starring Mikael Blomkvist and Lisbeth Salander.
Astrid Lindgren *Pippi Longstocking* (1945) Fantastic series of children's books about a girl who does exactly as she pleases.
John Ajvide Lindqvist *Let the Right One In* (2007) A bestseller in Sweden, this is a unique fusion of social novel and vampire legend.

Henning Mankell Best-selling crime writer most famous for his series of detective stories starring Inspector Kurt Wallander from southern Sweden.
Vilhelm Moberg *The Emigrants* (1949) Moving story about what it was like to emigrate from Sweden to the US in the 19th century, later made into a film.
Mikael Niemi *Popular Music* (2004). A witty, compelling coming-of-age story set in northern Sweden in the 1960s.
August Strindberg *Miss Julie and Other Plays* (1998) Contains some of the dramatist's key plays: *Miss Julie*, *The Father*, *A Dream Play*, *Ghost Sonata* and *The Dance of Death*.
Mary Wollstonecraft *Letters Written during a Short Residence in Sweden, Norway and Denmark* (2004) Early feminist Wollstonecraft describes her travels through Scandinavia in 1795.

History, politics & society

Peter Berlin *The Xenophobe's Guide to the Swedes* (1999) An amusing book explaining the complex rules that govern Swedish social interaction.
Michael Booth *The Almost Nearly Perfect People: The Truth about the Nordic Miracle* (2014) A wry look at what really makes the Scandinavians tick.
Lisa Werner Carr & Christina Johansson Robinowitz *Modern-day Vikings: A Practical Guide to Interacting with the Swedes* (2001) Discussion of the Viking beginnings of the Swedish character.
Ake Daun *Swedish Mentality* (1996) Focuses on the development of Swedish culture and society.
Matz Erling *Glorious Vasa: The Magnificent Ship and 17th-century Sweden* (2001) Fascinating book that provides a great insight into what life was like in 17th-century Stockholm.
Stig Hadenius *Swedish Politics during the 20th Century* (1999) Authoritative treatment of all the dramatic political changes that took place between 1900 and 1999.
Istvan Hargittai & James Watson *The Road to Stockholm: Nobel Prizes, Science and Scientists* (2002) Discusses the selection process for the scientific laureates and the ingredients for scientific discovery and recognition.

Herman Lindqvist *A History of Sweden: From Ice Age to Our Age* (2006) An entertaining introduction to the history of Sweden.
Byron J Nordstrom *The History of Sweden* (2002) Swedish history from prehistoric times to the present.
Jan Öjvind Swahn *Maypoles, Crayfish and Lucia: Swedish Holidays and Traditions* (1997) A guide to Swedish customs and festivals.

FILM

Before the Storm (Reza Parsa, 2000) Excellent thriller.
The Best Intentions (Bille August, 1992) The story of Ingmar Bergman's parents, written by Bergman himself.
Elvira Madigan (Bo Widerberg, 1967) Beautiful-looking film about a doomed love affair.
The Emigrants (Jan Troell, 1970) First of two films dealing with Swedish emigrants to America.
Evil (Mikael Håfström, 2004) Oscar-nominated film about a young rebel in a Swedish private school in the late 1950s.
Fanny and Alexander (Ingmar Bergman, 1982) Family saga seen through the eyes of a young boy.
The Father (Alf Sjöberg, 1969) Film version of Strindberg's play about a battle between husband and wife, descending into madness and death.
Four Shades of Brown (Tomas Alfredson, 2004) Black comedy interweaving four lives.
Fucking Åmål (US title *Show Me Love*, Lukas Moodysson, 1998) All-girl twist to the high-school romance genre, which won multiple awards.
House of Angels (Colin Nutley, 1992) Prejudice and conflict in rural Sweden.
I am Curious: Yellow (Vilgot Sjöman, 1967) Sexually frank but morally involved tale.
Jalla! Jalla! (Josef Fares, 2000). Culture clash comedy.
Let the Right One In (Tomas Alfredson, 2008). Vampire horror set in the suburbs of Stockholm.
Lilja 4-ever (Lukas Moodysson, 2002) Moodysson darker than usual but very popular in Sweden.
My Life as a Dog (Lasse Hallström, 1985) A witty and touching story of a young boy in 1950s rural Sweden.
Persona (Ingmar Bergman, 1966) An actress refuses to speak, while her nurse chats away about her sex life.
The Seventh Seal (Ingmar Bergman, 1956) Unforgettable medieval allegory, with plague sweeping through an apocalyptic Sweden and Max von Sydow's knight playing chess with Death.

Songs from the Second Floor (Roy Andersson, 2000) Loosely connected vignettes deal with traffic jams and redundancy in a surreal black comedy.
Together (Lukas Moodysson, 2000) Excellent comedy about life and love in a 1970s commune.
The Treasure of Arne (Mauritz Stiller, 1919) Bravura premonition-laden drama set in the 16th century.
Tsatsiki, Mum and the Policeman (Ella Lemhagen, 1999) Engaging story of a young Stockholmer who longs to meet his Greek father.
Under the Sun (Colin Nutley, 1998) Sweet and satisfying film based around an unconventional love story.
We are the Best! (Lukas Moodysson, 2013) Tale of 1980s teen rebellion in Stockholm.
Wild Strawberries (Ingmar Bergman, 1957) Warm story of an academic who rediscovers his youth.
Wings of Glass (Reza Bagher, 2000) A Swedish-Iranian family's conflict between their Muslim roots and Swedish environment.

MUSIC

Classical

Hugo Alfvén (1872-1960) Composer of the ballet *Bergakungen*, five symphonies and numerous songs.
Franz Berwald (1796-1868) Wrote operas, chamber music and four symphonics.
Daniel Börtz (born 1943) Composer whose contemporary chamber music and solo pieces reflect earlier periods.
Anders Eliasson (born 1947) Composer of complex works.
Håkan Hardenberger (born 1961) Internationally renowned trumpeter.
Anders Hillborg (born 1952) Most famous for his *Celestial Mechanics* for solo strings.
Christian Lindberg (born 1958) Trombone virtuoso.
Wilhelm Peterson-Berger (1867-1942) Composer of operas and piano miniatures with a folk influence.
Allan Pettersson (1911-80) Composer most renowned for his *Symphony No. 7*.
Hilding Rosenberg (1892-1985) Wrote numerous string quartets.
Wilhelm Stenhammar (1871-1927) Composed chamber music, operas and orchestral pieces.
Jan Sandström (born 1954) Renowned for his *Motorbike Concerto* for trombone and orchestra.
Sven-David Sandström (born 1942) Composer of complex orchestral works, ballets and percussion pieces.

Anne Sofie von Otter (born 1955) The world-famous mezzo-soprano.

Pop & rock

Abba Their phenomenally successful albums include *Waterloo* (1974) and *Super Trouper* (1980).
The Cardigans Pop band formed in 1992, with *Life* probably their most well-known album.
The Concretes *Hey Trouble* (2007) was the third album from eccentric Stockholm-based rockers.
Europe Remembered for the terrible 1986 hit 'The Final Countdown'.
The Hellacopters US-tinged Swedish rock.
The Hives Successful punk fivesome; albums include *Your New Favourite Band*, *Barely Legal* and *Tyrannosaurus Hives*.
Lykke Li Hypnotic indie star, whose new album, *I Never Learn*, was released in 2014.
Robyn Hugely popular mainstream popster. Her last album, *Body Talk*, came out in late 2010.
Sahara Hotnights Garage-rock girl band.
Soundtrack of Our Lives Successful six-piece rock outfit hailing from Gothenburg.

WEBSITES

City of Stockholm
www.stockholm.se Official information on the city's government, services and history.
Destination Stockholm
www.destination-stockholm.se Discounted accommodation, plus restaurant reviews and useful city information. In multiple languages.
Nobel Prizes
www.nobel.se Everything you ever wanted to know about the Nobel Prize.
Scandinavian Design
www.scandinaviandesign.com The products and personalities of Nordic design, plus museums, magazines and design schools.
Stockholm Guide
www.stockholmtown.com Official site with good information on events and attractions in the city and archipelago.
Sweden
www.sweden.se 'The official gateway to Sweden', with well-written articles and fact-sheets on Swedish culture.
Swedish Institute
www.si.se Essential source of information about Sweden, Swedes and Swedish culture, plus information about studying in Sweden.

ESSENTIAL INFORMATION

Index

Written by
local experts,
rated 'Top
Guidebook
Brand'
by Which?

Do
some
local
insight
seeing

All new
2014
guidebook.
Rewritten,
redesigned
and better
than ever.

Keep up, join in Time Out

INDEX

Maps

Tåg på andra plattformen mot →

MAPS

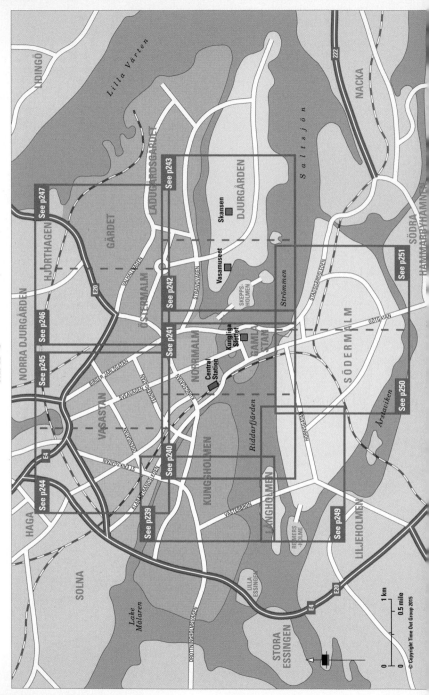

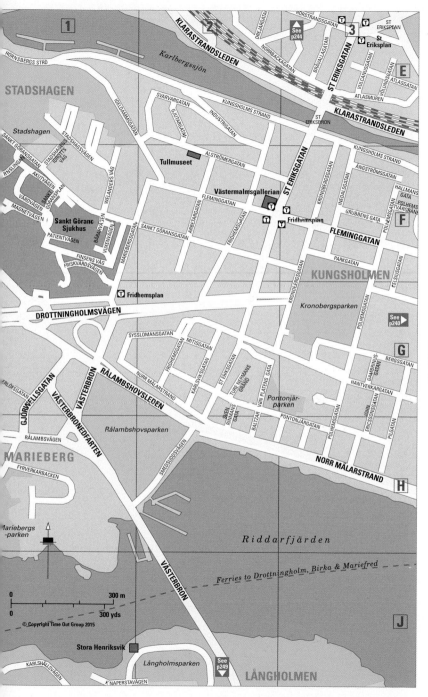

STADSHAGEN

Stadshagen

Karlbergssjön

Tullmuseet

Västermalmsgallerian

Sankt Görans Sjukhus

Fridhemsplan

KUNGSHOLMEN

Kronobergsparken

DROTTNINGHOLMSVÄGEN

Fridhemsplan

VÄSTERBRON

RÅLAMBSHOVSLEDEN

VÄSTERBRONEDFARTEN

Rålambshovsparken

Pontonjär-parken

MARIEBERG

NORR MÄLARSTRAND

Mariebergs-parken

Riddarfjärden

VÄSTERBRON

Ferries to Drottningholm, Birka & Mariefred

0   300 m
0   300 yds
© Copyright Time Out Group 2015

Stora Henriksvik

Långholmsparken

LÅNGHOLMEN

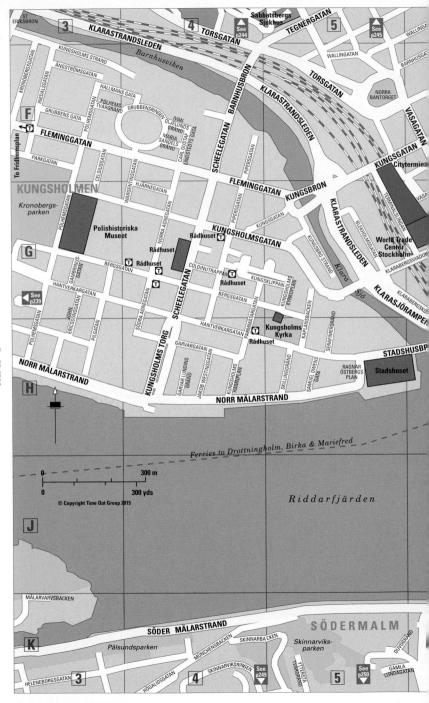

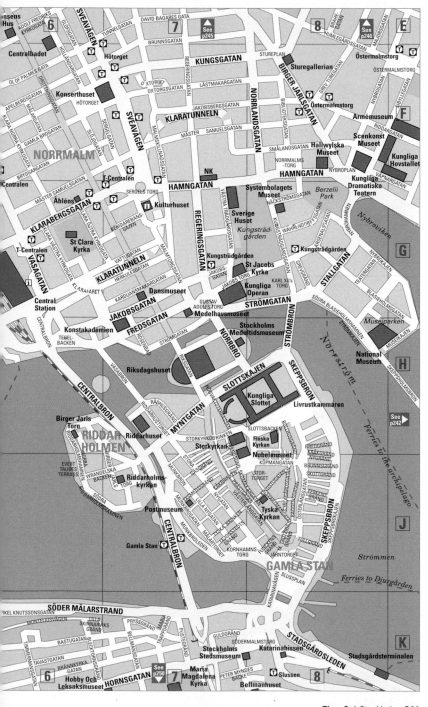

MAPS

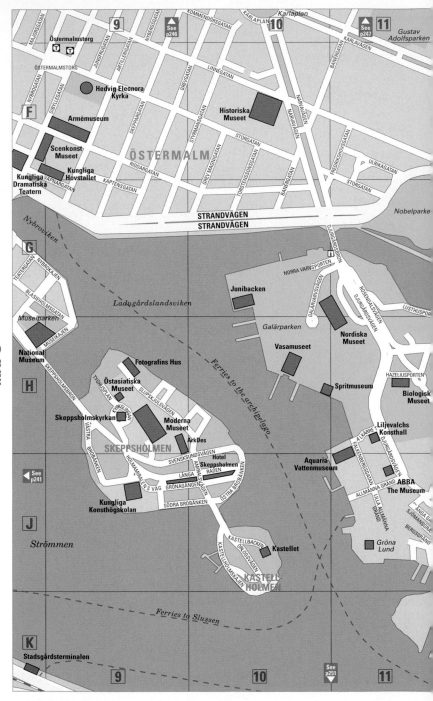

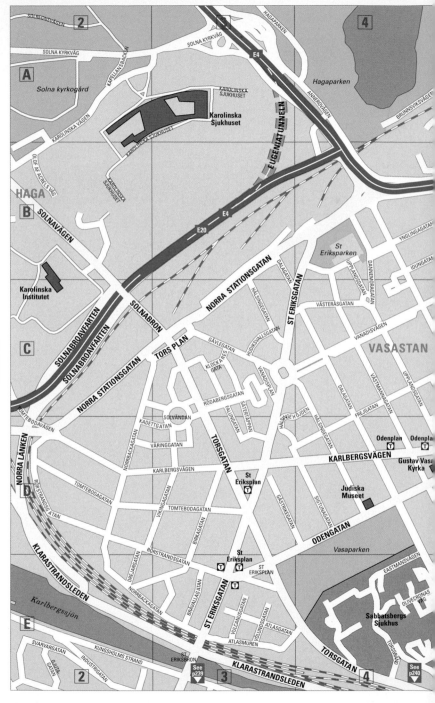

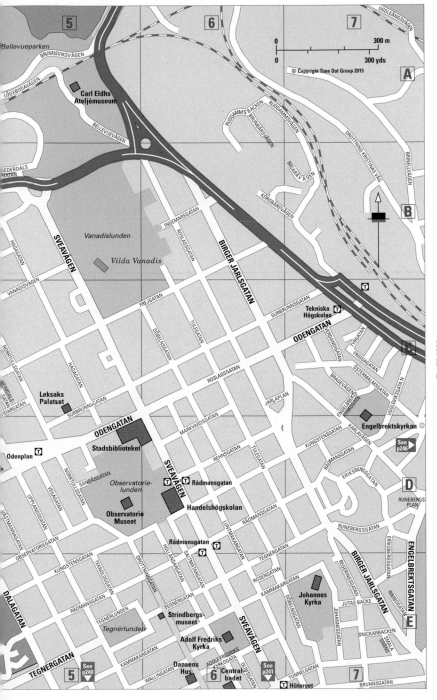

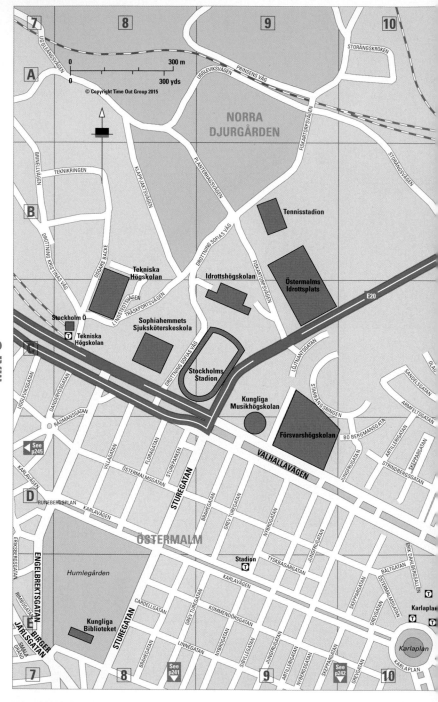

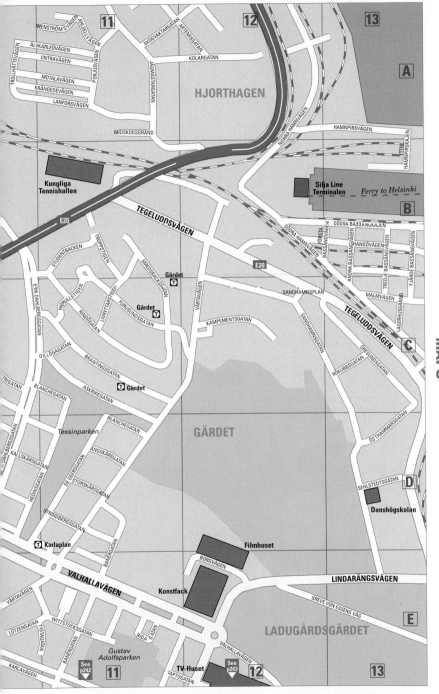

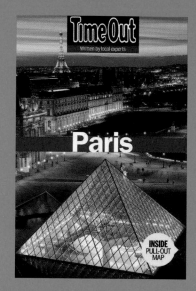

Paris

INSIDE PULL-OUT MAP

Written by
local experts,
rated 'Top
Guidebook
Brand'
by Which?

Travel
beyond
the
clichés

All new 2014 guidebook.
Rewritten, redesigned
and better than ever.

Keep up, join in

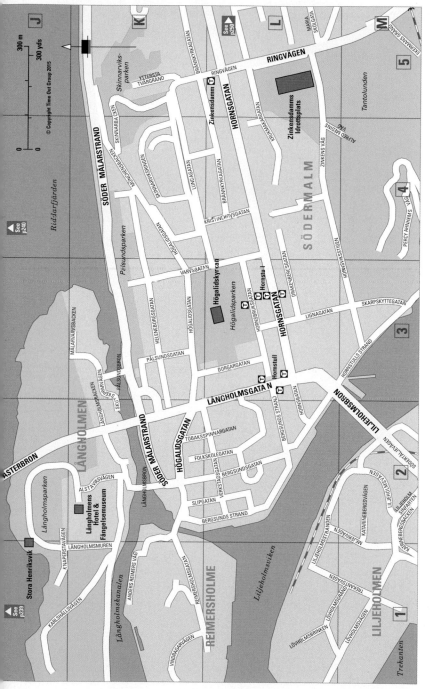

MAPS

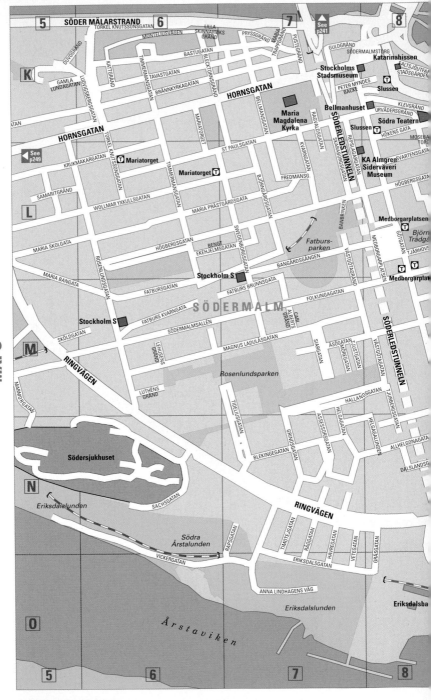

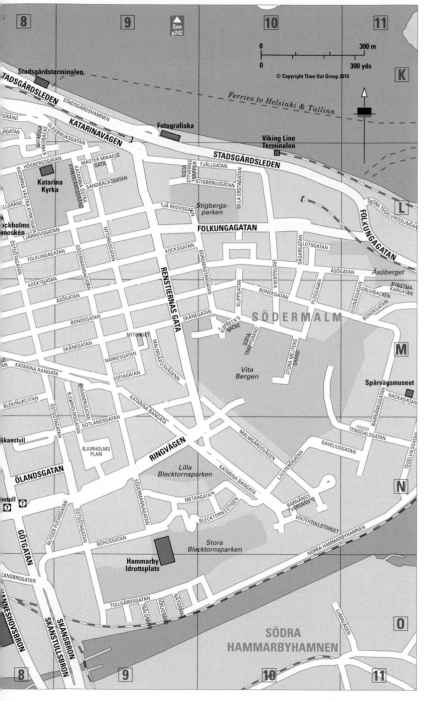

Street Index

STREET INDEX

Tunnelbana · Metro · U-Bahn

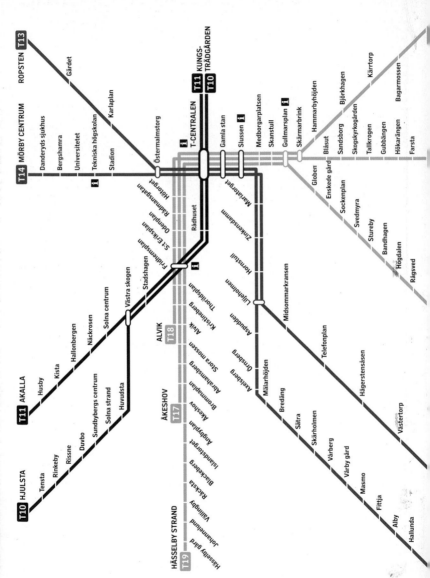